Strategic Alliances for Value Creation

A volume in
Research in Strategic Alliances
T. K. Das, *Series Editor*

Research in Strategic Alliances

T. K. Das
Series Editor

Researching Strategic Alliances: Emerging Perspectives
Edited by T. K. Das

Strategic Alliances in a Globalizing World
Edited by T. K. Das

Behavioral Perspectives on Strategic Alliances
Edited by T. K. Das

Strategic Alliances for Value Creation
Edited by T. K. Das

Strategic Alliances for Value Creation

Edited by

T. K. Das

City University of New York

IAP

INFORMATION AGE PUBLISHING, INC.
Charlotte, NC • www.infoagepub.com

Library of Congress Cataloging-in-Publication Data

Strategic alliances for value creation / edited by T.K. Das
p. cm. – (Research in strategic alliances)
Includes bibliographical references and index.
ISBN 978-1-61735-692-6 (pbk.) – ISBN 978-1-61735-693-3 (hbk.) – ISBN 978-1-61735-694-0 (ebook)
1. Strategic alliances (Business) 2. Strategic planning. 3. Value. I. Das, T. K.
HD69.S8S774 2011
658'.046–dc23

2011043739

Printed and bound by CPI Group (UK) Ltd, Croydon, CR0 4YY

CONTENTS

FOREWORD TO THE SERIES

Relationships have been important to commercial activity and economic transactions for thousands of years. Yet the development of a global competitive landscape has substantially enhanced the importance of partnerships between economic entities. These partnerships, referred to as strategic alliances, provide access to resources and capabilities that allow firms to gain economies of scope and to increase their productivity and innovation. The economies, productivity, and innovations are necessary to at least maintain competitive parity and especially to achieve a competitive advantage in the often highly competitive global markets. Strategic alliances have also become a prominent means of entering new markets, especially foreign markets. Therefore, alliances and the networks of firms of which they are a part have become essential for the conduct of business for all types of firms, large, small, established, and new.

Because of their growing importance, research on strategic alliances has increased markedly in the last two decades. Yet there is need for an authoritative compendium of strategic alliance research and knowledge. This book series on *Research in Strategic Alliances* fills this critically important gap in our field. It provides a thorough examination of significant topics that provide complete and up-to-date knowledge on strategic alliances. This book series will serve as a catalyst for more effective management of strategic alliances and will guide future research on them. I commend it to you.

—Michael A. Hitt

Distinguished Professor and Joe B. Foster Chair in Business Leadership at Texas A&M University, and Past President of the Academy of Management and the Strategic Management Society

Strategic Alliances for Value Creation, page vii

ABOUT THE SERIES

The globalization of markets has led to increased interdependence among business firms, leading to an explosion in the number of strategic alliances. Strategic alliances, briefly, are cooperative arrangements aimed at achieving the strategic objectives of two or more partner firms. These interfirm arrangements can range from joint R&D to equity-based joint ventures. However, the scholarship relating to strategic alliances remains largely dispersed in the literatures of traditional academic disciplines such as strategic management, marketing, economics, and sociology. This book series on strategic alliances will cover the essential progress made thus far in the literature and elaborate upon fruitful streams of scholarship. More importantly, the book series will focus on providing a robust and comprehensive forum for new scholarship in the field of strategic alliances. In particular, the books in the series will cover new views of interdisciplinary theoretical frameworks and models (dealing with resources, risk, trust, control, cooperation, learning, opportunism, governance, developmental stages, performance, etc.), significant practical problems of alliance organization and management (such as alliance capability, interpartner conflict, internal tensions, use of information technology), and emerging areas of inquiry. The series will also include comprehensive empirical studies of selected segments of business, economic, industrial, government, and nonprofit activities with a wide prevalence of strategic alliances. Through the ongoing release of focused topical titles, this book series will seek to disseminate theoretical insights and practical management information that will enable interested professionals to gain a rigorous and comprehensive understanding of the field of strategic alliances.

Strategic Alliances for Value Creation, page ix

CHAPTER 1

LEVERAGING MULTIPARTNER ALLIANCES IN TECHNOLOGY-DRIVEN INDUSTRIES

Dovev Lavie
Christoph Lechner
Harbir Singh

ABSTRACT

Multipartner alliances have become a popular vehicle for coordinating firms' strategies in technology-driven industries. They play an important role in promoting industry standards, yet very few firms have been able to successfully leverage their involvement in these complex organizations. Apparently, a firm's experience with bilateral alliances is insufficient for managing the tradeoffs entailed in engagement in multilateral relationships. This chapter analyzes the benefits, costs, and risks associated with multipartner alliances. It offers guidance for five key decisions throughout the alliance lifecycle: whether to join a multipartner alliance, which multipartner alliance to join, when to enter a multipartner alliance, how to become involved in a multipartner alliance, and when to exit a multipartner alliance. The case of multipartner alliances in the Wireless Local Area Network (WLAN) industry serves to illustrate the insights. For instance, firms are advised to join a multipartner alliance either at an early stage or later in their lifecycle in order to gain from their

Strategic Alliances for Value Creation, pages 1–21

membership in the alliance. Furthermore, extensive organizational involvement in the multipartner alliance generates common benefits to all partners, yet does not guarantee private benefits to the firm that assumes a leadership role. Firms that carefully consider their steps instead of following the herd in making these decisions can find the right balance between contributing to the overall success of the multipartner alliance and capturing value from their involvement in that alliance.

INTRODUCTION

In recent years, a broad range of industries has witnessed the emergence of multipartner alliances (MPAs), which bring multiple firms together to collaborate in the development and promotion of emerging technologies or innovative products and services. Some examples include NSP in the nanotechnology industry, VESA in the video industry, IDSP in the identity theft protection industry, JEDEC in the semiconductor industry, and Wi-Fi in the WLAN industry. According to Thomson Financial records, more than 13,000 MPAs were formed between 1990 and 2007. An MPA is a collective voluntary organization that interactively engages its multiple corporate members in multilateral value-chain activities, such as collaborative research; development; sourcing; production; or the marketing of technologies, products, or services. Some common forms of MPAs include R&D consortia, official and de facto standard-setting associations, multiparty production joint ventures, supplier networks, co-marketing arrangements, and industry constellations. MPAs are typically established as nonprofit associations and welcome all firms with shared interests. They operate through a hierarchical structure with a governing board and multiple layers of membership. The board appoints committees that focus, for example, on defining and formalizing needs and their solutions, testing and certifying products in accordance with mutually agreed-upon standards, or promoting the adoption of a sponsored technology in the industry.

An MPA can operate as an efficient vehicle for guiding the product development efforts of partner firms, establishing a dominant industry design, sharing investments, and avoiding competition between proprietary technologies, which has been widespread since the days of VHS versus Betamax to the days of Blu-Ray versus HD-DVD. Nevertheless, very few firms manage to benefit from this emerging form of collaborative organizations. According to most industry surveys, alliances are failure-prone, with typical failure rates ranging between 40% and 70% (Park & Ungson, 2001). The large number of partners involved in an MPA creates unique coordination challenges due to increasing complexity and the need to reconcile partners' divergent objectives and interests. Even in a successful MPA, most partners fail to leverage the MPA's success. MPAs impose strategic constraints and risks related to antitrust liability or infringement of intellectual property. Thus, many firms, even those that have become very experienced in managing traditional forms of dyadic alliances, face difficulties in coordinating collaborative activities in MPAs.

Considering the primary role of MPAs in driving the evolution of technology-driven industries, managers in such industries confront a range of critical managerial issues. In particular, they debate whether to establish a new MPA, join an existing MPA, or instead continue pursuing their firms' independent strategies. When several MPAs compete for dominance in a particular industry, managers also need to carefully consider which MPA their firms should support. Furthermore, they need to reach decisions about when their firms should enter an MPA in order to minimize investments and maximize gains. Should they join early on or rather wait until a certain technology becomes dominant? Once they enter, should they assume a leadership role or remain passive observers in the MPA? In making such decisions, firms must strike the right balance between underinvesting and overinvesting in MPAs. Whereas some firms hope to free-ride on their partners' investments, others end up subsidizing their partners and fail to earn appropriate return on their investments. Identifying the right time to exit an MPA is also far from trivial since, unlike traditional dyadic alliances, an MPA can maintain its operations even after certain members have left. Thus, engaging in MPAs is a challenging endeavor given the complex set of tradeoffs that firms face (Gomes-Casseres, 1994). Managers need to develop unique capabilities for managing their firms' engagements in MPAs. Our filed interviews suggest that in many cases, managers lack the appropriate means to evaluate the benefits and costs of their firms' memberships in MPAs and therefore tend to follow the herd in making these strategic decisions, which may come at great cost.

Based on our in-depth research and interviews with managers and industry experts, we offer essential guidelines for coping with the far-reaching decisions and challenges that managers face when seeking to manage and leverage their firms' engagements in MPAs. We examine the tradeoffs that arise during the MPA lifecycle and identify some approaches that can enable firms to effectively collaborate with partners while benefiting from their engagements in MPAs. These suggestions are often overlooked by studies that focus on managing dyadic alliances. The case of the WLAN industry serves to illustrate our main points.

RESEARCH DESIGN

Our empirical research employed quantitative and qualitative methods for studying the WLAN industry and the Wi-Fi (an acronym for Wireless

Fidelity) alliance in particular. In selecting a setting for our study, we considered several criteria: (a) appropriateness of the context, (b) representativeness of the alliance, and (c) accessibility and suitability of data for analysis. After searching press items on MPAs and reviewing alliance listings of technical associations, we selected the Wi-Fi Alliance as the subject of our inquiry. First, in terms of context appropriateness, we examined MPAs in technology-driven industries that competed against other MPAs and produced benefits for their partners. The fact that the Wi-Fi Alliance competed in the emerging WLAN industry and was successful in establishing the IEEE 802.11 standard as the dominant design in this industry suggests that at least some Wi-Fi partners were able to extract benefits from this alliance. Second, the Wi-Fi Alliance is representative with respect to its activities and governance structure. This alliance operated both technical and marketing committees, thus covering R&D and marketing activities. Additionally, its governance structure incorporated a sponsoring board, specialized democratic committees, and multiple layers of membership, all of which are typical in technology-driven industries. Finally, most alliances had fewer members or offered limited archival information concerning membership, time of entry, and certified products. In the case of the Wi-Fi Alliance, 250 member partners were identified, thus providing a sufficient number of observations for empirical analysis. This alliance has received extensive media coverage, and it offered abundant archival information for measuring the study's variables. It also constituted a well-defined network with clear boundaries, since any firm that sought to certify Wi-Fi products was required to join the alliance. Detailed background information on the Wi-Fi Alliance has been documented and is available from the authors.

We followed four stages in carrying out our research. In the first stage we gathered archival data from various sources for all the firms that joined the Wi-Fi Alliance since its formation in August 1999. We relied on the corporate Web site of the Wi-Fi Alliance (www.wi-fi.org), which offered detailed listings of partners and their certified products. Additionally, we obtained membership listings of the HiperLAN, HomeRF, and Bluetooth alliances from their respective Web sites or directly from their representatives. The Factiva database offered press releases, including periodical announcements of membership and announcements of partners joining the alliance, which were used to establish the approximate date of entry to the alliance as well as to compute our market exposure measure. The U.S. Patent & Trademark Office database provided full-text access to issued patents and patent applications, and was used for determining whether partners patented WLAN technologies. The Compustat and Dun & Bradstreet databases offered industry classification and financial data for public and private firms in our sample. We also relied on firms' corporate Web sites as well as on the Gartner Dataquest, Corporate Affiliations, Gale's Business & Company Resource Center, and Mergent Online databases.

In the second stage, we elaborated our research design by conducting personal interviews with the marketing director of HomeRF, the managing director of the Wi-Fi Alliance, the vice chairman of the Wi-Fi Alliance board of directors, industry analysts, managers of partners participating in these alliances, as well as representatives of Wi-Fi Alliance committees. We also issued a survey to several industry experts in order to assess the market success of Wi-Fi partners.

In the third stage, we quantitatively tested a broad range of hypotheses with our integrated database. We ran hierarchical negative binomial regressions as well as moderated hierarchical regressions in order to disentangle the complex set of factors affecting the benefits to partners in MPAs. We focused on three types of benefits: (a) productivity in terms of the number of certified products per year involvement in the MPA, (b) market exposure based on counts of press releases in which partners were mentioned in connection with their affiliation in the Wi-Fi Alliance, and (c) market success based on the assessments of industry experts that evaluated the success that partners gained with the development, introduction, and marketing of Wi-Fi products. We further considered alternative types of benefits, such as market share, to test the robustness of our analyses. We developed measures for internal organizational involvement based on board membership and product certification, studied external involvement in competing alliances by tracking partners' membership in each of the four alliances in this industry, and also analyzed the timing of entry of partners by calculating the order in which they entered the focal MPA. We took care to control for the duration of involvement in the alliance, the industry sector of the partner, its product diversity, innovativeness, and various other aspects that might account for the benefits that a partner extracted from the MPA.

As we mention in this chapter, our findings revealed that Wi-Fi partners that also took part in HiperLAN, Bluetooth, or HomeRF certified more Wi-Fi products and were more successful with the development, introduction, and marketing of these products. They also gained better reputation in the market relative to partners that lacked such experience. Our findings also show that early entrants to the Wi-Fi Alliance gained greater success with the development, introduction, and marketing of Wi-Fi products. However, late entrants were productive even more than early entrants, with the lowest productivity observed among intermediate entrants. Thus, intermediate entrants were stuck in the middle while early entrants explored new opportunities, and late entrants exploited the cumulative alliance resources. Finally, we found that board members in the Wi-Fi Alliance who sought to exert influence by investing a large amount of resources gained recognition and were more successful with the introduction of their products in the market. Yet they were unable to enhance their productivity relative to less involved partners. Additionally, partners that were involved in product development gained greater market success than those that were not directly involved in the process, although less involved partners still enjoyed certain benefits as much as active partners, for example, with respect to their exposure and reputation in the market. Overall, these findings highlight the implications of involvement in competing MPAs, timing of entry to the MPA, and organizational processes within the MPA.

Finally, to validate our conclusions, we presented our findings at several conferences and integrated our empirical data with additional feedback that we received from managers and consultants with expertise in the relevant domains. The scientific report that we generated from this study has gone through a rigorous peer-review process (Lavie, Lechner, & Singh, 2007). Next, we provide some insights from our study of the Wi-Fi Alliance and the WLAN industry before discussing our main conclusions.

THE CASE OF MPAs IN THE WLAN INDUSTRY

The WLAN industry has grown considerably in the past few years. Firms that operate in this industry offer products such as wireless access points, PC cards, USB modules, PDAs, and printers that connect users to data networks in the home, office, and public areas such as airports, hotels, and coffee shops. The IEEE 802.11 standard, supported by the Wi-Fi Alliance, is a common household name in this industry today, but it was neither the most advanced technology nor the first to gather industry support. At the outset, there was significant uncertainty about the prospects of wireless technologies, as an executive at Nokia noted:

> There was lots of doubt about what wireless LAN, if any, would be successful. There was uncertainty about the prospects. From the perspective of a cellular phone supplier, the question was, "Here comes 3G, why do you need wireless LAN?" HiperLAN was in discussion in those days. There was also the Bluetooth scenario, whether Bluetooth or Wi-Fi would go out.

Indeed, the HiperLAN Alliance was the first MPA formed in August 1996 to promote a technology that had been in development by ETSI (the European Telecommunications Standards Institute) since 1991. Initially backed by Apple, Advanced RISC Machines, and GECPlessey Semiconductors, the HiperLAN technology was arguably more advanced than the Wi-Fi technology, but was late to market and unable to make inroads into the United States, given that its first product was shipped 2 years after the first Wi-Fi product hit the market. In March 1998, Intel began to gather support from Compaq, Motorola, and more than 100 other firms around the HomeRF

Alliance that relied on the technology of chip maker Proxim. Industry analysts praised the merits of this technology, which integrated voice and data transmission, and solved security, quality of service, and interference problems. In December 2000, approximately 8 months after the release of the first HomeRF product, a PC Data Report revealed that HomeRF reached a 90% market share in the wireless home networking market. Still, the flux in the WLAN industry continued, and a couple of months after HomeRF was formed, the Bluetooth Special Interest Group began to attract members like Nokia and Ericsson, offering a point-to-point alternative for transmitting voice and data between handheld devices and wired computers. Despite its ability to attract more than 200 partners and 4,000 adopters, the short range and low power of the Bluetooth technology supported only a few commercial applications such as those used in cellular phones. It was only in August 1999 that the Wi-Fi Alliance was founded by 3COM, Agere, Cisco, Intersil, Nokia, and Symbol Technologies with the objective of promoting the IEEE 802.11 standard among consumers and manufacturers that certified the interoperability of WLAN products. Finally, after a couple of years of intensive competition between these technologies, the HomeRF and HiperLAN alliances were dissolved, which paved the way for Wi-Fi to emerge as the de facto industry standard since 2004.

Why did Wi-Fi emerge as a winner in this competition among MPAs? One success factor was Wi-Fi's ability to gain traction by adopting an open standard instead of relying on a proprietary technology. Such an open standard was unavailable when HomeRF emerged, which made the HomeRF partners highly dependent on the manufacturing capacity and the cooperation of Proxim. The benefits of open standards in the information technology sector are well documented (Gawer & Cusumano, 2002). Additionally, unlike HiperLAN, which sought to produce a superior technology, the Wi-Fi Alliance gave priority to rapidly releasing products to the market rather than perfecting the technology. The overturn, however, may have been related to Intel's decision to defect from HomeRF and join Wi-Fi in September 2001. Indeed, the Wi-Fi Alliance can be considered a success story, but not all Wi-Fi partners benefited equally from this success. In 2004, a Gartner Dataquest report suggested that 20 firms of the 250 Wi-Fi partners accounted together for about 85% of the worldwide WLAN market. As Proxim had to discover when eventually joining the Wi-Fi Alliance, allying with the winning MPA is no guarantee for a firm's own success. Subsequently, the unrest in the WLAN industry has continued, with the next generation technology promoted by the WiMAX Forum threatening to undermine the success of Wi-Fi producers. It has become clear that long-term success in emerging technology markets requires mastering competition both within and between MPAs. While the competition between MPAs has received some attention (Lazzarini, 2007), the inner workings of an MPA remain much of a mystery.

ASSESSING BENEFITS AND COSTS

The case of the WLAN industry suggests that MPAs can thrive and play a productive role in emerging technology markets under high levels of technical risk and market uncertainty as product life cycles become shorter and demand for product interoperability and R&D investments increases (Hagedoorn, 1995). These conditions limit the ability of any single firm to independently gain success in the market, yet allow MPAs to offer three types of benefits to partner firms.

Technological Benefits

MPAs enable partners to pool their engineering skills and R&D resources. They offer easy access to technical information beyond the reach of any individual partner (Gulati & Kletter, 2005). They provide a platform for enhancing interoperability among complementary products as well as testing and certifying solutions (Rosenkopf, Metiu, & George, 2001). By sharing knowledge with other partners in the MPA, partners can learn how to enhance the quality of their products.

Marketing Benefits

MPAs let partners focus their marketing efforts and share promotion and advertising investments. They provide access to market data and grant a seal of approval to certified products, which enhances partners' legitimacy in the market (Stuart, Hoang, & Hybels, 1999). By fostering awareness and common brand recognition, MPAs help partners build their reputation and increase their market penetration.

Strategic Benefits

MPAs serve as a platform for exchanging ideas and shaping the evolution of industries (Sgourev & Zuckerman, 2006). By joining forces and creating a critical mass, partners improve their competitive positions and leverage network externalities (Katz & Shapiro, 1986). This reduces uncertainty about the features of the emerging technology. In addition, MPA partners can avoid appropriation claims from owners of proprietary technologies, enjoy collective lobbying with regulatory bodies, and network with industry leaders.

As is so often in business, these benefits do not come without costs (see Figure 1.1). A careful examination of MPAs reveals that they create unique

MPA benefits

- **Technological**
  - Pooled R&D
  - Access to technical info
  - Interoperability
  - Certification
  - Knowledge sharing
  - Product quality
- **Marketing**
  - Shared promotion
  - Shared advertising
  - Access to market data
  - Legitimacy
  - Brand recognition
  - Reputation
  - Market penetration
- **Strategic**
  - Competitive position
  - Network externalities
  - Reduced uncertainty
  - Dominant design
  - Appropriation
  - Networking

MPA costs

- **Visible costs**
  - Annual membership dues
  - Certification fees
- **Hidden costs**
  - Human resource investments
  - Engineering resources
  - Managerial resources
  - Demanding committee work
  - Leakage of proprietary knowledge
  - Modification of technology
  - Reconciliation of strategic objectives
- **Risks**
  - Failure to establish a dominant technology
  - Failure to capitalize on a dominant technology
  - Standardization of inferior technology
  - Insufficient IP protection
  - Litigation claims

Figure 1.1 The benefits and costs of multipartner alliances.

challenges, often acting as a double-edged sword from the perspective of the individual partner firm (McAfee & Oliveau, 2002). Not all firms realize how to best explore and exploit the opportunities that MPAs provide. The gains of firms that take part in MPAs may vary, since ultimately it is the customers that decide which vendor to purchase their products from. Additionally, in recent years, multiple MPAs have emerged to promote competing technologies in certain industries, which reduces the chances of success for each MPA. The proliferation of MPAs attests to the attractiveness of this organizational form, but firms should be aware of the pitfalls that involve not only visible costs but also hidden costs and risks.

Visible Costs

MPAs impose monetary and nonmonetary obligations on their membership in the form of membership dues and indirect resource investments. They also constrain the strategic decisions of partners by enforcing common rules through such means as voting procedures and certification programs that do not always serve the interests of individual partners. Annual membership dues can become considerable for small firms or those involved in many MPAs. Membership dues are typically proportionate to a partner's status in the MPA. For example, in the Wi-Fi Alliance, regular corporate members traditionally paid $25,000 in annual dues, while board members paid $125,000 for the right to set the agenda for the alliance committees, decide about the allocation of marketing funds, and approve technical proposals. In the HomeRF Alliance, a more fine-grained classification was used, with Promoters paying $100,000 in annual dues, Contributors $20,000, Implementers $7,500, and Supporters $2,500. This membership dues structure reflects hierarchical leadership roles in the MPA. It is not uncommon to find MPAs that charge additional fees for product certification or for running test labs.

Hidden Costs

Membership dues are mostly overshadowed by managerial and engineering resources as well as other dedicated human resources that firms allocate to MPA committees and task groups. Some partners play a role in the MPA board that sets the agenda and approves the work of committees and task groups to which other partners also send their representatives. Additionally, partners may find themselves sponsoring their industry rivals if their proprietary knowledge leaks to their competitors through the MPA (Hamel, 1991). Even when competition does not pose an imminent threat, partners may witness declines in autonomous innovation efforts because of their reliance on MPAs as a primary source of emerging technologies. At times, partners may be required to invest in acquiring skills and modifying their product designs in accordance with technologies that are inconsistent with their engineering platforms and technical capabilities. Similarly, some partners may need to reconcile their strategic objectives with those of other partners in the MPA in order to advance common goals. These types of costs are difficult to quantify and thus easy to overlook.

Risks

MPAs have better chances of gaining industry support than individual firms under conditions of uncertainty, yet partners' investments in joint research and product development can be compromised if the MPA fails to establish a dominant design in the industry. Moreover, to gather broad industry support, some MPAs discourage technologies that implicate current intellectual property rights or are based on patented technology, which may lead to inefficiencies in technology development or to the endorsement of inferior technologies. Some MPAs even establish bylaws that require new members to disclose and share their patents. Firms that join MPAs without having thoroughly investigated these bylaws may bear substantial legal hazards (Jakobsen, 2004). Put differently, insufficient intellectual property protection can endanger the competitive positions of member firms.

A careful assessment of the above benefits and costs may help managers reach informed decisions about joining an MPA, but the challenges do not end there. Managers must decide which MPA to join, when to enter that MPA, how to become involved in the MPA, and when to exit it. Our research shows that some firms bet on the wrong MPA, and that even in the most successful MPAs, some firms are able to capture a larger slice of the value pie, leaving crumbs to other partner firms. Differences in firms' decisions and strategic behavior within the MPA can explain much of the performance differences among partners. In particular, we identify the choice of an MPA, the timing of entry to the MPA, and the type of involvement in the MPA as key decision factors (Lavie et al., 2007).

DECISION 1: TO JOIN OR NOT TO JOIN?

Managers often base their decisions to join an MPA on industry trends and hype rather than on careful cost-benefit analysis. What suits one firm may not suit another. Managers must recognize the unique benefits and costs that matter to their firms. In some cases, a firm may be better off going it alone. If a firm owns a superior technology and has exclusive market access, it may not need to leverage the externalities furnished by an MPA. In other cases, it may decide to establish a new MPA and gather industry support around it to counter the efforts of its competitors. For example, in June 2001, Simplex Solutions and Toshiba joined forces with 10 other firms to launch the X-Initiative, a consortium of semiconductor supply-chain firms that was created to advance the usage of diagonal routing technology called the X Architecture. This MPA challenged the hegemony of the "Manhattan" architecture, which had been the de facto industry standard for chip design. Since MPAs have begun to proliferate, the real question is not whether but which MPA to join.

DECISION 2: WHICH MPA TO JOIN?

Clearly, with hindsight, joining a successful MPA generates greater potential benefits than joining an MPA that eventually loses in battle against other MPAs and can only offer more or less useful experience to its partner firms. Betting on the wrong horse endangers a partner's resource endowments and its competitive position. While it is quite easy to recognize the "right" MPA once it has established an industry standard, this task is very challenging at the outset owing to uncertainty about the prospects of competing MPAs.

We found that firms can enhance their foresight by considering a range of factors. As illustrated with the case of MPAs in the WLAN industry, when firms select an MPA to join, they should benchmark MPAs with respect to the merits of the technologies that they promote (short transmission range and limited applications were Bluetooth's main drawbacks), their stage in the product development lifecycle vis-à-vis windows of opportunity (HiperLAN was late to market, while HomeRF's vision of integrated voice, data, and video communication preceded its time), their installed base of adopters (HiperLAN gathered limited support relative to its competition), the availability of complementary products, and the reputation and capabilities of partners that have already joined each MPA (whom does Intel support?). This case also suggests that firms should take into account the geographical market in which a technology is prevalent and which governments sponsor the standards that MPAs promote (the European Telecommunications Standards Institute sponsored HiperLAN, while the U.S. Institute of Electrical and Electronics Engineers sponsored the IEEE802.11 standard). MPAs that support an open standard are typically preferable to those promoting a proprietary technology even for the owner of that technology (as evident in the case of Proxim in the HomeRF Alliance), unless that technology has already emerged as a dominant design (Anderson & Tushman, 1990; Shapiro & Varian, 1999). These benchmarks can help managers decide which MPA to place their bets on.

However, betting on what seems to be the right horse is not necessarily the best strategy. An unforeseen technology may emerge, and the benchmark may not reveal a consistent winner (Cares, 2006). In such cases, when MPAs do not require exclusive membership, firms should consider spreading their bets by joining multiple MPAs. Participation in multiple MPAs may lead to redundant investments in R&D, dispersal of corporate resources and attention, and potential conflicts of interest among partners that promote competing technologies. Nevertheless, our research shows that the benefits of engaging in competing MPAs outweigh efficiency losses for several reasons: reduced uncertainty, complementarity, interoperability, and hedging.

Reduced Uncertainty

A firm can better cope with technical risk and reduce market uncertainty by gathering information and learning about competing technologies, prospective markets, and potential competitors (McGrath, 1997) through its involvement in competing MPAs.

Complementarity

A firm can offer better products by benchmarking technologies, combining knowledge, and integrating best-of-breed solutions that originate from competing MPAs. Despite the incompatibility of the alternative technology architectures, competing MPAs may offer complementary designs for peripheral components or services.

Interoperability

A firm can gain by ensuring compatibility across multiple technologies. The availability of multisystem televisions, multizone DVDs, and multimode cellular phones compatible with TDMA, GSM, and CDMA technologies demonstrates the demand for such interoperable products.

Hedging

Investments in competing technologies can be considered real options whose value appreciates with the levels of technological and market uncertainties that the industry faces (McGrath & Nerkar, 2004). Participation in multiple MPAs provides favorable exit options in case an MPA loses its dominance to a competing MPA.

Overall, these merits outweigh the challenges of managing a firm's involvement in multiple MPAs, as an executive at Dell remarked when referring to his firm's involvement in the Wi-Fi Alliance, "We are members of a number of alliances, which does not preclude us at all from participation in the Wi-Fi Alliance. It brings in a lot of positives because you certainly are aware of different industries and segments.... You can bring best practices from each trade association and leverage relationships."

Our findings suggest that Wi-Fi partners that also took part in HiperLAN, Bluetooth, or HomeRF certified more Wi-Fi products and were more successful with the development, introduction, and marketing of these products. They also gained better reputation in the market relative to partners that lacked such experience.

DECISION 3: WHEN TO ENTER AN MPA?

Once a firm has decided which MPAs to enter, it must figure out the best timing for entry. Should it enter early in the MPA lifecycle, at an intermediate stage, or perhaps later when uncertainty unfolds? Our research shows that early and late entrants gain much more from their membership in MPAs than intermediate entrants. Interestingly, however, the opportunities that MPAs offer to entrants at the outset of the alliance differ from those available to late entrants.

Advantages of Early Entry

At the early stage of alliance formation, partners make fundamental decisions that determine the subsequent organizational and technological progress of the MPA. Late entrants may not be able to overturn such decisions, for example, since to ensure interoperability, technical specifications build upon formally defined standards (David & Greenstein, 1990). Thus, the modular nature of technology development leads to persistence in alliance decisions. Also, early entrants are well-positioned to leverage formal and informal ties to other partners. This allows them to build internal coalitions and create rich information channels for their use before subsequent partners join the MPA. Further, since the governance body of the MPA is being defined early on, early entrants can set rules and procedures that best fit their own needs (Zollo, Reuer, & Singh, 2002). Finally, early entrants can pioneer with the introduction of alliance-reliant products. Such first-mover advantage (Lieberman & Montgomery, 1998) is especially critical in emerging technology markets, where innovation is frequent but firms cannot fully protect their technologies from imitators.

Advantages of Late Entry

Unlike the founding partners, late entrants can avoid setup investments that are needed at the stage of alliance formation, such as those required for seeking and negotiating with like-minded partners in order to set the objectives and organize the MPA. Partners often underestimate the "heavy lifting" needed to initiate alliance operations. More importantly, late entrants can save on R&D costs, which are higher in the early stages of developing emerging technologies. They can also limit investments in educating the market, since the most crucial technical and marketing efforts are typically made at earlier stages of the MPA lifecycle. Based on feedback about prior performance of the MPA, late entrants can make more informed decisions about which MPA to join and thus minimize investments in technologies that turn out to be unproven or unsuccessful in gaining market acceptance. Thus, late entrants can fully concentrate on the opportunities provided by an established alliance instead of contributing to the collaborative effort. While pioneering firms may excel in technological invention, late entrants that possess complementary assets and managerial expertise (Teece, 1986) can leverage the accumulated knowledge and free-ride on the efforts of incumbent partners.

In conclusion, both early and late entrants to an MPA can benefit by pursuing a somewhat different strategy, either by pioneering and exploring new opportunities or by exploiting the accumulated resource base of the alliance, as one manager noted:

> Earlier entrants are companies that look at things more futuristically...perhaps the companies with a longer strategic horizon. Then those companies with a shorter strategic horizon might become more involved when it becomes obvious that it is going to be a success and they want to get in or they can now afford to get in. So the early adopters are either betting heavily on their R&D and making it happen or have a view that it is something that needs to be monitored; and then the guys that come late tend to be opportunistic.

Our research shows that early entrants to the Wi-Fi Alliance gained greater success with the development, introduction, and marketing of Wi-Fi products. However, late entrants were even more productive than early entrants, with the lowest productivity observed among intermediate entrants. Thus, intermediate entrants were stuck in the middle while early entrants explored new opportunities, and late entrants exploited the cumulative resources of the MPA.

DECISION 4: HOW TO BECOME INVOLVED IN AN MPA?

Once a decision to enter an MPA has been reached and the right timing has been chosen, firms are often overwhelmed by the various ways in which they can become involved in the operations of an MPA. Partners may become involved in the exchange of information, in negotiation and evaluation of proposals, in the design and certification of new products, and by taking an active role in governing the MPA and monitoring other partners' compliance with alliance decisions (Farrell & Saloner, 1988). Frequently, these activities are tied to the type of alliance membership, which defines the privileges and obligations of partners (Ring, Doz, & Olk, 2005). For example, partners that serve on the board of an MPA typically have stronger voting power and can influence decisions by setting the agenda for committees and approving their proposals. In the case of HomeRF, promoters were sitting on the board of directors, were involved in all initiatives, drove the technology trajectory, and approved decisions. Contributors could submit proposals to the board and actively engaged in committees and collaborative projects. Implementers were involved in the design and manufacture of products based on the approved technical specifications, while supporters could access these specifications and information without any active role in the MPA. The question then is how involved should a firm become in an MPA?

Common wisdom suggests that greater involvement carries greater benefits. One would expect that partners will gain from the ability to set the alliance agenda, align the alliance objectives, control the decision-making process, access and influence the flow of information, and exploit alliance resources (Rosenkopf et al., 2001). However, our research reveals a more complex picture. We found, for example, that board members in the Wi-Fi Alliance that sought to exert influence by investing a large amount of resources, gained recognition and were more successful with the introduction of their products in the market. Yet they were unable to enhance their productivity relative to less involved partners. This may be the case since board members direct most of their resources and attention to achieving the common objectives of the MPA, i.e., creating an ecosystem and winning in competition against other MPAs. Such sponsorship may limit their capacity to pursue private initiatives. Less involved partners can benefit from the collective effort of other partners by freely accessing technology and marketing resources without adequately sharing the burden of managing and promoting the MPA. In sum, organizational involvement in an MPA contributes to the overall success of the MPA in competition against other MPAs; but while it enhances the market reputation of highly involved partners, it does not necessarily improve their competitiveness relative to other partners in the MPA. This realization is akin to the distinction between common benefits and private benefits (Gulati, Khanna, & Nohria, 1994). As a board representative in the Wi-Fi Alliance reflected,

> There is a significant difference in the financial support that board members give relative to the general membership. The board members pay a much heavier burden in keeping the Wi-Fi alliance running. Board membership requires much more commitment... providing dedicated resources. It comes down to the belief in building the Wi-Fi ecosystem. If we build the largest ecosystem, then the competitive world will decide which companies get which slice of that pie, but everyone will be better off with a slice of a very large pie.

Besides joining the board of an MPA, firms might become involved in committees and task groups, where technical proposals are submitted for evaluation, and issues such as specification, certification, and interoperability are resolved. However, not all firms engage in product development and certification. Whereas some partner firms develop new products and successfully introduce them to the market, others are mostly interested in the licensing and production of third-party products, in complementary infrastructure or service, or in integrated systems that embed standardized components. Firms that do not engage in product development can still benefit from the opportunity to evaluate and monitor the emerging technology and influence its future development and usage while building a capacity for a more active role in the future. They can network with technology providers and enjoy the reputation and marketing advantages associated with the MPA's brand much like active developers. In sum, partner firms that do not actively engage in product development can indirectly benefit from their membership in MPAs.

Of course, while all partners enjoy certain opportunities by virtue of their membership in MPAs, some partners can leverage their involvement in MPAs more than others. For example, in our study of the Wi-Fi Alliance, we found that partners that gained experience by developing broad product portfolios were more successful than partners that concentrated on narrow product lines. In emerging technology markets, large clients such as Dell, may prefer to work with few vendors that can offer integrated solutions that work. In addition, our research suggests that partners that are more innovative gain better market recognition. Thus, the success of individual partners depends not only on their collaboration with other partners in an MPA but also on their individual skills and capabilities.

DECISION 5: WHEN TO EXIT AN MPA?

One of the challenges that managers face is to figure out when to exit an MPA. In technology-driven industries, it is only a matter of time until emerging technologies render their predecessors obsolete. Intel was a founding member of the HomeRF Alliance, but after the Wi-Fi Alliance was established, it decided to join it and monitor its progress. Having witnessed the increasing dominance of the IEEE 802.11 standard, in September 2001, Intel became a board member in Wi-Fi and disassociated itself from HomeRF. In turn, Proxim, another sponsor of the HomeRF Alliance, while joining the Wi-Fi Alliance in December 2000, continued to chair the board of HomeRF until it was shut down. Proxim's Wi-Fi products did not gain much traction, perhaps because the market associated Proxim with the competing MPA. The market does not salute firms that fail to abandon a sinking ship. Managers that can overcome organizational resistance to change and write off sunken costs can better manage their firms' engagements in MPAs. Managers should continuously monitor the progress of the MPAs that their firms are involved in, watching out for emerging MPAs that can overturn the formers' dominance. Figure 1.2 summarizes our main points concerning the key decisions that managers face in managing their firms' engagements in MPAs.

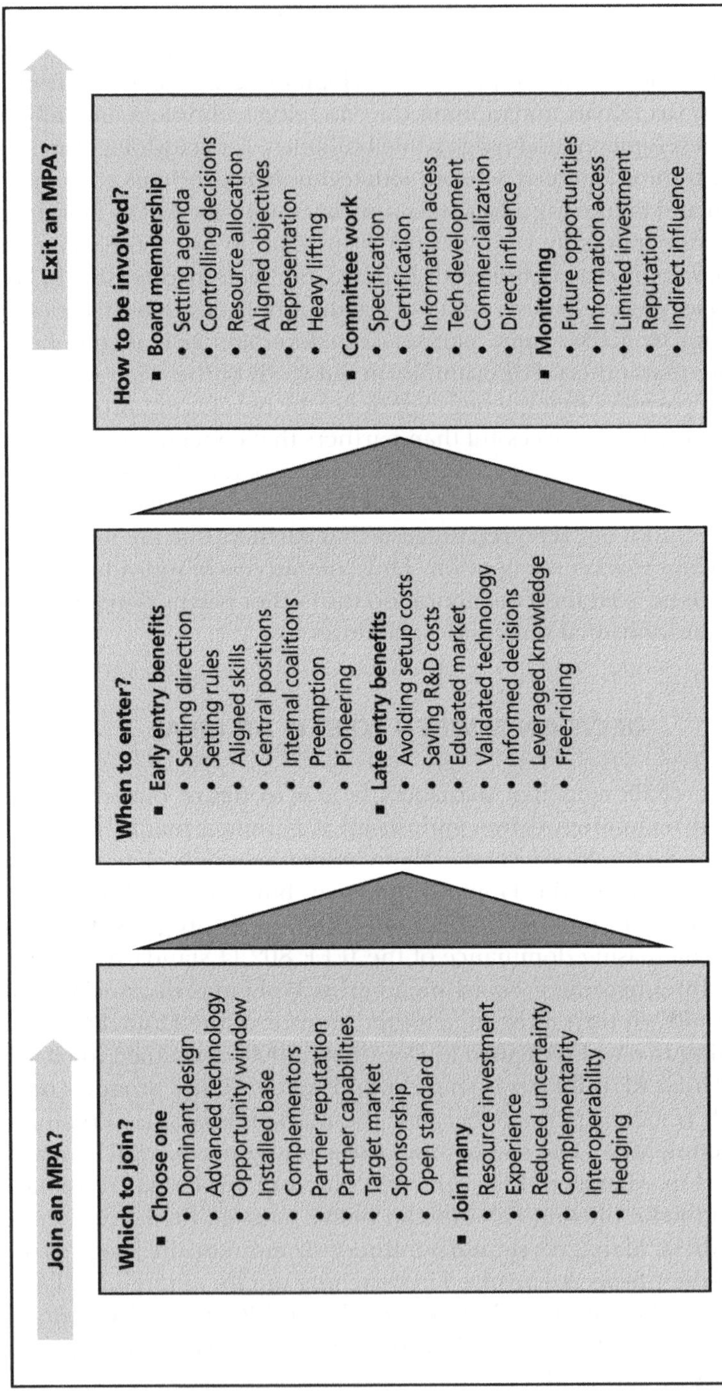

Figure 1.2 Key decisions for partners in MPAs.

CONCLUSION

As technology-driven industries witness increasing reliance on collaborative arrangements, firms must improve their abilities to strategize within and between MPAs. These organizational settings offer technological, marketing, and strategic benefits in industries characterized by short product–life cycles, increasing requirements for R&D investments, and high levels of technical risk and market uncertainty. However, in addition to their benefits, MPAs impose visible and hidden costs as well as risks that are often underestimated.

Our research shows that in competition between MPAs, only few MPAs can survive and fulfill their mission. Even when the objectives of an MPA are met, the benefits to partners vary. A firm that joins an MPA buys a ticket to the game, but without careful maneuvering, it cannot win that game. Therefore, we urge managers to carefully consider their firms' engagements in MPAs throughout the life cycle of these alliances: first, whether to join an MPA; second, which MPA to join and how to spread the bets across multiple MPAs; third, when to enter an MPA, given the tradeoffs between early entry opportunities and late entry advantages; fourth, how involved to become and what role to play in the MPA; and finally, when to exit an MPA.

These five decisions are challenging since they are typically made under high degrees of uncertainty. Their outcomes depend in part on the strategic behavior of other partners in MPAs and are therefore not within the full managerial discretion of any firm. For instance, to increase its relative gains in an MPA, a partner firm may seek to maximize its share of proceeds from the MPA while minimizing its investments. However, if all partners follow the same strategy, the MPA may lose in competition against other MPAs, and no partner will gain. Thus, partners need to walk the fine line between exploiting the MPA and overcontributing to the MPA's success, taking into consideration feedback following their actions. Managing a firm's engagements in MPAs is not trivial, and firms may lose their way in the MPA setting unless they develop unique capabilities for managing these complex organizational arrangements. As MPAs increasingly become the way of the future in technology-driven industries, managers must learn their merits and liabilities.

ACKNOWLEDGMENTS

This research was supported by the Mack Center for Technological Innovation at the Wharton School. Dovev Lavie also acknowledges the support of the Alfred P. Sloan Foundation. We thank Pankaj Dinodia, Mike Hendron, Lydia Jones, Ekant Kohli, Nicola Malcherek, Joel Silverman, and Brett

Smith for their research assistance, and also acknowledge the useful information received from our industry contacts: Shantam Biswas, Soumitra Das, Wayne Caswell, Jonathan Gaw, Frank Hanzlik, Paul Meche, Jens Milnikel, Liam Quinn, Kurt Scherf, and Phil Solis.

REFERENCES

Anderson, P., & Tushman, M. L. (1990). Technological discontinuities and dominant designs: A cyclical model of technological change. *Administrative Science Quarterly, 35,* 604–633.

Cares, J. (2006). Battle of the networks. *Harvard Business Review, 84*(2), 40–41.

David, P. A., & Greenstein, S. (1990). The economics of compatibility standards: An introduction to recent research. *Economics of Innovation and New Technology, 1,* 3–41.

Farrell, J., & Saloner, G. (1988). Coordination through committees and markets. *Rand Journal of Economics, 19,* 235–252.

Gawer, A., & Cusumano, M. A. (2002). *Platform leadership: How Intel, Microsoft, and Cisco drive industry innovation.* Boston: Harvard Business School Press.

Gomes-Casseres, B. (1994). Group versus group: How alliance networks compete. *Harvard Business Review, 72*(4), 62–66.

Gulati, R., Khanna, T., & Nohria, N. (1994). Unilateral commitments and the importance of process in alliances. *Sloan Management Review, 35*(3), 61.

Gulati, R., & Kletter, D. (2005). Shrinking core, expanding periphery: The relational architecture of high-performing organizations. *California Management Review, 47*(3), 77–104.

Hagedoorn, J. (1995). Strategic technology partnering during the 1980s: Trends, networks, and corporate patterns in non-core technologies. *Research Policy, 24,* 207–231.

Hamel, G. (1991). Competition for competence and interpartner learning within international strategic alliances. *Strategic Management Journal, 12,* 83–103

Jakobsen, K. A. (2004). Revisiting standard-setting organization patent policies. *Northwestern Journal of Technology and Intellectual Property, 3*(1), 43–60.

Katz, M., & Shapiro, C. (1986). Technology adoption in the presence of network externalities. *Journal of Political Economy, 94,* 822–841.

Lavie, D., Lechner, C., & Singh, H. (2007). The performance implications of timing of entry and involvement in multipartner alliances. *Academy of Management Journal, 50,* 578–604.

Lazzarini, S. G. (2007). The impact of membership in competing alliance constellations: Evidence on the operational performance of global airlines. *Strategic Management Journal, 28,* 345–367.

Lieberman, M. B., & Montgomery, D. B. (1998). First mover (dis)advantages: Retrospective and link with the resource-based view. *Strategic Management Journal, 19,* 1111–1125.

McAfee, A., & Oliveau, F. X. (2002). Confronting the limits of networks. *MIT Sloan Management Review, 43*(4), 85–87.

McGrath, R. G. (1997). A real options logic for initiating technology positioning investments. *Academy of Management Review, 22,* 974–996.

McGrath, R. G., & Nerkar, A. (2004). Real options reasoning and a new look at the R&D investment strategies of pharmaceutical firms. *Strategic Management Journal, 25,* 1–21.

Park, S. O., & Ungson, G. R. (2001). Interfirm rivalry and managerial complexity: A conceptual framework of alliance failure. *Organization Science, 12,* 37–53.

Ring, P. S., Doz, Y. L., & Olk, P. M. (2005). Managing formation processes in R&D consortia. *California Management Review, 47*(4), 137–156.

Rosenkopf, L., Metiu, A., & George, V. P. (2001). From the bottom up? Technical committee activity and alliance formation. *Administrative Science Quarterly, 46,* 748–772.

Sgourev, S. V., & Zuckerman, E. W. (2006). Improving capabilities through industry peer networks. *MIT Sloan Management Review, 47*(2), 33–38.

Shapiro, C., & Varian, H. R. (1999). Information rules: A strategic guide for the network economy. Boston: Harvard Business School Press.

Stuart, T., Hoang, H., & Hybels, R. (1999). Interorganizational endorsements and the performance of entrepreneurial ventures. *Administrative Science Quarterly, 44,* 315–349.

Teece, D. J. (1986). Profiting from technological innovations: Implications for integration, collaboration, licensing, and public policy. *Research Policy, 15,* 285–303.

Zollo, M., Reuer, J. J., & Singh, H. (2002). Interorganizational routines and performance in strategic alliances. *Organization Science, 13,* 701–713.

CHAPTER 2

KNOWLEDGE MANAGEMENT IN INTERNATIONAL R&D ALLIANCES

A Cultural Perspective

Dan Li
Lorraine Eden
Michael A. Hitt
R. Duane Ireland

ABSTRACT

Drawing on transaction cost economics and the cultural distance literature, we explore how knowledge management mechanisms vary across three types of international R&D alliances differentiated by partner nationality and alliance location: Home-Home (both partners are from the same home country and the R&D alliance activity takes place in the host country), Home-Host (one partner is from the home country and the other from the host country where the alliance activity occurs), and Home-Foreign (one partner is from the home and the other from a third country, with the alliance activity taking place in the host country). We argue that cultural difference (a) between partner firms and/or (b) between partner firms and alliance location increas-

Strategic Alliances for Value Creation, pages 23–49

es the difficulties of knowledge management for the alliance partners and affects partner decisions about alliance governance structure and scope. We expect that the uncertainty of tasks intended for the alliance moderates these relationships. Our analysis of 531 international R&D alliances over a 10-year period demonstrates that the Home-Foreign alliance is most likely to have an equity-based governance structure, whereas the Home-Home alliance is most likely to have a broad scope. The degree of task uncertainty weakens these relationships. We also find that governance structure and alliance scope can substitute for each other as knowledge management mechanisms.

INTRODUCTION

Prior research emphasizes the importance of balancing open knowledge exchange to further technological development with controlling knowledge flows to avoid unintended leakages in R&D alliances (Kale & Barnes, 1992; Li, Eden, Hitt, & Ireland 2008; Oxley & Sampson 2004; Sampson 2007). Knowledge management, which involves both knowledge exchange and protection, is particularly difficult in the international context. International R&D alliances pose additional difficulties of knowledge sharing and concerns of knowledge leakage for partner firms because of greater political, policy, economic, and social complexity associated with unfamiliar host markets (McCutchen, Swamidass, & Teng, 2004). Therefore, alliance partners typically encounter more challenges of knowledge management in international R&D alliances, increasing the salience of decisions about governance structure and scope.

Our study examines how cultural differences between alliance partners' nationalities and alliance location affect the partners' choice of governance structure and alliance scope in international R&D alliances. We draw insights from transaction cost economics (TCE) and the literature on national cultural distance to explore knowledge-management mechanisms in three types of international R&D alliances that are differentiated by partner nationality and alliance location. The first objective is to investigate *how governance structure and alliance scope decisions vary across international R&D alliances involving different degrees of cultural difference.* We argue that cultural differences affect partner firms' concerns about knowledge exchange and leakage during collaboration and therefore affect their choices of governance structure and alliance scope. We move beyond the dyadic cultural distance between the partners, typically discussed in prior research, to look at both cultural differences created by activities that (a) involve parties from different countries and that (b) involve activities in different countries.

Further, R&D alliances can engage in tasks with differing uncertainty (e.g., radical vs. incremental innovations). The different levels of uncertainty can affect partners' expectations regarding collaboration. Thus, our second objective is to investigate *how task uncertainty moderates the decisions of governance structure and alliance scope in the three types of international R&D alliances.* We test our arguments on a sample of 531 international R&D alliances involving companies in high-technology industries where survival and profitability depend critically on the ability to efficiently create and commercialize new technologies.

Our research extends the application of TCE to governance and scope decisions in international R&D alliances and provides greater precision and enhanced understanding of how firms manage knowledge in these alliances. First, our study enriches the cultural distance literature by showing how different dimensions of cultural difference affect partner firms' decisions of governance and scope in their international R&D alliances through the lens of transaction cost theory.

Second, while prior research has typically emphasized the benefits of international R&D collaboration, we examine the risks and challenges arising from multifaceted cultural differences in international R&D alliances. In a globalized business environment, it is tempting for firms to ally with others in order to capture market opportunities located in different countries. However, our study shows that cultural differences are complicated and can affect firms' alliance formation and management decisions at a fundamental level, particularly in terms of how partner firms' technological assets are managed through governance structure and alliance scope decisions.

Third, prior research has primarily focused on the traditional type of international strategic alliance formed between a foreign entrant and a host country partner. Our research examines the cultural differences involved in different types of international R&D alliances and their implications to knowledge management for partner firms. Fourth, our findings on the weakening moderating effects of task uncertainty reveal the additional difficulties of managing knowledge in international alliances involving high task uncertainty. Lastly, our research confirms the substitution effects between governance structure and alliance scope as knowledge management mechanisms in international R&D alliances.

The remainder of the chapter is organized as follows. We define three types of international R&D alliances by partner nationality and discuss the cultural difference associated with each type. We examine how alliance governance and scope as knowledge management mechanisms vary with cultural difference, and propose associated hypotheses on governance structure and alliance scope decisions. These discussions are followed by hypotheses on the moderating effects of task uncertainty. We test our hypotheses and conclude with a discussion of implications, limitations, and potential research questions that are suggested by the findings.

CULTURAL DIFFERENCES IN INTERNATIONAL R&D ALLIANCES

Culture refers to patterns of beliefs and values that are manifested in practices, behaviors, and various artifacts shared by members of an organization or a nation (Hofstede, 1980) and permeates all aspects of life within a society (for a review, see Kirkman, Lowe, & Gibson, 2006). Scholars have found that cultural differences create ambiguities in collaborative relationships, leading to conflicts and poor performance (e.g., Barkema, Bell, & Pennings, 1996; Brouthers & Brouthers, 2001; Lee, Shenkar, & Li, 2008; Tihanyi, Griffith, & Russell, 2005). Further, cultural differences exist at different levels (e.g., national, subnational, organizational, and intra-organizational). Prior research has examined how national cultural differences dominate/interact with more microlevel cultural differences (e.g., Hofstede, 1980; Javidan, House, Dorfman, Hanges, & de Luque, 2006; Pothukuchi, Damanpour, Choi, Chen, & Park, 2002; Sirmon & Lane, 2004). National cultural difference arises from activities involving different national cultures (that is, the partners have different nationalities and/or activities occur in different countries). In this study, we focus only on national cultural differences in international R&D alliances.

Cultural Difference and Alliance Type

Following Makino and Beamish (1998), we differentiate among three types of international alliances and examine the cultural differences involved in each. The first type is a Home-Host alliance (HSA) in which one partner is from the home and the other from the host country where the alliance activity occurs. An R&D alliance between Ford (a U.S. company) and Mitsubishi (a Japanese company) that takes place in Japan (host country) is an example. This is the conventional form of international alliance studied most frequently in the literature (Makino & Beamish, 1998). The second is a Home-Home alliance (HHA) where both partners come from the same home country and form an alliance in a host country; an example is Ford and General Motors opening a joint R&D lab in Germany. The third is a Home-Foreign alliance (HFA) between a home-country firm and a firm from a second country, with the alliance taking place in a third (host) country. An R&D alliance between Ford and Toyota in China is an example.[1] The percentage of Home-Home and Home-Foreign R&D alliances has risen sharply in recent years, from 8% in 1994 to almost 45% in 2003.[2]

Cultural distance refers to the cultural gap or difference between two cultures. Thus, cultural distance is a dyadic concept that is typically measured by an entropy measure (Kogut & Singh, 1988). We argue that in international alliances, cultural difference is multidimensional and involves cultural distances between two or more cultures. A few researchers have examined the issue of multiple national cultures faced by firms (e.g., Barkema & Drogendijk, 2007; Barkema & Vermeulen, 1997; Hutzschenreuter & Voll, 2008; Vermeulen & Barkema, 2002); these works actually analyze sequential cultural difference because the firms studied add more alliance locations over time. Our work is perhaps closest in spirit to Barkema et al.'s (1996) study of double-layered acculturation where firms adjust to two layers of cultural distance in their joint ventures and acquisitions: working in a foreign environment and working with foreign partners.

A Cultural Difference Metric

Table 2.1 develops a cultural difference metric for proxying cultural differences between our three international alliance types. The actual cultural difference for a particular alliance, which depends on the specific nationalities of the partners and alliance location, can be calculated using well-known cultural characteristics measures such as the Hofstede and Globe indexes, although we recognize that these measures do have their own problems (Shenkar, 2001). Still, our underlying theoretical argument about cultural differences between alliance types should be robust with respect to these measures, particularly since we focus more on *ranking* differences rather than calculating *absolute* difference measures.

We argue that cultural difference can rise in two ways: between alliance partners and/or from alliance location. Considering first only the partner firms and ignoring alliance location (see column 5 in Table 2.1), cultural distance is, in the first instance, zero for HHA because both partners in the dyad are from the same home country. (We recognize, of course, that there can be cultural differences within countries, but these are ignored here for simplicity.) Cultural distance is positive for both HSA and HFA, but more information about the partners' cultural characteristics is needed to be able to rank HSA relative to HFA in terms of cultural difference.

Turning to the second source of cultural difference, alliance location, we examine the nationality(ies) of the partner firms relative to alliance location (see column 6 in Table 2.1). In HHA, the foreign location of the alliance means that while cultural distance is zero between the partner firms, it is positive between the home and host country locations. For example, the cultural distance in an international alliance involving Ford and GM going to Japan depends on the cultural distance between each partner and the alliance location.

Next, we need to aggregate the individual dyadic cultural distances in order to determine the cultural difference of the alliance as a whole, taking

TABLE 2.1 Cultural Difference in International Alliances

Alliance Type	Nationality of Partner 1	Nationality of Partner 2	Alliance Location	Culture Difference between the Partner Firms (Ignoring Alliance Location)	Cultural Difference between the Partner Firms (Taking Alliance Location into Account)
HHA	Home (H)	Home (H)	Host (S)	$\lvert H - H \rvert = \text{zero}$	$w(\lvert H - S \rvert) + (1 - w)(\lvert H - S \rvert) = (\lvert H - S \rvert)$
HSA	Home (H)	Host (S)	Host (S)	$\lvert H - S \rvert$	$w(\lvert H - S \rvert) + (1 - w)(\lvert S - S \rvert) = w(\lvert H - S \rvert)$
HFA	Home (H)	Foreign (F)	Host (S)	$\lvert H - F \rvert$	$w(\lvert H - S \rvert) + (1 - w)(\lvert F - S \rvert)$

Note: "w" is a weighting factor capturing the relative importance of the focal firm in the international alliance.

into account cultural difference due to both partner nationality and to alliance location. We can simply add the three difference proxy measures, or we can use a weighting factor to take differences in alliance characteristics into account. For example, an alliance dominated by one large partner with a small partner performing a minor role is clearly different from a 50–50 partnership. We therefore use "w" as a weighing device for the relative contribution or share of the first partner in the alliance and "1 – w" for the second partner's contribution or share.

Using this approach, the cultural difference of the HHA alliance, taking into account both partner nationality and alliance location, is $w(|H-S|) + (1-w)(|H-S|) = (|H-S|)$. For example, in the case of Ford and GM going to Japan, overall alliance cultural difference would be only that between the United States and Japan because both partners are U.S. firms.

In HSA, the partners are from different home countries and the alliance location is in one of the two partners' countries. Therefore, we must consider the cultural distance of each home partner firm relative to the alliance location. For example, in the case of Ford and Mitsubishi in Japan, cultural distance for Ford, relative to alliance location, is that between the United States and Japan; for Mitsubishi, it is zero. The only cultural difference is that faced by the foreign partner (Ford) in the host country alliance location (Japan). If Ford is the home alliance partner, cultural difference can be illustrated by Ford's alliance contribution or share multiplied by the cultural distance between the United States and Japan (that is, $w(|H-S|)$ in column 6 of Table 2.1). Because cultural difference for HHA is $(|H-S|)$, which is larger than $w(|H-S|)$ for $w < 1$, there is a clear benefit in terms of reduced cultural difference when an international R&D alliance involves a local partner in the host country.

In HFA, the partners are from different home countries and the alliance location is in a third, host country (Ford and Toyota in China). Thus, cultural difference is the sum of that between each partner firm and the alliance location, where each distance is weighted by the partner firm's contribution to the alliance, which is $w(|H-S|) + (1-w)(|F-S|)$.

We can now use our cultural difference metric to rank the cultural differences of the three alliance types. For HSA, overall cultural difference, taking into account alliance location, is clearly the smallest because $w(|H-S|)$ is less than $|H-S|$ and also less than $w(|H-S|) + (1-w)(|H-F|)$. Thus, as long as $w < 1$, the cultural difference ranking is HHA > HSA and HFA > HSA. However, the ranking of HHA versus HFA depends on their relative cultural distances from the host country location; that is, $|H-S|$ can be greater or less than $w(|H-S|) + (1-w)(|F-S|)$.[3] Normally, one could expect the additional challenges of managing three cultures would matter in addition to the distances between them. Thus, we expect the sequence of cultural difference incorporating both partner nationality and alliance location to be HFA > HHA > HSA. Using this cultural difference ranking of different alliance types, we now build our hypotheses linking cultural difference to the alliance partners' decisions about alliance governance and scope.

GOVERNANCE AND SCOPE AS KNOWLEDGE MANAGEMENT MECHANISMS

Governance Structure

Transaction cost economics (TCE) suggests that an appropriate governance structure is a mechanism that firms can use to promote knowledge sharing and reducing partners' knowledge leakage concerns in an alliance (Kale & Barnes, 1992; Oxley, 1997; Shimizu, Hitt, Vaidyanath, & Pisano, 2004). On one hand, R&D alliances are designed to encourage *intended* knowledge sharing as alliance linkages are key channels to obtain accesses to external knowledge (e.g., Ahuja, 2000; Shan, Walker, & Kogut, 1994). Equity investments from both partners encourage commitment and willingness to share knowledge to ensure the performance of an alliance. Researchers drawing from both TCE (e.g., Oxley, 1999; Pisano, 1989) and from the knowledge-based view (e.g., Kogut & Zander, 1992) have suggested the important role of hierarchy in promoting knowledge sharing.

On the other hand, however, firms expose their valuable technological assets to opportunism hazards while encouraging intended knowledge sharing, resulting in *unintended* knowledge sharing. Appropriation concerns are based on behavioral uncertainty, combined with the difficulties of specifying intellectual property rights, and by the challenges of contractual monitoring and enforcement (Oxley, 1997). The "mutual hostage" positions offered by equity-based governance structures, to an extent, guarantee alliance performance as part of the internalization process to avoid opportunism (Hennart, 1982, 1991; Teece, 1986). Hierarchical structures are thus thought to be more applicable when concerns of appropriation are potentially high because more hierarchical controls are believed to provide greater incentive alignment than fewer hierarchical controls.

Comparing the three types of international R&D alliances, we expect the highest cultural differences with HFAs and the lowest with HSAs, based on the arguments above (HFA > HHA > HSA). Therefore, knowledge sharing challenges and knowledge leakage concerns stemming from potential partner opportunism conflicts and incompatibilities should be highest for HFAs and lowest for HSAs. Thus, to address these challenges and concerns in international R&D alliances, HFA partner firms are the most likely to choose an equity-based governance structure, while HSA partner firms are the least likely to adopt an equity-based governance structure.

Hypothesis 1a: *HFA partner firms are more likely to adopt an equity-based governance structure than HSA partner firms; i.e., HFA(equity) > HSA(equity).*

Hypothesis 1b: *HHA partner firms are more likely to adopt an equity-based governance structure than HSA partner firms; i.e., HHA(equity) > HSA(equity).*

Hypothesis 1c: *HFA partner firms are more likely to adopt an equity-based governance structure than HHA partner firms, i.e., HFA(equity) > HHA(equity).*

Alliance Scope

Oxley and Sampson (2004) define alliance scope as the extent to which the partners combine multiple and sequential functions or value-chain activities within the alliance such as R&D, manufacturing, and/or marketing. Alliance scope is one of the most important decisions partner firms make when forming an alliance (Khanna, 1998).

A broad alliance scope (that is, an alliance with not only R&D, but also manufacturing and/or distribution) creates knowledge management challenges for an international R&D alliance (Khanna, 1998; Li et al., 2008; Oxley & Sampson, 2004; Reuer, 2002). First, broad alliance scope implies that various types of knowledge are intended for transfer (Khanna, 1998; Oxley & Sampson, 2004). The increased number of knowledge types generates complicated contents to be transferred between partners, imposing additional challenges to effective knowledge exchange. Second, broad alliance scope generates more challenges to craft the boundary between partners and thus more challenges to protect partner firms' technological assets. It is almost impossible to effectively manage mixed activity in R&D alliances without extensive sharing of tacit knowledge embedded in operational routines (Reuer, 2002). Such extensive knowledge sharing can possibly alter the relative competitive position of partner firms.

Decisions to restrict alliance scope can be a response to the elevated leakage concerns associated with knowledge sharing in particular competitive contexts. Considering the cultural difference of international R&D alliances, scope decisions are likely to vary by alliance types. Because the degree of cultural difference is the highest in HFAs and lowest in HSAs in the sequence HFA > HHA > HSA, knowledge exchange challenges and leakage concerns about partner opportunism are the least in HSAs. HSA partners are therefore more likely to vertically expand their collaboration to include manufacturing and/or marketing activities than are HFA or HHA partner firms. That is, an HSA is more likely to be formed with a broader scope than HFA and HHA, allowing this type of alliance to potentially achieve more synergies.

Further, comparing HFA and HHA, we argue that HFA is more complicated because it involves three nationalities (two foreign partner firms and one host market). This substantial cultural difference complicates the collaboration between partner firms, thereby creating more challenges and opportunism concerns. To effectively manage these concerns, partner firms are likely to allow only a small number of contact points in HFAs, in contrast to HHAs.

> **Hypothesis 2a:** *HFA partner firms are more likely to choose a narrow alliance scope than HSA partner firms; i.e., HFA (narrow) > HSA (narrow).*

> **Hypothesis 2b:** *HHA partner firms are more likely to choose a narrow alliance scope than HSA partner firms; i.e., HHA (narrow) > HSA (narrow).*

> **Hypothesis 2c:** *HFA partner firms are more likely to choose a narrow alliance scope than HHA partner firms; i.e., HFA (narrow) > HHA (narrow).*

Impact of Task Uncertainty

R&D alliances can be used to develop at least two types of innovations: radical and incremental (Dewar & Dutton, 1986; Sheremata, 2004). Incremental innovations are based on minor changes or improvements in the current technology, which help incumbent firms derive maximum value from their current capabilities by providing customers with similar goods or services that are marginally improved or provided at a lower cost (Sheremata, 2004). In contrast, radical innovations are based on new design concepts that break existing paradigms and possibly change the basis of competition in the industry.

In addition to uncertainty arising from the task *per se,* international R&D alliances designed to develop radical innovations involve even more uncertainty due to the potential knowledge transfer difficulties and greater partner opportunism. For example, alliances focused on developing radical innovations have more challenges of knowledge sharing coupled with risks of knowledge leakage than those targeting incremental innovations (Li et al., 2008). For incremental innovations, the preexisting product or process technology enables partner firms to delineate property rights at the beginning of an alliance with far less ambiguity than is the case of radical innovations in which the relevant technology does not preexist (Pisano, 1989). As a result, alliances developing radical innovations involve more potential partner opportunism and greater uncertainty than those developing incremental innovations.

Thus, we argue that task uncertainty increases partner firms' concerns about knowledge management and encourages the adoption of equity-based governance structures and the restriction of alliance scope for *all* three types of international R&D alliances. A firm's concern regarding knowledge control is greater when the innovation task of an international R&D alliance is radical and the contact points between partner firms are greater in number. To address this concern, firms have a stronger preference for an equity structure and narrow scope.

Hypothesis 3a: *Greater task uncertainty encourages the adoption of an equity-based governance structure for all types of international R&D alliances.*

Hypothesis 3b: *Greater task uncertainty encourages the adoption of a narrower alliance scope for all types of international R&D alliances.*

We argued in previous sections that in order to protect their valuable knowledge in international R&D alliances, partner firms are likely to adopt an equity-based governance structure and to engage in a narrow alliance scope in the sequence HFA > HHA > HSA. Task uncertainty moderates these relationships by reducing preference differences across alliance types. Task uncertainty increases partner firms' preference for equity-based governance structures and narrow alliance scope, regardless of alliance type. However, HFA partners are likely to have adopted both governance and scope protective mechanisms—even in the absence of task uncertainty—because HFAs have the highest level of cultural difference. As a result, we hypothesize that preference differences across alliance types should shrink (that is, the preference ordering is unchanged—HFA > HHA > HSA—but the gaps shrink) as task uncertainty increases. Therefore, task uncertainty leads to smaller preference differences across alliance types in terms of selecting protective mechanisms (i.e., governance structure and alliance scope).

Hypothesis 4: *Task uncertainty moderates the relationship between governance structure and type of international R&D alliance such that the difference in governance preference across alliance type narrows as task uncertainty increases.*

Hypothesis 5: *Task uncertainty moderates the relationship between alliance scope and type of international R&D alliance such that the difference in scope preference across alliance types narrows as task uncertainty increases.*

Figure 2.1 summarizes and illustrates our main arguments, which are tested below.

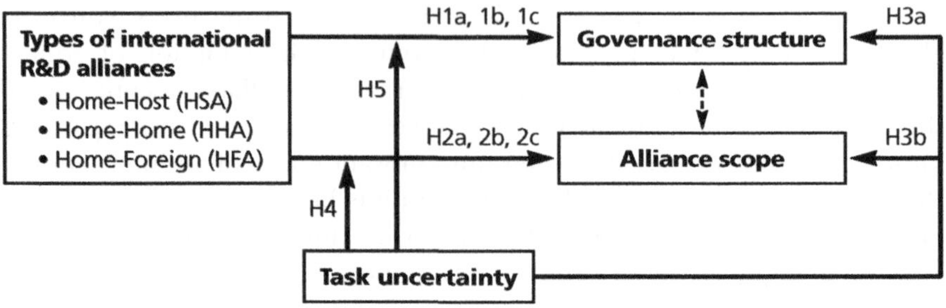

Figure 2.1 Conceptual framework. *Note:* Relationship represented by broken line has been investigated in prior literature (see Li et al., 2008 and Oxley & Sampson, 2004) and therefore is not formally hypothesized in our chapter.

METHODOLOGY

Sample

We test our hypotheses on a sample of international R&D alliances in which (a) all the partner firms are from high-technology industries;[4] (b) the alliance takes place in a high-technology industry; and (c) the alliance involves R&D activities. Firms in high-technology industries are ideal for our study because profitability and survival are critically dependent on a firm's ability to create and commercialize innovations quickly and efficiently. We consider an alliance international if partners are from different countries or if partners are from the same home country but the alliance is located in a country different from their home country. We used the Securities Data Corporation (SDC) Platinum database to retrieve sample alliances and their information. After the deletion of observations with incomplete information, our final sample is composed of 531 international R&D alliances formed between 1994 and 2003.

Measures

Dependent Variables

The first dependent variable, *governance*, is set to 1 when the international R&D alliance is an equity-based alliance and 0 when it is a contractual alliance. The second dependent variable, *scope*, is set to 1 when alliance activities only include collaborative R&D and 0 when the alliance also involves manufacturing and/or marketing.

Independent Variables

Three dummy variables are generated, with 1 representing *HSA*, *HHA*, and *HFA*, respectively; and 0 otherwise. The identification of each type of international R&D alliance is based on the theoretical definition presented in the previous section.

Information to create the variable *task uncertainty* is coded from synopses of alliance activities provided by the SDC Platinum database, the Lexis-Nexis Database, and the RDS Business Reference Suite, with a scale from 1 (highly incremental innovation) to 7 (highly radical innovation). Two independent coders evaluated the synopses of alliance activities. The percentage agreement between the coders was 73% and Cohen's kappa was 0.79, which is well above the satisfactory level of 0.70. Disagreements were discussed and resolved by the two coders. We standardized the coding by year to eliminate possible time bias by the coders.

Control Variables

While our theoretical framework focuses on three types of international R&D alliances, we include in the analyses the cultural distance involved in each alliance based on its location in order to control for within-group variances. The weight w, representing each partner's contribution to the alliance (see Table 2.1), is proxied by its equity share.[5, 6] We measure cultural distance using two major cultural dimensions—*power distance* and *uncertainty avoidance*—as they have been recognized as more relevant for management purposes than other cultural dimensions (i.e., individualism and masculinity) (Hennart & Larimo, 1998; Hofstede, 1991). The inclusion of two more relevant cultural dimensions instead of all four also avoids multicollinearity problems.[7]

We include several control variables for partner firm characteristics. First, we control for *firm size,* because larger firms have more resources to engage in equity-based governance and to offer a wide range of collaborative opportunities (broader scope) than do smaller firms. The proxy for firm size is the logged number of employees, which is an appropriate measure given our high-technology sample. Second, we include the logged number of prior alliances between partner firms during the past 5 years to control for *prior alliances between partner firms.* There is evidence (although mixed) in the literature that trust develops in repeated alliances such that the hazards of opportunism can be reduced, thereby affecting the governance structure and scope decisions (Gulati, 1995). Third, we include the logged number of prior alliances by each partner during the past 5 years to control for *general alliance experience of partner firms.* Experience through repeated engagements in various collaborative formats with diverse partners likely help the firm in selecting appropriate governance structures and in designing the scope of future alliances (Hoang & Rothaermel, 2005; Kale, Dyer, & Singh, 2002).

We also control for alliance characteristics. First, the distinction of scale alliances from link alliances reflects different objectives by partner firms and therefore is likely to affect partners' intent to cooperate (Dussauge, Garrett, & Mitchell, 2000). *Scale alliance* is set to 1 if the contributions by partner firms to an alliance are similar and overlap, and 0 otherwise. Second, the direct competition between partners is likely to influence their strategies of collaboration as well as the governance structures and scopes; *competitor* is set to 1 if partner firms have the same 3-digit SIC codes, and 0 if not. Third, we add a dummy variable, *industry,* for the alliance, because technologies in some industries involve more uncertainty than others and therefore may face different levels of concerns regarding protection of their technological assets. *Industry* is set to 1 if the sample alliance is of a high-tech service industry, and 0 if high-tech manufacturing.

At the country level, we control for the *intellectual property protection* provided by the markets where the alliances are located. When external markets cannot provide effective protection of intellectual properties, partner firms are likely to absorb the residual costs to protect their IPR by adopting more protective mechanisms such as equity-based governance structures or narrow scopes (Li et al., 2008). Information on intellectual property protection in the local market is from the World Competitiveness Yearbook. We also control for *host market size* using its annual GDP (US$ at PPP). Larger market size in a host country may attract more equity-based alliances and alliances with broader scope to realize potential synergies between alliance partners in the host country. The logged format is used in our analysis.

Lastly, because the dataset covers R&D alliances over a 10-year period, we must be concerned with the possibility that firms and industries have changing preferences regarding partner selection. Thus, we include a dummy variable for each year in our analysis.

Design and Procedure

The endogenous relationship between governance structure and alliance scope is well-known (Li et al., 2008; Oxley & Sampson, 2004). Because a Hausman test indicates there is endogeneity in our analysis ($\chi^2 = 85.72$, $p < 0.001$), we adopt a three-stage least squares (3SLS) regression approach. Following Arellano and Bover (1995), we select three instrumental variables (scale alliance, competitor, and host country GDP) for the 3SLS regression technique.

RESULTS

Table 2.2 presents the descriptive statistics. We carefully explored the potential for multicollinearity, which does not threaten our coefficient estimates as indicated by the highest variance inflation factor (VIF) of 5.50 and the average VIF below 2.

Table 2.3 presents five sets of 3SLS models. Model 1 includes control variables only. Models 2 and 3 report results where HSAs are the base case compared with HFAs and HHAs alliances. Model 2 includes the control and independent variables; Model 3 adds interaction terms. Models 4 and 5 report results where HHAs are the base case compared with HFAs and HSAs alliances. Model 4 includes the control and independent variables; Model 5 adds interaction terms. The partial correlation is 0.60 between HFA and HSA (see Table 2.2). However, VIF scores for Models 4 and 5 did not suggest a multicollinearity problem. In addition, we included these independent variables separately in the regression models and the statistical significance levels of estimated coefficients remain largely the same. Therefore, we concluded that multicollinearity did not threaten the coefficient estimates in Models 4 and 5.

We hypothesized that HFAs are more likely to be governed by an equity-based structure than HSAs (Hypothesis 1a) and HHAs (Hypothesis 1c) and that HHAs are more likely to be governed by equity-based structure than HSAs (Hypothesis 1b). Hypothesis 1a receives support because the coefficient for HFA, where HSA is the base case (Model 2), is positive and statistically significant ($\beta = 0.162$, $p < 0.05$) in the Governance equation, indicating that HFA partner firms are more likely to choose equity-based governance than HSA partner firms. However, we do not find empirical support for Hypothesis 1b, suggesting that HHAs are more likely to be governed by equity-based structures than HSAs. The coefficient for HHA, where HSA is the base case (Model 2), which is the same coefficient with the reversed sign on HSA in Model 4), is not statistically significant. Hypothesis 1c receives support as indicated by the positive and statistically significant coefficient for HFA relative to the HHA base case (Model 4) in the Governance equation ($\beta = 0.227$, $p < 0.05$), suggesting that HFA partner firms are more likely to engage in equity-based governance than HHA partner firms. In sum, the results suggest that HFA partner firms are most likely to choose equity-based governance structure; but we cannot determine whether HHA or HSA partner firms are the least likely to choose equity-based governance structure.

We hypothesized that HFAs are more likely to involve narrow alliance scope than HSAs (Hypothesis 2a) and HHAs (Hypothesis 2c), and that HHAs are more likely to involve narrow alliance scope than HSAs (Hypothesis 2b). For Hypothesis 2a, the coefficient for HFA in the Scope equation relative to HSA as the base case (Model 2) is not statistically significant, offering no support for this hypothesis. The coefficient for HFA relative to HHA as the base case (Model 4) in the Scope equation is positive and statistically significant ($\beta = 0.343$, $p < 0.05$), supporting Hypothesis 2c, suggesting that HFAs are more likely to engage in narrow scope than HHAs.

TABLE 2.2 Descriptive Statistics

Variables	Mean	S.D.	Min	Max	1	2	3	4	5	6	7	8
1. Governance	0.284	0.452	0	1	1.000							
2. Scope	0.565	0.496	0	1	–0.171	1.000						
3. Home-Foreign R&D alliance (HFA)	0.083	0.233	0	1	0.133	0.019	1.000					
4. Home-Host R&D alliance (HSA)	0.847	0.309	0	1	–0.097	0.042	–0.660	1.000				
5. Home-Home R&D alliance (HHA)	0.070	0.215	0	1	0.006	–0.074	–0.049	–0.718	1.000			
6. Task uncertainty	–0.023	0.977	–2.178	2.186	–0.151	0.113	–0.065	0.075	–0.040	1.000		
7. Cultural distance: Power distance	8.322	7.353	0	55	0.322	0.028	0.159	–0.163	0.069	–0.096	1.000	
8. Cultural distance: Uncertainty avoidance	15.051	10.757	0	54	–0.016	0.089	0.124	–0.198	0.149	0.023	0.371	1.000
9. Firm size: Partner 1	3.690	2.042	–4.269	6.541	0.082	–0.001	0.090	–0.096	0.044	0.052	0.116	0.114
10. Firm size: Partner 2	4.125	1.558	–4.510	5.945	0.118	–0.064	0.071	–0.049	0.000	–0.031	0.055	–0.026
11. Prior alliances between partner firms	0.357	0.583	0	2.773	–0.135	–0.021	0.002	–0.026	0.032	0.129	–0.119	0.121
12. General alliance experience: Partner 1	2.239	1.093	0	6.244	0.075	–0.022	0.033	–0.002	–0.028	0.035	0.009	0.098
13. General alliance experience: Partner 2	2.303	1.067	0.693	6.217	–0.071	0.033	–0.050	0.028	0.010	–0.012	0.011	0.054
14. Scale alliance	0.670	0.470	0	1	–0.135	0.177	0.011	0.007	–0.020	0.087	–0.012	–0.026
15. Competitor	0.207	0.406	0	1	0.028	–0.030	0.051	–0.026	–0.013	–0.002	0.054	0.017
16. IPR protection	7.210	1.419	1.340	8.950	–0.451	0.039	–0.002	0.039	–0.050	0.173	–0.467	0.002
17. Industry	0.356	0.479	0	1	0.028	0.113	–0.023	–0.016	0.043	–0.141	–0.008	–0.167
18. Host country GDP	7.951	1.241	4.140	9.256	–0.371	0.056	–0.151	0.106	0.000	0.083	–0.246	–0.053
19. Year	1995.239	1.595	1994	2003	0.107	–0.145	0.090	–0.081	0.024	–0.025	0.037	0.003

Variables	Mean	S.D.	9	10	11	12	13	14	15	16	17	18	19
9. Firm size: Partner 1	3.690	2.042	1.000										
10. Firm size: Partner 2	4.125	1.558	−0.124	1.000									
11. Prior alliances between partner firms	0.357	0.583	0.144	−0.041	1.000								
12. General alliance experience: Partner 1	2.239	1.093	0.293	0.011	0.023	1.000							
13. General alliance experience: Partner 2	2.303	1.067	−0.022	0.217	0.001	0.017	1.000						
14. Scale alliance	0.670	0.470	−0.065	−0.001	0.002	0.008	0.062	1.000					
15. Competitor	0.207	0.406	−0.072	0.045	−0.010	−0.018	0.083	0.052	1.000				
16. IPR protection	7.210	1.419	−0.115	−0.089	0.099	−0.051	−0.026	0.103	−0.067	1.000			
17. Industry	0.356	0.479	−0.111	0.081	−0.122	−0.074	0.038	−0.039	0.067	0.020	1.000		
18. Host country GDP	7.951	1.241	−0.114	−0.100	0.049	−0.069	−0.002	0.096	−0.024	0.349	−0.029	1.000	
19. Year	1995.239	1.595	0.036	−0.011	0.031	−0.054	−0.090	−0.005	0.002	0.044	−0.131	0.040	1.000

Note: N = 531; correlations with absolute value greater than 0.08 are statistically significant at the level of $p < .05$.

TABLE 2.3 Three-Stage LeastSquares Regression

			HSA as base case				HHA as base case			
	Model 1		Model 2		Model 3		Model 4		Model 5	
	Governance	Scope	Governance	Scope	Governance	Scope	Governance	Scope	Governance	Scope
Governance	—	–0.327***	—	–0.326***	—	–0.343***	—	–0.326***	—	–0.343***
Scope	–0.217***	—	–0.219***	—	–0.228***	—	–0.219***	—	–0.228***	—
HFA	—	—	0.162*	0.132	0.112†	0.108	0.227*	0.343*	0.157	0.281*
HSA	—	—	-	-	-	-	0.065	0.210*	0.046	0.173†
HHA	—	—	–0.065	–0.210*	–0.046	–0.173†	-	-	-	-
Task uncertainty	—	—	–0.009	0.051*	–0.009	0.041†	–0.009	0.051*	0.105	0.252**
HFA*Task uncertainty	—	—	—	—	–0.168†	–0.071	—	—	–0.282*	–0.281*
HSA*Task uncertainty	—	—	—	—	—	—	—	—	–0.114†	–0.211*
HHA*Task uncertainty	—	—	—	—	0.114†	0.211*	—	—	—	—
Cultural distance: Power distance	0.008**	0.004	0.007**	0.004	0.007**	0.004	0.007**	0.004	0.007**	0.004
Cultural distance: Uncertainty avoidance	–0.001	0.004*	–0.001	0.005*	–0.001	0.005*	–0.001	0.005*	–0.001	0.005*
Firm size: Partner 1	0.003	0.010	0.002	0.008	0.001	0.007	0.002	0.008	0.001	0.007
Firm size: Partner 2	0.017	–0.010	0.015	–0.012	0.013	–0.014	0.015	–0.012	0.013	–0.014
Prior alliances between partner firms	–0.058*	–0.051	–0.056*	–0.057	–0.060*	–0.060†	–0.056*	–0.057	–0.060*	–0.060†

General alliance experience: Partner 1	0.022	–0.005	0.021	–0.007	0.021	–0.005	0.021	–0.007	0.021	–0.005
General alliance experience: Partner 2	–0.031*	–0.001	–0.029†	0.001	–0.029†	–0.002	–0.029†	0.001	–0.029†	–0.002
Scale alliance	—	0.169**	—	0.160**	—	0.164**	—	0.160**	—	0.164**
Competitor	—	–0.054	—	–0.06	—	–0.045	—	–0.060	—	–0.045
IPR protection	–0.096***	–0.025	–0.099***	–0.035†	–0.100***	–0.037†	–0.099***	–0.035†	–0.100***	–0.037†
Industry	0.054	0.137**	0.055	0.158**	0.059	0.164**	0.055	0.158**	0.059	0.164**
Host country GDP	–0.079***	—	–0.075***	—	–0.075***	—	–0.075***	—	–0.075***	—
Year 1995	0.087*	–0.127**	0.089*	–0.122*	0.089*	–0.122*	0.089*	–0.122*	0.089*	–0.122*
Year 1996	0.180**	0.081	0.179**	0.086	0.184**	0.088	0.179**	0.086	0.184**	0.088
Year 1997	–0.001	–0.073	–0.004	–0.078	–0.014	–0.091	0.093	–0.073	0.114	–0.036
Year 1998	0.098	–0.117	0.093	–0.073	0.114	–0.036	0.114	–0.221	0.117	–0.218
Year 1999	0.109	–0.259	0.114	–0.221	0.117	–0.218	0.112	–0.277†	0.129	–0.258
Year 2000	0.126	–0.262	0.112	–0.277†	0.129	–0.258	0.279	–0.496†	0.280	–0.490†
Year 2001	0.322	–0.476†	0.279	–0.496†	0.280	–0.490†	0.170	–0.289†	0.156	–0.287†
Year 2002	0.176	–0.298†	0.170	–0.289†	0.156	–0.287†	0.757*	–0.068	0.758	–0.054
Year 2003	0.766*	–0.125	0.757*	–0.068	0.758	–0.054	0.007**	0.004	0.007**	0.004
Intercept	1.563***	0.681	1.559***	0.765***	1.582	0.791***	1.494***	0.555***	1.536***	0.618***
N	531	531	531	531	531	531	531	531	531	531
χ^2	304.42***	110.35	312.40***	125.47	323.82***	134.63***	312.40***	125.47***	323.82***	134.63***
F-value	15.22***	2.25***	13.58***	5.23***	12.95***	5.18***	13.58***	5.23***	12.95***	5.18***

Note: $^{\dagger}p < .10$, $^{*}p < .05$, $^{**}p < .01$, $^{***}p < .001$.

Findings for Hypothesis 2b are contrary to the hypothesized relationship. The estimated coefficient for HHA relative to the HSA as the base case in the Scope equation (Model 2) is statistically significant but negative ($\beta = -0.210$, $p < 0.05$). This is also reported in Model 4 as the coefficient for HSA with the reversed sign. Thus, HSAs are more likely to involve narrow alliance scope than HHAs, which is the opposite of that hypothesized. In sum, the results suggest that HHA partner firms are most likely to engage in broad scope; but we cannot determine whether HFA or HSA partner firms are the least likely to engage in broad scope.

Hypotheses 3a and 3b suggest that greater task uncertainty increases the likelihood that alliance partners adopt equity-based governance structures (3a) and narrow alliance scope (3b). We find support for Hypothesis 3b as indicated by the positive and statistically significant coefficients in all Scope equations, indicating that task uncertainty encourages partner firms to develop a narrower alliance scope. However, Hypothesis 3a, on the positive relationship between task uncertainty and the adoption of equity-based governance structures, receives no support.

Lastly, we examine our hypotheses about the preference gap shrinking as task uncertainty increases (Hypotheses 4 and 5). In Model 3, the coefficient for the interaction term between HFA and task uncertainty is negative and marginally statistically significant in the Governance equation ($\beta = -0.168$, $p < 0.10$). The coefficient for the interaction term between HHA and task uncertainty is positive and also marginally statistically significant in the Governance equation ($\beta = 0.114$, $p < 0.05$); see also the same effect with the reverse sign in Model 5. In Model 5, the coefficient for the interaction term between HFA and task uncertainty is negative and statistically significant in the Governance equation ($\beta = -0.282$, $p < 0.01$). In Figure 2.2a, we graph the moderating effect of task uncertainty on governance for each alliance type. Because alliance type is a categorical variable proxied by three dummy variables, instead of graphing the relationship between governance and alliance type and showing the shifts as task uncertainty changes, we graph governance against task uncertainty for each alliance type. Figure 2.2a clearly shows that HFA is more likely to engage in equity-based governance than HHA or HSA, across all levels of task uncertainty, supporting Hypotheses 1a and 1c. However, because HHA > HSA exists at low levels of task uncertainty and HSA > HHA exists at high levels of task uncertainty, the lack of support for Hypothesis 1b (HHA > HSA) is likely due to the moderator effect. As task uncertainty rises, the preference gap between HFA and HSA and between HFA and HHA declines, providing partial support for Hypothesis 4.

In Model 3, the coefficient for the interaction term between HHA and task uncertainty is positive and statistically significant in the Scope equation ($\beta = 0.211$, $p < 0.05$). The coefficient for the interaction term between

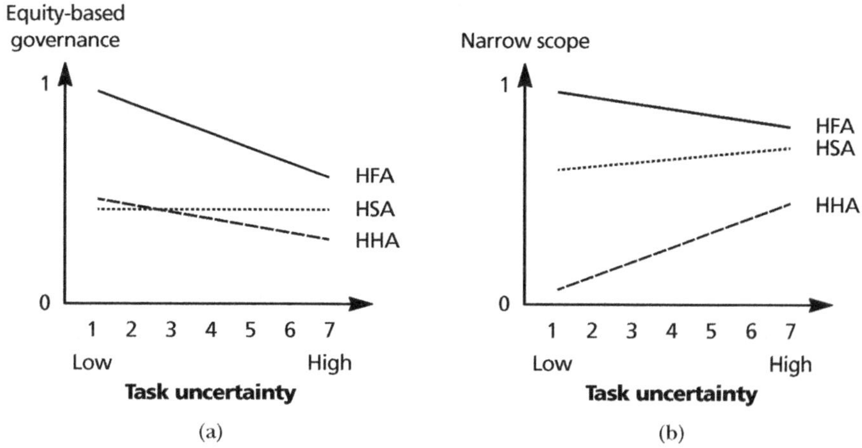

Figure 2.2 Moderating effect of task uncertainty by alliance type.

HFA and task uncertainty is negative and marginally statistically significant in Model 5 ($\beta = -0.281$, $p < 0.10$). The coefficient for the interaction term between HSA and task uncertainty is positive and marginally statistically significant in Model 3 ($\beta = 0.211$, $p < 0.10$); see also Model 5 with the reverse sign. Figure 2.2b shows that HHA is more likely to engage in narrow alliance scope than HFA, supporting Hypothesis 2c, across all levels of task uncertainty. The lack of support for Hypothesis 2b is evident as HSA > HHA, which is contrary to our arguments. While the direction of HFA > HSA shown in the figure is as expected in Hypothesis 2a, the test was not statistically significant. As Figure 2.2b shows, the preference gap between the three alliance types clearly narrows as task uncertainty rises, supporting Hypothesis 5. These results provide evidence that partner firms are careful to protect their technological assets when task uncertainty is high and are more likely to choose a narrow alliance scope.

DISCUSSION AND CONCLUSION

Cultural difference creates knowledge management challenges for international R&D alliance partners. The firms can reduce their knowledge management concerns by altering the alliance's governance structure and scope. Our analyses show that Home-Foreign alliances are the most likely to be governed by equity-based structures, and Home-Home alliances are the most likely to have broad alliance scope. Greater task uncertainty induces alliance partners to maintain a narrow alliance scope and reduces the preference differences across alliance types.

The finding that HSA partner firms are more likely to engage in narrow scope (that is, more likely to include only R&D and not include manufacturing or distribution) than HHA partner firms is the opposite of the prediction in Hypothesis 2b. Our speculation attributes this finding to concerns about local partners' opportunism regarding knowledge leakage. Prior research has typically recommended "going with a local" as an entry mode for better understanding the host market and quicker entry (which is important for sales and distribution) and for lower transaction costs for postentry operation (which is important for managing the local workforce). However, our analysis shows that while a local partner may help with entering a host market quickly, firms are concerned about knowledge leakage to their local partners. Alternatively, partnering with a "friend from home" may reduce opportunism concerns.

Contributions

Our study extends transaction cost theory in the explanation of governance and scope decisions in international R&D alliances. This extension offers enhanced understanding of how firms form and manage R&D alliances in international contexts. In the current global environment, it is tempting to encourage firms to capture opportunities located in different countries. Prior research has largely emphasized the benefits of international R&D collaboration; however, we argue that firms should be cautious in engaging in and managing international R&D alliances because of their heightened cultural differences. The cultural differences between partner firms as well as those between partner firms and alliance locations complicate the effective exploitation and exploration of partners' technological assets due to enhanced concerns of knowledge leakage. As a result, the goals of developing new technology or exploiting existing technology in new markets may be compromised.

Moreover, while prior research has typically focused on the traditional international alliance of a foreign and a host company, our research offers a more in-depth examination of cultural differences in three types of international R&D alliances. Such an examination advances our understanding not only of the variance of risks and transaction costs associated with different types of international R&D alliances, but also of the decision-making process likely used in each type of such an alliance to effectively balance knowledge sharing and knowledge control.

Further, our findings on the weakening moderating effects of task uncertainty reveal the complexity of R&D alliances. On one hand, it is necessary for both partner firms to commit to developing radical innovation in the alliance, which requires equity investment and a broad scope of shared activities. On the other hand, partner firms should be very cautious about their equity investment abroad when the uncertainty involved is high and may have to narrow the scope of shared activity to reduce the concern about partner opportunism.

Finally, our research confirms the substitution effects between governance structure and alliance scope in international R&D alliances. While many prior studies have assumed either governance or scope to be exogenous with the other endogenous variables, we considered both as endogenous and investigated how these two mechanisms can be utilized simultaneously to govern knowledge control in international R&D alliances.

Limitations and Future Research Avenues

Our study has several limitations that yield opportunities for future research. Our focus on R&D alliances leads to a relatively constrained sample where the number of Home-Home and Home-Foreign R&D alliances is relatively small. While the topic of focus and sample eliminate alternative explanations for the proposed causal relationships, these characteristics also limit our ability to further examine the composition of these two types of alliances. Future research can broaden the context and examine various combinations of, for example, Home-Foreign alliances.

We measured cultural distance using two cultural dimensions—power distance and uncertainty avoidance. It is interesting to note that power distance within an international R&D alliance is associated with governance-structure decisions, and uncertainty avoidance affects alliance scope decisions. It is probably because governance structure reflects the degree to which partner firms desire formal mechanisms of collaboration, and alliance scope mirrors the level of risks that partner firms are willing to accept. Further, in a post-hoc analysis, we controlled for the overall cultural difference between the alliance and the host market and between partner firms. We found that the cultural distance between the alliance and the host country, weighted by partner ownership, is positively related to the likelihood that the alliance was narrow in scope; whereas the simple measure of cultural distance between partners does not produce effects in our analysis of governance structure selection. Therefore, echoing Shenkar (2001), Shenkar, Luo, and Yeheskel (2008), and Ailon's (2008) challenge of current theoretical and methodological properties of cultural distance, we call for a comprehensive examination of the effects of cultural difference and both formal and informal institutional distance.

Investigating the role of partner selection as a possible knowledge protection mechanism in international R&D alliances is a promising avenue for future research. Li et al. (2008) recently argued that partner selection is a critical component of alliance management, and that these three decisions are substitutive and represent a dynamic and endogenous system. However, one could expect that the role of partner selection *per se* and the dynamic relationships among the three protective mechanisms are likely to be complicated when partner firms are from different home countries. For instance, partner firms from collectivistic countries may value prior interactions more than those from individualistic countries. Therefore, how prior relationships affect partner firms' decisions on governance structure and scope in future alliances is likely highly complex.

Moreover, examining international alliances (R&D or non-R&D) by geographic region is a promising avenue for future research; for example, how do North American alliances differ from European ones? We also recognize that cultural difference is derived not only from differences in, but also the direction of, its international activity (for example, moving from an OECD country to an emerging market [e.g., the focal partner is an OECD firm and the smaller partner(s) from an emerging market] versus when an emerging market firm is the focal partner and it has an OECD partner that has taken a small stake in the alliance).

In conclusion, international R&D alliances have grown in number and become more complicated over the past decade. The findings from this study suggest that cultural difference is an important construct for understanding strategic decision making in these alliances.

NOTES

1. When the number of alliance partners exceeds two, mixed forms are possible. For example, two foreign (home country) firms ally with one domestic (host country) firm would be a mixture of HSA and HHA. Our analysis is restricted to two-firm alliances.
2. Data were compiled from the Securities Data Corporation (SDC) Platinum database.
3. For example, assume H = 2, S = 1, F = 3 and w1 = ½, then the overall cultural complexity (the last column in Table 2.1) is HHA = 1, HSA = .5 and HFA = 1.5 so HFA > HHA > HSA. However, if F = 1.5, then HHA > HFA > HSA. We indeed empirically control the distance in our regression analyses.
4. See AeA's list of high-tech industries at http://www.aeanet.org/Publications/IDMK_definition.asp
5. If a sample alliance is non–equity based, the assigned weights for partners are as 50% each.
6. We also tested robustness by assigning 50–50 weights for partners as substitution for the actual ownership percentage. These two sets were highly correlated and similar results were observed.
7. We replicated our analyses by including overall cultural distance based on Kogut and Singh's (1988) index for four Hofstede cultural dimensions. Over-

all cultural distance was not statistically significant in the Governance equations, indicating the need to consider cultural distance as a multidimensional concept, at least in the empirical context of this study.

REFERENCES

Ahuja, G. (2000). The duality of collaboration: Inducements and opportunities in the formation of interfirm linkages. *Strategic Management Journal, 21,* 317–343.

Ailon, G. (2008). Mirror, mirror on the wall: Culture's consequences in a value test of its own design. *Academy of Management Review, 33,* 885–904.

Arellano, M., & Bover, O. (1995). Another look at the instrumental variables estimation of error-component models. *Journal of Econometrics, 68*(1), 29–51.

Barkema, H., Bell, J. H., & Pennings, J. M. (1996). Foreign entry, cultural barriers, and learning. *Strategic Management Journal, 17,* 151–166.

Barkema, H. G., & Drogendijk, R. (2007). Internationalizing in small, incremental or larger steps? *Journal of International Business Studies, 38,* 1132–1148.

Barkema, H. G., & Vermeulen, F. (1997). What differences in the cultural backgrounds of partners are detrimental for international joint ventures? *Journal of International Business Studies, 28,* 845–864.

Brouthers, K. D., & Brouthers, L. E. (2001). Explaining the national cultural distance paradox. *Journal of International Business Studies, 32,* 177–189.

Dewar, R. D., & Dutton, J. E. (1986). The adoption of radical and incremental innovations: An empirical analysis. *Management Science, 32,* 1422–1433.

Dussauge, P., Garrette, B., & Mitchell, W. (2000). Learning from competing partners: Outcomes and durations of scale and link alliances in Europe, North America and Asia. *Strategic Management Journal, 21,* 99–126.

Gulati, R. (1995). Does familiarity breed trust? The implications of repeated ties for contractual choices in alliances. *Academy of Management Journal, 38,* 85–112.

Hennart, J-F. (1982). *A theory of the multinational enterprise.* Ann Arbor, MI: University of Michigan Press.

Hennart, J-F. (1991). Control in multinational firms: The role of price and hierarchy. *Management International Review, 31*(1), 71–96.

Hennart, J-F., & Larimo, J. (1998). The impact of culture on the strategy of multinational enterprises: Does notional origin affect ownership decisions? *Journal of International Business Studies, 29,* 515–538.

Hoang, H., & Rothaermel, F. T. (2005). The effect of general and partner-specific alliance experience on joint R&D project performance. *Academy of Management Journal, 48,* 332–345.

Hofstede, G. (1980). *Culture's consequences, international differences in work-related values.* Beverly Hills, CA: Sage.

Hofstede, G. (1991). *Culture and organizations: Software of the mind.* London: McGraw-Hill.

Hutzschenreuter, T., & Voll, J. C. (2008). Performance effects of "added cultural distance" in the path of international expansion: The case of German multinational enterprises. *Journal of International Business Studies, 39,* 53–70.

Javidan, M., House, R. J., Dorfman, P. W., Hanges, P. J., & de Luque, M. S. (2006). Conceptualizing and measuring cultures and their consequences: A comparative review of GLOBE's and Hofstede's approaches. *Journal of International Business Studies, 37,* 897–914.

Kale, S. H., & Barnes, J. W. (1992). Understanding the domain of cross-national buyer-seller interactions. *Journal of International Business Studies, 23,* 101–132.

Kale, P., Dyer, J. H., & Singh, H. (2002). Alliance capability, stock market response, and long-term alliance success: The role of alliance function. *Strategic Management Journal, 23,* 747–767.

Kirkman, B. L., Lowe, K. B., & Gibson, C. B. (2006). A quarter century of culture's consequences. *Journal of International Business Studies, 37,* 285–320.

Khanna, T. (1998). The scope of alliances. *Organization Science, 9,* 340–355.

Kogut, B., & Singh, H. (1988). The effect of national culture on the choice of entry mode. *Journal of International Business Studies, 19,* 411–432.

Kogut, B., & Zander, U. (1992). Knowledge of the firm, combinative capabilities and the replication of technology. *Organization Science, 3,* 383–397.

Lee, S-H., Shenkar, O., & Li, J. (2008). Cultural distance, investment flow, and control in cross-border cooperation. *Strategic Management Journal, 29,* 1117–1125.

Li, D., Eden, L., Hitt, M. A., & Ireland, R. D. (2008). Friends, acquaintances or strangers? Partner selection in R&D alliances. *Academy of Management Journal, 51,* 315–334.

Makino, S., & Beamish, P. W. (1998). Performance and survival of joint ventures with non-conventional ownership structures. *Journal of International Business Studies, 29,* 797–818.

McCutchen, W. W., Jr., Swamidass, P. M., & Teng, B. (2004). R&D risk-taking in strategic alliances: New explanations for R&D alliances in the biopharmaceutical industry. *Management International Review, 44*(1), 53–67.

Oxley, J. E. (1997). Appropriability hazards and governance in strategic alliances: A transaction cost approach. *Journal of Law, Economics and Organization, 13,* 387–409.

Oxley, J. E. (1999). Institutional environment and the mechanisms of governance: The impact of intellectual property protection on the structure of inter-firm alliances. *Journal of Economic Behavior & Organization, 38,* 283–309.

Oxley, J. E., & Sampson, R. C. (2004). The scope and governance of international R&D alliances. *Strategic Management Journal, 25,* 723–749.

Pisano, G. (1989). Using equity participation to support exchange: Evidence from the biotechnology industry. *Journal of Law, Economics and Organization, 5*(1), 109–126.

Pothukuchi, V., Damanpour, F., Choi, J., Chen, C. C., & Park, S. H. (2002). National and organizational culture differences and international joint venture performance. *Journal of International Business Studies, 33,* 243–256.

Reuer, J. J. (2002). Incremental corporate reconfiguration through international joint venture buyouts and selloffs. *Management International Review, 42,* 237–260.

Sampson, R. (2007). R&D alliances and firm performance: The impact of technological diversity and alliance organization on innovation. *Academy of Management Journal, 50,* 364–386.

Shenkar, O. (2001). Cultural distance revisited: Towards a more rigorous conceptualization and measurement of cultural differences. *Journal of International Business Studies, 32,* 519–535.

Shenkar, O., Luo, Y., & Yeheskel, O. (2008). From "distance" to "friction": Substituting metaphors and redirecting intercultural research. *Academy of Management Review, 33,* 905–923.

Sheremata, W. A. (2004). Competing through innovation in network markets: Strategies for challengers. *Strategic Management Journal, 29,* 359–377.

Shan, W., Walker, G., & Kogut, B. (1994). Interfirm cooperation and startup innovation in the biotechnology industry. *Strategic Management Journal, 15,* 387–394.

Shimizu, K., Hitt, M. A., Vaidyanath, D., & Pisano, V. (2004). Theoretical foundations of cross-border mergers and acquisitions: A review of current research and recommendations for the future. *Journal of International Management, 10,* 307–353.

Sirmon, D. G., & Lane, P. (2004). A model of cultural differences and international alliance performance. *Journal of International Business Studies, 35,* 306–319.

Teece, D. J. (1986). Transactions cost economics and the multinational enterprise: An assessment. *Journal of Economics, Behavior & Organization,* 7(1), 21–45.

Tihanyi, L., Griffith, D. A., & Russell, C. J. (2005). The effect of cultural distance on entry mode choice, international diversification, and MNE performance: A meta-analysis. *Journal of International Business Studies, 36,* 270–283.

Vermeulen, F., & Barkema, H. (2002). Pace, rhythm, and scope: Process dependence in building a profitable multinational corporation. *Strategic Management Journal, 23,* 637–653.

CHAPTER 3

SHARING INTELLECTUAL PROPERTY RIGHTS IN CONTRACTUAL R&D ALLIANCES

Exchange Hazards and Cooperation

Hélène Delerue

ABSTRACT

Why do some firms choose to share foreground intellectual property rights (IPR) through joint patents while others do not? Joint patenting often results from R&D alliances. Under joint ownership, the contracting parties share ownership of an asset and the property rights to it. A joint patent can therefore be considered a means to allocate appropriable control rights. However, these rights are owned by different entities. This creates boundary overlaps that go beyond temporary organizational ones. To understand IPR sharing, therefore, we must investigate boundary decisions. In this chapter, we look at joint intellectual property ownership by extending the perspectives—which have been used mainly to explain organizational boundaries—to the firm's property rights boundaries. Although there are many reasons for a firm to set

Strategic Alliances for Value Creation, pages 51–71

organizational boundaries, we focus on (a) exchange hazards regarding asset-specific investments and (b) cooperation motives. Our findings indicate that joint patent activity depends mainly on contextual factors such as partners' technological portfolios and their anticipations of future interactions, rather than partners' contribution.

INTRODUCTION

The practice of joint ownership in biotechnology alliances continues to puzzle researchers. A joint patent is the output of a strategic alliance[1] and is increasingly common in research and development (R&D). Joint patenting is a potential indicator of success for interfirm cooperation (Hagedoorn, van Kranenburg, & Osborn, 2003). Nevertheless, because joint ownership results in the partition of rights (Kim & Mahoney, 2005) and increases the other party's freedom of action beyond the temporary R&D project, it may have important economic implications. Hagedoorn (2003) points out that "Joint patenting by companies, the sharing of property rights on inventions, is a relatively unknown phenomenon that is generally seen by patent lawyers and firms alike as a second-best option that, if possible, should be avoided" (p. 1035). Why do some firms share their patents with other firms? Joint patenting raises the issue of firm boundaries. Among the many definitions of firm boundaries, property rights theory defines a firm as a bundle of rights that delimits its boundaries (e.g., Grossman & Hart, 1986). Joint intellectual property (IP) ownership creates overlapping boundaries. Consequently, to understand intellectual property rights (IPR) sharing, we must look at boundary decisions.

It was traditionally argued that firms set boundaries due to fear of opportunism and the holdup problem (Holmström & Roberts, 1998). Thus, firm boundaries are driven by the exchange hazards that affect contractual completeness. PR theory emphasizes the allocation of *ex ante* control rights—distinguishing residual rights (e.g., ownership) from specific rights included in the contract—and considers that the contract may allocate the residual rights to either party (Grossman & Hart, 1986). In this perspective, the allocation of ex ante control rights may explain the allocation of *ex post* control rights. Hence, property rights theory can also interpret the role of rights to residual income. Due to contract incompleteness, the ex ante allocation of control rights and subsequent variables (e.g., investments) is limited by the indispensability of the parties in the ex post R&D process (Tirole, 1999). Put differently, a partner's incentive to invest in the relationship is contingent upon guarantees of some claim to the expected future income attributable to the discovery (Grossman & Hart, 1986; Hart & Moore, 1990).

A second argument is that joint IP ownership results from high levels of cooperation and trust (Rocha, 1997; Slowinski & Sagal, 2006). The greater the cooperation, the less reluctance to hold the informal and open idea exchanges between partners that are required for joint patenting (Slowinski & Sagal, 2006). From this perspective, we may explore the firm's boundaries in terms of the firm's willingness to cooperate. First, several studies have emphasized the social basis of boundary decisions (e.g., Eisenhardt & Schoonhoven, 1996; Gulati, 1995; Leiblein & Miller, 2003). For instance, the firm's boundaries depend on its routines, historical patterns, and experience (Pisano, 1990). Prior history between partners may explain alliance formation and firm boundaries. Second is the strategic role of self-interest in cooperation (Eisenhardt & Schoonhoven, 1996; Heide & Miner, 1992; Parkhe, 1993). Firms are driven to cooperate by the assignment of net positive values to expected outcomes (Axelrod, 1984; Parkhe, 1993; Skaperdas & Syropoulos, 1996). Astley (1984) calls this voluntaristic, organic cooperation.

This chapter investigates joint IP ownership by taking the perspectives that have traditionally explained organizational boundaries and extending them to property rights boundaries. Whereas there are many potential reasons for a firm to set organizational boundaries (e.g., Araujo, Dubois, & Galde, 2003; Pisano, 1990; Poppo & Zenger, 1998), we focus here on (a) asset specificity and (b) cooperation motives in terms of partnership experience and relationship continuity. We test our hypotheses using data on 104 R&D alliances in the U.S. biotechnology sector.

The remainder of this chapter is organized as follows: In the next section, we develop our hypotheses about the key motivations for joint ownership activity in R&D alliances. We then describe the research design in the methodology section. We end by discussing the results and drawing conclusions.

R&D ALLIANCES AND PROTECTION OF FOREGROUND KNOWLEDGE

An R&D alliance is defined as any voluntarily initiated interfirm cooperative agreement (Gulati, 1995) "which seeks to leverage the resources and competencies of partners in order to exchange or develop technology" (Li & Zhong, 2003, p. 101). The benefits of R&D alliances are many: R&D alliances provide dedicated funding, reduce uncertainty and costs, enable skills sharing, and complement internal resources and assets for innovation development (Hagedoorn, 1993). However, alliances are complex organizational arrangements characterized by overlapping organizational boundaries that pose appropriability hazards and risks (Das & Teng, 1996). These hazards increase with the degree of asset specificity due to contract incompleteness (e.g., Oxley, 1997). The higher the appropriability hazards in interfirm partnering, the more companies will prefer a joint venture mode (Oxley, 1997). In this perspective, ex post ownership of R&D output is implicitly explained by ex ante ownership and the governance structure. What is not clear is the extent to which the partner firms should share, for example, the unanticipated gains of the joint venture. Moreover, the empirical evidence reveals no difference in the number of joint patents between contractual alliances and joint ventures (Hagedoorn et al., 2003).

Most studies on R&D alliances focus on background knowledge protection (existing technologies as the firms enter into an R&D alliance); few authors focus on foreground knowledge (the technology created during the alliance). Hertzfeld, Link, and Vonortas (2006) show that patents are the most frequently used mechanisms to protect foreground knowledge, but they make no distinction between sole patents and joint patents. At the end of the collaborative process, the division of rights may result in mainly individual IP ownership or joint IP ownership.[2] If individual ownership results, either the partner firms split the R&D outputs or one partner ends up owning all the IP arising from the joint R&D (Teng, 2007). Under individual ownership, the joint R&D project results in either two separate assets owned by the two firms, or the appropriable control rights are concentrated in the hands of one agent, along with the residual rights to income, thereby minimizing dissipation (Foss & Foss, 1999). Under joint ownership, the contracting parties share ownership of and the property rights to the same asset. Thus, joint patenting can be a way to allocate appropriable control rights.

The division of intellectual property may result from the negotiation phase, in which the partners define their respective contributions. Alternatively, the partners may decide to leave the contract incomplete for a more informal division. Nevertheless, according to Guffey (2004), intellectual property rights have to be accounted for. He stresses that

> Joint ownership of patents can trap the unwary into a false sense of security. Often parties to a strategic alliance believe that joint ownership means that the parties will jointly control the patents and share the profits from the alliance in proportion to contributions or at least will share equally in such profits. The interplay between the laws governing joint inventorship and the laws governing joint ownership for patents can produce unexpected and disastrous results when parties enter into strategic alliances without anticipating how these laws affect the parties' rights to profit from the resulting patents. (p. 1)

IPR sharing refers to both the legal and economic concepts of property rights. From a legal standpoint, national jurisdictions have different statutory rules governing legal relationships between co-owners. These differences may affect whether firms engage in joint patenting. From the late 1970s to the late 1980s, about 4.6% of American firms had at least one joint patent, compared to 40.1% of firms in Japan and 13.1% in Germany (Gauvin, 1992). In the United States, the general rules are codified under 35 U.S.C. § 262, which states, "In the absence of any agreement to the contrary, each of the joint owners of a patent may make, use, offer to sell, or sell the patented invention... without the consent of and without accounting to the other owners" (Merges & Locke, 1990). Without a specific agreement to protect against problems associated with the general rules, co-owners are at each other's mercy.

According to Barzel (1997), economic rights are the more relevant concept in terms of property rights. "Property rights affects the allocation and use of resources in specific and predictable ways... it is understood to consist of the right to use, to change the form and substance, and to transfer all rights in the asset through sales, or through rental" (Furubotn & Pejovich, 1972, p. 1139). Co-ownership and the sharing of intellectual property rights raise the issue of the firm's boundaries. Under property rights theory, a firm is a collection of assets over which managers enjoy residual control rights, including the right to decide how the assets are to be used under circumstances that are not specified in a contract (Grossman & Hart, 1986). The allocation of property rights affects the firm's boundary decisions (Arora & Merges, 2004).

So why do some firms choose to share foreground IPR through joint patenting while others do not?

JOINT PATENTING AND ECONOMIC RATIONALES

Joint Patenting and Asset-Specific Investment

Both transaction cost (TC) theory and the resource-based (RB) view address specificity. Two kinds of specific assets are important in alliances: the firm-specific assets central to the RB view and the transaction-specific assets central to TC theory. Firm-specific assets are described as imperfectly mobile. That is, "They are tradable but more valuable within the firm that currently employs them than they would be in other employ" (Peteraf, 1993, p. 183). Firm-specific resources could be gainfully applied to multiple uses in various product markets, through internal or external transactions, and in combination with various complementary assets (Teece 1986; Madhok & Tallman, 1998). Transaction-specific assets, on the other hand, refer to "the degree to which the assets used can be redeployed to alternative uses and by alternative users without sacrifice of productive value" (Williamson, 1991, p. 282). Specific assets have important value-creation properties, and at the same time, by generating opportunistic behavior, they influence transaction costs (Riordan & Williamson, 1985). The greater the transaction asset specificity, the greater the switching costs for the firm, and the greater the partner's ability to expropriate transactional quasi-rent, or the excess above the returns required to maintain a resource in current operation. Williamson does not suggest that all actors behave opportunistically. Rather, he contends that the probability of opportunism increases with increasing asset specificity. Due to bounded rationality and uncertainty, it is difficult to distinguish between actors who will cooperate and those who will behave opportunistically. Williamson (1975) therefore concludes that when the degree of asset specificity is not significant, the probability of opportunistic behavior is low.

Economic value creation is the outcome of economizing on transaction costs (Foss & Foss, 2005). In order to reduce transaction costs, it has been suggested that vertical integration, defined as internal organization or joint venturing, is more likely to become the preferred governance structure when specific investments become important (Oxley, 1997; Teece, 1986). The reason is that specific ex ante investment generate ex post bargaining situations in which the other party has an opportunity to extract a portion of the quasi-rent associated with the specific investment. Consequently, according to TC theory, asset specificity could increase the opportunistic potential and induce the parties to jointly own resources. Nevertheless, in an analysis of General Motors' reasons for acquiring Fisher Body, Coase (2000) noted that the asset specificity problem was satisfactorily solved through contractual arrangements, and that vertical integration was not the chosen solution. Contractual arrangements become more complex with increasing protective provisions, according to neoclassic contract law, whereas investment becomes more specific (Joskow, 1988; Poppo & Zenger, 2002; Reuer & Ariño, 2002). Parties insert contract clauses in anticipation of future contingencies that are based on current perceptions. According to Foss and Foss (2005), firms can appropriate more of the economic value created by resource utilization in the transaction by clearly defining property rights. Property rights generate "new rules of the game" (Kim & Mahoney, 2005). Specific resources can be viewed in terms of property rights: "the more economically valuable the resources, the more economic incentives there are to make property rights of resources more precise and the more precisely delineated the property rights of resources, the more valuable resources become" (p. 235). Consequently, Kim and Mahoney argue that making property rights more precise can be another way of looking at the value creation process. That is, resource management must take into account the transformation from an ex ante competitive situation to an ex post joint situation in order to maximize the quasi-rent. Asset specificity may therefore explain joint patent activity.

Asset-specific investments can be more or less balanced between the partners. According to Williamson (1996), asymmetric investments may appear as myopic, as well as poor managerial practice. More recently, another debate has arisen as to whether firms realize benefits from asymmetric commitment (Gulati, Khanna, & Norhia, 1994; Kang, Mahoney, & Tan, 2009). Kang et al. showed that unilateral investments are not strategic mistakes, but rather sound value-maximizing strategies. Unilateral-specific investments are logically motivated by a firm's self-interest. This self-interest stems from the firm's ability to strategically anticipate outcomes of the project alliance that go beyond the current relationship.

These ideas appear to be consistent with property rights theory. The proposal is that unilateral investments may divide control rights to the advantage of the party that invests the most. "The ex ante allocation of ownership, with its accompanying residual rights of control over the productive asset, is performed to maximize the ex post gains from trade" (Elfenbein & Lerner, 2003, p. 358). According to Hart and Moore's model (1990), the party whose noncontractible investments are indispensable for the project should hold the property rights. Aghion and Tirole (1994) analyzed the basic contractual relationship between the research unit and the customer, and demonstrated that the ownership of the research output will be efficiently allocated to the research unit if the marginal impact of the research unit's effort on the innovative output is greater than the marginal impact of the customer's effort. The empirical evidence confirms this argument (Elfenbein & Lerner, 2003; Leiponen, 2008; Ryall & Sampson, 2009). In a study on ownership and the specification of ex ante control rights in alliances between Internet portals, Elfenbein and Lerner reported that ownership division is highly sensitive to the allocation of critical efforts between the parties, suggesting that unilateral investments may lead the firm to retain the overall ex post control rights. Leiponen found that the party whose noncontractible investments are indispensable for the project generally obtains overall control rights to the output project assets. Jap (2001) also suggested that the organization that contributes more resources than the partner will be motivated to use an equity rule to ensure a larger portion of the expanded pie for itself. It is therefore reasonable to expect that partners would be less likely to share output control rights when one of them invests more specific assets than the other.

Underlying this argument is the concept of appropriability, which refers to the intellectual asset owner's ability to obtain a return equal to the value generated by that asset (Levin, Klevorick, Nelson, & Winter, 1987). Leiponen (2008) reported that firms with innovative capacity generally retain overall control rights to intellectual assets and are more reluctant to accept partial rights. Such firms are also more likely to innovate in the future. In fact, firms that do not retain the control rights to their accumulated knowledge are constrained in terms of innovation opportunities, because it appears that maintaining IP ownership is a prerequisite for developing the IP into core competencies (Teng, 2007). The problem in joint ownership is not that the firm does not retain the rights, but that the firm does not have a monopoly on the rights to the underlying assets, as it shares ownership with the partner.

IPR sharing under a joint patent can be viewed as the result of a joint R&D project in which both parties have made indispensable investments in the project, creating a balance. Balanced asset specificity creates mutual dependence, or mutual safeguards and a collective incentive to maintain the relationship (Kogut, 1988; Young-Ybarra & Wiersema, 1999), which in turn increases joint created value (Blankenburg, Eriksson, & Johanson, 1999). Recently, Gulati and Sytch (2007) noted that even when each of two separate relationships are perfectly balanced in terms of actor investment, there may be different behavioral implications if they are balanced at different levels of investment. The more assets invested in the relationship by both partners, the more the partners are embedded in the relationship. Consequently, we may reasonably assume that (a) asymmetric-specific investments are negatively related to joint patent behavior; and (b) the greater the joint investments, the lower the partner's reluctance to share the IPR on the R&D output under a joint patent. Thus,

> **Hypothesis 1a:** *The greater the asymmetric relationship-specific investments, the less the parties will share IP ownership under a joint patent.*

> **Hypothesis 1b:** *The greater the joint relationship-specific investments, the more the parties will share IP ownership under a joint patent.*

JOINT PATENTING AND COOPERATION

Joint patenting results from high levels of cooperation (Rocha, 1997; Slowinski & Sagal, 2006). Cooperation may result from prior experience (Gulati, 1995) or relationship continuity (Heide & Miner, 1992; Poppo, Zhou & Rhu, 2008).

The Effect of Previous Specific Experience

Firms gain experience of alliances from previous interactions and mutual undertakings with partners. This increases their capacity to handle alliances (Doz, 1996; Levinthal & Fichman, 1988). Pisano (1990) showed how the R&D procurement pattern affects the current R&D procurement decision. Increased relational orientation and the development of relational capabilities result in more joint action, which in turn leads to joint creation value (Gulati & Sytch, 2007; Wu & Cavusgil, 2006). Gulati and Sytch defined joint action as "the degree of dyadic cooperation and coordination across a wide array of organizational activities, such as design, cost control, and quality improvement" (p. 40). Joint action therefore conveys the interpenetration of an organizational partner's boundaries (Heide & Miner, 1992). Through repeated ties, partners develop critical resources that become embedded in interfirm routines and processes, such as knowledge sharing, which increase relational rent (Dyer & Singh, 1998). In fact, firms' valuable resources often extend beyond their organizational boundaries. For instance, as a logical continuity, partners may extend their IPR boundaries beyond the alliance process. Several studies have shown that a previous relationship between partners increases alliance complexity (e.g., Heide & Miner, 1992). Hagedoorn et al. (2003) suggested that IPR sharing through joint patenting is an additional collaborative dimension that may be encouraged by shared experience. Ryall and Sampson (2009) noted that Fujitsu had multiple deals with Ross Technology surrounding Fujitsu's development of a microprocessor core based on Ross' proprietary microcontroller technology. The second contract differed from the first in several respects. For instance, the intellectual property rights on jointly developed technologies were jointly owned.

Nevertheless, a screening of U.S. biotechnology contracts suggest that the first contract often stipulates that all inventions made jointly under the agreement by the employees of the two partners will be owned jointly by the two partners, and that each party shall retain full ownership under any patents resulting therefrom. Moreover, Hagedoorn et al. (2003) show that companies' experience of specific R&D alliances is not predictive for more jointly owned patents between comparable company pairs. Thus,

> **Hypothesis 2a:** *There will be a negligible relationship between the cooperation history between firms and shared IP ownership under a joint patent.*

The Effects of Relationship Continuity

From the perspective of property rights theory, a firm's boundaries coincide precisely with its decisions on asset ownership (Arora & Merges, 2004). Joint IP ownership increases the boundaries of partner firms beyond a temporary alliance relationship, creating boundary overlap. Consequently, joint IP ownership guarantees access to the IP of all the owners (Teng, 2007). A jointly owned asset also gives all the owners a sustainable competitive advantage. As Amit and Shoemaker (1993) noted, "Resources are converted into final products or services by using a wide range of other firm assets" (p. 35). Consequently, it is understood that the firms, not the individual resources, appropriate the economic rents. Therefore, in an alliance relationship, the economic rent of the R&D output can be higher when the asset ownership is shared rather than divided as distinct assets between the two partners. Moreover, when two firms jointly own an IP asset, they can exploit it more efficiently together than separately. Joint patents therefore favor the continuity of the relationship.

Expectations of continuity are closely related to relationship stability (Olk & Ring, 2010), and less opportunism (Poppo et al., 2008). Future interactions allow the players to reward or punish each other. In this type of game, Axelrod (1984) shows that if one player cooperates in one round, the other player can reward that move by cooperating in the next round. The empirical research has shown that the more strongly the parties expect the relationship to continue in the future and the more indeterminate the end point, the more they will cooperate (Heide & Miner, 1992). In an open-ended alliance, the partners may anticipate long-term efforts, which may lengthen the shadow of the future (Reuer & Ariño, 2007).

In a similar vein, Hagedoorn et al. (2003) show that joint ownership can lock partners into long-term relationships with a succession of joint patents: the specific experience with joint patenting in particular pairs of companies is positively associated with the number of jointly owned patents for company pairs at a later date.

We therefore suggest that in open-ended compared to time-limited alliances, partners more easily share ownership of foreground knowledge under a joint patent. In other words, the expectation of continuity may favor joint ownership. Thus,

> **Hypothesis 2b:** *There will be a positive relationship between relationship continuity and joint patent activity.*

METHODOLOGY

We tested our hypotheses on data obtained from a firm we call BioCosmos, a large U.S. biotechnology company with more than 7,000 employees. The biotechnology sector is undergoing rapid technological development and uses a high degree of IPR protection. Moreover, the probability of co-assignment and co-assignment growth varies across technologies. For example, chemical firms almost never co-assign their patents (0.08%), whereas about 8% of biotechnology patents are co-assigned (Pleggenkuhle-Miles & Khoury, 2009). BioCosmos contracted 272 alliances from 1997 to 2007. Of the 272 alliances, 121 are contractual R&D agreements. Contracts and internal docu-

TABLE 3.1 Sample Characteristics

	Number of R&D alliances	Percent
R&D only	44	42.3%
R&D plus manufacturing	18	17.3%
R&D plus marketing	30	28.8%
R&D plus manufacturing & marketing	14	13.5%
Asymmetric alliances	84	80.8%
Joint patent	22	21.2%

ments were obtained and coded to construct the variables. After removing 17 alliances for missing data, our final sample is composed of 104 alliances. Table 3.1 summarizes the alliances in the final sample. Differences between international and national partners might affect the joint patenting behavior (Hagedoorn et al., 2003). Odagiri (2003) analyzed R&D alliances among Japanese pharmaceutical firms and found that joint patent applications with a foreign partner accounted for less than 10%, whereas the proportion of R&D alliances with a foreign partner was 50%. In our sample, all alliances are domestic. Only 6% are with another pharmaceutical company. Nearly 56% of alliances were discontinued for various reasons, such as commercial or therapeutic considerations or trials that did not meet primary endpoints. Of the alliance contracts, 55.8% specified that all joint inventions would be jointly owned by BioCosmos and its partners.

For each alliance, we determined whether the partners had jointly applied for a patent. Joint patent is therefore a dummy variable. As a proxy for partner experience, we used the number of alliances contracted by BioCosmos and its partners prior to the latest alliance from 1997 to 2007. As a proxy for relationship continuity, we coded the presence or absence of time bounds on collaborative agreements. Time-bounded alliances do not feature the shadow of the future (Reuer & Ariño, 2007). Open-ended alliances were coded 0 for contracts that specified a duration for the alliance and 1 for contracts with open-ended duration. Investment in a specific asset was measured by the number of employees that the two partners specifically assigned to the alliance. Our first conceptual model targeted imbalanced investments. To create a measure of asymmetric relationship-specific investment, we calculated the absolute value of the difference between the number of employees assigned by BioCosmos and by its partner. We constructed the joint investment relationship variable based on previous conceptualizations (e.g., Gulati & Sytch, 2007) and hence added measures of the firm's and the partner's number of dedicated employees.

We sought to develop a model of the factors that potentially influence joint ownership in R&D alliances, but we also wanted to control for relevant contingencies. We introduced three control variables: technological overlap, alliance performance, and partners' joint patenting experience. Following Mowery, Oxley, and Silverman (1998), technological overlap was measured by patent cross-citations—a measure of the relative importance of patents held by BioCosmos in its partner's technology portfolio and vice versa—as firms with a higher cross-citation rate show higher technological overlap. Following Rothaermel and Deeds (2004), we consider that the progression into the next development stage reflects alliance success. Hence, an alliance that evolved to the next stage was coded 1. If the alliance was unsuccessfully terminated, it was coded 0. Partners can jointly apply for a patent at the end of or during the collaborative process. Consequently, our sample includes both ongoing and terminated alliances. We also introduced joint ownership experience, measured by the number of patents the partners had jointly filed in the past. Some organizational factors, such as the partners' experience and expertise in managing IP, may explain the decision choice regarding IP ownership (Teng, 2007). The number of the partners' joint patents proxies for the partners' experience. Table 3.2 presents a summary of the measures.

TABLE 3.2 Measurement of Variables

Variables	Measures
Theoretical variables	
Asymmetric specific investment	The difference between the number of employees assigned to the alliance by BioCosmos and by its partner
Joint Specific Investment	Total number of employees specifically assigned to the alliance by BioCosmos and its partner
Partner-specific experience	Number of prior alliances between BioCosmos and its partner
Expectation of continuity	Dummy variable: coded 0 for contracts specifying alliance duration and 1 for contracts with open-ended duration
Control variable	
Technological overlap	$\frac{\text{Citations to partner firm's patents in BioCosmos' patents}}{\text{Total citations in BioCosmos' patents}} + \frac{\text{Citations in BioCosmos' patents to patents cited in partner firm's patents}}{\text{Total citations in partner firm's patents}}$
Alliance performance	Dummy variable: coded 1, if the alliance evolved to the next stage and 0 if the alliance was unsuccessful.
Joint patenting experience between BioCosmos and its partner	The number of patents jointly filed with partners in the past

RESULTS

Because our dependent variable was binary, we applied a logistic regression.[3] Results are summarized in Table 3.3. The results do not support Hypothesis 1a, which predicts a negative relationship between asymmetric relationship-specific investments and joint patenting behavior. In the models containing this variable (Models 2 and 3), the coefficient is negative but not significant, suggesting that partners' asymmetric contributions have no apparent bearing on the willingness to share IPR under a joint patent. Hypothesis 1b predicts a positive effect of joint relationship investment on joint patenting behavior. The coefficient is negative in Model 2 and Model 4 ($\beta = -.03$ in the two models, $p < .05$) and hence does not support Hypothesis 1b. Hypothesis 2a predicts a negligible relationship.[4] As shown in Models 3 and 4, there is no apparent bearing between partner-specific experience and joint patenting behavior. Hypothesis 2b, which proposes a positive impact of open-ended relationship on the likelihood of a joint patent, is supported. The coefficient for relationship continuity is positive and significant in Models 3 and 4 ($\beta = 2.35$, $p = .029$, Model 3; $\beta = 2.07$, $p = .069$, Model 4).

CONCLUSION AND DISCUSSION

As the rapidly changing architecture of global business attests, and given the high costs of R&D, firms are forming alliance relationships as never before. When firms pool their financial resources, human resources, and competencies to jointly develop products and innovations, they tend to share IPR during or at the end of the collaborative process. Nevertheless,

TABLE 3.3 Logistic Regression Results

	Probability of joint patenting			
	Model 1	Model 2	Model 3	Model 4
Control variable				
Alliance success	$(+)^{**}$	$(+)^{**}$	$(+)^{**}$	$(+)^{**}$
Joint patenting experience	$(+)^{*}$	$(+)^{*}$	$(+)^{*}$	$(+)^{*}$
Technological overlap	$(+)^{***}$	$(+)^{***}$	$(+)^{**}$	$(+)^{**}$
Key variables				
Asymmetric specific investment		n.s.		n.s.
Joint specific investment		$(-)^{*}$		$(-)^{*}$
Partner specific experience			n.s.	n.s.
Relationship continuity			$(+)^{*}$	$(+)^{\dagger}$

$^{\dagger}\,p < .10$; $^{*}p < .05$; $^{**}p < 0.01$; $^{***}p < 0.001$; $N = 104$; n.s. = not significant from the perspective of IPR theory, and in the traditional view of interfirm cooperation in the pursuit of individual competitive advantage, this decision challenges the boundaries of firms. The relationship between joint ownership and cooperation poses an interesting puzzle. First, joint patenting does not increase with previous relationships. On the other hand, joint ownership under a joint patent appears to be favored by open-ended alliances in which future interaction is more likely to be anticipated. Cooperation that follows previous collaborative experience stems mainly from attachment and includes an affective component (Poppo et al., 2008). In contrast, cooperation that follows expectations of continuity is independent of the partners' well-being (Kondo, 1990). Consequently, on the one hand, cooperation is driven by social norms; on the other hand, cooperation is described as a rational choice (Kondo, 1990). Hence, joint patenting may depend on neither social norms nor institutional trust; these are based on prior history, and they are more explanatory of organizational boundary decisions and therefore alliance formation. Instead, joint patenting may depend on the parties' willingness to enter into a long-term relationship, with a lengthier shadow of the future. Generally, open-ended relationship contracts are less likely to include enforcement provisions and more likely to include coordination provisions (Reuer & Ariño, 2007). Coordination provisions can be used to verify whether firms uphold their promises (Ryall & Sampson, 2009). They also provide mechanisms that are supposedly in place in hierarchical exchanges (Noordewier, John, & Nevin, 1990), but which operate invisibly within the private decision-making realms of firms. These clauses define the operating procedures that govern the exchange and resolve potential disputes among partners (Sobrero & Schrader, 1998). They foster greater use of interest-based negotiation, which increases cooperation (Lumineau & Malhotra, 2011). Joint patenting behavior is one possible result of cooperative behavior, and it is more likely to occur when the partners anticipate future interactions. Moreover, joint patenting also locks the partners into the relationship and can lay the groundwork for a continuing relationship.

Figure 3.1 presents a collaborative R&D timeline for joint patenting between BioCosmos and one of its partners. After a failed bioequivalent test in the phase III clinical trial, the partners jointly applied for two patents and initiated a third phase III to resolve the problem.

Grossman-Hart-Moore's model—whereby the allocation of control rights is driven by ex ante investment—mainly analyzed the allocation of control rights to one or the other partner, and not joint ownership as such. Our results show that asymmetric-specific investment has no apparent bearing on joint patent activity. Nevertheless, we found a negative relationship between joint-specific investment (the total amount of specific assets) and the probability of joint patenting. This result confirms Aghion and Tirole's

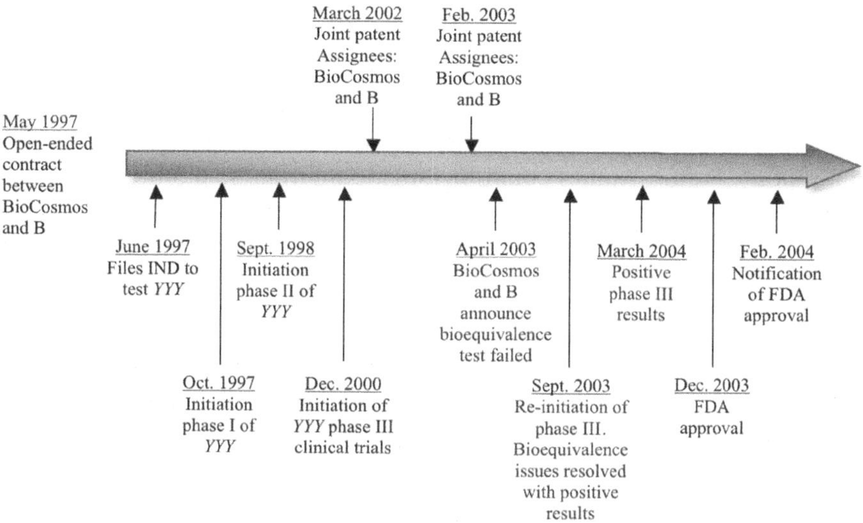

Figure 3.1 Example of a collaborative R&D timeline.

(1994)'s model, according to which joint ownership generally leads to sub-investment by the parties to the contract. Lerner and Merges (1998) also suggest that "The most profound effect on the allocation of control rights, at least in technology alliances,... is the financial condition of the R&D firm, rather than mutual concern about maximizing joint value" (p. 153).

Although successful alliances are associated with joint patenting behavior, joint R&D may not always result in a joint patent application. The number of joint applications therefore underestimates the success of joint inventions. Joint applications may result from the exploratory nature of R&D activities, but they also depend on organizational factors such as the partners' own technology at the time of the alliance formation. Teng (2007) suggests that when the risk of patent interference is high, partner firms tend to be concerned about the possibility that the party owning the IP may not provide due access to it in the future. In such cases, joint ownership would be more desirable. Indeed, the analysis of technological overlap between BioCosmos and its partners shows that high overlap in technological expertise appears to favor joint patent behavior. There is also another possible explanation for this behavior. When alliance partners are much closer in terms of technological expertise and have high potential absorptive capacity, it is easier to share knowledge in order to achieve a joint project (Sampson, 2007). In this case, technological overlap may favor cooperation and joint patenting behavior. We also found that joint ownership activity stems from the partners' knowledge and experience of joint ownership. Our results are consistent with those of Hagedoorn et al. (2003), who found a positive and significant link between joint patenting experience and the probability of a joint patent.

This study contains a few limitations that can lead to future research. First, because the empirical evidence is limited to a sample of R&D alliances entered into by one firm, further investigation is needed to provide external validity. Future studies could investigate international joint patenting. Research is also needed on joint patenting differences across countries. Finally, longitudinal studies could look at the anticipation of IP distribution in R&D alliances and how IP is actually divided at the end of the collaborative process.

Notwithstanding certain data limitations, our study has important implications. Whereas the literature has highlighted the theoretical determinants of ex ante control rights based on property rights theory, our study introduces strategic and social variables and indicates that the division of rights, and specifically IPR sharing, results mainly from a strategic decision and the firms' willingness to pursue future exchanges. Our results suggest that joint patenting behavior depends on initial conditions such as the long-term perspective of the relationship and the technological expertise of the partner-firms.

NOTES

1. Multinational firms and their national and foreign subsidiaries might also apply as joint patent owners.
2. Teng (2007) noted that there are four possible ways to allocate R&D outputs: joint, individual, public, and third-party ownership. Public ownership occurs when the innovation is considered public knowledge. The last IP ownership option is to sell the innovation to a third party, for instance at a public auction.
3. The empirical results suggest an overall good fit of the regression equation for all models, with a log-likelihood ratio significant at the 0.001 level. Model 1 is the base model and includes the three control variables. Models 2, 3, and 4 include the key variables. Model 4 is a full model and represents an improvement over Model 1 (pseudo-adjusted R^2 increases from .38 to .45). Model 4 correctly classified over 82.23% of the sample observations. The χ^2 (39.41, significant at the 0.001 level.) indicates that all coefficients depart from zero. In addition, the Hosmer–Lemeshow goodness-of-fit statistic (1.41) is not statistically significant, indicating no significant misspecification in the full model (Hosmer, Hosmer, Le Cessie, & Lemeshow, 1997). Results are similar for the other models.
4. Our Hypothesis 2 is stated in the null form. It is generally incorrect to test null hypotheses, but there are circumstances in which the absence of relationship is of interest in itself (Cohen, 1988). Nevertheless, it is important to reject the null hypothesis when it is in fact false, thus avoiding a Type II error (Murphy & Myors, 2004). We use Cohen's approximations for medium effect size and

the multiple regression power table (Cohen, 1988, p. 421) to determine the minimum sample size required to test a null hypothesis. Tables provided by Cohen indicate a required sample size of 103 ($R^2 = .13$; the desired power of the test = .80).

ACKNOWLEDGMENT

This research was supported by Le Fonds Québécois de la Recherche sur la Société et la Culture (FQRSC) (# 128106) awarded to the author.

REFERENCES

Aghion, P., & Tirole, J. (1994). The management of an innovation. *Quarterly Journal of Economics, 109,* 1185–1209.

Amit, R., & Schoemaker, P. J. H. (1993). Strategic assets and organizational rent. *Strategic Management Journal, 14,* 33–46.

Arora, A., & Merges, R. P. (2004). Specialized supply firms, property rights and firm boundaries. *Industrial and Corporate Change, 13,* 451–475.

Araujo, L., Dubois, A., & Galde, L-E. (2003). The multiple boundaries of the firm. *Journal of Management Studies, 40,* 1255–1277.

Astley, W. G. (1984). Toward an appreciation of collective strategy. *Academy of Management Review, 9,* 526–535.

Axelrod, R. (1984). *The evolution of cooperation.* New York: Basic Books.

Barzel, Y. (1997). *Economic analysis of property rights* (2nd ed.). Cambridge, UK: Cambridge University Press.

Blankenburg, H. D., Eriksson, K., & Johanson, J. (1999). Creating value through mutual commitment to business network relationships. *Strategic Management Journal, 20,* 467–486.

Coase, R. H. (2000). The acquisition of Fisher Body by General Motors. *Journal of Law and Economics, XLIII,* 15–31.

Cohen, J. (1988). *Statistical power test for the behavioral sciences.* Hillsdale, NJ: Lawrence Erlbaum.

Das, T. K., & Teng, B. (1996). Risk types and inter-firm alliance structures. *Journal of Management Studies, 33,* 827–943.

Doz, Y. L. (1996). The evolution of cooperation in strategic alliances: Initial conditions or learning processes? *Strategic Management Journal, 17,* 55–83.

Dyer, J. H., & Singh, H. (1998). The relational view: Cooperative strategy and sources of interorganizational competitive advantage. *Academy of Management Review, 23,* 660–679.

Elfenbein, D., & Lerner, J. (2003). Ownership and control rights in Internet portal alliances, 1995–1999. *RAND Journal of Economics, 32,* 356–369.

Eisenhardt, K. M., & Schoonhoven, C. B. (1996). Resource-based view of strategic alliance formation: Strategic and social effects in entrepreneurial firms. *Organization Science, 7,* 136–150.

Foss, K., & Foss N. J. (1999). *Understanding ownership: Residual rights of control and appropriable control rights* (Working paper, Copenhagen Business School, Denmark).

Foss, K., & Foss, N. J. (2005). Resources and transaction costs: How property rights economics furthers the resource-based view. *Strategic Management Journal, 26,* 541–553.

Furubotn, E. G., & Pejovich, S. (1972). Property rights and economic theory: A survey of recent literature. *Journal of Economic Literature, 10,* 1137–1162.

Gauvin, S. (1992). *Cooperative R&D benefits to society—Does it benefit firms?* (Unpublished working paper, Université Laval, QC, Canada).

Grossman, S. J., & Hart, O. (1986). The costs and benefits of ownership: A theory of vertical and lateral ownership. *Journal of Political Economy, XCIV,* 691–719.

Guffey, W. R. (2004). *Joint ownership of patents: A trap for the unwary.* Working paper available at http://www.intelproplaw.com/Articles/cgi/download.cgi?v=1091393695

Gulati, R. (1995). Does familiarity breed trust? The implications of repeated ties for contractual choice in alliances. *Academy of Management Journal, 38,* 85–112.

Gulati, R., Khanna, T., & Nohria, N. (1994). Unilateral commitments and the importance of process in alliances. *Sloan Management Review, 35,* 61–69.

Gulati, R., & Sytch, M. (2007). Dependence asymmetry and joint dependence in interorganizational relationships: Effects of embeddedness on a manufacturer's performance in procurement relationships. *Administrative Science Quarterly, 52,* 32–69.

Hagedoorn, J. (1993). Understanding the rationale of strategic technology partnering: Interorganizational modes of cooperation and sectoral differences. *Strategic Management Journal, 14,* 371–385.

Hagedoorn, J. (2003). Sharing intellectual property rights: An exploratory study of joint patenting. *Industrial and Corporate Change, 12,* 1035–1050.

Hagedoorn, J., van Kranenburg, H., & Osborn, R. N. (2003). Joint patenting amongst companies: Exploring the effects of inter-firm R&D partnering and experience. *Managerial and Decision Economics, 24,* 71–84.

Hart, O., & Moore, J. (1990). Property rights and the nature of the firm. *Journal of Political Economy, 98,* 1119–1158.

Heide, J. B., & Miner, A. S. (1992). The shadow of the future: Effects of anticipated interaction and frequency of contact on buyer-seller cooperation. *Academy of Management Journal, 35,* 265–291.

Hertzfeld, H. R., Link, A. L., & Vonortas, N. S. (2006). Intellectual property protection mechanisms in research partnerships. *Research Policy, 35,* 825–838.

Holmström, B., & Roberts, J. (1998). The boundaries of the firm revisited. *Journal of Economic Perspectives, 12,* 73–94.

Hosmer, D. W., Hosmer, T., Le Cessie, S., & Lemeshow, S. (1997). A comparison of goodness-of-fit tests for the logistic regression model. *Statistics in Medicine, 16,* 965–980.

Jap, S. D. (2001). "Pie sharing" in complex collaboration contexts. *Journal of Marketing Research, 38,* 86–99.

Joskow, P. (1988). Asset specificity and the structure of vertical relationships: Empirical evidence. *Journal of Law, Economics, and Organization, 4,* 95–118.

Kang, M-P., Mahoney, J. T., & Tan, D. (2009). Why firms make unilateral investments specific to other firms: The case of OEM suppliers. *Strategic Management Journal, 30,* 117–231.

Kim, J., & Mahoney, J. T. (2002). Resource-based and property rights perspectives on value, creation: The case of oil field unitization. *Managerial and Decision Economics, 23,* 225–245.

Kim, J., & Mahoney, J. T. (2005). Property rights theory, transaction costs theory, and agency theory: An organizational economics approach to strategic management. *Managerial and Decision Economics, 26,* 223–242.

Kogut, B. (1988). Joint venture: Theoretical and empirical perspectives. *Strategic Management Journal, 9,* 319–332.

Kondo, T. (1990). Some notes on rational behavior, normative behavior, moral behavior, and cooperation. *Journal of Conflict Resolution, 34,* 495–530.

Leiblein, M. J., & Miller, D. J. (2003). An empirical examination of transaction and firm-level influences on the vertical boundaries of the firm. *Strategic Management Journal, 24,* 839–859.

Leiponen, A. (2008). Control of intellectual assets in client relationships: Implications for innovation. *Strategic Management Journal, 29,* 1371–1394.

Lerner, J., & Merges, R. P. (1998). The control of technology alliances: An empirical analysis of the biotechnology industry. *Journal of Industrial Economics, 46,* 125–156.

Levin, R. C., Klevorick, A. K., Nelson, R. R., & Winter, S. G. (1987). Appropriating the returns from industrial research and development. *Brookings Papers on Economic Activity, 3,* 783–820.

Levinthal, D. A., & Fichman, M. (1988). Dynamics of interorganizational attachments: Auditor-client relationships. *Administrative Science Quarterly, 33,* 345–369.

Li, J., & Zhong, J. (2003). Explaining the growth of international R&D alliances in China. *Managerial and Decision Economics, 24,* 101–115.

Lumineau, F., & Malhotra, D. (2011). Shadow of the contract: How contract structure shapes interfirm dispute resolution. *Strategic Management Journal, 32*(5), 532–555.

Madhok, A., & Tallman, S. B. (1998). Resources, transactions and rents: Managing value in interfirm collaborative relationships. *Organization Science, 9,* 326–339.

Merges, R. P., & Locke, A. L. (1990). Co-ownership of patents: A comparative and economic view. *Journal of Patent and Trademark Office Society, 72,* 586–610.

Mowery, D. C., Oxley, J. E., & Silverman, B. S. (1998). Technological overlap and interfirm cooperation: Implications for the resource-based view of the firm. *Research Policy, 27,* 507–523.

Murphy, K. R., & Myors, B. (2004). *Statistical power analysis. A simple and general model for traditional and modern hypothesis tests.* Mahwah, NJ: Lawrence Erlbaum.

Noordewier, T. G., John, G., & Nevin, J. R. (1990). Performance outcomes of purchasing arrangements in industrial buyer-vendor relationships. *Journal of Marketing, 54,* 80–93.

Odagiri, H. (2003). Transaction costs and capabilities as determinants of the R&D boundaries of the firm: A case study of the ten largest pharmaceutical firms in Japan. *Managerial and Decision Economics, 24,* 187–211.

Olk, P. M., & Ring, P. S. (2010). Alliances as sources of legitimacy. In T. K. Das (Ed.), *Researching strategic alliances: Emerging perspectives* (pp. 27–55). Charlotte, NC: Information Age Publishing.

Oxley, J. E. (1997). Appropriability hazards and governance in strategic alliances: A transaction cost approach. *Journal of Law, Economics and Organization, 13,* 387–409.

Parkhe, A. (1993). Strategic alliance structuring: A game theory and transaction cost examination of interfirm cooperation. *Academic of Management Journal, 36,* 794–829.

Peteraf, M. (1993). The cornerstone of competitive advantage: A resource-based view. *Strategic Management Journal, 14,* 179–191.

Pisano, G. (1990). The R&D boundaries of the firm: An empirical analysis. *Administrative Science Quarterly, 35,* 153–176.

Pleggenkuhle-Miles, E. G., & Khoury, T. A. (2009, August 7–11). *How do different strategic alliances expand a firm's technological breadth? A study of joint patenting within biotechnology 1980–2007.* Paper presented at the annual meeting of the Academy of Management, Chicago.

Poppo, L., & Zenger, T. (1998). Testing alternative theories of the firm: Transaction cost, knowledge-based, and measurement explanations for make-or-buy decisions in information services. *Strategic Management Journal, 19,* 853–877.

Poppo, L., & Zenger, T. (2002). Do formal contracts and relational governance function as substitutes or complements? *Strategic Management Journal, 23,* 707–725.

Poppo, L., Zhou, K. Z., & Rhu, S. (2008). Alternative origins to interorganizational trust: An interdependence perspective on the shadow of the past and the shadow of the future. *Organization Science, 19,* 39–55.

Reuer, J. J., & Ariño, A. (2002). Contractual renegotiations in strategic alliances. *Journal of Management, 28,* 47–68.

Riordan, M. H., & Williamson, O. E. (1985). Asset specificity and economic organization. International Journal of Industrial Organization, 3, 365–378.

Rocha, F. (1997). *Inter-firm technological cooperation: Effects of absorptive capacity, firm size and specialization.* Discussion paper No. 07, United Nations University Institute for New Technologies.

Rothaermel, F. T., & Deeds D. L. (2004). Exploration and exploitation alliance in biotechnology: A system of new product development. *Strategic Management Journal, 25,* 201–221.

Ryall, M. D., & Sampson, R. C. (2009). Formal contracts in the presence of relational enforcement mechanisms: Evidence from technology development projects. *Management Science, 55,* 906–925.

Sampson, R. C. (2007). R&D alliances and firm performance: The impact of technological diversity and alliance organization on innovation. *Academy of Management Journal, 50,* 364–386.

Skaperdas, S., & Syropoulos, C. (1996). Can the shadow of the future harm cooperation? *Journal of Economic Behavior and Organization, 29,* 355–372.

Slowinski, G., & Sagal, M. W. (2006). Allocating patent rights in collaborative research. *Research Technology Management, 49,* 51–53.

Sobrero, M., & Schrader, S. (1998). Structuring inter-firm relationships: A meta-analytic approach. *Organization Studies, 19,* 585–615.

Teece, D. J. (1986). Profiting from technological innovation: Implications for integration, collaboration, licensing and public policy. *Research Policy, 15,* 285–305.

Teng, B. (2007). Managing intellectual property in R&D alliances. *International Journal of Technology Management, 38,* 160–177.

Tirole, J. (1999). Incomplete contracts: Where do we stand? *Econometrica, 67,* 741–781.

Williamson, O. E. (1975). *Markets and hierarchies.* New York: Free Press.

Williamson, O. E. (1991). Comparative economic organization: The analysis of discrete structural alternatives. *Administrative Science Quarterly, 36,* 269–296.

Williamson, O. E. (1996). *The mechanisms of governance.* New York: Oxford University Press.

Wu, F., & Cavusgil, S. T. (2006). Organizational learning, commitment, and joint value creation in interfirm relationships. *Journal of Business Research, 59,* 81–89.

Young-Ybarra, C., & Wiersema, M. (1999). Strategic flexibility in information technology alliances: The influence of transaction cost economics and social exchange theory. *Organization Science, 10,* 439–459.

CHAPTER 4

R&D ALLIANCES IN SCIENCE AND TECHNOLOGY PARKS

The Advantages of Location

Ángeles Montoro-Sánchez
Eva-María Mora-Valentín
Marta Ortiz-de-Urbina-Criado

ABSTRACT

The purpose of this study is to analyze the factors relating to R&D cooperation among companies located in science and technology parks (STPs), and the effects of that cooperation. First, we analyze the factors that may determine firm propensity to cooperate, such as innovative behavior and knowledge flows, or spillovers. Second, we analyze the impact of R&D cooperation on innovation and on firm performance. To do so, we have used a sample of 363 industrial and services companies located in STPs. The results show that the innovative behavior of firms in STPs and the related spillovers encourage the establishment of cooperation agreements. We also observed that R&D cooperation has a significant positive effect on firm propensity to innovate on product and organizational aspects, and that companies who cooperate on R&D file more patents and achieve better business results in the medium term.

Strategic Alliances for Value Creation, pages 73–99

INTRODUCTION

Innovation is essential to corporate development and survival. However, some companies, especially small and medium enterprises (SMEs), encounter grave difficulties when they attempt to carry out R&D on their own. For this reason, R&D cooperation is a strategy that is much used to improve innovative capability because, among other things, it reduces complexity and lowers the risks and costs associated with innovation (Hagedoorn, 2002). Furthermore, cooperation with other companies makes it easier to gain access to the external resources needed to carry out R&D activities and makes it possible to exchange resources and transfer knowledge more efficiently (Becker & Dietz, 2004; Das & Teng, 2000). Consequently, in recent years, there has been growing academic interest in the study of R&D cooperation (Tether, 2002). Research has focused, on the one hand, on factors that determine cooperation (Becker & Dietz 2004; Belderbos, Caree, Diederen, Lokshin, & Veugelers, 2004; López, 2008; Tether, 2002) and, on the other hand, on their effects on results or performance, and in general, on company value creation (Ariño, 2003; Mora-Valentín, Montoro-Sánchez, & Guerras-Martín, 2004; Reuer & Zollo, 2005).

Recent decades have brought significant growth of science and technology parks (STPs) worldwide (Bakouros, Mardas, & Varsakelis, 2002). In Spain, most STPs are promoted by the regional governments in order to boost regional development by modifying the traditional industrial fabric (Ondategui, 2000). STPs are an essential tool for developing corporate research, innovation, and development. They are consequently one of the most heavily used innovation support infrastructures worldwide. Furthermore, they seek to fulfill two distinct but complementary objectives: to promote regional economic development by producing innovative firms and to encourage the dissemination and transfer of technology from the research centers to the firms (Löfsten & Lindelöf, 2003). Previous literature has paid particular attention to the relation between innovation and STPs (Felsenstein, 1994; Lindelöf & Loftsen, 2004; Link & Scott, 2003).

However, few studies have thus far attempted to look at the decision by firms located in STPs to cooperate on R&D in conjunction with the effect of cooperation on firm results and on the results of innovation. The purpose of the study is thus twofold. On the one hand, we shall analyze the factors that determine the propensity of firms located in STPs to establish R&D alliances. Based on the advantages of agglomeration arising from location in an STPs, we believe that there are two significant factors: (a) the firm's innovative behavior; and (b) knowledge flows, or spillovers. On the other hand, we shall analyze the effect of R&D cooperation among firms located in STPs on innovation and firm results. The chapter thus makes several significant contributions. First, it looks at R&D cooperation taking firm location into account, while many previous studies consider that location does not have a significant impact on technology and knowledge exchanges among firms (Narula & Santangelo, 2009). Furthermore, the prior literature has not focused on the specific aspects determining that cooperation within the context of STPs. Although both innovative behavior and spillovers are topics that have been sufficiently studied, either within the context of cooperation or within STPs, there is as yet insufficient empirical evidence combining both aspects into a joint analysis in order to delve into the specific characteristics of these locations and of the strategic options implemented by firms to increase their innovative activity. On the other hand, we complete our analysis by carrying out a study of the effects of cooperation on firm performance or value creation. Thus, this study allows us to determine whether R&D collaboration does indeed allow firms to achieve their strategic objectives and improve their competitive position and, if so, whether being located in STPs makes it easier for them to achieve these objectives.

In order to do so, the following section contains an analysis of cooperation in STPs and the hypotheses that we wish to test. The third section contains an empirical comparison, followed in the next section by the results of the empirical study. The final section sets out our discussion of the results, and we conclude with some considerations and possible future research lines.

R&D COOPERATION IN SCIENCE AND TECHNOLOGY PARKS

Location in Science and Technology Parks

According to the International Association of Science Parks (IASP, 2002), the term "park" encompasses both science parks and technology parks and is defined as

> a project that occupies a physical space, that maintains collaborative relations with universities, research centers and other institutions of higher learning, and that has been conceived in order to promote the creation or installation of innovative technology-based industries or of tertiary sector companies providing high value-added services, all from within the park's own management system, that plays an active role in transferring technology and increasing the value of firms within the park.

As the breadth of this definition shows, finding an adequate explanation to reflect the true essence of STPs can be complex and difficult.

There are differences between a technology park and a science park in terms of size, links with universities, technological intensity, and type of activity engaged in by the firms located in them (IASP, 2002). Thus, technology parks are medium-sized or large projects that are not necessarily linked to a university, that are oriented toward technology companies, and that may, within limits, contain productive activities. Science parks, on the other hand, are medium-sized or small projects that are linked and occasionally developed by universities, which focus on the creation of new companies (usually university spin-offs) and tend to sell or rent premises that are already equipped. Studies such as Malairaja and Zawdie (2008) analyzed the differences between science parks and industrial parks, concluding that while the former contain highly innovative companies with a highly skilled workforce, industrial parks are basically composed of manufacturing companies that employ unskilled labor. The breadth of the concept of a park and the fact that it has gradually evolved, has resulted in different terms such as "innovation park," "technological innovation park," "technopolis," and "technology infrastructure," which are often used to refer to the same phenomenon.

In our field, we define STPs as a project that is generally associated with a specific physical space and that has an implicit formal relation with a university, research center, or institution of higher learning. Its purpose is to promote the creation and growth of knowledge-based firms and other high-value-added services companies, usually within STPs. STPs also participate actively in technology-transfer activities, promoting innovation among the organizations located within them.

STPs play an essential role in the development of policies on research, innovation, and corporate development, simultaneously providing a theoretical and practical laboratory for both public and private organizations located within its physical space or its networks (Ondategui, 2002). They are therefore one of the most widely used infrastructures worldwide to support innovation, addressing two distinct but complementary objectives: to foster regional economic development by creating innovative businesses, and to promote the diffusion and transfer of technology from the research centers to the firms (Löfsten & Lindelöf, 2003). At this point, it becomes clear that STPs assist the organizations located in them in their innovation processes, thereby also helping the region (Löfsten & Lindelöf, 2003). In other words, STPs have a positive impact both within the park and beyond it.

First, considering the role of STPs in national economic development and on the competitiveness of firms, both regionally and nationally, much of the literature has focused on studying the effect of parks at the macroeconomic level. Such studies analyze the influence of STPs on certain national economic indicators such as job creation or university-industry relations.

Second, there is another, no less significant, body of literature that analyzes the effects of STPs on organizations located within the parks themselves. These studies tend to analyze the benefits accruing to businesses located within STPs. This is because these parks provide the perfect habitat to promote competitiveness and a culture of innovation among the institutions that comprise them, encouraging the exchange of knowledge and technology flows with universities, research centers and firms (Squicciarini, 2009). In STPs, organizations share not only geographical space, but also a set of common services such as security, suppliers, telecommunications networks, reception areas, administrative services, restaurants, banks, parking, internal transport, etc., all of which permit considerable cost savings.

On the other hand, an important feature of these spaces is the interaction that occurs among organizations located in the park. This interaction can translate into cooperative agreements on innovation, i.e., into R&D cooperation agreements (Castells & Hall, 1994). European Union initiatives launched with the aim of promoting the establishment of cooperation networks between STPs-based firms is an example of this. Within this context, numerous studies show that firm location in STPs facilitates business networking and the formation of cooperation agreements with other organizations, particularly universities and other research organizations (Fukugawa, 2006; Löfsten & Lindelöf, 2005; Phillimore, 1999; Vedovello, 1997).

In this chapter, we shall focus on the latter. Nevertheless, considering the large number of studies that examine the advantages and benefits that might accrue to organizations located in STPs, our purpose is first, to identify the factors that increase the propensity to cooperate among institutions located in STPs and second, to show that STPs-based organizations that do cooperate outperform those that do not.

Factors that Increase the Propensity to Cooperate on R&D

Today, innovation plays a key role in helping companies to develop and maintain their competitive advantage. Consequently, more and more organizations are engaging in R&D activities. However, not all companies are able to perform these activities independently. That being so, cooperation on R&D can help businesses to supplement their R&D deficiencies, affording theme access to certain external resources that they need and cannot always set up in-house.

As we reviewed the literature, we identified several studies that analyze the factors that affect firm propensity to cooperate on R&D (Becker & Dietz, 2004; López, 2008; Un, Romero-Martínez, & Montoro-Sánchez, 2009). At a wider level, studies such as Belderbos et al. (2004) or López (2008) refer to factors such as cost and risk sharing, complementarity, absorptive capacity, forms of appropriation and protection of inventions or innovation, etc. Other papers look at various fundamental business variables such as size, sector, age, and external relations (Buesa & Molero, 1998), or at certain characteristics relating to firm innovative behavior such as type of innovation, R&D intensity, knowledge flows, or firm location (Becker & Dietz, 2004; Belderbos et al., 2004; Fritsch & Lukas 2001; López, 2008). Another research current has focused on studying some of the factors that increase a company's propensity to cooperate, i.e., the impact that prior collaboration experiences have on choice of partner (Hagedoorn, Van Kranenburg, & Osborn, 2003; Oxley & Sampson, 2004).

What we propose is that the propensity to cooperate on R&D for firms located in STPs will depend on two factors: the firm's innovation performance, and knowledge flows or spillovers. Our proposal is built on several premises: (a) R&D collaboration within STPs, (b) innovative behavior by firms located in STPs, (c) knowledge flows or spillovers generated within STPs. Thus, the model we posit allows us to analyze in conjunction several factors that previously had been analyzed in isolation in the literature.

Firm Innovative Behavior

According to existing empirical research, companies innovate in various different ways. This has resulted in various models of innovative behavior based on a specific combination of activities that are aimed at creating and appropriating knowledge, and on the actual characteristics of the technological field or sector within which these activities take place (Buesa & Molero, 1998). This has led firm innovative behavior to be tested according to various indicators.

Studies such as that by Segarra-Blasco and Arauzo-Carod (2008) use several measures to refer to firm innovative capacity: product innovation, process innovation, R&D activities, outsourcing of R&D, and cooperation with other companies in R&D. Numerous studies show that the propensity to collaborate in R&D is higher among firms operating in high-tech sectors (Bayona, García-Marco, & Huerta, 2001; Cohen, Goto, Nagata, Nelson, & Walsh, 2002; Fritsch & Lukas, 2001; Segarra-Blasco & Arauzo-Carod, 2008; Tether, 2002). For Piga and Vivarelli (2004), cooperation with other partners is more frequent the greater the complexity of the process innovation carried out by the firms (e.g., those that combine product and process innovation).

On the other hand, an important part of the literature on cooperative R&D looks at the cooperation between companies and research organizations (universities, innovation, and technology centers or research groups). These studies analyze the innovative behavior of firms that cooperate with universities, and they demonstrate that the firms who make the greatest R&D effort also cooperate more with universities (Arundel & Geuna, 2004; Fontana, Geuna, & Matt, 2006; Giuliani & Arias, 2009; Schartinger, Rammer, Fischer, & Frohlich, 2002). Veugelers and Cassiman (2005) argue that cooperation with universities is a form of cost sharing that complements the R&D performed by firms.

These arguments are reinforced if location in STPs is introduced into the analysis. For decades, the empirical evidence has shown that firms located in STPs show greater intensity in conducting R&D activities (Westhead, 1997). Specifically, the author shows that both R&D spending and the percentage of scientists and engineers engaged in R&D are higher in firms located within STPs. In the same vein, Löfsten and Lindelöf (2003) argue that firm resources channelled into process innovation and its intensity are both greater when located inside STPs.

In summary, as our review shows, most of the literature analyzed indicates that companies who show distinctly innovative behavior are more likely to enter into R&D cooperation agreements. This leads us to posit our first hypothesis:

> **Hypothesis 1:** *In STPs, the propensity to cooperate on R&D is higher the greater a company's innovative behavior.*

Knowledge Flows or Spillovers

An analysis of knowledge flows, or spillovers, and their impact on firm propensity to establish R&D cooperation agreements is a topic that has attracted enormous interest in recent years. Knowledge flows, known also as spillovers, can be defined as the intangible knowledge that originates inside the firms and the commercial transactions or exchanges that occur among companies or between these companies and other types of institutions (Verspagen & De Loo, 1999). The knowledge generated as a result of a firm's innovative behavior (Kaiser, 2002) becomes available to other organizations so that they may use it freely (Kafouros & Buckley, 2008). Thus, the knowledge and technology generated by one company may be useful to other firms (Griliches, 1992). Furthermore, given that sometimes knowledge can be easily transferred through various media (journals, reverse engineering, cooperation, etc.), companies can avail themselves of this knowledge without having to pay for it (Verspagen, 1997). Such free appropriation of knowledge flows generated by another firm is the result of the failure of these firms to implement appropriate mechanisms to protect their innovation.

There are several different ways of classifying knowledge flows. The first, based on the type of exchange that occurs between the parties, are rent spillovers. These flows arise as a result of the exchange of goods between businesses. When a company uses an input from another firm in its production process, the former may reap the advantages of any resulting product innovation when using that input (Verspagen, 1997). Second, we find pure knowledge flows. These occur when the result of research carried out by company i improves the technology in firm j without j having to pay for it (Griliches, 1992). Such flows generally improve a company's in-house R&D capacity (Verspagen, 1997). Third, the work of Belderbos et al. (2004) distinguishes between entry and exit knowledge flows. Whereas entry knowledge flows are external information flows into the company that increase the appeal of cooperation for it, exit knowledge flows are flows of information from the company that limit the appropriability of the results of its innovation processes. Fourth, some studies refer to horizontal knowledge flows vs. vertical knowledge flows.

Thus, when the company who receives knowledge operates in a different sector from that of the company that produces the knowledge, the flows are considered intra-industry or vertical, whereas flows are interindustry or horizontal when the company receiving the knowledge operates in the same sector as the knowledge producer (Kaiser, 2002). Finally, it should be noted that knowledge flows may be analyzed from different points of view: company, industry, nation, and world markets. In our study, we analyze every type of knowledge flow, but always from the firm perspective.

In the prior literature, some studies have analyzed the effects of knowledge flows on economic growth, business concentration, R&D expenditure, R&D productivity, and propensity to cooperate on R&D projects (Kaiser, 2002). Within all of these, we shall focus on the effect of such flows on propensity of firms located in STPs to collaborate on R&D.

When companies have easy access to knowledge flows generated by other firms, they generally spend less on R&D investment. However, another way of internalizing these knowledge flows is through R&D alliances, so companies obtain greater benefits than if they do not cooperate. In this context, the exchange of knowledge flows often translates into cooperative relations between the involved parties. Moreover, once the companies move beyond the initial stages of the relationship, partnerships often develop that are far more complex and formal. Of all the possible types of interorganizational relationship, R&D cooperation is the one that requires the greatest amount of face-to-face contact to ensure its success. This is because such relationships require a high degree of commitment and trust between the parties (Mora-Valentín et al., 2004; Simonen & McCann, 2008).

Looking at the relationship between knowledge flows and R&D cooperation, several studies have focused on how such flows influence the decision to initiate a cooperative R&D relationship or on propensity to collaborate in R&D (Belderbos et al., 2004; Cassiman & Veugelers 2002; Kaiser, 2002; López, 2008, López-Fernández, Serrano-Bedia, & García-Piqueres, 2008). Authors of papers such as Belderbos et al. (2004), Cassiman and Veugelers (2002), as well as López (2008) have shown that organizations that consider external knowledge flows an important resource in their innovation processes are more likely to enter into cooperative R&D agreements. This is because companies thereby have greater access to existing knowledge, benefitting from their partners' technological skills. This increases the expected benefits of collaboration, thus increasing its likelihood. Furthermore, the greater the amount of knowledge exchanged, the greater the possibility of learning from the agreement and increasing the marginal benefit arising from it (López, 2008).

Now, such spillovers occur with greater intensity and therefore encourage its appropriation by means of collaboration agreements when companies are in close geographical proximity as a result of being located in a common STPs. Thus, a significant portion of the literature has underscored the increased propensity of collaborating among companies located in the same STPs due to their physical proximity. Consequently, the transfer of knowledge related to R&D tends to be more intense among organizations that are in close physical proximity (Jaffe, Trajtenberg, & Henderson, 1993; Maurseth & Verspagen, 2002).

Based on these arguments, we posit our second hypothesis:

> **Hypothesis 2:** *The propensity to engage in R&D cooperation by companies located in STPs is proportional to the knowledge flows or spillovers.*

Creating Value in R&D Cooperation in Science and Technology Parks

As we mentioned at the beginning of the section setting out the theoretical framework, STPs are an essential tool to economic development and to the generation of innovation. They thus have a significant positive impact on the performance of firms located within them. This, together with the prior argument that R&D alliances will tend to occur more frequently within STPs allows us to predict that the outcomes of said cooperation should be greater.

While looking at the results of cooperation, a significant body of research on cooperative relations in general, and R&D alliances in particular, has looked with great interest into whether this strategic option increases enterprise value or not; i.e., whether it is successful (García Canal & Valdés Llaneza, 2000; Mohr & Spekman, 1994; Mora-Valentín et al., 2004). In this regard, measuring the performance of strategic alliances has been the subject of significant discussion and controversy (Ariño, 2003). Several studies have highlighted the problems that can arise when the measures employed do not reflect the actual results yielded by the agreement.

The success of a cooperative relationship can be measured using both objective and subjective measures. Among the objective measures are financial indicators such as growth or costs (Hu & Chen, 1996), or exceptional returns accruing to a company, further to the announcement of the alliance (Merchant & Schendel, 2000). Other objective measures of operating success include survival, duration of the agreement (Glaister & Buckley, 1999), sustained stability of ownership (Geringer & Hebert, 1991), sales volume among partners (Mohr & Spekman, 1994), technical quality, and commercial success (Dussauge & Garrette, 1995). Subjetive measures refer to degree of satisfaction of the partners and achievement of the objectives set by them (García Canal & Valdés Llaneza, 2000; Mohr & Spekman, 1994). These measures measure organizational efficiency; i.e., global assessment of a firm's satisfaction with the performance of a cooperative relationship (Ariño, 2003). Here, most studies used satisfaction as a measure of success, and even as a complement to other objective measures (Dussauge & Garrette, 1995; Glaister & Buckley, 1999).

Now, much of the more recent literature measures success by measuring the achievement of the objectives of the alliance (Montoro Sánchez & Mora Valentín, 2010; Pearce & Hatfield, 2002; Reuer & Zollo, 2005). In any case, no performance indicator is perfect, because either they are subjective, as is the case of using management's perceptions, or they are specific to a certain type of cooperation agreement, which limits the sample that can be constructed and hence, the scope of any possible conclusions (Montoro Sánchez, 2005). In the case of R&D partnerships, their main objective is to develop stable cooperation relations within which to develop new technologies that might translate into new products, processes, organizational methods; or company product marketing methods, higher sales, access to the technology of their partners and to other types of technological resources, business growth in order to develop these innovations, increased company market share, and increased profit (Fryxell, 1990; George, Zahra, & Wood, 2002).

There is extensive literature that analyzes and confirms the positive correlation between R&D alliances and innovation. Much of the literature focuses on product innovation (Becker & Dietz, 2004; Fritsch & Lukas, 2001; Haeussler, Patzelt, & Zahra, in press), followed by commercial innovation and process innovation (Cassiman & Veugelers, 2002; López, 2008). Therefore, the channelling of resources into R&D cooperation has a positive impact on results in the form of innovation (Fontana et al., 2006; Mohnen & Hoareau, 2003; Segarra-Blasco & Arauzo-Carod, 2008; Tether, 2002). As for organizational innovation, there is as yet no evidence in this regard.

In any case, the arguments that support the positive correlation between cooperation agreements and firm performance through innovation are based on the fact that alliances allow partners to share the costs, risks, and uncertainty associated with innovation (Das & Teng, 2001; George et al., 2002; Liebeskind, Oliver, Zucker, & Brewer, 1996). This means that companies that engage in R&D collaboration are more likely to succeed in their innovation projects (Becker & Dietz, 2004; Belderbos et al., 2004; Faria, Lima, & Santos, 2010).

There are also abundant studies in which the results of innovation are measured by the number of patents awarded to the partners. Companies must protect the results of their R&D alliances from being imitated or copied by competitors (George et al., 2002). Patents are the mechanism most widely used for this (Liebeskind et al., 1996). At the same time, they help to protect the company's competitive position. Thus, one of the positive effects of R&D collaboration and hence, of the value thereby achieved is the number of patents filed by the partners. Patents capture the results of R&D development by the partners (George et al., 2002). Again, there is empirical evidence proving that firms located in STPs tend to file more patents (Monck, Porter, Quintas, Storey, & Wynarczyk, 1988; Westhead, 1997).

Finally, partnerships are also an instrument that allows companies, particularly small and medium-sized ones, to strengthen their competitive position vis-à-vis domestic and foreign markets. Such alliances are therefore expected to increase company sales and exports (Glaister & Buckley, 1999; Mohr & Spekman, 1994). Exports are the first step before moving into markets outside the home country. According to the latter, companies that establish R&D agreements are better placed to sell abroad and consequently, their exports can be expected to be greater (Haahti, Madupu, Yavas, & Babakus, 2005). This advantageous position is reinforced when the company has the additional resources needed as a result of its location in STPs to support its move abroad.

Based on the aforementioned factors, under Hypothesis 3, we suggest that STPs provide a setting that allows companies involved in R&D alliances to achieve better results and thus greater value creation, insofar as they are more likely to achieve their aims in terms of the results of innovation and market position.

Hypothesis 3: *In STPs, the results obtained by the companies will be better if the companies participate in R&D cooperative agreements.*

Figure 4.1 sets out the four variables we used in our model, namely, innovative behavior, spillovers, R&D cooperation and performance or success,

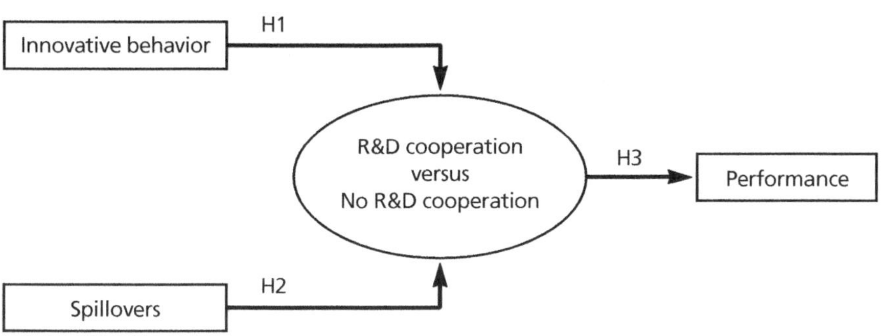

Figure 4.1 Analysis model and hypotheses.

as well as the relations we propose among these variables as reflected in the three above hypotheses.

METHODOLOGY: SAMPLE AND VARIABLES

Sample

For the empirical study, a sample of companies was selected from the Technological Innovation Panel (PITEC) drawn up by the Instituto Nacional de Estadística (INE). This panel originated from the Technological Innovation survey. This survey is part of the General Plan for Statistics on Science and Technology approved by the Statistical Office of the European Union (Eurostat). The panel's information collection tool was a questionnaire that included all relevant aspects of the company profile (turnover, staff, activity type, geographic market, etc.) and of the possible innovative activities (their conditions and effects). PITEC has been employed in pioneering studies performing analysis on innovations in the manufacturing and services sectors (e.g., see Castro, Montoro-Sánchez, & Ortiz-de-Urbina-Criado, 2011; Romero-Martínez, Ortiz-de-Urbina-Criado, & Ribeiro-Soriano, 2010; Un et al., 2009; Vega-Jurado, Gutiérrez-Gracia, & Fernández-de-Lucio, 2009).

The sample was chosen using PITEC data for the last 3 years (2006–2008), which spans a 5-year period for purposes of analysis (2004–2008). From among the companies contained in PITEC, we selected those that were located in STPs, giving a total of 392 companies. We then proceeded to filter the sample by removing companies that did not answer the question on R&D cooperation, leaving a final sample of 363 companies, of which 59.2% cooperated on R&D and the rest did not.

The sample presents the following characteristics. The majority of companies (63.4%) do not belong to a business group and are well-established companies (99.4%). Looking at company size, we observe that 59.5% (216) of companies are small, 34.2% (124) are medium-sized, and 6.3% (23) are large. By activity sectors, 71.1% (258) of companies belong to the services sector. Most of the companies are privately held (84%), only 11.6% are research centers, and only 4.4% are public enterprises.

Variables

Table 4.1 sets out the variables along with a description. To analyze the factors that determine the propensity among firms located in STPs to establish R&D alliances, the dependent variable is a category variable (ALLIANCE)

TABLE 4.1 Measures of Variables

Variables	Abreviation	Measurement	Source	Descriptives (frequency or mean/td)
Innovative behavior	INNOBEH*	Total innovation expenditures in 2006	Adapted from Belderbos, Carree, Diedersen, & Lokshin (2006) PITEC 2006	3425277.34/ 8149627.41
		Number of R&D personnel in 2006	Adapted from Belderbos et al. (2004) PITEC 2006	29.82/ 81.41
Spillovers	SPILLOVER*	Competitor Spillover: Importance of competitors as source of knowledge for the firm's innovation process during 2004–2006 (values 1 = "no importance" to 4 = "high importance")	Adapted from Belderbos et al. (2004) and López (2008) PITEC 2006	2.38/1.204
		Customer Spillover: Importance of customers as source of knowledge for the firm's innovation process during 2004–2006 (values 1 = "no importance" to 4 = "high importance")		2.89/1.099
		Supplier Spillover: Importance of suppliers as source of knowledge for the firm's innovation process during 2004–2006 (values 1 = "no importance" to 4 = "high importance")		2.51/0.953
		Institutional Spillover: Average of importance of universities, innovation centers, and research institutions as source of knowledge for the firm's innovation process during 2004–2006 (values 1 = "no importance" to 4 = "high importance")		2.20/1.024
		Public Spillover: Average of importance of patents, databases, trade literature, and fairs as source of knowledge for the firm's innovation process during 2004–2006 (values 1 = "no importance" to 4 = "high importance")		2.33/0.91

(continued)

TABLE 4.1 (continued) Measures of Variables

Variables	Abreviation	Measurement	Source	Descriptives (frequency or mean/td)
R&D alliances	ALLIANCE 2006	Dummy: Firm has cooperated on R&D during 2004–2006: value 1: yes; value 0: no	PITEC 2006	No (152)/Yes (211)
	ALLIANCE 2007	Dummy: Firm has cooperated on R&D during 2005–2007: value 1: yes; value 0: no	PITEC 2007	No (148)/Yes (215)
Patents	NUMPAT	Number of requested patents during 2006–2008	PITEC 2008	1.656/6.450
Turnover	TURNOVER	Turnover in 2008	PITEC 2008	39249662.408/ 184253259.314
Exportation	EXPORT	Export expenditures in 2008	PITEC 2008	7.211/18.818
Product innovation	PRODINN	Dummy: The firm has product innovation during 2006–2008: value 1: yes; value 0: no	PITEC 2008	No (97)/Yes(266)
Process innovation	PROCINN	Dummy: The firm has process innovation during 2006–2008: value 1: yes; value 0: no	PITEC 2008	No (117)/Yes (246)
Organizational innovation	ORGAINN	Dummy: The firm has organizational innovation during 2006–2008: value 1: yes; value 0: no	PITEC 2008	No (126)/Yes (237)
Commercial innovation	COMINN	Dummy: The firm has commercial innovation during 2006–2008: value 1: yes; value 0: no	PITEC 2008	No (221)/Yes (142)
Size	SIZE	Categorical variable: value 1 for small firms (less than 50 employees); value 2 for medium-size firms (between 50 and 500 employees) and value 3 for large firms (more than 500)	Adapted from Belderbos et al. (2004); López (2008) and López-Fernández et al. (2008) PITEC 2008	Small (216)/ Medium-size (124)/Large (23)
Sector	SECTOR	Categorical variable: value 0: industrial & agriculture (CNAE93: 1–45) and value 1: service sector (CNAE93: 50–92).	PITEC 2008	Industrial & Agriculture (105)/Services (258)

* These variables are the result of factorial analysis: see Table 4.2.

TABLE 4.2 Factorial Analysis

Variables		Loads	Variance explained (%)	Kaiser-Meyer-Olkin (KMO)	Bartlett (Chi-squared)
Innovative behavior (INNOBEH)	Total innovation expenditures	0.851	72.418	0.500	80.909 (sig. 0.000)
	Number of R&D personnel	0.851			
Spillovers (SPILLOVER)	Competitor	0.756	50 .913	0 .748	427 .136 (sig. 0 .000)
	Customer	0.754			
	Institutional	0.710			
	Public	0.705			
	Supplier	0.635			

that takes two values: a value of 1 if the company has engaged in R&D cooperation, and a value of 0 if it has not.

We analyzed the effect on cooperation of the following variables: innovative behavior, and spillovers. To create the innovative behavior variable, we created a factor based on two variables (INNOBEH): innovation expenditure and number of employees engaged in R&D activities. To create the external knowledge flows or spillovers variable, we carried out further factor analysis that produced a single factor (SPILLOVER) that includes every type of spillover: competitors, customers, suppliers, institutional, and public (see Table 4.2). We also considered two control variables, size (SIZE) and the company's activity sector (SECTOR).

To analyze the effects of R&D cooperation on the performance or results (value creation) of firms located in STPs, we used the following measures. First, we classified innovation outputs into five categories under five variables: four of them indicate whether the firm has innovated or not in each of these areas: product, process, organizational and commercial (PRODINN, PROCINN, ORGINN, COMINN), and a fifth variable indicating the number of patents filed by the company during that period (NUMPAT). On the other hand, we used two measures of firm performance: total sales (TURNOVER) and export sales (EXPORT).

RESULTS

To analyze the effect of innovative behavior and knowledge spillovers on the propensity to cooperate of firms located in STPs, we used logistic regression. Before calculating these models, we analyzed the correlations between the independent variables. The tests show a moderate correlation

TABLE 4.3 Logistic Regression Models

Variables	Model 1 B	Model 1 Wald	Model 1 Exp(B)	Model 2 B	Model 2 Wald	Model 2 Exp(B)
INNOBEH	0.644**	4.769	1.904	—	—	—
SPILLOVER	—	—	—	0.648***	30.073	1.911
SIZE (Small)	n.s.			n.s.		
SIZE (Medium)	n.s.			n.s.		
SIZE (Large)	n.s.			n.s.		
SECTOR (Services)	n.s.			n.s.		
Constant	0.428***	13.821	1.534	0.401***	12.782	1.494
Chi squared		9.701***			33.468***	
–2 loglikelihood		481.086			457.320	
R^2 Cox and Snell		0.026			0.088	
R^2 Nagelkerke		0.036			0.119	
Matrix of Classification		59.23%			63.09%	

*** $p < 0.01$; ** $p < 0.05$; * $p < 0.1$
Note: The dependent variable is ALLIANCE 2007

between innovative behavior and knowledge spillovers (0.416, sig. 0.000). Based on these correlations, we estimated various regression models analyzing the effect of each variable separately. Table 4.3 shows the results of the logistic regression models. All the regression models display good fit.

The results show that innovative behavior has a significant positive effect on firm propensity to cooperate, supporting Hypothesis 1. Model 1 of Table 4.3 shows that more innovative firms (higher spending on innovation and R&D personnel) are 1,904 times more likely to cooperate on R&D. Model 2 of Table 4.3 shows that spillovers also have a significant positive impact; i.e., companies that give greater importance to spillovers are 1,911 times more likely to cooperate on R&D than those who give less importance to these sources of information and knowledge, as posited in Hypothesis 2.

To analyze the effects of cooperation on innovation and on the results of cooperation, we calculated the descriptive statistics and analyzed the difference between firms located in STPs who cooperate, and those who do not (Table 4.4). Most of the companies in the sample that cooperated on R&D engaged in product innovation (48.76%), process innovation (41.32%), and organizational innovation (42.98%), whereas only 23.69% engaged in commercial innovation. On the other hand, difference testing shows that there are significant differences in product innovation, organizational innovation, number of patents filed, and exports.

TABLE 4.4 Effects of R&D Alliances: Differences

Variables	Frequencies (%)/Mean R&D alliance	Frequencies (%)/Mean No R&D alliance	Test for differences†
PRODINN: Yes	177 (48.76%)	89 (24.52%)	22.04***
PRODINN: No	38 (10.47%)	59 (16.25%)	
PROCINN: Yes	150 (41.32%)	96 (26.45%)	0.96
PROCINN: No	65 (17.91%)	52 (14.33%)	
ORGINN: Yes	156 (42.98%)	81 (22.31%)	12.29***
ORGINN: No	59 (16.25%)	67 (18.46%)	
COMINN: Yes	86 (23.69%)	56 (15.43%)	0.17
COMINN: No	129 (35.54%)	92 (25.34%)	
NUMPAT	199.595	156.439	12127.00***
TURNOVER	184.61	178.21	14469.00
EXPORT	188.70	172.26	14683.50*

† Chi-square test for categorical variables and U of Mann-Whitney for quantitative variables; $^{***}p < 0.001$; $^{*}p < 0.10$

Having analyzed the differences, we proceeded to study the effect of R&D cooperation on each of the outcomes (Hypothesis 3). For the dichotomous variables, we used binomial logistic regression models (Table 4.5), while for the continuous variables, we used simple regression models (Table 4.6). Table 4.5 shows that firms that cooperated on R&D in the period 2005–2007 were more likely to innovate by product and by organizational aspect in subsequent periods (2006–2008). The same effects were obtained for cooperation agreements carried out in the previous period (2004–2006). It also follows that R&D cooperation during the period 2005–2007 had a significant positive effect on the number of patents filed by the company in the period 2006–2008. However, cooperation does not have a significant effect on business turnover and export sales in 2008 (Table 4.6). On the other hand, in order to study the effect of cooperation on the outcomes over a longer time period, we looked at the effect of firm's R&D cooperation over the period 2004–2006 on performance in 2008 (Table 4.6). Here, the significant positive effect of cooperation on business turnover and number of patents filed was observed. In conclusion, it can be stated that R&D cooperation in STPs has a positive impact on innovation outputs and on the propensity to file patents, and furthermore, the effect of cooperation on company turnover tends to be seen in the medium term.

TABLE 4.5 Effects of R&D Alliances: Output of Innovation, Logistic Regression

	PRODINN		PROCINN		ORGINN		COMINN	
Variables	**B**	**Wald**	**B**	**Wald**	**B**	**Wald**	**B**	**Wald**
ALLIANCE 2007	1.127***	21.13	0.223 (sig. 0.326)	0.96	0.783***	12.10	0.091 (sig. 0.678)	0.172
Constant	0.411**	5.99	0.613***	12.68	0.19	1.32	–0.496***	8.579
Chi squared	21.814***		0.961		12.218***		0.172	
–2 loglikelihood	399.609		455.404		456.515		485.721	
R^2 Cox and Snell	0.058		0.003		0.033		0.000	
R^2 Nagelkerke	0.085		0.004		0.046		0.001	
Matrix of Classification	73.3%		67.8%		65.3%		60.9%	
ALLIANCE 2006	0.942***	15.060	0.361 (sig. 0.111)	2.535	0.759***	11.423	0.309 (sig. 0.160)	1.978
Constant	0.511***	9.296	0.539***	10.275	0.211	1.678	–0.625***	13.477
Chi squared	15.382***		2.532		11.545***		1.993	
–2 loglikelihood	406.040		453.832		457.188		483.901	
R^2 Cox and Snell	0.041		0.007		0.031		0.005	
R^2 Nagelkerke	0.060		0.010		0.043		0.007	
Matrix of Classification	73.30%		67.80%		65.30%		60.90%	

*** $p < 0.001$; ** $p < 0.05$

TABLE 4.6 Effects of R&D Alliances: Patents and Firm's Performance, Simple Regression

Dependent variables	Independent variables	B	Sig.	R^2	Corrected R^2
NUMPAT	ALLIANCE 2007	1.301	0.059	0.010	0.007
	Constant	0.885	0.095		
TURNOVER	ALLIANCE 2007	26305257.595	0.182	0.005	0.002
	Constant	23669413.419	0.119		
EXPORT	ALLIANCE 2007	1.353	0.502	0.001	–0.002
	Constant	6.409	0.000		
NUMPAT	ALLIANCE 2006	1.630	0.019	0.015	0.013
	Constant	0.716	0.177		
TURNOVER	ALLIANCE 2006	38269271.662	0.054	0.010	0.008
	Constant	16870424.432	0.267		
EXPORT	ALLIANCE 2006	1.208	0.552	0.001	–0.002
	Constant	6.581	0.000		

DISCUSSION

The purpose of this study is to provide a broad overview of the importance of R&D cooperation for companies located in STPs, and the positive effect of location in STPs on building up a larger number of cooperative R&D relations. To do so, we analyzed how the innovative behavior of firms (measured as investment in innovation and personnel engaged in R&D) affects their propensity to establish cooperative R&D agreements with other companies. In the existing literature, we find studies analyzing the cooperation between firms and research centers that suggest that firms that make a greater R&D effort cooperate to a greater degree with universities (Giuliani & Arias, 2009). Then, authors such as Tether (2002) found that R&D investment has a significant positive effect on firm propensity to cooperate on R&D. Furthermore, we also find studies that conclude that companies located in STPs exhibit greater intensity in their R&D activities (Löfsten & Lindelöf, 2003; Westhead, 1997). The results of our study expand and complement the existing empirical evidence, and following previous research lines, we were able to show that STPs-based firms that exhibit more innovative behavior are also those that cooperate most with other companies on R&D.

On the other hand, we observed that knowledge spillovers affect R&D cooperation. Working along this research line, some authors (Belderbos et al., 2004; Kaiser, 2002; López, 2008) have shown that firms that attach the greatest importance to external knowledge flows in their innovation processes have a greater propensity to initiate R&D cooperation agreements. The existing literature suggests that firm technological skills are often associated with their location, because innovation depends on the availability of specific assets to a large degree. The tacit nature of knowledge associated with production and innovation often involves physical or geographical proximity, which facilitates the transfer of that knowledge. Moreover, knowledge spillovers tend to be higher among firms that are located in neighboring areas (Jaffe et al., 1993; Maurseth & Verspagen, 2002). Narula and Santangelo (2009) support these ideas and emphasize that having firms in close proximity, as is the case in STPs, facilitates the transfer of knowledge. By confirming that knowledge spillovers determine the propensity to cooperate on R&D of companies located in STPs, our results provide new empirical evidence.

Companies cooperate on R&D with the aim of, among other things, obtaining better results from innovation (development of new products, processes, organizational methods, or company product marketing) to increase their sales and financial results (Fryxell, 1990; George et al., 2002). Although some authors have found a positive link between cooperation and innovation performance (Segarra-Blasco & Arauzo-Carod, 2008; Tether, 2002), few studies look at the effect of R&D cooperation on the propensity to innovate on organizational aspects. In this study, we found that companies who cooperate on R&D are more likely to engage in product innovation and organizational innovation. However, we have not found a significant impact on process or commercial innovation. In process innovation, the explanation may lie in the fact that most of the companies are service sector companies, which tend to engage in process innovation, regardless of whether R&D is carried out alone or in conjunction with other firms. Commercial innovation, on the other hand, presents fewer difficulties than other types of innovation, which makes cooperation less necessary.

Other studies have measured the results of innovation through patents, which allow companies to protect themselves from competitors who might imitate or copy them (Liebeskind et al., 1996). Furthermore, the empirical evidence shows that firms in STPs tend to file more patents (Monck et al., 1988; Westhead, 1997). In this chapter, we combine both arguments and show that STPs-based companies who cooperate on R&D provide the greatest protection for their innovation. This may stem from the fact that cooperation usually involves a higher risk of appropriation of knowledge and thus a greater likelihood that one of the partners may behave opportunistically (Das & Rahman, 2010; Narula & Santangelo, 2009). Hence, companies that cooperate on R&D have a greater tendency to use mechanisms to protect their technological knowledge and resources.

CONCLUSIONS

For decades, the literature has reflected growing interest in the study of R&D partnerships. We find numerous studies that build or focus on aspects such as the reasons and factors that determine cooperation, analyzing the cooperation process or analyzing the effects of cooperation. Moreover, often these studies have been context specific, studying domestic or international partnerships, or looking at alliances between companies from different sectors, or at companies of different sizes, or taking into account company location and the links that arise between different types of companies on account of their proximity. Within the latter, it is interesting to analyze the behavior of companies located in STPs, especially with regard to innovation and cooperation.

The conclusions of our study concur with those of previous work highlighting the importance of cooperation and intercompany relations within STPs and the growing trend among these companies to establish R&D partnerships over time. STPs are spaces that foster innovation, technology transfer, and knowledge, promoting research and R&D cooperation. To do so, STPs themselves constitute complex structures that rely on the coordinated action of the various agents to function and achieve their objectives. And it is the intrinsic complexity of STPs that constitutes a key tool in R&D and the dissemination of innovation (Ortiz-de-Urbina Criado & Montoro Sánchez, 2011).

The results of a sample of 392 firms located in STPs confirm the relations presented in this study. This research therefore makes a significant contribution to the empirical evidence on the relationship between firm location in STPs, innovation, and R&D cooperation. Our results confirm that innovative behavior and knowledge spillovers have a positive effect on the propensity to cooperate on R&D of firms in STPs. Furthermore, companies who cooperate are more likely to innovate and perform better than those that do not cooperate, even if these are located in STPs. This has important implications for firm decisions to establish themselves in STPs. Thus, companies that are innovative or wish to become more so can benefit from STPs location and the increased likelihood of cooperating on R&D with other firms, since such agreements benefit innovative behavior and company performance.

Thus, our results show that there is a significant link between innovative behavior and spillovers in the context of STPs. Although both factors have previously been studied in the literature, there is some disagreement as to the direction of the relationship or even as to whether it might work in both directions; i.e., that it might be a circular relationship. One conclusion we can draw is that both factors may be reinforcing one another, so it would be necessary to make a more in-depth analysis and study in greater detail the potential mediating or moderating effects of both variables, especially with regard to the results of collaboration.

As for the relationship between participation in R&D alliances and the success of these alliances, our results show that the relationship is significant and positive for firms located in STPs. This link is borne out for most of the various indicators used to represent the aims of the alliance, those related both to the results of innovation (number of patents, product and organizational innovation) and to sales turnover. According to most of the existing literature, these effects are far more significant in the case of product innovation (Becker & Dietz, 2004). Both for generating patents and for different types of innovation, it is understandable that cooperation with suppliers, customers, competitors, or other institutions within the STPs allow companies to capture or share necessary or complementary resources and knowledge to achieve better results through their innovation processes (Tether, 2002). Similarly, companies can reap the benefits of alliances during the distribution and sale of their products, or when entering foreign markets through exports. Thus, cooperation within the framework of STPs is a stimulus that allows firms to improve their performance or that places them in a better position to achieve their objectives.

Finally, bearing in mind the importance of STPs in the current system of innovation, our results should provide guidance to governments and public institutions when managing STPs. Thus, if the aim is for proximity to promote partnerships between organizations located within STPs, special care must be taken when looking for institutions to promote the establishment of cooperative relationships that generate benefits, not only in terms of their own results, but also at the regional and even national level.

However, as in all research, the results should be interpreted taking into account the limitations imposed by using secondary information sources. Future studies will try to overcome these constraints by obtaining additional disaggregated information on each of the variables analyzed in the study and carrying out an in-depth study in each Spanish STPs. It would be of great interest to study these relationships and effects based on the nature of the partner with which the company cooperates or to make a detailed study of the origin of the spillovers; i.e., if they are vertical or horizontal, or detailing each of its types. It would also be interesting to perform similar analyses in STPs in other geographic areas in order to compare the results and make them more generally applicable.

ACKNOWLEDGMENT

This study was financed under Project ECO2009-13818 and Project ECO2009-10358 of the Ministry of Science and Innovation, the Cátedra

Bancaja Jóvenes Emprendedores Complutense University of Madrid, and the Cátedra Iberdrola de Investigación en Administración y Dirección de Empresas of the Rey Juan Carlos University.

REFERENCES

Ariño, A. (2003). Measures of strategic alliance performance: An analysis of construct validity. *Journal of International Business Studies, 34,* 66–79.

Arundel, A., & Geuna, A. (2004). Proximity and the use of public science by innovative European firms. *Economics of Innovation & New Technology, 13,* 559–580.

Bakouros, Y. L., Mardas, D. C., & Varsakelis, N. C. (2002). Science park, a high tech fantasy?: An analysis of the science parks of Greece. *Technovation, 22,* 123–128.

Bayona, C., García-Marco, T., & Huerta, E. (2001). Firms' motivations for cooperative R&D: An empirical analysis of Spanish firms. *Research Policy, 30,* 1289–1307.

Becker, W., & Dietz, J. (2004). R&D cooperation and innovation activities of firms—Evidence for the German manufacturing industry. *Research Policy, 33,* 209–223.

Belderbos, R., Carree, M., Diederen, B., & Lokshin, B. (2006). Complementarity in R&D cooperation strategies. *Review of Industrial Organization, 28,* 401–426.

Belderbos, R., Carree, M., Diederen, B., Lokshin, B., & Veugelers, R. (2004). Heterogeneity in R&D cooperation strategies. *International Journal of Industrial Organization, 22,* 1237–1263.

Buesa, M., & Molero, J. (1998). The innovative stability in Spanish firms. *Revista de Economía Aplicada, 6,* 111–134.

Cassiman, B., & Veugelers, R. (2002). R&D cooperation and spillovers: Some empirical evidence from Belgium. *American Economic Review, 92,* 1169–1184.

Castells, M., & Hall, P. (1994). *Technopoles of the word. The making of twenty-first-century industrial complexes.* London: Routledge.

Castro, L. M., Montoro Sánchez, M. A., & Ortiz-de-Urbina-Criado, M. (2011). Innovation in service industries: Current and future trends. *Service Industries Journal, 31,* 7–20.

Cohen, W. M., Goto, A., Nagata, A., Nelson, R. R., & Walsh, J. P. (2002). R&D spillovers, patents and the incentives to innovate in Japan and the United States. *Research Policy, 31,* 1349–1367.

Das, T. K., & Rahman, N. (2010). Determinants of partner opportunism in strategic alliances: A conceptual framework. *Journal of Business Psychology, 25,* 55–74.

Das, T. K., & Teng, B. S. (2000). A resource based theory of strategic alliances. *Journal of Management, 26,* 31–61.

Das, T. K., & Teng, B. S. (2001). Trust, control, and risk in strategic alliances: An integrated framework. *Organization Studies, 22,* 251–283.

Dussauge, P., & Garrette, B. (1995). Determinants of success in international strategic alliances: Evidence from the global aerospace industry. *Journal of International Business Studies, 26,* 505–530.

Faria, P., Lima, F., & Santos, R. (2010). Cooperation in innovation activities: The importance of partners. *Research Policy, 39,* 1082–1092.

Felsenstein, D. (1994). University-related science parks—"Seedbeds" or "enclaves" of innovation? *Technovation, 14,* 93–110.

Fontana, R., Geuna, A., & Matt, M. (2006). Factors affecting university–industry R&D projects: The importance of searching, screening and signalling. *Research Policy, 35,* 309–323.

Fritsch, M., & Lukas, R. (2001). Who cooperates on R&D? *Research Policy, 30,* 297–312.

Fryxell, G. (1990). Multiple outcomes of product R&D: Profitability under different strategic orientations. *Journal of Management, 16,* 633–646.

Fukugawa, N. (2006). Science parks in Japan and their value-added contributions to new technology-based firms. *International Journal of Industrial Organization, 24,* 381–400.

García Canal, E., & Valdés Llaneza, A. (2000). Influence of the initial conditions on the joint venture performance: Theory and evidence. *Cuadernos de Economía y Dirección de la Empresa, 5,* 25–49.

George, G., Zahra, S. A., & Wood, D. R. (2002). The effects of business–university alliances on innovative output and financial performance: A study of publicly traded biotechnology companies. *Journal of Business Venturing, 17,* 577–609.

Geringer, J. M., & Hebert, L. (1991). Measuring performance of international joint ventures. *Journal of International Business Studies, 22,* 249–263.

Giuliani, E., & Arias, V. (2009). What drives the formation of "valuable" university–industry linkages? Insights from the wine industry. *Research Policy, 38,* 906–921.

Glaister, K. W., & Buckley, P. J. (1999). Performance relationships in UK international alliances. *Management International Review, 39*(2) 123–147.

Griliches, Z. (1992). The search for R&D spillovers. *Scandinavian Journal of Economics, 94,* 29–47.

Haahti, A., Madupu, V., Yavas, U., & Babakus, E. (2005). Cooperative strategy, knowledge intensity and export performance of small and medium sized enterprises. *Journal of World Business, 40,* 124–138.

Haeussler, C., Patzelt, H., & Zahra, S. A. (in press). Strategic alliances and product development in high technology new firms: The moderating effect of technological capabilities. *Journal of Business Venturing* (doi:10.1016/j.jbusvent.2010.10.002).

Hagedoorn, J. (2002). Inter-firm partnership: An overview of major trends and patterns since 1960. *Research Policy, 31,* 477–492.

Hagedoorn, J., Van Kranenburg, H., & Osborn, R. N. (2003). Joint patenting amongst companies—Exploring the effects of inter-firm R&D partnering and experiences. *Managerial and Decision Economics, 24,* 71–84.

Hu, M. Y., & Chen, H. (1996). An empirical analysis of factors explaining foreign joint venture performance in China. *Journal of Business Research, 35,* 165–173.

International Association of Science Parks (IASP). (2002). Retrieved from http://www.iasp.ws/

Jaffe, A., Trajtenberg, M., & Henderson, R. (1993). Geographical localization of knowledge spillovers, as evidenced by patent citations. *Quarterly Journal of Economics, 58,* 577–598.

Kafouros, M. I., & Buckley, P. J. (2008). Under what conditions do firms benefit from the research efforts of other organizations? *Research Policy, 37,* 225–239.

Kaiser, U. (2002). An empirical test of models explaining research expenditures and research cooperation: Evidence from the German service sector. *International Journal of Industrial & Organization, 20,* 747–774.

Liebeskind, J. P., Oliver, A. L., Zucker, L., & Brewer, M. (1996). Social networks, learning and flexibility: Sourcing scientific knowledge in new biotechnology firms. *Organization Science, 7,* 428–443.

Lindelöf, P., & Loftsen, H. (2004). Proximity as a resource base for competitive advantage: University–industry links for technology transfer. *Journal of Technology Transfer, 29,* 311–326.

Link, A. N., & Scott, J. T. (2003). U.S. science parks: The diffusion of an innovation and its effects on the academic missions of universities. *International Journal of Industrial Organization, 21,* 1323–1356.

Löfsten, H., & Lindelöf, P. (2003). Determinants for an entrepreneurial milieu: Science parks and business policy in growing firms. *Technovation, 13,* 51–64.

Löfsten, H., & Lindelöf, P. (2005). R&D networks and product innovation patterns—Academic and non-academic new technology-based firms on science parks. *Technovation, 25,* 1025–1037.

López, A. (2008). Determinants of R&D cooperation: Evidence from Spanish manufacturing firms. *International Journal of Industrial Organization, 26,* 113–136.

López-Fernández, M. C., Serrano-Bedia, A. M., & García-Piqueres, G. (2008). Exploring determinants of company-university R&D collaboration in Spain. *Journal of Manufacturing Technology Management, 19,* 361–373.

Malairaja, C., & Zawdie, G. (2008). Science parks and university-industry collaboration in Malaysia. *Technology Analysis & Strategic Management, 20,* 727–739.

Maurseth, P., & Verspagen, B. (2002). Knowledge spillovers in Europe: A patent citations analysis. *Scandinavian Journal of Economics, 104,* 531–545.

Merchant, H., & Schendel, D. (2000). How do international joint ventures create shareholder value? *Strategic Management Journal, 21,* 723–737.

Mohnen, P., & Hoareau, C. (2003). What type of enterprise forges close links with universities and government labs? Evidence from CIS 2. *Managerial and Decision Economics, 24,* 133–146.

Mohr, J. J., & Spekman, R. E. (1994). Characteristics of partnership success: Partnership attributes, communication behavior, and conflict resolution techniques. *Strategic Management Journal, 15,* 135–152.

Monck, C. S. P., Porter, R. B., Quintas, P., Storey, D. J., & Wynarczyk, P. (1988). *Science parks and the growth of high technology firms.* London: Croom Helm.

Montoro Sánchez, M. A. (2005). R&D international cooperation. An organizational factors analysis. *Revista de Economía Aplicada, 23,* 21–45.

Montoro Sánchez, M. A., & Mora Valentín, E. M. (2010). Measures of performance in cooperative relationships: The effect of objectives achievement on partner satisfaction. *Revista Europea de Dirección y Economía de la Empresa, 19,* 147–164.

Mora-Valentín, E. M., Montoro-Sánchez, M. A., & Guerras-Martín, L. A. (2004). Determining factors in the success of R&D cooperative agreements between firms and research organisms. *Research Policy, 33,* 17–40.

Narula, R., & Santangelo, G. D. (2009). Location, collocation and R&D alliances in the European ICT industry. *Reseach Policy, 38,* 393–403.

Ondategui, J. (2000). Evolution and actual context of science and technological parks in Spain. Madrid, Spain: Cotec.

Ondategui, J. (2002). Science and innovation parks in Spain: Fifteen years of experience. *Economía Industrial, 346,* 147–160.

Ortiz-de-Urbina Criado, M., & Montoro Sánchez, M. A. (2011). The role of Spanish science and technological parks in the generation of R&D. *Boletín Económico del ICE, 3005,* 55–64.

Oxley, J. E., & Sampson, R. C. (2004). The scope and governance of international R&D alliances. *Strategic Management Journal, 25,* 723–749.

Pearce, J. A., & Hatfield, L. (2002). Performance effects of alternative joint venture resource responsability structures. *Journal of Business Venturing, 17,* 343–64.

Phillimore, J. (1999). Beyond the linear view of innovation in science park evaluation: An analysis of Western Australian Technology Park. *Technovation, 19,* 673–680.

Piga, C., & Vivarelli, M. (2004). Internal and external R&D: A sample selection approach. *Oxford Bulletin of Economics and Statistics, 66,* 457–482.

Reuer, J. J., & Zollo, M. (2005). Termination outcomes of research alliances. *Research Policy, 34,* 101–115.

Romero Martínez, A. M., Ortiz-de-Urbina Criado, M., & Ribeiro Soriano, D. (2010). Evaluating European Union support for innovation in Spanish small and medium enterprises. *Service Industries Journal, 30,* 671–683.

Schartinger, D., Rammer, C., Fischer, M. M., & Frohlich, J. (2002). Knowledge interactions between universities and industry in Austria: Sectoral patterns and determinants. *Research Policy, 31,* 303–328.

Segarra-Blasco, A., & Arauzo-Carod, J. M. (2008). Sources of innovation and industry-university interaction: Evidence from Spanish firms. *Research Policy, 37,* 1283–1295.

Simonen, J., & McCann, P. (2008). Innovation, R&D cooperation and labor recruitment: Evidence from Finland. *Small Business Economics, 31,* 181–194.

Squicciarini, M. (2009). Science parks: Seedbeds of innovation? A duration analysis of firms' patenting activity. *Small Business Economics, 32,* 169–190.

Tether, B. S. (2002). Who co-operates for innovation, and why. An empirical analysis. *Research Policy, 31,* 947–967.

Un, C. A., Romero-Martínez, A. M., & Montoro-Sánchez, M. A. (2009). Determinants of R&D collaboration of service firms. *Service Business, 3,* 373–394.

Vedovello, C. (1997). Science parks and university–industry interaction: Geographical proximity between the agents as a driving force. *Technovation, 17,* 491–502.

Vega-Jurado, J., Gutiérrez-Gracia, A., & Fernández-de-Lucio, I. (2009). Does external knowledge sourcing matter for innovation? Evidence from the Spanish manufacturing industry. *Industrial & Corporate Change, 18,* 637–670.

Verspagen, B. (1997). Measuring intersectoral technology spillovers: Estimates from the European and US patent office databases. *Economic Systems Research, 9,* 47–65.

Verspagen, B., & De Loo, I. (1999). Technology spillovers between sectors and over time. *Technological Forecasting and Social Change, 60,* 215–235.

Veugelers, R., & Cassiman, B. (2005). R&D cooperation between firms and universities. Some empirical evidence from Belgian manufacturing. *International Journal of Industrial Organization, 23,* 355–379.

Westhead, P. (1997). R&D "inputs" and "outputs" of technology-based firms located on and off science parks. *R&D Management, 27,* 45–62.

CHAPTER 5

INTERORGANIZATIONAL LEARNING IN ALLIANCES AND NETWORKS

Amalya L. Oliver
Yuval Kalish

ABSTRACT

While interorganizational alliances among firms and between firms and universities have been the subject of rigorous research in the past 2 decades, the understanding of the inherent complexities of interorganizational learning processes is relatively limited both theoretically and empirically. One of the main areas that needs further exploration is how organizational actors balance the tension between knowledge generation and knowledge protection in learning through networks. In this chapter, we offer a review of the literature on interorganizational learning in the context of knowledge generation and protection. Our aim is to develop a theoretical framework that brings together the complex tensions regarding knowledge exchange across organizational boundaries and how they are or can be balanced. Our model includes different types of knowledge exchanges in learning alliances that are based on content and relational learning mechanisms. These learning mechanisms are related to different types of value creation for organizations. Further, we review the network literature that refers to various network structures (the

Strategic Alliances for Value Creation, pages 101–118

most prominent will be the concepts of triadic closure and structural holes as they apply to single and multiple relationships). Finally, we explain what network methodologies can be used to study and analyze complex network structures. We show how univariate and multivariate exponential random graph (ERG) models can provide evidence that can test the proposed theoretical framework for studying learning collaborations.

COMPLEXITIES IN LEARNING ALLIANCES

Knowledge exchange and interorganizational learning are crucial for organizational survival in many knowledge-intensive industries. Therefore, it is not surprising that most of the organizational literature on interorganizational exchange networks focuses on the biotechnology industry in the United States and other countries. Oliver (2009) and Powell, White, Koput, and Owen-Smith (2005) suggest that several conditions account for the emergence of learning alliances as the dominant learning form in the industry. These conditions include the limited resources and high competition, the importance of collaborating with universities and research institutes, and the large number of small firms that lack the capabilities to bring a product from the invention stage to the market.

However, despite the fact that learning alliances are crucial for the survival of organizations, such alliances are not simple, and many complexities are associated with them (Oliver, 2004). The first complexity associated with learning alliances is that the literature has many different definitions of interorganizational learning. Generally, the literature uses broad definitions that view such learning as a crucial element for the organization's strategic renewal (Crossan, Lane, & White, 1999) and survival (Oliver 2001; Powell, Koput, & Smith-Doer, 1996). Thus, the learning in alliances is defined as an element in the complex puzzle that comprises renewal and survival. Specifically, the underlying commonality in such definitions is the recognition that interorganizational learning exchanges can bring about changes in the knowledge structures of the organization. The organizational knowledge structures are embodied in an organization's routines and are stored in an ambiguous form in the organization's collective memory. Within this ambiguous organizational knowledge structure, firms form alliances that eventually lead to changes in knowledge structures of the firm.

The second main complexity is that there are different *types* of learning that occur in alliances. From the literature, we learn that it is important to account for the different analytical types of organizational learning in the effort to understand the complexities associated with learning alliances. One main distinction is offered by Das and Kumar (2007, p. 286), who refer to three main elements regarding learning: nature, process, and effectiveness. As described in their work, "The first issue is a definitional one, namely the nature of organizational learning. The second focuses on the processes of learning, namely how does learning occur? The third deals with the fundamental question of learning to learn effectively, i.e., the factors that impede the reliability and validity of the learning."

As Das and Kumar (2007) explain, it is important to make the analytic distinction in learning alliances between what needs to be learned from the partner firm and the extent to which a firm can acquire and internalize the new knowledge negotiated through the alliance. The distinction focuses on the partner for the alliance and refers to two main components: learning from a partner and learning about a partner. In alliances, there is an important aspect of "learning from," yet Das and Kumar provide an important additional clarification: that in alliances, partners also need to learn about each other regarding capabilities, norms and values, trustworthiness, etc. Finally, the third distinction refers to the degree to which the firm is effective in the management of their alliances and to the degree to which they utilize them effectively in absorbing the needed new learning.

These three elements jointly compose three stages within the learning process (Das & Kumar, 2007). At the formation stage, a "sense-making" process leads to a contractual arrangement. During this stage, the partners define the learning process they wish to establish in the alliance and possible contingencies regarding the process. During this phase, they evaluate the compatibility of the knowledge of the two firms, the risks associated with sharing the needed knowledge, and define the scope and boundaries of the learning. At this stage, the firms usually try to gather information on the reputation of their partner and the firm's past performance in other alliances. The second phase is when they need to learn about their partner. Thus, the focus is on learning about a partner if the relations are newly initiated, or even if these are repeated relations, yet not all actors in the collaboration are familiar with each other. Actors differ in their integrity, trustworthiness, and openness. It takes time to learn about such characteristics, yet learning about them may be crucial for establishing a successful learning process.

The third part of the learning process incorporates turning the tacit knowledge of the two alliance partners into some concrete knowledge that can be translated into a patent, a technology, or a product. This stage is where the alliance partners start the operation of the joint learning activities, and the content-specific components of their knowledge become crucial for the process. Das and Kumar (2007) argue that the degree to which the joint learning is effective in generating the anticipated learning integration depends on the successful preestablished interactional aspects of the two partners, including reputation and trustworthiness (Larsson, Bengtsson, Hendriksson, & Sparks, 1998).

To these three elements of learning, we add another distinction: a process-based complexity, based on the Borgatti and Cross (2003) model of knowledge search. Their assumption is that the need for learning is associated with three main stages in the search process for knowledge. We argue that this is a gradual process where every stage is an antecedent to the following stage. In the first stage, actors need to *learn where* the relevant knowledge is—searching for who knows what they need for their learning collaboration. Once they've found potential knowledge partners, they need to *learn what* the knowledge is and to be able to assess how well it is compatible with what they need. Finally, they need to *learn how* to access and exchange this knowledge while ensuring that the exchange is not too costly for them. At this last stage, firms learn to manage any specific alliance so as to maximize the gains of the new knowledge acquired. At this stage, it is expected that firms with multiple alliances and a history of successful alliances may have established a better capacity for learning absorption as well as be able to store new knowledge and practices for the dissemination of learning outcomes throughout the firm. Thus, we argue that knowledge exchanges are formed only after of a set of different search behaviors are enacted and performed in a satisfactory manner by both partners.

Obviously, there is also a gradual increase in clarity once we move from one level of the search process to another. During the first phase, when organizations are *learning where* they can find the needed compatible knowledge for the missing parts in their internal capabilities, they are searching for knowledge that is not well-defined and are often unclear as to what exactly they are searching for. Once the potential sources of knowledge are found, it becomes a more specific and clear search. At this stage, organizations are *learning what* the knowledge is and what it entails. At the *learning how* phase of the search, organizations need to see how this knowledge can be implemented in their learning process. They focus on how they can best incorporate the new knowledge with what they know and implement it into their internal learning process. At this stage, the search for knowledge becomes highly specific and is characterized by a higher level of clarity regarding what is needed to absorb it into the product development process.

In the following model, presented in Table 5.1, we claim that the three elements of learning are associated with the three stages we offer regarding the search elements in learning processes. Each cell in the table illustrates the main strategic question that can be asked by the firm.

At this point, we add an additional complexity regarding value creation through networks of learning. This complexity is associated with the organizational levels of learning. We know from the literature that organizational learning is based both on internal and external exchanges between individuals, which is a complex process due to its multilevel nature (Argote, McEvily, & Reagens, 2003; Holmqvist, 2003; Oliver & Liebeskind, 1998). It

TABLE 5.1 Focus and Process Issues Regarding Learning and Related Strategic Questions Based on Das & Kumar (2007) and Borgatti & Cross (2003)

	Learning where	Learning what	Learning how
Nature of knowledge	What do we need to learn, and who may have this knowledge?	What do we need to learn, and what does the potential partner know?	What do we need to learn, and how can we do this?
Process—knowing about the partner	Who are the potential knowledge holders, and what do we know about their reputation and trustworthiness?	What do we know about the potential partners, and what do we need to do in order to maintain a learning alliance with them?	What do we know about the potential partners, and how can we manage this learning alliance so it will fit our internal purposes?
Outcome effectiveness	What do we see as an effective alliance outcome, and where are the alliance partners that can fit such anticipated outcome?	What do we see as an effective alliance outcome, and what do we need to learn for achieving it?	What do we see as an effective alliance outcome, and how do we manage the learning process in the alliance?

also involves a collective integrative process of individuals, groups, and organizations and thus, is a highly costly and complex process (Das & Kumar, 2007). Yet it is clear that learning occurs on the individual and team levels, and thus, the basic unit for understanding organizational learning through alliances is at the individual level.

We have suggested that learning alliances encompass different dimensions and thus require a complex view of the different strategic processes they entail. We will offer another distinction regarding the complementarity or the distinctness of the exchanged knowledge between the alliance partners, and we will review the literature on interorganizational learning mechanisms in strategic alliances at both relational and content levels. Next, we will show how the relational and the content levels are associated with different types of value creation for organizations. Since network research and methodologies for analyzing structure are not only relevant for studying alliances but can also enhance the understanding of their theoretical implications, we will introduce various network structures that are of value within the context of learning. In doing so, we will elaborate on different structures that emerge in networks and their meaning, and exemplify the most prominent structural concepts: triadic closure and structural holes. Since these two concepts can apply to single and multiple relationships, they are of great importance for further research on alliances and value creation. Finally, we will explain how new network methods have a powerful ability to be applied for the study of complex learning network structures. These methods include univariate and multivariate exponential random graph (ERG) models that can test theoretical frameworks and thus contribute to the development of interorganizational networks theories.

MECHANISMS FOR BALANCING KNOWLEDGE GENERATION AND KNOWLEDGE PROTECTION

Our starting point is to claim that learning alliances are based on two main components: knowledge generation and knowledge protection. Firms who seek alliances need to learn in order to generate new knowledge that is highly needed for their product development. On the other hand, alliances expose internal knowledge to external partners and can lead to appropriation and leakages of knowledge (Oliver, 2004). So the challenge for studying learning alliances is to understand how firms manage to balance the two opposing challenges of knowledge "generation" and "protection" and the tensions between these challenges.

Since alliances provide both risks and opportunities to organizations, network actors have to balance the tension between knowledge generation and knowledge protection. Through knowledge generation, organizations aim at expanding their knowledge base through others by absorbing knowledge developed elsewhere ("content learning"; Das & Kumar, 2007). Knowledge protection involves securing the organizations' own valuable knowledge from appropriation by others, through compartmentalizing (Liebeskind, 1996) or selectively disclosing their knowledge (Perkmann, 2009) or through other, external governance mechanisms (Nooteboom, 2004). However, researchers found that governance mechanisms, whether contractual (Majewski, 2004), hierarchical (Mintzberg, 1984), incentives based (Nooteboom, 2004), based on organizational structures (e.g., R&D consortia; Majewski, 2004), or based on trust-generating mechanisms (Sydow, 1996), may not suffice to protect knowledge from appropriation or leakage (Majewski, 2004).

We suggest that organizational actors who establish learning alliances form different network structures to balance knowledge generation and knowledge protection while controlling the type of knowledge exchanged with others. We argue that firms alternate between two mechanisms exemplified by typical network structures: a network for generating learning and a network for controlling knowledge exchanged and protecting it.

Balancing Knowledge Generation and Protection through Selection of Partners

Previous research treated knowledge exchange relationships as unidimensional—network actors have either exchanged or did not exchange knowledge. Yes, since the argument is about the inherent tensions between knowledge protection and knowledge creation, we suggest treating knowledge exchange as a multidimensional construct. In doing so, we follow the model proposed by Borgatti and Cross (2003) that claims that in seeking information from others, network actors seek different types of information. They need to know what other network actors know—a general screening of knowledge is needed. They need to evaluate the other network actors' knowledge; they need to ascertain that the information others have is relevant and complementary to their own; and they need to be able to access the other network actors' knowledge. Finally, they need to perceive that seeking information from other network actors will not be too costly.

Thus, as indicated above, based on Borgatti and Cross (2003), we offer the three classifications regarding knowledge exchanges and learning and presented them above: *learn where, learn what,* and *learn how.* Knowledge exchanges therefore are composed of a set of different search behaviors aimed at achieving different types of information, defined by level of specificity and clarity. When organizations are *learning where* knowledge is, they are searching for knowledge that is nonspecific, and they are often unclear as to what exactly they are searching for. When organizations are *learning what* the knowledge is, their search becomes clearer as they are searching for more specific information. Finally, when organizations are *learning how* to implement knowledge, their search for knowledge is highly specific, and they are very clear about what they are trying to achieve (see also Oliver, 2004).

Conjointly, we claim that the risks associated with knowledge leakage and opportunism as well as the costs associated with information exchange are much higher for *learning how* relationships compared with *learning where* relationships (see Borgatti & Cross, 2003). Thus, we propose that network actors will balance knowledge generation and protection through the number of relationships of each type they have (see also Ahuja, 2000). They will have more low-risk (*learning where* relationships) and fewer high-risk (*learning how*) relationships. This leads to the following proposition.

Proposition 1: *Network actors will have more learning where and learning what relationships compared with learning how relationships.*

Balancing Knowledge Generation and Protection through Network Structure

We argue that the study of network structures can enhance our understanding of how actors can balance the tensions between knowledge generation and protection. We focus on the discussion of triadic structures[1] in social network analysis. We refer to the two main types of triadic structures that bestow different opportunities on network actors. On the one hand, forming redundant relationships (forming relationships to two network actors who are already connected to each other: *triadic closure*) is associated with the development of strong group norms and pressures toward conformity (Friedkin, 2004). Actors embedded in these structures enjoy enhanced trust, stricter norms, and control over misbehavior (Krackhardt, 1999), a stronger sense of "group identity" (Kalish & Robins, 2006), and higher efficiency (Burt, 2005). In interfirm relationships, having multiple nonredundant contacts has been shown to create value by exploiting knowledge that has been created elsewhere (DeFillippi, Arthur, & Lindsay, 2007) and to enhance governance of relational risk (Gulati, Nohria, & Zaheer, 2000; Nooteboom, 1999). Thus, when an actor wishes to secure proprietary knowledge while minimizing nonnormative opportunistic behavior, *triadic closure* (see Figure 5.1) may be the optimal structure.

On the other hand, structural-holes theory (Burt, 1992) presents a second set of benefits to actors. A structural hole is defined as a situation where one actor is connected to two others that are not themselves connected to each

Strategic objective:	**Control over knowledge**	**Knowledge generation and competitive advantage**
Level of analysis		
Dyadic learning ties	Few limited to only the most important	Many widescale, unbounded "fishing expeditions"
Triadic learning ties	Triadic closure 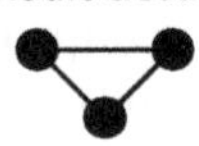	Structural holes 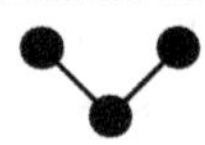
Multiplex learning ties	Dyadic embedding and multiplex triadic closure 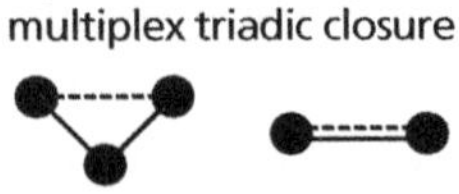	Odyadic disembedding and multiplex structural holes 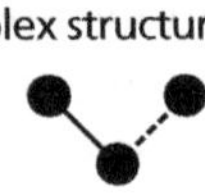

Figure 5.1 Dyadic, triadic, and multiplex network structures for enhancing knowledge generation and knowledge protection.

other (Figure 5.1). Simmel (1955) was the first to argue that occupying structural holes allows for opportunities to enhance self-interests by brokering relationships and therefore to enhance one's knowledge and power compared with others'. Research suggests that actors who occupy structural holes enjoy earlier access to more diverse information, greater innovation and creativity, and higher recognition (Burt, 2005). In the same line of argument, Hibbert and Huxham (2007, p. 128) suggest that when network actors are "competitive" in a collaborative learning setting, they "engage in particular learning patterns... in which the 'selfish' partner seeks to control the [learning] processes in a way that preserves the learning opportunity." We conclude that when actors seek to maximize their competitive advantage and to generate knowledge, they should form networks that are composed of many structural holes (Gilsing, Nooteboom, Vanhaverbeke, Duysters, & van den Oord, 2008).

Assuming that actors are aware of potential network allies,[2] we expect that they will form network configurations that will maximize their knowledge generation while controlling knowledge protection. As a result, actors may shape the relations they have with alliance partners in order to improve the returns they receive. We thus argue that when knowledge is less specific and organizations are unclear about what it is they are looking for (e.g., *learning where* and *learning what* relationships), they will seek to position themselves in network structures that create opportunities for diverse information sources and competitive advantage (e.g., structural holes), while when knowledge exchanges becomes more specific and focused (e.g., *learning how* relationships), triadic closure will secure the advancement of proprietary knowledge. We therefore propose the second and the third propositions:

> **Proposition 2:** *Learning where and learning what relationships will be characterized by structural holes.*

> **Proposition 3:** *Learning how relationships will be characterized by triadic closure.*

Now we add another dimension to the claim regarding the advantage of studying triads, beyond the study of dyads in learning networks. We need to study multiple learning networks rather than assuming uniformity in the nature of learning in strategic alliances. In doing this, we join the call of network scholars to offer simultaneous analysis of different inter- and intraorganizational (multiplex) relationships (Oliver & Liebeskind, 1998), since "No single type of relationship constitutes 'the' network of an organizational field" (Kenis & Knoke, 2002, p. 276). Similarly, Kilduff, Tsai, and Hanke (2006) claimed that "future research is more likely to emphasize multiple contingencies and fascinating exceptions that characterize the complex interweaving of social networks"; and Nohria (1992, p. 4) argued that "the structure of any organization must be understood and analyzed in terms of multiple networks of relations."

But why would different networks become interdependent (see Robins & Pattison, 2006 for a discussion on this topic)? First is the issue of embeddedness. Network relationships often become embedded within each other. For example, Granovetter (1985) and Uzzi (1997, 1999) suggest that accounting for relational interdependence enhances the explanation of economic transactions, since friendship relationships facilitate economic transactions. Similarly, Das and Teng (2002a, 2002b) suggest that in alliances, having good interpersonal relationships between participants enhances the learning of general topics together. Second, relationships can develop from each other, one relationship being a precursor to the other. Examining multiple relationships can therefore capture the dynamic nature of networks. For example, the literature on interorganizational alliances suggests that previous successful alliances lead to future alliances (Gulati, 1995) through enhancing partner trustworthiness and better knowledge of the integrity and the reputation of both partners (Das & Teng, 1998, 2001; Nooteboom, 2006). As a result, future relationships between partners tend to be deeper and more trusting (Kapmeier, 2008). Finally, exchanges of various types of resources among actors can be understood as different networks (Lazega & Pattison, 1999). Blau (1964), who founded "social exchange" theory, suggests that actors exchange resources with each other and expect returns (cf. Borgatti & Cross, 2003). Such reciprocity generates trust, which then leads to the expansion of the domains of the exchange: "firms commit themselves to provide resources and receive *other* resources in return" (Das & Teng, 2002b, p. 445, italics added). Thus, exchange of one type of resource or relationship may lead to reciprocation in another type of resources or relationship, creating interdependence between exchange networks.

The logic of brokerage and closure described above also operates at a multiplex (multiple relationship) level. We propose that when firms search for new knowledge, it will be beneficial for them to form multiplex structures that enhance brokerage. The logic of brokerage suggests that being the only actor to connect others provides opportunities for knowledge generation and competitive advantage because the actor is exposed to nonredundant sources of information and can control its flow. This logic of value creation and protection, within the context of the dyadic level of analysis claims that actors should avoid forming dyadic multiplex relationships. This is because having multiple types of learning alliances with the same actor increases the actors' constraint and reduces his ability to benefit from information advantages (Burt, 1992). Thus, in order to maximize their exposure to nonredundant information, network actors should de-couple and *disembed*[3] their relationships. This is especially relevant to the *learning how* and *learning where* relationships, both at the extremes of the types of learning range. While the former is characterized by specific exchanges and clarity for the allies, the latter is nonspecific and lacks clarity. The argument that follows is that if network actors wish to continue their search for new knowledge while exchanging more specific knowledge with another actor, they should separate their contacts from each other. In other words, they should search for new information (*learning where*) from those that they are not exchanging specific, practical (*learning how*) information with. This leads us to the fourth proposition:

> **Proposition 4:** *The learning where and learning how relationships will be disembedded, so that the existence of one type of relationship negatively predicts the existence of the other.*

The argument about brokerage at a multiplex triadic level suggests that disembedding network relationships may not suffice. Since two actors that are exchanging information with each other are already sharing some information, having a learning relationship with both provides the focal actor with redundant information (Burt, 1992). Therefore, in order to enhance exposure to new knowledge and create competitive advantage value, firms should exchange knowledge with two other firms that are not themselves connected through a learning relationship: the focal firm should try to form *multiplex structural holes* (Figure 5.1). This will be especially relevant to the two relationships at the extreme end of the learning continuum—*learning where* and *learning how* networks. Multiplex structural holes means that organizations prefer that their *learning where* and *learning how* partners are not exchanging either general (*learning where*) or specific (*learning how*) knowledge with each other. This brings us to the fifth proposition:

> **Proposition 5:** *When analyzed in tandem, learning where and learning how relationships will be characterized by multiplex structural holes.*

Now we move from knowledge generation to the issue of knowledge protection. This part of the argument claims that that when network actors seek to secure their knowledge, they will form closure between learning partners by forming *dyadic embedding* and *multiplex triadic closure* (Figure 5.1). The more specific the exchanged knowledge, the more important is the control over opportunism and leakage. Thus, we propose that network actors will opt for closure in the two relationships that entail exchange of more specific information: learning "what" and "how." At a dyadic, multiplex level, the logic of closure suggests that network actors will prefer to have multiple learning relationships with the same partner. Embedding relationships allows for greater control over the partner (Granovetter, 1985), and to more cooperative learning (Das & Teng, 2002b; Larsson et al., 1998). Thus, when network actors value control over knowledge leakage (which is becoming highly relevant when the learning becomes more specific as it is with the *learning how* and *learning what* in exchange relationships), they will benefit from forming multiplex dyads (Figure 5.1). This leads us to the sixth proposition:

> **Proposition 6:** *When actors wish to protect their knowledge in learning exchanges, they will form dyadic embedding for their learning what and learning how collaborative relationships.*

The logic of closure proposed above also operates at a triadic, multiplex level of network structures. We define multiplex triadic closure as situations in which an actor has one type of relationship to two others that have a different type of relationship between themselves (Figure 5.1). If, as Das and Teng (2002b, p. 443) suggest, network actors "take explicit cognizance of the level of trust between [their partners] in constructing the alliance," the existence of a relationship between a focal firm's partner and a second partner may signal to the focal firm that the third actor is trustworthy, leading to the development of a relationship between the focal actor and the third actor. Therefore, when trust is important, network actors will prefer to form triadic closure not only within networks but also between networks (forging multiplex triadic closure, Figure 5.1). This will be especially important in the learning alliances in which relatively specific knowledge is being exchanged: if a focal organization's trusted, *learning how* partner is already *learning what* with a third actor, this can signal to the focal actor that the third actor is also trustworthy and competent, and that its knowledge base is relevant. The likelihood of a *learning what* or *learning how* relationship developing between the focal actor and the third party is greatly enhanced. Thus the seventh proposition:

> **Proposition 7:** *Learning relations that wish to protect knowledge, such as learning what and learning how, will be characterized by triadic closure.*

The next section offers a short overview of a new network methodological approach that can assist scholars of strategic alliances in testing new models of complex networks that can enhance new theoretical development.

ANALYTIC TECHNIQUE: EXPONENTIAL RANDOM GRAPH MODELS

For testing hypotheses that are exerted from our propositions, one needs to apply a method that will estimate the probabilities for each structure that emerges in any data of learning-based networks. Exponential Random Graph (ERG) Model frameworks can analyze network data (for a more technical introduction, see Robins, Pattison, Kalish, & Lusher, 2007). Contrary to standard statistical techniques, which assume independence of observations, ERG models are based on the assumption that network ties are conditionally dependent on each other, so that given one network tie, others will be observed. This framework is especially useful for our purposes since our hypotheses relate to the interdependencies within and between networks. Moreover, this technique allows us to deduce actors' agency from observed network configurations (Monge & Contractor, 2003; Robins et al., 2007).

Briefly, the ERG framework models the observed (collected) network based on underlying "motifs" or "building blocks" specified by the researcher. The typical motifs used in ERG models using Markov dependence assumptions (Frank & Strauss, 1986) are depicted in Figure 5.2.

Parameter name	**Graphical representation**	**Parameter interpretation**
Edge		*Both actors have a learning relationship*
2-star	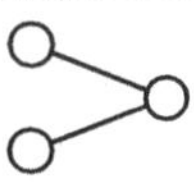	*A structural hole between 2 actors:* Actor *i* is in a learning relationship with actors *j* and *k,* who are not in a learning relationship with each other.
Triangle	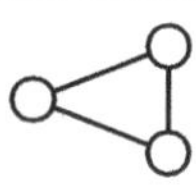	*Triadic closure between 3 actors:* Actor *i* is in a learning relationship with actor *j* and *k,* who are in a learning relationship with each other.
Multivariate Markov Configurations		
Edge AB		*Multiplex dyadic embedding:* Both actors share two learning relationships of different types.
2-star AB	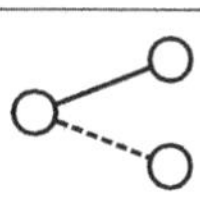	*Multiplex structural hole:* An actor has one type of learning relationship to one partner and a second type of learning relationship to a second partner, with both partners not having a learning relationship of either type with each other.
AAB triangle	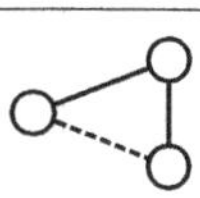	*Multiplex triadic closure:* An actor has one type of learning relationship (A) and another type of learning relationship to another actor (B), who has a learning relationship of type A to each other.
BAB triangle	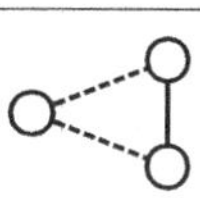	*Multiplex triadic closure:* An actor has one type of learning relationship (B) with two other actors, who have a different type of relationship (A) with each other.

Figure 5.2 Markov Configurations used for univariate (top panel) and multivariate (bottom panel) nondirected networks.

Robins and Pattison (2006) extended the univariate ERG framework to include multivariate parameters. Multivariate ERG models have the same general form as univariate ERG models, except that they add some additional parameters that depict the interdependence of ties between networks. In the multivariate network model, both within-network parameters (i.e., parameters used in univariate networks, such as the parameters in the top panel of Figure 5.2) and across-network parameters (i.e., parameters in the lower panel of Figure 5.2) are included.

The building blocks presented in Figure 5.2 represent the occurrence of dyads, structural holes, triadic closure, multiplex structural holes, and multiplex triadic closure. By modeling an observed learning-alliance network with these blocks, we obtain statistical answers as to whether, given all other configurations in the model, our learning network has more or fewer of each type of structure. The presence (at above/below chance levels) of particular structures implies that forces (such as the need to generate knowledge or to protect it) are operating on actors in our sample. The ERG model methodology can therefore be used to directly test our propositions.

DISCUSSION

The theoretical framework we propose here integrates the work of Das and Kumar (2007) with work on knowledge seeking (Borgatti & Cross, 2003) and insights from social-network analysis. In the first part of the chapter, we showed how the two approaches can be synergized in order to present different strategic questions firms should confront in order to create value from their learning networks.

Further, based on the complexities we described in the current state of interorganizational network research, we claim that learning in strategic alliances is not a unidimensional construct, and that in order to capture and create value, network actors can utilize the different types of learning-based networks, which differ in the benefits and risks (Das & Kumar, 2007) to balance knowledge generation and protection. By extending Borgatti and Cross' (2003) analysis of interorganizational information sharing, we suggested that learning exchanges involve different processes: *learning where* information is located, *learning what* the information is, and *learning how* to access and utilize this information.

We further suggested that network actors utilize the opportunity structures that are associated with brokerage and closure. We suggested that in order to gain competitive advantage, network actors form networks characterized by univariate and multivariate structural holes, and that they do this for learning relationships for which risk is relatively low because they form relatively early exploration stages.

At this stage, we claim that such theoretical questions should be studied by using a newly developed network method that estimates the probability that certain network structures will emerge. This method allows us to study the dominant network structure that emerges from a large network of strategic alliances of a certain kind, and it allows us to study the interrelations between networks of learning. This method can also demonstrate that not only does each knowledge exchange network exhibit a distinct type of logic, but that there is also a logic for the interrelations between learning networks, and that this logic is also related to the ideas of brokerage and closure.

The proposed model follows the claim offered by Oliver (2004, p. 153), who argued that in exchanging knowledge with others, firms utilize different behaviors through time: "The [learning] process begins with *general screening and the search for new knowledge*... At this stage,... heterogeneity and diversity in capabilities and knowledge are required." Similar to Borgatti and Cross (2003), Oliver suggests that initially, firms screen their potential partners for new knowledge. However, she notes that as firms become aware of the knowledge that others have, they acquire more specific knowledge from the same set of network actors. Thus, we expect that over time, as network actors become clearer about the knowledge others have and firms wish to protect their knowledge within alliances, they will reform the structure of their networks. In general, we expect that firms will (a) deepen their learning relationships, (b) prune their other learning relationships, and (c) close the network so that they work on the important learning issues within closed structures of networks. In essence, when the learning becomes content-specific *learning how,* appropriation risks and potential benefits increase. This requires a change in the structure of the learning networks so that open structures of learning networks give in to dyadic, triadic, and multiplex structures that allow for greater control and monitoring over partner misbehavior and higher absorption of information.

NOTES

1. Structures where there are three actors and the relationships between them.
2. Snijders (2001), Das and Kumar (2007), and Janicik and Larick (2005) argue that actors are aware of the existence of relationships with, and between, their network partners; and Kalish (2008) shows that this knowledge informs the way they structure their own relationships.
3. Dyadic disembedding refers to a process that is the opposite of the processes of embeddedness (where economic activities are embedded in social relations; Granovetter, 1985). In our context, disembedding refers to the disconnection between one learning network and another to the same actor (for example, when a network actor does NOT learn general topics with their project partners).

REFERENCES

Ahuja, G. (2000). Collaboration networks, structural holes, and innovation: A longitudinal study. *Administrative Science Quarterly, 45,* 425–455.

Argote, L., McEvily, B., & Reagans, R. (2003). Managing knowledge in organizations: An integrative framework and review of emerging themes. *Management Science, 49,* 571–582.

Blau, P. M. (1964). *Exchange and power in social life.* New York: Wiley.

Borgatti, S. P., & Cross, R. (2003). A relational view of information seeking and learning in social networks. *Management Science, 49,* 432–445.

Burt, R. S. (1992). *Structural holes: The social structure of competition.* Cambridge, MA: Harvard University Press.

Burt, R. S. (2005). *Brokerage and closure: An introduction to social capital.* Oxford, UK: Oxford University Press.

Crossan, M., Lane, H., & White, R. (1999). An organizational learning framework: From intuition to institution. *Academy of Management Journal, 24,* 522–537.

Das, T. K., & Kumar, R. (2007). Learning dynamics in the alliance development process. *Management Decision, 45,* 684–707.

Das, T. K., & Teng, B. (1998). Between trust and control: Developing confidence in partner cooperation in alliances. *Academy of Management Review, 23,* 491–512.

Das, T. K., & Teng, B. (2001). Trust, control, and risk in strategic alliances: An integrated framework. *Organization Studies, 22,* 251–283.

Das, T. K., & Teng, B. (2002a). Alliance constellations: A social exchange perspective. *Academy of Management Review, 27,* 445–456.

Das, T. K., & Teng, B. (2002b). A social exchange theory of strategic alliances. In F. J. Contractor & P. Lorange (Eds.), *Cooperative strategies and alliances* (pp. 439–460). Oxford, UK: Elsevier Science.

DeFillippi, R. J., Arthur, M. B., & Lindsay, V. J. (2007). Brokerage, closure and community dynamics: Implications for virtual knowledge work collaborations. In T. Gossling, R. Jansen, & L. Oerlemans (Eds.), *Inside networks* (pp. 139–162). Northampton, MA: Edward Elgar.

Frank, O., & Strauss, D. (1986). Markov graphs. *Journal of the American Statistical Association, 81*(395), 832–842.

Friedkin, N. E. (2004). Social cohesion. *Annual Review of Sociology, 30,* 409–425.

Gilsing, V., Nooteboom, B., Vanhaverbeke, W., Duysters, G., & van den Oord, A. (2008). Network embeddedness and the exploration of novel technologies: Technological distance, betweenness centrality and density. *Research Policy, 37,* 1717–1731.

Granovetter, M. (1985). Economic action and social structure—The problem of embeddedness. *American Journal of Sociology, 91,* 481–510.

Gulati, R. (1995). Social structure and alliance formation patterns: A longitudinal analysis. *Administrative Science Quarterly, 40,* 619–652.

Gulati, R., Nohria, N., & Zaheer, A. (2000). Strategic networks. *Strategic Management Journal, 21,* 203–215.

Hilbbert, P., & Huxham, C. (2007). Collaboration, knowledge and learning: Integrating perspectives. In T. Gossling, L. Oerlemans, & R. Jansen (Eds.), *Inside networks: A process view on multi-organizational partnerships, alliances and networks* (pp. 117–138). Cheltenham, UK: Edward Elgar.

Holmqvist, M. (2003). A dynamic model of intra- and interorganizational learning. *Organization Studies, 24,* 95–103.

Janicik, G. A., & Larrick, R. P. (2005). Social network schemas and the learning of incomplete networks. *Journal of Personality and Social Psychology, 88,* 348–364.

Kalish, Y. (2008). Bridging in social networks: Who are the people in structural holes and why are they there? *Asian Journal of Social Psychology, 11*(1), 53–66.

Kalish, Y., & Robins, G. L. (2006). Psychological predispositions and network structure: The relationship between individual predispositions, structural holes and network closure. *Social Networks, 28*(1), 56–84.

Kapmeier, F. (2008). Common learning and opportunistic behaviour in learning alliances. *Systems Research and Behavioral Science, 25,* 549–573.

Kenis, P., & Knoke, D. (2002) How organizational field networks shape interorganizational tie-formation rates. *Academy of Management Review, 27,* 275–293.

Kilduff, M., Tsai, W., & Hanke, R. (2006). A paradigm too far? A dynamic stability reconsideration of the social network research program. *Academy of Management Review, 31,* 1031–1048.

Krackhardt, D. (1999). The ties that torture: Simmelian tie analysis in organizations. In S. B. Andews & D. Knoke (Eds.), *Networks in and around organizations* (Vol. 16, pp. 183–212). Stamford, CT: JAI Press.

Larsson, R., Bengtsson, L., Hendriksson, K., & Sparks, J. (1998). The interorganizational learning dilemma: Collective knowledge development in strategic alliances. *Organization Science, 9,* 285–304.

Lazega, E., & Pattison, P. E. (1999). Multiplexity, generalized exchange and cooperation in organizations: A case study. *Social Networks, 21,* 67–90.

Liebeskind, J. P. (1996, Winter). Knowledge, strategy, and the theory of the firm. *Strategic Management Journal, 17*(Special Issue), 93–107.

Majewski, S. E. (2004). *How do consortia organize collaborative R&D?: Evidence from the National Cooperative Research Act.* Discussion paper series # 483. Harvard Law School, John M. Olin Center for Law, Economics and Business.

Mintzberg, H. (1984). *Power in and around organizations.* Englewood Cliffs, NJ: Prentice Hall.

Monge, P. R., & Contractor, N. S. (2003). *Theories of communication networks.* New York: Oxford University Press.

Nohria, N. (1992). Introduction: Is a network perspective a useful way of studying organizations? In N. Nohria & R. G. Eccles (Eds.), *Networks and organizations: Structure, form, and action* (pp. 1–22). Boston: Harvard Business School Press.

Nooteboom, B. (1999). Innovation, learning and industrial organization. *Cambridge Journal of Economics, 23*(2), 127–150.

Nooteboom, B. (2004). Learning and governance in inter-firm relations. *Revue d Economie Politique, 114*(1), 55–76.

Nooteboom, B. (2006). *Learning and innovation in inter-organizational relationships and networks.* (Working paper, Tilburg University, The Netherlands).

Oliver A. L. (2001). Strategic alliances and the learning life-cycle of biotechnology firms. *Organization Studies, 22,* 467–489.

Oliver, A. L. (2004). On the duality of competition and collaboration: Network-based knowledge relations in the biotechnology industry. *Scandinavian Journal of Management, 20,* 151–171.

Oliver, A. L. (2009). *Networks for learning and knowledge creation in biotechnology.* Cambridge, UK: Cambridge University Press.

Oliver, A. L. & Liebeskind, J. P. (1998). Three levels of networking: Implications for the study of interorganizational networks. *International Studies in Management and Organization,* 27(4), 76–103.

Perkmann, M. (2009, August 7–11). *Trading off revealing and appropriating in drug discovery: The role of trusted intermediaries.* Paper presented at the annual meeting of the Academy of Management, Chicago.

Powell, W. W., Koput, K. W., & Smith-Doerr, L. (1996). Interorganizational collaboration and the locus of innovation: Networks of learning in biotechnology. *Administrative Science Quarterly, 41,* 116–145.

Powell, W. W., White, D. R., Koput, K. W, & Owen-Smith, J. (2005). Network dynamics and field evolution: The growth of interorganizational collaboration in the life sciences. *American Journal of Sociology, 110,* 132–205.

Robins, G., & Pattison, P. (2006). *Multiple networks in organisations.* Australian Defence Science and Technology Organization (DSTO).

Robins, G., Pattison, P., Kalish, Y., & Lusher, D. (2007). An introduction to exponential random graph (p*) models for social networks. *Social Networks, 29*(2), 173–191.

Simmel, G. (1955). *The sociology of Georg Simmel* (K. H. Wolff, Trans.). Glencoe, IL: Free Press.

Snijders, T. A. B. (2001). The statistical evaluation of social network dynamics. *Sociological Methodology, 31,* 361–395.

Sydow, J. (1996, July 8–19). *Understanding the constitution of inter-organizational trust.* Paper presented at the SASE Conference, Geneva.

Uzzi, B. (1997). Social structure and competition in interfirm networks: The paradox of embeddedness. *Administrative Science Quarterly, 42,* 35–67.

Uzzi, B. (1999). Embeddedness in the making of financial capital: How social relations and networks benefit firms seeking financing. *American Sociological Review, 64,* 481–505.

CHAPTER 6

VALUE ENHANCING IN THE GOVERNANCE DECISION PROCESS

A Portfolio Theory Perspective on Strategic Alliances and Mergers and Acquisitions

Anna Sabidussi
Harry J. Bremmers
Geert Duysters
Onno Omta

ABSTRACT

The present work discusses how the value generation potential from strategic alliances can be enhanced by adopting a portfolio perspective in the governance decision process. A growing research stream has argued that corporate performance is fostered not by a single link but by the entire portfolio of external relationships the company is engaged in. Recent developments also suggest that in a well-balanced view, various external sourcing modalities need to be considered. The main message from the above research stream

Strategic Alliances for Value Creation, pages 119–140

encourages companies to look at their external relationships in an integrated fashion as interdependencies emphasize the value-generation potential of strategic alliances (SAs) and other governance modalities. In the context of our study, we argue that the insights gained by the content-related literature on the key value drivers of external sourcing may be embedded in the governance-decision process. In order to contribute to both the literature and managerial practice, we go further than the mere elaboration of propositions and, by formalizing in an ordered sequence the decision steps that should be undertaken, we provide a conceptual decisional model to be used as a reference term. We ground our approach on financial Portfolio Theory, whose guidelines are interpreted in the context of the governance-decision process and integrated in a decision model. The present work contributes to the literature by proposing a model wherein the governance modes are not conceived as independent choices but as elements of balance and integration within a portfolio.

INTRODUCTION

In the last decades, we have witnessed an unprecedented increase in the use of external relationships to foster innovation (Chaudhuri, 2004; Vasudevan, Duysters, van den Oord, & Bakkes, 2001). The above trend confirms the widespread diffusion of an "open innovation" paradigm, where external technology sourcing contributes at different stages of the innovation process (Chesbrough, 2003). For companies, entering into external relationships entails multiple, complex choices that range from partner selection to the governance mode definition, i.e., the way this interfirm link is going to be organized.

In particular, choosing the organizational form of an external partnership represents a strategic and critical decision that may affect the success of the relationship (Cools & Roos, 2005). Companies aiming at fostering their innovative performance through external relationships engage in "the process of translating objectives into actions" (Tan & Platts, 2003, p. 569), and this process starts with understanding the consequences of the alternatives (Keeney, 1982). Decision makers should therefore be aware, first and foremost, of the key drivers enhancing the value-generating potential of external relationships and embed them into the decision process as they provide "empirically validated guidelines" for the governance choice (De Man & Duysters, 2005, p. 1377).

A growing body of research, especially developed in the alliance literature, has argued that innovative performance is enhanced not by a single link but by the entire portfolio of external relationships the company is engaged in (e.g., Belderbos, Carree, & Lokshin, 2006; Faems, Van Looy, & Debackere, 2005; Hoffman, 2005; Keil, Maula, Schildt, & Zahra, 2008).

Bamford and Ernst (2002) confirm the need for a portfolio approach, arguing that otherwise, companies collect over the years, a "random mix" of linkages whose contribution to corporate strategy is unclear. Alliances are, however, not the only option for external sourcing and in a well-balanced view, also other modalities need to be considered. A recent research line further expands this approach and calls for an application of a portfolio perspective to various governance modalities, as considering them jointly can better explain corporate performance (Keil et al., 2008). The main message from the above research stream encourages companies to look at their external relationships in an integrated fashion as interdependencies emphasize the value-generation potential of strategic alliances (SAs) and other governance modalities.

Surprisingly, little of this message shedding light on "what strategic positions of the firm lead to optimal performance" (Chakravarthy & Doz, 1992, p. 5) has crossed the borders of content research and has been embedded in process research to improve the "how to do" when dealing with governance choices (Khanna, Gulati, & Nohria, 2000, p. 783). As a consequence, to date, efforts to apply portfolio principles to the governance-decision process have remained unexplored. In the context of our study, we argue that the insights gained by the content-related literature on the performance consequence of external relationships may support the governance-decision process. In order to contribute to both the literature and managerial practice, we go further than the mere elaboration of propositions and, by formalizing in an ordered sequence the considerations that should be accounted for, we provide what Khanna et al. (2000) call a "benchmark model": a conceptual decisional model to be used as a reference term. In order to do so, we ground our approach in financial Portfolio Theory (hereafter, PT; Markowitz, 1952, 1959), whose guidelines are interpreted within the context of the governance-decision process and integrated in a decision model.

In the present work, we argue that the value-generating potential of strategic alliances can be fostered by adopting a portfolio perspective in the governance-decision process. The relevance of the present work resides in its two main contributions. First, by proposing an application of Portfolio Theory to the governance-decision process, the study enriches the literature of a new conceptual tool for approaching the organizational choices. Additionally, in line with Huff and Reger (1987) and Khanna et al. (2000), we attempt to bridge process and content perspectives by conjugating the literature on external technology, sourcing performance to the governance-decision process. Second, we suggest a new conceptualization of the decision process outcome. Typically, the literature has framed the governance decision in terms of choice between SAs and M&As. In this line, previous research followed three main lines. As highlighted by Wang and Zajac (2007), the first approaches SAs and M&As as interchangeable forms of governance, the second isolates one of the two alternatives and focuses on either SAs or M&As. A third research stream compares the circumstances under which an alliance should be preferred to an M&A or *vice versa* (Chiesa & Manzini, 1998; Garette & Dussauge, 2000; Hagedoorn & Duysters, 2002; Hennart & Reddy, 1997; Van de Vrande, Vanhaverbeke, & Duysters, 2009; Vanhaverbeke, Duysters, & Noorderhaven, 2002; Villalonga & McGahan, 2005; Yin & Shanley, 2008). We contribute to previous literature by proposing a fourth approach that conceives the governance choice not as a simple binary outcome, either M&As or SAs, but in terms of its balance and integration within a portfolio.

This chapter is structured as follows: The next section provides an overview of the organizational alternatives and their associated characteristics. Next, from the literature on partnerships performance, we derive the propositions that should be accounted for in the governance-decision process. Finally, an interpretation of the conceptual pillars from financial Portfolio Theory is proposed as a theoretical tool supporting the governance decision. The complementarities between the proposed conceptual approach and previous literature on the governance choice are discussed in the final remarks.

THE SPECTRUM OF ORGANIZATIONAL MODES

Although external relationships can come in a variety of forms, the literature has focused mainly on two broad categories of governance modes that can be chosen by companies: Strategic Alliances (SAs) and Mergers & Acquisitions (M&As) (Roberts & Liu, 2003; Wang & Zajac, 2007). Strategic Alliances refers to "cooperative efforts in which two or more separate organizations, while maintaining their own corporate identities, join forces to share reciprocal inputs" (Vanhaverbeke et al., 2002). According to Dussauge and Garette (1999, p. 22), an alliance can be qualified as strategic "when it contributes significantly to the strategies pursued by the partner companies." The term "strategic alliances" indicates many different partnering modalities, including equity as well as nonequity linkages (Osborn & Hagedoorn, 1997). In the present work, we will use the generic term "strategic alliances" to refer to the above range of diverse modalities. M&As refers to situations in which one company acquires the control over another corporate entity. In the case of a merger, the acquirer absorbs the other entity (that ceases to exist), while in the case of an acquisition, the two identities keep on functioning as juridical entities. Mergers are relatively rare, and many transactions called mergers are in fact acquisitions (Van de Vrande, Lemmens, & Vanhaverbeke, 2006). SAs and M&As can be conceived as organizational alternatives resting on a continuum, depicting various degrees of organizational integration (Chiesa & Manzini, 1998). If we approximate the level of integration by the degree of equity participation, the spectrum ranges from relatively simple contractual transactions to full equity integration in the form of M&As. The characteristics of SAs and M&As vary along the continuum (Table 6.1).

Governance modes on the left-hand side of the above scale, like SAs, present the characteristic of flexibility, allowing companies to adjust their course of actions to changing conditions (Chan, Kensinger, Keown, & Martin, 1997; Chiesa & Manzini, 1998). The downside of this flexibility is that, especially when the scope of the alliance is broad, the possibility to control the partners is limited, and the risk of opportunistic behavior is relatively high (Gulati & Singh, 1998). Governance modes lying on the left side of the continuum, like alliances, are concerned by the appropriability of the results achieved by the joint activities. The above implies that costs need to be sustained to control the opportunistic behavior of partners or to measure whether the goals of the relationship are met (Calantone & Stanko, 2007). More hierarchical forms of governance, like acquisitions, provide higher levels of control and present reduced levels of opportunism threat but, being less flexible, their possibility to adjust to changing conditions is constrained (Oxley, 1997). Increasing the degree of integration may also increase the termination costs of the partnership (Fontenot & Wilson, 1997). M&As represent typically a larger investment compared to SAs (Folta, 1998). Governance forms with higher levels of integration, like M&As, are typically associated with difficulties of integration that can jeop-

TABLE 6.1 Spectrum of Organizational Modes and Associated Characteristics

	SA			M & A	
	Non equity alliance (Joint R&D)	Equity alliance	Joint venture	Acquisition	Merger
Flexibility	High ←				→ Low
Control	Low ←				→ High
Integration	Low ←				→ High
Termination cost	Low ←				→ High
Life span	Low ←				→ High
Opportunistic behavior risk	High ←				→ Low
Formalization	Low ←				→ High

Source: Adapted and modified from Cools and Roos (2005) and Chiesa and Manzini (1998).

ardize innovation performance in the postmerger phase (Ahuja & Katila, 2001; Cloodt, Hagedoorn, & Van Kranenburg, 2006; De Noble, Gustafson, & Hergert, 1988). With respect to the time dimension, moving along the continuum, higher forms of integration are associated with a longer life span—M&As may even have an indefinite life (Chan et al., 1997). In M&As, the acquirer obtains immediate access and control over the required resources (Chiesa & Manzini, 1998), while in SAs, partners are committed to develop new technological knowledge through joint activities (Chan et al., 1997). Highly integrated forms, like M&As, however, typically need a longer time span to have an influence on innovation (around 5 years), while lower degrees of integration, like alliances, display their effects sooner (around 3 years or less) (De Man & Duysters, 2005).

THE VALUE DRIVERS

Each organizational mode leverages different mechanisms to enhance innovation (Keil et al., 2008). Studying the individual effects of SAs and M&As on innovation, however, would provide only limited guidance for the governance-decision process. Companies are involved at the same time in a web of a growing number of relationships (De Man, 2004). Firms' success is no longer determined by the achievements obtained from an individual external sourcing of technology or from a group of links of the same governance mode, but by leveraging the entire portfolio of multiple links (Parise & Casher, 2003). An increasing body of literature confirms that a portfolio perspective is appropriate for approaching the effects of external relationships (like SAs and M&As) on innovation (Duysters & Lokshin, 2011; Faems et al., 2005; George, Zahra, Wheatley, & Khan, 2001; Wuyts, Dutta, & Stremersch, 2004). To support innovation in front of rapid technological evolutions, companies need therefore to recognize that considering interfirm links as "one-offs"—"independent relationships pursued separately"—is perilous (Powell, Koput, & Smith-Doerr, 1996, p. 119).

If value is generated by the portfolio, it is critical to identify which mechanism can be exploited by the governance-decision process, and we focus on interactions effects. A portfolio approach allows firms to face the complexity of multiple and contemporaneous relationships (Hoffmann, 2005; Mahnke & Overby, 2005) by providing a better understanding of the interdependencies and complementarities among different corporate links (Belderbos et al., 2006; Parise & Casher, 2003). The interactions among the relations shape the competitive dynamics and determine the companies' value-creation potential (De Man, 2004). When positive interrelationships occur, the benefits of one relationship enhance the achievements of another link (Parise & Casher, 2003). We therefore elaborate the following:

Proposition: *A governance-choice process enhancing the value-creation potential of external relationships should aim at (a) the overall portfolio performance maximization and (b) adopt a perspective where interactions are accounted for.*

Summarizing, content research highlights that a portfolio perspective supports performance. A proper theoretical framework for supporting the governance-decision process should account for the above, and we propose Financial Portfolio Theory (PT) as a conceptual tool.

PORTFOLIO THEORY

Due to the conceptual similarity of the financial investment process with other fields where the allocation of limited resources and the balance of different objectives is critical, PT principles have been applied to the R&D investment selection (e.g., Chiesa, 2001) and extended to the management of technology (e.g., Yu, 2006) or to the selection of technologies (Jackson, Kloeber, Ralston, & Deckro, 1999). In expanding the range of application of PT reasoning, it has been argued that the portfolio logic may be applied to the context of the multiple alliances in which firms are involved (George et al., 2001). A motivation for the above extension is that firms enter into several relationships trying to achieve greater returns while minimizing risks from their alliances in a process that is comparable to the rationale followed in a PT framework (George et al., 2001). In the choice of our theoretical framework, we follow the same reasoning. When deciding which governance mode should be preferred in order to achieve technological innovation, the company is, conceptually, facing an investment-selection decision and financial Portfolio Theory principles may be applied.

In financial markets, managers face the challenge of allocating scarce resources to a limited set of assets. In a portfolio context, the investment process aims at determining in which assets (or class of assets) it is preferable to invest for the specific objectives and at finding an optimal balance among assets by shifting the composition of the portfolio itself over time (Farrell, 1997). Portfolio theory disciplines the investment process. It originates from the seminal work of Markowitz (1952, 1959). The cornerstone of PT is that an investor will select the combination of securities based on its *risk-return* profile: preference is given to the "efficient" portfolio that provides the highest expected return at the lowest level of variance (Farrell, 1997). In financial PT, the investors choose the assets that, when added to the portfolio, provide the highest return for a given level of risk and therefore, optimize the risk-return profile of the overall portfolio. To define which assets maximize the portfolio, the interactions among assets need to be accounted for. The reason for the above is that the contribution to the overall portfolio from each single security, in terms of risk and returns, is influenced by the interrelationship with all the other assets. The key contribution from the theory is therefore not that the specific characteristics of the individual asset be considered in isolation but "how each security co-moves with all the other securities" (Elton & Gruber, 1997, p. 1744). Optimizing the portfolio is not a one-point-in-time activity but a dynamic process that calls for continuous rebalancing (Ahmed & Hegazi, 2006).

Summarizing, the main PT conceptual pillars are (a) the risk-return profile of an asset, (b) the interdependencies among the components of the existing portfolio and the asset under consideration; (c) the maximization of the portfolio as final scope of the investment choice, and (d) the monitoring and rebalance of the portfolio composition over time. Since the 1950s, financial theory has evolved by increasing levels of detail and realism in the modeling process. The basic concepts provided by Markowitz remain, however, at the core of the investment selection techniques (Elton & Gruber, 1997). In our elaboration, we therefore propose to interpret the key PT pillars to support a value-enhancing governance-decision process.

THE GOVERNANCE-DECISION PROCESS: A PORTFOLIO THEORY-BASED MODEL

The present work proposes to widen the application of PT as a conceptual tool to support governance decisions. Changing the framework of application of the main PT principles from financial assets to partnerships activities requires a degree of adaptation and interpretation. The overall model applying the PT into a dynamic process that manages the governance-decision process is illustrated in Figure 6.1. The proposed decision model refers to a situation where the company decided to start an external relationship with a corporate entity.

Each phase of the decision process is associated with the interpretation in a governance-choice context of the PT conceptual pillars.

Phase 1

In Phase 1, the risk-return profile of a governance decision is defined as per the PT criteria previously indicated. At this initial stage, the governance alternatives are valued individually considering their specific nature and characteristics.

In an external technology-sourcing perspective, expected returns can be considered as the benefits foreseen from engaging in a relationship. Two

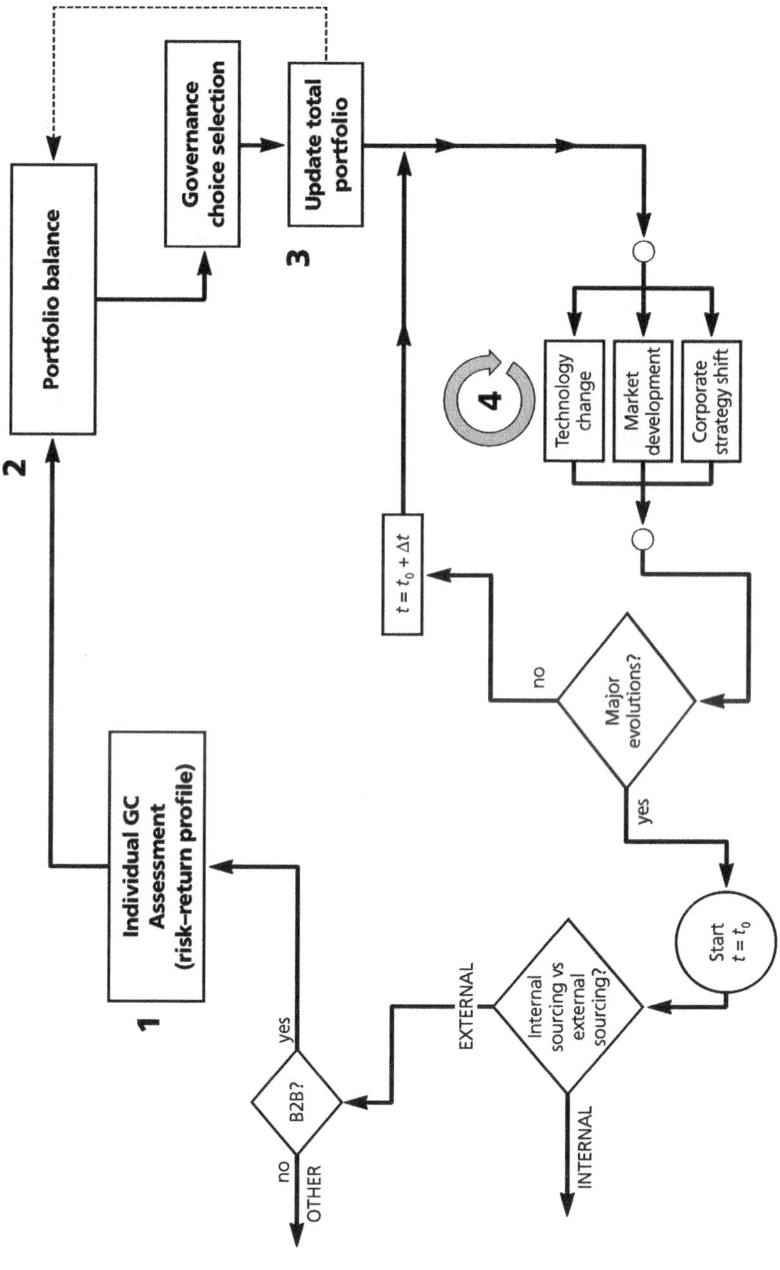

Figure 6.1 Decision process model.

broad scopes of interfirm agreements can be identified based on the dichotomy proposed by March (1991): technology exploration and technology exploitation (Faems et al., 2005; Granstrand, Bohlin, Oskarsson, & Sjoberg, 1992; Koza & Lewin, 1998). Explorative partnering is aimed at discovering new opportunities, while in exploitation, interfirm relationships are oriented to the maximization of the benefits deriving from existing knowledge (Faems et al., 2005). Nontechnological objectives of an external partnership refers to the access to new product markets or geographical areas in the case a company may need to use external partnerships to introduce an innovation in a foreign market through a local company that provides the required distribution channels (Hung & Tang, 2008; Sakakibara, 1997). Additionally, partnerships may be used for competitive purposes like blocking a rival in a specific technological or market field (Vanhaverbeke & Noorderhaven, 2001).

The benefits are balanced against the costs to achieve those (Wang & Zajac, 2007). Additionally, the time span that is necessary to achieve innovation is an additional element to consider when assessing the competitive benefits foreseen by a partnership (Cohen, Eliashberg, & Ho, 1996; Hagedoorn, 1993). The precise quantification of an expected return is, however, not straightforward. Expectations about returns can oscillate as they are affected by a series of factors that influence the prospected outcome. How much an expected return can fluctuate depends on the level of the associated risk. From a governance-choice point of view, the returns expected from partnering activities can fluctuate due to two types of uncertainties: endogenous and exogenous (Folta, 1998; Van de Vrande et al., 2006). Endogenous uncertainty refers to the possibility of failure of the relationship. Exogenous uncertainty refers to the unknown evolution of technologies and of market conditions. It increases proportionally to the level of technological newness and the novelty of the potential applications in the market. SAs and M&As are exposed in different measure to the above sources of risk as indicated in Table 6.1. Ultimately, risk exposure leads to higher costs due to the additional resources that need to be devoted to control uncertainty (e.g., higher coordination or monitoring costs).

Phase 2

In Phase 2, the analysis takes a portfolio perspective in line with the abovementioned second PT conceptual pillar. By compounding the governance alternatives in the portfolio, the interactions that take place between the new potential governance link and the existing relationships are emphasized. In order to clarify the mechanisms that play a role in the portfolio-compounding phase, we proceed in two steps. First, we discuss the kind of interdependencies that should be accounted for when a new potential governance form of external partnership has to be introduced into the portfolio. Second, we discuss the levels at which interdependencies may generate benefits.

The interactions among governance modes can affect the portfolio by means of two mechanisms: risk reduction through diversification and/or generation of synergies (Mahnke & Overby, 2005). As in Wilcox, Chang, and Grover (2001), diversification is obtained if a firm enters in diverse and unrelated relationships. Diversification mainly has an effect on spreading exogenous, technological, and market risks over different partnerships (Mahnke & Overby, 2005). Endogenous risk, however, can also be affected by interactions. The uncertainty surrounding an acquisition can be reduced by the existence of previous alliances with the same partner and by reciprocal knowledge. A recent study confirms that previous alliances with a target company increase the performance and the learning effect of the M&As (Porrini, 2004). Synergies are typically generated by links among a firm's activities (Kay & Diamantopoulos, 1987) and by the combination of complementary assets (Colombo, Grilli, & Piva, 2006). The benefit that is individually expected by the firm from an alliance is influenced by synergies and complementarities generated by and with other relationships (other alliances or other governance modes like M&As) that need therefore to be taken into account. As an example of positive interaction, acquiring KLM, which had at that time a partnership with Northwest Airlines, allowed Air France to better leverage the value of its existing alliances with Delta Airlines and achieve the coverage of the principal hubs of the North American market. As an example of potentially negative interaction, recently Continental had to withdraw from the alliance with SkyTeam prior to the M&A with United (which is linked to the StarAlliance partnership) so as to not obstruct the deal.

Adapting to our context, the distinction between private and common benefits (Khanna, Gulati, & Nohria, 1998), we distinguish two levels of the interactions effects. At a first level, individual benefits are defined as the gains from the interactions that increase the return or decrease the risk of the governance alternative directly. At a second level, common benefits refers to the situation where the gains from the interaction favor one or several of the other existing relationships by reducing their risk or enhancing their returns. By explicitly considering interactions among proposed governance choices and existing web of relationships, current governance decisions are influenced by the unique current corporate profile (technology and market positioning) and by past governance choices (Argyres & Liebeskind, 1999).

Phase 3

In a financial-portfolio approach and in line with the third PT conceptual pillar, once the interactions of a potential asset with other securities are defined, the final choice about which investment to prefer can be taken. Preference is given to the asset that optimizes the risk-return profile of the overall portfolio when the new security is added to the portfolio. Interpreting the above in a governance context, the governance modality that optimizes the portfolio is the one that offers the highest levels of private or common benefits after considering the interactions with the other links in the portfolio. It is worth noting that, in the proposed approach, the focus is not on identifying a governance choice with superior absolute qualities, but on selecting the organizational modality that provides the highest contribution to the whole portfolio over time. The governance-mode decision is therefore not conceived as an independent choice but as an element in the dynamic balance of the portfolio. Once the governance-mode decision is taken, the profile of the portfolio is altered by the new added relationship.

Phase 4

In Phase 4, after the governance decision is taken, the external conditions evolve over time simultaneously in terms of technology change, competitive and market conditions, corporate profile, and strategic orientation. The framework in which the companies operate is as fluid and dynamic as it is constantly changing, affected by the evolution of the markets, technology shifts, by the development of the company's profile, the competitive position, and by its web of relationships. A rich body of literature from different disciplines confirms that technologies (Anderson & Tushman, 1990), innovation patterns (Abernathy & Utterback, 1978; Mansfield, 1961; Utterback & Abernathy, 1975), markets and competitive situations (Porter, 1981; Schumpeter, 1942), and networks (Hite & Hesterly, 2001) change and progress over time. Efficient boundaries of the firm need to be dynamic to adjust to those continuous evolutions (Afuah, 2001). Adapting to changing environments is essential to sustain competitive advantage and corporate performance in the long run. For the above purpose, companies need to develop and exploit dynamic capabilities that include strategic alliances and M&As (Barney, Wright, & Ketchen, 2001; Eisenhardt & Martin, 2000). A governance-decision process, in order to sustain firms' achievements over time, should comfortably deal with the dynamic nature of external partnerships. The portfolio represents an intrinsically nonstatic tool that adjusts to new conditions by balancing its composition over time and by monitoring the effects of those changes (Cooper, Edgett, & Kleinschmidt, 1999;

Parise & Casher, 2003). By optimizing the entire portfolio, the governance-decision process is focused on the strategic, future-oriented interests of the firm. Strategy indeed deals with making choices for the future, and it can be defined as "the scope and direction of an organization over the long run" (Johnson & Scholes, 2002, p. 10). The entire corporate portfolio of relationships is not static but co-evolves with the firm's strategy (Koza & Lewin, 1998). Also, the portfolio is evolving. With the passing of time, for example, some of the less integrated governance modes (e.g., like R&D agreements) will come to an end. This will alter the profile of the portfolio and call for a rebalance through new governance decisions. As a consequence of time dynamics, the same company facing new governance decisions will have, as a starting point, a different portfolio that will affect the final choice in a different way. The process starts again, entering in a circular loop that is continuously repeated. In the proposed context, the governance-decision process is dynamic, as it cannot be considered independently of the previous choices, the past evolution of those choices, as well as of the strategic orientation the company embraces.

The approach presented in Figure 6.1 is, therefore, dynamic as it considers the effect of different time aspects in the decision process, considering jointly the current characteristics of the company (Phase 1), the past governance decisions that led to the present portfolio composition (Phase 2), and the future-oriented corporate strategic orientation (Phase 3). The proposed approach is also dynamic because it recognizes the need for rebalance over time (Phase 4) to account for the abovementioned evolutions.

DISCUSSION AND CONCLUSIONS

This chapter discusses how value-generation potential from strategic alliances can be enhanced by adopting a portfolio perspective in the governance-decision process. Our work is grounded in the alliance-portfolio literature and its recent extensions, arguing that the entire portfolio of external relationship fosters performance by leveraging interdependencies among various governance modalities. The present work identifies the value drivers elaborated by content-related research and embed those in the governance-decision process. By using PT as theoretical support, we elaborate a decision model where the governance modes are not conceived as independent choices but as elements of balance and integration within a portfolio.

In a theoretical context, by expanding the range of application of PT from economics to a managerial context, we contribute to the literature by proposing a new conceptual paradigm that supports the governance-decision process. To the best of our knowledge, this is the first attempt to apply PT to the governance decision of external partnerships. The suggested PT application represents a complement to and enrichment of previous literature. The contributions from previous models have been summarized according to their main underlying conceptual paradigms (Table 6.2). The present work proposes a new dimension of analysis: the portfolio. In this sense, our approach expands the previous literature that, according to Villalonga and McGahan (2005), has paid attention to the transaction (TCE, ROR), the company (RBV) or the network (NT). A portfolio perspective presents the advantage to account for interdependencies of governance modes, allowing the identification and the exploitation of synergistic and risk-diversification effects. Time considerations are central in the PT framework: present governance decisions are influenced by past choices, present corporate profile, and strategic orientation. From this point of view, the changing conditions in which the governance choice takes place (market/technological developments or evolution of strategic intents) are recognized in their dynamic nature, and their influence on the governance decision are acknowledged. In a portfolio context, the discussion is centered on two key attributes of the governance decision: the risk and the return profile. The systematic consideration of the trade-off between the benefits and their associated risks complements the models based on Resource Based View (RBV) and on the Network Theory (NT), where the effects of exogenous and endogenous uncertainty are not central. Similarly, a Real Option Reasoning (ROR) perspective is enhanced by the PT-based observation that the impact of risks on the governance decision is not absolute but contextual to the interrelations with the other existing corporate links. Finally, the Transaction Costs Economics (TCE) profit maximization logic is expanded by a PT approach by suggesting that the maximization of the individual transaction is secondary to the optimization of the overall portfolio. Assessing the relative advantage of models from one paradigm compared to those from others, represents an issue to be addressed by empirical investigation (Khanna et al., 2000). For the governance-decision model, an empirical test of the "effectiveness of decisional guidance" (in line with Parikh, Fazlollahi, & Verma, 2001, p. 303) of the proposed portfolio perspective could pave the way to a fruitful research line.

From a managerial perspective, the chapter provides a sort of "best practice" model that accounts for the key value drivers of external technology sourcing for innovation. In order to have preliminary feedback about the relevance of the conceptual framework we propose, we conducted 35 interviews with high-level decision makers from global companies. All the selected companies excel in innovation. Approximately 23% of the sample may be defined as "best-in-class," being listed among the top three in their sector of reference worldwide. During the semistructured interviews, the respondents were presented with a governance-decision case. The respondents were asked to simulate the decision process and to "think aloud" their thoughts and considerations as they would have occurred in a real-life situation. The comments from the interviews confirmed that a portfolio perspective, where interactions and time dynamics are accounted for, is relevant in the decision process.

In particular, with respect to the need of a portfolio perspective in the governance-decision process, our respondents commented, "The key is to combine the new relationship with the existing ones: the complete picture has to make sense." By leveraging the interdependencies and the time dynamic effects in the governance-decision process, companies optimize their portfolio of technology-sourcing modalities and enhance innovation performance. Indeed, synergistic effects were reported by the respondents to be of critical importance. One of our respondents said, "Of course, the choices are not independent of each other, they are always integrated in order to achieve synergies among them. It is not a matter of piling them up without interconnections. We develop one piece of a technology with one relationship, another piece with another partner, we develop certain aspects ourselves and then we integrate the whole." With respect to risk considerations, a respondent stated, "There must be a risk balance in the portfolio." From the comments of our respondents, it was also confirmed that SAs and M&As display different profiles in terms of expected benefits (costs, access to new knowledge, time horizon of the expected returns, etc.) and risks, and that those aspects have to be considered for the governance choice. Indeed, in the consideration of our respondents risk-benefit trade-offs are key decision drivers. Our respondents pointed out that the governance decision has to be interpreted as an element of a dynamic process. The portfolio of relationships has to follow the evolution of the corporate strategic orientation. In the words of one of our respondents, "We decide where we want to be in the future and then we see if the new alliances and acquisitions are in line with these objectives."

From the interviews, it emerged that companies do not dispose of a standardized approach when taking a governance decision but proceed with a case-by-case approach. Following a standardized protocol, however, may be fruitful, as it eases the learning effects from experience and the building of appropriate routines. The present work provides a concrete managerial tool by explicitly formalizing a series of steps that are critical to ensuring the success of the external relationships. Matching the practice with the model's benchmark is beneficial for the management of the technology sourcing modalities as it encourages the companies to look at their relationships in an integrated fashion. A portfolio perspective helps to determine the potential interactions among different relationships. Overall, we argue that a protocol providing decision guidelines and serving at different phases of the decision process (e.g., from the initial choice to the monitoring phases) offers support to managerial practice. Future research may further advance our current contribution by providing an empirical validation of the proposed approach.

TABLE 6.1 Complementary Governance Choice Principles

	Resource-based view (RBV)	Transaction cost economics (TCE)	Real options approach (ROR)	Network approach (NT)
Basic context	In an RBV perspective, the type and nature of the resources combinations involved in the relationship provide the criteria to identify the most suitable form of governance.	TCE predicts that managers should prefer the governance mode that carries the lowest costs for coordination and control.	In ROR, the main criterion for the governance choice is the level of uncertainty. High levels of uncertainty suggest the use of flexible governance modes.	In an NT approach, the governance choice is influenced by the position of the company in its web (network) of relationships and by the nature of these links.
Criteria	**Acquisitions** • If resources are core for the company. Synergies come from hard resources (like manufacturing plants). • If high levels of integration are required among the partners' activities (i.e., in case reciprocal synergies are needed, when resources need to be generated by integrated activities of the two companies). • If technologies are initial phases of the life cycle (fluid or transitional)	**Acquisitions** • If time pressure great • If low degree of cultural distance between partners • If high level of relative power/size of one partner over the other • If low appropriability regimes • If high levels of specificity of assets • In sectors with high need for control (low tech) **Alliances** • If time pressure not significant	**Acquisitions** • If low level of endogenous uncertainty • If exogenous uncertainty is low/medium (mature technologies) • If learning about the value of the uncertain investment is endogenous (obtained within the governance) **Alliances** • If high need for flexibility • If high level of endogenous uncertainty • If high level of exogenous uncertainty (in the early	**Acquisitions** • If prior direct ties exist • If companies were previously positioned at the center of a network • If the relationship is intra-industry **Alliances** • If prior indirect ties exist • If relationship is interindustry • If networks are vertical (relationships with suppliers and/or customers)

	• If the content of the collaboration is very familiar to the company or if content of the collaboration can be clearly defined **Alliances** • If resources refer to mature technologies. Synergies come from soft resources (as human resources) • If low level of integration in partners' activities is required (i.e., in the case of modular synergies where resources are independently managed and then combined) • If content of the collaboration cannot be clearly defined or if the content of the collaboration is not familiar to the company	• If high degree of cultural distance between partners • If low level of relative power/size of one partner over the other • If high appropriability regimes • If low levels of specificity of assets • If high costs of integration with the target firm • In sectors with low need for control (high tech)	phases of the technological development). • If learning about the value of the uncertain investment is exogenous (depends on factors external to the governance) • If longer project duration (higher uncertainty about the potential developments)	
Focus	The company	The transaction	The transaction	The network
References	Barney & Lee, 1998; Chiesa & Manzini, 1998; Dyer, Kale & Singh, 2004; Folta & Leiblein, 1994; Garette & Dusssage, 2000; Hagedoorn & Duysters, 2002; Hennart & Reddy, 1997; Hoffmann & Schaper-Rinkel, 2001; Leiblein, 2003; Roberts & Liu, 2001, 2003; Van de Vrande et al., 2006; Vanhaverbeke et al., 2002; Vilallonga & McGahan, 2005; Yoshikawa, 2003			

REFERENCES

Abernathy, W. J., & Utterback, J. M. (1978). Patterns of industrial innovation. *Technology Review, 80*(7), 40–47.

Afuah, A. (2001). Dynamic boundaries of the firm: Are firms better off being vertically integrated in the face of a technological change? *Academy of Management Journal, 44,* 1211–1228.

Ahmed, E., & Hegazi, A. S. (2006). On different aspects of portfolio optimization. *Applied Mathematics and Computation, 175*(1), 590–596.

Ahuja, G., & Katila, R. (2001). Technological acquisitions and the innovation performance of acquiring firms: A longitudinal study. *Strategic Management Journal, 22,* 197–220.

Anderson, P., & Tushman, M. L. (1990). Technological discontinuities and dominant designs: A cyclical model of technological change. *Administrative Science Quarterly, 35,* 604–633.

Argyres, N. S., & Liebeskind, J. P. (1999). Contractual commitments, bargaining power, and governance inseparability: Incorporating history into transaction cost theory. *Academy of Management Review, 24,* 49–63.

Bamford, J., & Ernst, D. (2002). Managing an alliance portfolio. *McKinsey Quarterly, 3,* 29–39.

Barney, J. B., & Lee, W. (1998, August). *Governance under uncertainty: Transaction costs, real options, and property rights.* Paper presented at the annual meeting of the Academy of Management, San Diego, CA.

Barney, J. B., Wright, M., & Ketchen, D. J. (2001). The resource-based view of the firm: Ten years after 1991. *Journal of Management, 27,* 625–641.

Belderbos, R., Carree, M., & Lokshin, B. (2006). Complementarities in R&D cooperation strategies. *Review of Industrial Organization, 28,* 401–426.

Calantone, R. J., & Stanko, M. A. (2007). Drivers of outsourced innovation: An exploratory study. *Journal of Product Innovation Management, 24,* 230–241.

Chakravarthy, B. S., & Doz, Y. (1992). Strategy process research: Focusing on corporate self-renewal. *Strategic Management Journal, 13*(Special Issue), 5–14.

Chan, S. H., Kensinger, J. W., Keown, A. J., & Martin, J. D. (1997). Do strategic alliances create value? *Journal of Financial Economics, 46,* 199–221.

Chaudhuri, S. (2004). Can innovation be bought? Managing acquisitions in dynamic environments. Unpublished doctoral dissertation, Boston.

Chesbrough, H. W. (2003). *Open innovation: The new imperative for creating and profiting from technological innovation.* Boston: Harvard Business School Press.

Chiesa, V. (2001). *R&D strategy and organization: Managing technical change in dynamic contexts.* London: Imperial College Press.

Chiesa, V., & Manzini, R. (1998). Organizing for technological collaborations: A managerial perspective. *R&D Management, 28,* 199–212.

Cloodt, M., Hagedoorn, J., & Van Kranenburg, H. (2006). Mergers and acquisitions: Their effect on the innovative performance of companies in high-tech industries. *Research Policy, 35,* 642–654.

Cohen, M. A., Eliashberg, J., & Ho, T. H. (1996). New product development: The performance and time to market tradeoff. *Management Science, 42,* 173–186.

Colombo, M. G., Grilli, L., & Piva, E. (2006). In search of complementary assets: The determinants of alliance formation of high-tech start-ups. *Research Policy, 35,* 1166–1199.

Cools, K., & Roos, A. (2005, November). *The role of alliances in corporate strategy.* Boston: Boston Consulting Group Report.

Cooper, R., Edgett, S. J., & Kleinschmidt, E. J. (1999). New product portfolio management: Practices and performance. *Journal of Product Innovation Management, 16,* 333–351.

De Man, A. P. (2004). *The network economy. Strategy, structure and management.* Cheltenham, UK: Edward Elgar.

De Man, A. P., & Duysters, G. M. (2005). Collaboration and innovation: A review of the effects of mergers, acquisitions and alliances on innovation. *Technovation, 25,* 1377–1387.

De Noble, A. F., Gustafson, L. T., & Hergert, M. (1988). Planning for post-merger integration: Eight lessons for merger success. *Long Range Planning, 21*(4), 82–85.

Dussauge, P., & Garrette, B. (1999). *Cooperative strategy: Competing successfully through strategic alliances.* Chichester, UK: Wiley.

Duysters, G., & Lokshin, B. (2011). Determinants of alliance portfolio complexity and its effect on innovative performance of companies. *Journal of Product Innovation Management, 28,* 570–585.

Dyer, J. H., Kale, P., & Singh, H. (2004). When to ally and when to acquire. *Harvard Business Review, 82*(7), 108–115.

Eisenhardt, K. M., & Martin, J. A. (2000). Dynamic capabilities, what are they? *Strategic Management Journal, 21,* 1105–1121.

Elton, E. J., & Gruber, M. J. (1997). Modern portfolio theory, 1950 to date. *Journal of Banking and Finance, 21,* 1743–1759.

Faems, D., Van Looy, B., & Debackere, K. (2005). Interorganizational collaboration and innovation: Toward a portfolio approach. *Journal of Product Innovation Management, 22,* 238–250.

Farrell, J. L. (1997). *Portfolio management, theory and applications* (2nd ed.). New York: McGraw-Hill/Irwin.

Folta, T. B. (1998). Governance and uncertainty: The trade-off between administrative control and commitment. *Strategic Management Journal, 19,* 1007–1028.

Folta, T. B., & Leiblein, M. J. (1994). Technology acquisition and the choice of governance by established firms: Insights from option theory in a multinominal logit model. *Academy of Management Proceedings,* 27–31.

Fontenot, R. J., & Wilson, E. J. (1997). Relational exchange: A review of selected models for a predication matrix of relationship activities. *Journal of Business Research, 39,* 5–12.

Garette, B., & Dussauge, P. (2000). Alliances versus acquisitions: Choosing the right option. *European Management Journal, 18*(1), 63–69.

George, G., Zahra, S. A., Wheatley, K. K., & Khan, R. (2001). The effect of alliance portfolio characteristics and absorptive capacity on performance. A study of biotechnology firms. *Journal of High Technology Management Research, 12,* 205–226.

Granstrand, O., Bohlin, E., Oskarsson, C., & Sjoberg, N. (1992). External technological acquisition in large multi-technology corporations. *R&D Management, 22,* 111–133.

Gulati, R., & Singh, H. (1998). The architecture of cooperation: Managing coordination costs and appropriation concerns in strategic alliances. *Administrative Science Quarterly, 43,* 781–814.

Hagedoorn, J. (1993). Understanding the rationale of strategic technology partnering: International modes of cooperation and sectoral differences. *Strategic Management Journal, 14,* 371–385.

Hagedoorn, J., & Duysters, G. (2002). External sources of innovative capabilities: The preference for strategic alliances or mergers and acquisitions. *Journal of Management Studies, 39,* 167–88.

Hennart, J.-F., & Reddy, S. (1997). The choice between mergers/acquisitions and joint ventures: The case of the Japanese investors in the United States. *Strategic Management Journal, 18,* 1–12.

Hite, J. M., & Hesterly, W. S. (2001). The evolution of firm networks: From emergence to early growth of the firm. *Strategic Management Journal, 22,* 275–286.

Hoffmann, W. H. (2005). How to manage a portfolio of alliances. *Long Range Planning, 38,* 121–143.

Hoffmann, W. H., & Schaper-Rinkel, W. (2001). Acquire or ally?—A strategy framework for deciding between acquisition and cooperation. *Management International Review, 41,* 131–159.

Huff, A. S., & Reger, R. K. (1987). A review of strategic process research. *Journal of Management, 13,* 211–236.

Hung, S. W., & Tang, R. H. (2008). Factors affecting the choice of technology acquisition mode: An empirical analysis of the electronic firms of Japan, Korea and Taiwan. *Technovation, 28,* 557–563.

Jackson, J. A., Kloeber, J. M., Jr., Ralston, B. E., & Deckro, R. F. (1999). Selecting a portfolio of technologies: An application of decision analysis. *Decision Sciences, 30,* 217–238.

Johnson, G., & Scholes, K. (2002). *Exploring corporate strategy. Text and cases* (6th ed.). London: Financial Times Prentice Hall.

Kay, N. M., & Diamantopoulos, A. (1987). Uncertainty and synergy: Toward a formal model of corporate strategy. *Managerial and Decision Economics, 8,* 121–130.

Keil, T., Maula, M., Schildt, H., & Zahra, S. A. (2008). The effect of governance modes and relatedness of external business development on innovative performance. *Strategic Management Journal, 29,* 895–907.

Keeney, R. L. (1982). Decision analysis: An overview. *Operations Research, 30,* 803–838.

Khanna, T., Gulati, R., & Nohria, N., (1998). The dynamics of learning alliances: Competition, cooperation and relative scope. *Strategic Management Journal, 19,* 193–210.

Khanna, T., Gulati, R., & Nohria, N. (2000). The economic modeling of strategy process: "Clean models" and "dirty hands." *Strategic Management Journal, 21,* 781–790.

Koza, M. P., & Lewin, A. Y., (1998). The co-evolution of strategic alliances. *Organization Science, 9,* 255–264.

Leiblein, M. J. (2003). The choice of organizational governance form and performance: Predictions from transaction cost, resource-based, and real options theories. *Journal of Management, 29,* 937–961.

Mahnke, V., & Overby, M. L. (2005, June 27–29). *Portfolio management of R&D-collaborations: The case of mobile services.* Presentation at the DRUID tenth anniversary summer conference on Dynamics of Industry and Innovation: Organizations, Networks and Systems, Copenhagen, Denmark.

Mansfield, E. (1961). Technical change and the rate of imitation. *Econometrica, 29,* 741–766.

March, J. G. (1991). Exploration and exploitation in organizational learning, *Organization Science, 2,* 71–87.

Markowitz, H. (1952). Portfolio selection. *Journal of Finance, 7,* 77–91.

Markowitz, H. (1959). *Portfolio selection: Efficient diversification of investments.* New York: Wiley.

Osborn, R. N., & Hagedoorn, J. (1997). The institutionalization and evolutionary dynamics of interorganizational alliances and networks. *Academy of Management Journal, 40,* 261–278.

Oxley, J. E. (1997). Appropriability hazards and governance in strategic alliances: A transaction cost approach. *Journal of Law Economics and Organization, 13,* 387–409.

Parikh, M., Fazlollahi, B., & Verma, S. (2001). The effectiveness of decisional guidance: An empirical evaluation. *Decisions Sciences, 32,* 303–331.

Parise, S., & Casher, A. (2003). Alliance portfolios: Designing and managing your network of business partner relationships. *Academy of Management Executive, 17*(4), 25–39.

Porrini, P. (2004). Can a previous alliance between an acquirer and a target affect acquisition performance. *Journal of Management, 30,* 545–562.

Porter, M. E. (1981). The contribution of industrial organization in strategic management. *Academy of Management Review, 6,* 609–620.

Powell, W. W., Koput, K. W., & Smith-Doerr, L. (1996). Interorganizational collaboration and the locus of innovation: Network of learning in biotechnology. *Administrative Science Quarterly, 41,* 116–145.

Roberts, E. B., & Liu, W. K. (2001). Ally or acquire? *MIT Sloan Management Review, 43*(1), 26–34.

Roberts, E. B., & Liu, W. K. (2003). Ally or acquire? Case studies of Compaq and Cisco as additional tests of the external technology life cycle model. (Working Paper 4421-03, MIT Sloan School of Management).

Sakakibara, M. (1997). Heterogeneity of firm capabilities and cooperative research and development: An empirical examination of motives. *Strategic Management Journal, 18,* 143–164.

Schumpeter, J. (1942). *Capitalism, socialism and democracy.* New York: Harper & Row.

Tan, K. H., & Platts, K. (2003). Linking objectives to actions: A decision support approach based on cause-effect linkages. *Decision Sciences, 34,* 569–593.

Utterback, J. M. & Abernathy, W. J. (1975). A dynamic model of process and product innovation. *Omega, 3,* 639–656.

Van de Vrande, V., Lemmens, C., & Vanhaverbeke, W. (2006). Choosing governance modes for external technology sourcing. *R&D Management, 36,* 347–363.

Van de Vrande, V., Vanhaverbeke, W., & Duysters, G. (2009). External technology sourcing: The effect of uncertainty on governance mode choice. *Journal of Business Venturing, 24,* 62–80.

Vanhaverbeke, W., Duysters, G., & Noorderhaven, N. (2002). External technology sourcing through alliances or acquisitions: An analysis of the application-specific integrated circuits industry. *Organization Science, 13,* 714–733.

Vanhaverbeke, W., & Noorderhaven, N. G. (2001). Competition between alliance blocks: The case of the RISC microprocessors technology. *Organization Studies, 22,* 1–30.

Vasudevan, A., Duysters, G. M., van den Oord, A., & Bakkes, S. (2001). The changing face of alliance management: Managerial imperatives for the network economy. In A. P. De Man, G. M. Duysters, & A. Vasudevan (Eds.), *The allianced enterprise: Global strategies for corporate collaboration* (pp. 9–30). London: Imperial College Press.

Villalonga, B., & McGahan, A. M. (2005). The choice among acquisitions, alliances, and divestitures. *Strategic Management Journal, 26,* 1183–1208.

Wang, L., & Zajac, E. J. (2007). Alliance or acquisition? A dyadic perspective on interfirm resource combinations. *Strategic Management Journal, 28,* 1291–1317.

Wilcox, H. D., Chang, K-C., & Grover, V. (2001). Valuation of mergers and acquisitions in the telecommunications industry: A study on diversification and firm size. *Information & Management, 38,* 459–471.

Wuyts, S., Dutta, S., & Stremersch, S. (2004). Portfolios of interfirm agreements in technology-intensive markets: Consequences for innovation and profitability. *Journal of Marketing, 68*(2), 88–100.

Yin, X., & Shanley, M. (2008). Industry determinants of the "merger versus alliance" decision. *Academy of Management Review, 33,* 473–491.

Yoshikawa, T. (2003). Technology development and acquisition strategy. *International Journal of Technology Management, 25,* 666–674.

Yu, O. (2006). *Technology portfolio planning and management. Practical concepts and tools.* New York: Springer.

CHAPTER 7

COMPARING INTERNATIONAL AND DOMESTIC JOINT VENTURES

Aspects of Management and Performance

Merve Bener
Keith W. Glaister

ABSTRACT

This study investigates some core aspects of the management of domestic joint ventures and international joint ventures with parent firms from Europe, North America, and Australia. The study examines the following research questions: To what extent do perceptions of culture differences between the JV partners lead to variation in JV performance, trust between JV partners, and autonomy granted to the JV management? To what extent does the level of autonomy granted to the JV management vary with the level of trust between the JV partners? To what extent does the performance of the JV vary with the level of autonomy granted to the IJV management and conversely, to what extent does the level of autonomy granted to the JV management

Strategic Alliances for Value Creation, pages 141–170

influence the performance of the JV? To what extent does performance of the JV influence trust between the JV partners, and conversely, to what extent does trust between the JV partners influence performance of the JV? More fundamentally, the overriding question addressed by this study is the extent to which these aspects of management and performance differ between international joint ventures and domestic joint ventures.

INTRODUCTION

The joint venture (JV) is one of the most frequently used contractual forms in strategic alliances. Joint ventures are superior to markets and hierarchies when firms face uncertainty about future development or when information is inadequate (Balakrishnan & Koza, 1993). International joint ventures (IJVs) are a major means of global expansion for multinational enterprises (UNCTAD, 2004). Nevertheless, the inherent complexity of having two or more owners who may be competitors and collaborators leads to certain difficulties in management. Such problems are magnified when an IJV is operating in a risky and uncertain setting in which political and opportunistic behavior is rife, as this increases the transaction costs due to increased monitoring, communication, and negotiation requirements (Beamish & Kachra, 2004; Frayne & Geringer, 1990). Hence, IJVs are considered more risky and more difficult to manage than domestic joint ventures (DJVs); i.e., joint ventures formed with partners from the same country. In general, however, joint ventures can only be justified when the benefits of joining outweigh the increased governance costs and possible leakage of know-how (Beamish & Banks, 1987).

Research on joint ventures continues to attract the attention of business scholars in light of both the popularity of JVs and the largely unsatisfactory performance of JVs (Choi & Beamish, 2004; Luo, Shenkar, & Nyaw, 2001). An important stream of research on JVs seeks to identify factors that enhance or impede their performance. This research suggests that the success of JVs may be a function of several factors. This chapter examines the following factors that have been given particular prominence in the literature as determinants of joint venture performance: corporate culture differences (Pothukuchi, Damanpour, Choi, Chen, & Park, 2002; Sirmon & Lane, 2004; Weber, Shenkar & Raveh, 1996), JV autonomy (Hill & Hellriegel, 1994; Lyles & Reger, 1993; Newburry & Zeira, 1999; Zeira & Parker, 1995), and trust between partners (Madhok, 1995). Although examination of these factors is important in its own right, what has been neglected in prior studies is a comparison of IJVs and DJVs across these factors. A distinguishing feature of this chapter is the empirical examination of these factors for both IJV and DJVs, with a view to highlighting how the importance of these factors varies between the two organizational forms.

The focus of this study is the investigation of the relationships between the factors influencing the management and the performance of JVs. Figure 7.1 provides an overall model of the factors for the focus of this study and the predicted interrelationships between them.

Although prior research has also suggested other factors that might be critical to joint venture success, the factors that have been consistently identified as being important to joint venture performance were selected for consideration in this study. Further, these factors are meaningful to the conceptual framework proposed in this chapter as they potentially can have varying effects on joint venture performance. A distinguishing feature of this study is that it examines the perspectives of the respondent companies with respect to the influence of "soft" variables, such as culture, autonomy, and trust, on the effective management of these interfirm relationships.

As indicated in Figure 7.1, the main aim of this study is to address the following research questions: To what extent do perceptions of culture differences between the JV partners lead to variation in JV performance, trust between JV partners, and autonomy granted to the JV management? To what extent does the level of autonomy granted to the JV management vary with the level of trust between the JV partners? To what extent does the performance of the JV vary with the level of autonomy granted to the IJV management, and conversely, to what extent does the level of autonomy granted to the JV management influence the performance of the JV? To what extent does performance of the JV influence trust between the JV partners, and conversely, to what extent does trust between the JV partners influence performance of the JV? More fundamentally, as previously noted,

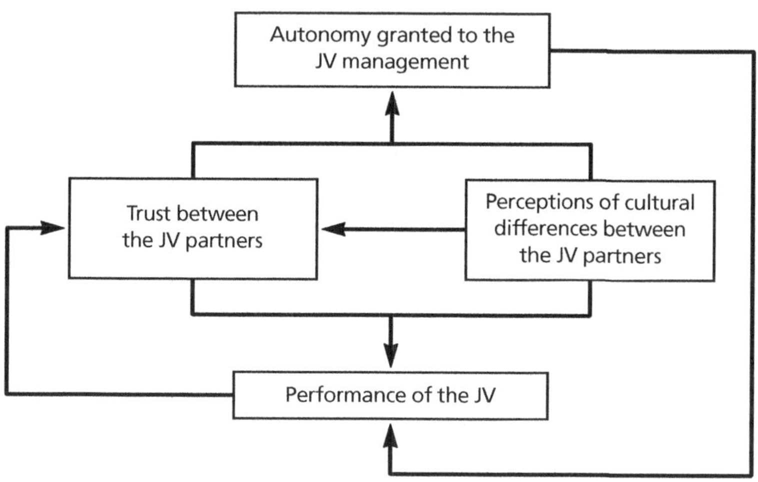

Figure 7.1 Model of the management and performance of JVs.

the overriding question addressed by this study is the extent to which these aspects of management and performance differ between IJVs and DJVs.

The rest of this chapter is organized as follows: The next section identifies relevant literature and sets out the hypotheses of the study. The third section describes the research methods employed. The fourth presents the findings and discussion. Conclusions are in the final section.

LITERATURE REVIEW AND HYPOTHESES DEVELOPMENT

Organizational culture differences differentiate partners based on their management practices, which are deemed essential for the functioning of their respective organizations. Differences in practices represent conflicting expectations and incompatible organizational processes. Partners with dissimilar organizational cultures may expend time and energy to establish managerial practices and routines to facilitate interaction and may incur high costs and more mistrust than culturally similar partners (Park & Ungson, 1997). Brown, Rugman, & Verbeke (1989) also concur that compatibility in partners' organizational cultures and practices could be a significant determinant of the performance of JVs. Research on organizational climate similarity and performance also indicates that firms selecting a partner that has a similar organizational climate will have superior performance (Fey & Beamish, 2001).

Differences in the cultural backgrounds of the partners generally have been perceived as a threat to the survival of JVs (Brown et al., 1989; Harrigan, 1988; Shenkar & Zeira, 1992). Wilkof, Brown, and Selsky (1995) noted that cultural clash has caused many JVs to fail due to the inability of the partners to work seamlessly. Lane and Beamish (1990) argued that cultural compatibility between the partners is the most important factor in the endurance of an international alliance. Consistent with this view, various studies (for instance, Barkema, Bell, & Pennings, 1996; Barkema, Shenkar, Vermeulen, & Ben, 1997) have found that the chances of survival of IJVs are lower when the cultural distance between the home country of the expanding firm and the host country is large. Li and Guisinger (1991) found that U.S. affiliates whose partners came from culturally dissimilar countries were more likely to fail.

Despite claims that cultural difference is detrimental to JV success, empirical work relating to the issue is mixed. For instance, Park and Ungson (1997) examine the effects of partner nationality, organizational dissimilarity, and economic motivation on the dissolution of JVs. They reported that cultural distance in general did not have an effect on dissolution, but U.S.-Japanese JVs lasted longer than U.S.-U.S. JVs. Prior relationships between partners appeared to negate some complexities arising from cultural differences. Opportunistic threat and rivalry appeared to be a stronger indication of the dissolution of JVs than organizational variables.

Aulakh and Madhok (2002) found corporate cultural congruence had a significant positive impact on JV flexibility, but did not have a direct impact on alliance performance; they also reported no significant effect of national cultural congruence on JV flexibility or performance. They comment that this is notable given that, ever since Hofstede's (1980) landmark study, national psychic distance has commanded the bulk of the attention in international business research rather than organizational culture. The assumption that differences in cultures produce lack of "fit" has been questioned. Shenkar (2001, p. 524) notes that not every cultural gap is critical to performance, with different aspects of culture being differentially critical to operations (Tallman & Shenkar, 1994). This leads to the following hypothesis:

> **Hypothesis 1:** *The greater the corporate culture differences perceived by the parent firms, the greater the impact of corporate cultural differences on JV performance.*

In the context of both mergers and joint ventures, scholars have generally argued that alliances between culturally similar partners are more likely to be successful than alliances between culturally dissimilar partners. Cartwright and Cooper (1993, p. 57) state that in alliances, "selection decisions are generally driven by financial and strategic considerations, yet many organizational alliances fail to meet expectations because the cultures of partners are incompatible." Different culture types create different psychological environments for the joint venture or the merged company, and differences in practices have a negative influence on performance (Cartwright & Cooper, 1993). Thus, "the degree of culture fit that exists between combining organizations is likely to be directly correlated to the success of the combination" (Cartwright & Cooper, 1993, p. 60).

It was found that cultural similarity among parent organizations is positively correlated with the success of many IJVs (Goldenberg, 1988; Lin & Germain, 1998). High levels of cultural dissimilarity may make it impossible for parent companies to achieve a strategic fit, a fit that is needed for venture success. Saxton (1997) found that similarities between partners with respect to specific organizational characteristics, including culture and human resources, were negatively related to alliance outcomes, and that organizational process similarities were negatively related to initial satisfaction. Saxton's findings contradict the popular idea that "culture clash" negatively influences alliance potential. For Saxton, the negative relationship suggests that although similarities in strategic factors such as manufacturing activities and markets are important to alliance success, it is not as important for a company to pick a partner that thinks in the same way. Furthermore,

Saxton (p. 456) argues that "It is also possible, perhaps even likely, that these relationships are not linear. A certain degree of similarity may be necessary and desirable for understanding a partner. Too much similarity though could limit the benefits because nothing novel is being brought to the relationship." This leads to the following hypothesis:

> **Hypothesis 2:** *The greater the corporate cultural differences contributing to different views on the management of the JV, the less satisfied will be the parent firms with JV performance.*

It has been widely assumed that the degree of distance between the culture to which a firm is accustomed and that of the environment in which it is planning to invest will influence the kind of organizational arrangement it is willing to accept for that investment. However, there are conflicting arguments and inconclusive evidence concerning the effect that cultural distance will have (Shenkar, 2001). A high cultural distance is likely to generate additional risk and uncertainty in the perceptions of the investing company's decision makers, especially if the other culture is unfamiliar to them.

Part of the risk lies in the need, in a culturally different environment, to depend on agents and partners that it does not know well. It is therefore argued that a firm will seek to compensate for this risk by exercising greater control in its dealings with foreign agents and partners. If the presence of greater cultural distance between prospective alliance partners is associated with low levels of trust between them, they might be encouraged to seek managerial as well as legal safeguards for their crucial interests (Shane, 1994). This implies that in cases of high cultural distance, the main investor or provider of key resources is likely to prefer direct foreign investment rather than licensing and in forming a JV in order to hold a majority equity share that provides the right to managerial control.

The counterargument is that when there is high cultural distance, a firm may prefer to rely on a local partner to contribute local knowledge, and it will therefore be willing to opt for limited control over their cooperative venture. This may be a particularly important consideration in the early stages of entering an unfamiliar environment, such as that of many emerging economies in which many parameters of doing business are subject to local negotiation (Beamish, 1988). Also, insofar as limited control is associated with committing limited investment, this alternative will reduce the company's financial exposure in an unfamiliar environment. The inconclusive nature of the evidence on this issue probably reflects complexities that require further investigation. For example, high control may be more efficient when the firm entering a new market through a cooperative alliance enjoys a specific advantage that its partner cannot easily imitate or apply (Anderson & Gatignon, 1986). A firm that is already experienced in working within another culture may feel more confident about assuming dominant control over the management of an alliance. This leads to the following hypothesis:

> **Hypothesis 3:** *The smaller the corporate culture differences contributing to differing views on JV management, the greater the autonomy granted to JV management.*

Hofstede, Neuijen, Ohavy, and Sanders (1990) found that while organizations from different nations differ in fundamental values, organizations from the same nation differ only in organizational practices. The authors therefore concluded that when both national and organizational cultures are examined, the former should be operationalized in terms of values, and the latter in terms of core organizational practices. Corporate culture refers to a pattern of shared basic assumptions about the environment, human nature, social relationships, and reality that employees have learned as they addressed and resolved problems of external adaptation and internal integration (Schein, 1992). Since a joint venture is typically a hybrid of two independent firms, dissimilarities in organizational structures and processes can create problems in coordination that can lead to dissolution of the joint venture. In contrast, similarity in partners' organizational structures and processes can facilitate mutual understanding and collaboration. This view is consistent with that of Bleeke and Ernst (1993), who found that cross-border joint ventures per se are not as problematic as joint ventures between companies with strong and weak cultures or those between companies with asymmetric financial ownership.

Jemison and Sitkin (1986) introduced the concept of organizational fit to describe the similarities between organizations in terms of organizational culture, human resource policies, and administrative processes. In the JV context, Saxton (1997) argued that organizational similarities between the partners help establish trust and enhance the appropriability of knowledge necessary to form the basis for a common frame of reference. In turn, learning can help offset cultural differences (Barkema et al., 1996) that often exist in international JVs. Inkpen (1995) found that a lack of compatibility between JV partners, particularly with regard to expectations about venture profitability, frustrated learning processes, which in turn, contributed to breakdowns in trust. This discussion leads to the following hypothesis:

> **Hypothesis 4:** *The smaller the perceptions of corporate cultural differences between the JV partner firms, the greater the level of trust between the JV partner firms.*

Shenkar and Zeira (1992) noted that IJV general managers suffer from serious role conflict and ambiguities, with over commitment to one parent often leading to the rebellion of the other parent. Similarly, Frayne and Geringer (1990) reported that foreign general managers face such challenges as divided loyalty, pressure for a quick response, the presence of multiple parents, limited preparation and support, and excessive responsibility. The general manager can be considered to be the agent of the parents in managing a JV. According to agency theory, agents are more risk-averse than principals, as they have invested themselves wholly in the company, whereas the shareholders of the parents can diversify their stakes (Eisenhardt, 1989). This situation may be even worse when there is a high level of uncertainty caused by conflict between parents. Although experienced executives alone can generate better performance, they will be more productive still when there is also trust between parents. As many experienced executives of IJVs are local people who are culturally more sensitive to the influence of trust, especially in transitional economies, they are likely to be more effective when the level of trust between parents is high (Jolly, 2005).

Inkpen and Currall (2004) argue that the greater the initial level of trust between partners, the more they can rely on informal social controls and the lower will be the initial costs of monitoring and controlling the JV. If trust develops over time, it should come to serve as a stabilizing influence on relations between the partners, helping them to cope with shifts in bargaining power and other crises. As the fear of opportunism fades because of the development of mutual trust, there may be a reduction in coordination and monitoring costs. Dyer (1997) argued that trust itself should be viewed as an efficient governance mechanism in interfirm relationships. Gulati (1995) made a similar argument, suggesting that firms may substitute trust for contractual safeguards when they form repeat alliances. In certain instances, contractual and bureaucratic arrangements may not be as useful as mutual trust in controlling the opportunistic behavior of the other party in a business relationship.

Whereas localization enables local senior managers to enjoy a high degree of task autonomy and independence, the extensive monitoring of their behavior and outcomes by overseas headquarters makes local senior managers unable to make decisions autonomously (Roth & Nigh, 1992). Overseas headquarters delegate more responsibilities and decision-making authorities to the local senior managers through increased localization (Wong & Law, 1999). The local staff is a valuable resource for foreign firms through which they can gain access to local knowledge and the local market. Without such knowledge, it is difficult for foreign firms to penetrate existing personal and business networks in an unfamiliar market (Wong & Law, 1999). However, by granting autonomy, foreign firms and local staff can gain a better understanding of each other, which leads to familiarity and the grounds for trust development (Luhmann, 1988). Localization signals a foreign firm's commitment to a local market. Presumably, its willingness to increase its vulnerability by relying on local managers reflects the firm's trust in the local staff and should lead to reciprocal trust from local employees (Child & Mollering, 2003). There is a paucity of prior studies that have examined the relationship between autonomy and trust, but based on the arguments in the literature, it is reasonable to argue the following hypothesis:

Hypothesis 5: *The greater the level of trust between the JV partner firms, the greater the degree of autonomy granted to the JV management.*

The performance of the JV is likely to be a moderating variable on JV autonomy. Killing (1983) noted that JV parents loosen or increase control over their ventures as a response to their performance. Yan and Gray (1994) reported data that suggests that performance also shapes the relative levels of bargaining power and the pattern of the sharing of management control between parents. In general, it may be argued that where the parents perceive the performance objectives of the JV to be at least satisfactory and to be improving beyond some minimum requirement, then they are more likely to grant greater decision-making autonomy to the JV management. In contrast, where JV performance is unsatisfactory in terms of objectives or generally declining, then the parent firms are more likely to withhold or withdraw autonomy and take a greater role in the decision making of the JV. A key finding from Glaister, Husan, and Buckley's (2003) study is that in general, greater IJV autonomy is positively associated with perceived performance of the IJV, but that the nature of this autonomy needs to be carefully specified. It appears that partners allow JV management autonomy as long as performance is acceptable to them, but only in certain areas of decision making. The following hypothesis therefore concerns the extent to which satisfaction with JV performance is related to the perceived extent of JV autonomy.

Hypothesis 6: *If the JV is performing well (poorly) then the JV management will be afforded a high (low) level of autonomy: JV autonomy will be positively associated with the perceived performance of the JV.*

In the context of strategic alliances, the positive link between trust and performance is validated by several systematic research efforts (e.g., Inkpen & Currall, 1997; Mohr & Spekman, 1994; Saxton, 1997; Seabright, Levinthal, & Fichman, 1992; Tsai & Ghoshal, 1998). Although it has generally been argued that trust leads to performance (e.g., Harrigan, 1986; Saxton, 1997), the argument that performance leads to trust has merit as well. Using perception of opportunistic behavior as a proxy for trust, Parkhe (1993) found a strong relationship between perception of opportunistic behavior and alliance performance. Yan and Gray (1994) suggested that performance may have a feedback effect on trust. Poor performance may cause distrust between the partners, which leads to poor long-term JV performance (Killing, 1983). A firm's review of past JV performance results, in comparison with expectations, can lead to a firm's prediction of the extent to which the partner firm will follow through on its current promises (i.e., is trust in the partner warranted?). If JV performance is worse than expected, JV partners are likely to question the competence and capabilities of their partners. The level of trust in the relationship will therefore suffer accordingly.

In a reciprocal manner, trust ensures a sound and cooperative working relationship between the JV partner firms. The greater the level of trust, the more efficient the JV will be in transforming an input of cooperation into a collaborative output (Buckley & Casson, 1988). Madhok (1995) suggests that a foundation of trust, although time-consuming and expensive to create, can contribute to the sustained continuation of cooperative relationships. Parkhe (1993) argues that as trust increases and the fear of opportunism fades, there is a declining role for contractual safeguards, leading to lower compliance and coordination costs. A lack of trust in a cooperative relationship can lead to a situation in which one or both partners believe their alliance efforts are unproductive, resulting in a downward spiral of poor performance, and dissatisfaction with the relationship (Smith & Barclay, 1997).

Li, Zhou, Lam, and Tse (2006) also found that the development of trust in overseas headquarters among local senior managers in uncertain environments is important for JV performance, and Wang and Nicholas (2005) suggested that process-based trust affects the performance of contractual joint ventures. Trust encourages partners to transfer tacit knowledge, which is considered a key contributor to sound JV performance (Dhanaraj, Lyles, Steensma, & Tihanyi, 2004). Finally, an expectancy effect may accompany the actual impact of trust on performance: trust in the other party will make the focal party feel secure about positive outcomes, and this evaluation leads to high level of satisfaction (Andaleeb, 1995). This discussion leads to the following hypothesis:

> **Hypothesis 7:** *There will be a positive significant correlation between the level of trust between the JV partner firms and the satisfaction with JV performance.*

RESEARCH METHODS

Sampling Frame and Data Collection Method

Particular characteristics of the mail questionnaire method militated strongly in favor of collecting survey data through this procedure. In order to avoid many of the common pitfalls of the questionnaire design, the research instrument was developed taking into account the guidelines laid down by Churchill (1987), Foddy (1994) and Oppenheim (1992). From a review of the literature, the main issues relating to the control of the JV, autonomy granted to the JV management, level of trust between partner firms, national and corporate cultural differences between partner firms, and performance of JVs were identified. Other questionnaires dealing with the similar issues were also consulted (see for example, Dong & Glaister, 2007a; 2007b; Glaister & Buckley, 1998; 1999; Tatoglu & Glaister, 1998c). This provided a sketch of the key questions to be asked. A pilot study of semistructured interviews was conducted with the senior managers of three UK firms involved in international joint venture operations in order to confirm understanding of the main research issues on the part of potential respondents and to make sure that the items on the questionnaire were clear and unambiguous.

The final research instrument incorporated questions of two broad types: categorical questions of a factual nature and questions designed to measure the attitude and perceptions of the respondents. In line with prior research, the latter set of questions were of an ordinal nature. Ordinal classification of attitude and perception was considered a more realistic task for respondents than the use of interval or ratio measures (Geringer, 1991). Given the limited available time of senior executives to complete the questionnaire, an easily understood Likert-type scale appeared to be appropriate, and questions were restricted to 5-point scales.

The starting point for obtaining a sample of parent firms was the OSIRIS database. OSIRIS is a comprehensive database of financial information, ratings, earnings estimates, stock data, ownership data, and news on global publicly listed companies, banks, and insurance firms around the world. With coverage of over 125 countries, OSIRIS contains information on over 37,000 companies.

It was decided to target "Western" companies; i.e., those in the UK, the rest of Europe, the United States, Canada, and Australia, in part because this would facilitate the use of a single questionnaire in English, and it was assumed these countries would be more likely to respond to a UK study than would companies in other countries. OSIRIS does not contain JV data and so does not provide any information on whether or not a particular company owns a joint venture. Therefore, the only way to identify whether the companies had any joint ventures was through the history pages of the individual company Web sites or through a search for the company on a search engine. This process resulted in a total of 931 companies with the possibility of having a joint venture. This does not constitute a definitive figure for the sampling frame because, as previously noted, it was not possible to identify with certainty whether or not the companies had joint ventures.

Since the desired information was highly specific in nature, the study required respondents with specialized knowledge of all facets of JV activity. These requirements identify respondents as senior executives who had intimate involvement in JV activities and had access to the requisite data. Potential respondents were identified after a thorough assessment of the professional information on them provided by each company's Web site. Most of the potential respondents occupied positions within their organizations as chairman, chief executive officer, business development manager, managing director, and commercial manager. If the respondent company had more than one joint venture or the respondent was involved in more than one joint venture, the respondent was requested to answer the questionnaire with reference to the joint venture he/she was the most familiar with.

During June 2007, paper copies of the questionnaires were sent to potential respondents in 931 companies. This was followed by an e-mail to the same potential respondents with the questionnaire attached. Therefore, the e-mail follow-up served as a reminder to participate in the survey (Schaefer & Dillman, 1998). A total of 41 paper questionnaires were returned from the postal survey and 90 questionnaires were returned from the follow-up e-mail. In total, 131 usable questionnaires were completed and returned by respondent companies that had established joint ventures, resulting in a response rate of 14.1%. Out of a total of 131 questionnaires, 22 of the questionnaires were completed with regard to domestic joint ventures and 109 questionnaires were completed with regard to international joint ventures. It should be noted that although 931 questionnaires were distributed, it is not known how many of the companies contacted actually had a JV. Clearly, for those that did not have a JV, the questionnaire would not be relevant and they would not have responded. Even so, given the well-documented difficulties of obtaining questionnaire responses from executives (Harzing, 1997) and the decreasing rate of response from executives (Cycyota & Harrison, 2006), the study's response rate of 14.1% can be considered satisfactory.

Sample Characteristics

The sample comprises 58 UK parent companies (44.3%), 36 U.S. and Canadian parent companies (27.5%), 18 Australian parent companies (13.7%), and 19 European companies (14.5%). The industry sector of the respondent companies was as follows: 68 in manufacturing (51.9%) and 63 in services (48.1%). Of the 131 joint ventures, 38 (29%) respondent companies held more than 50% of the joint venture's equity, 42 (32.1%) had less than 50% of the joint venture's equity, and 51 (38.9%) had equal to 50% share of the joint venture equity. The time period of IJV formation for

TABLE 7.1 Sample Characteristics

		International Joint Ventures		Domestic Joint Ventures	
		n	%	*n*	%
Respondent company nationality	UK	41	37.6	17	77.3
	Rest of Europe	19	17.4	—	—
	North America (U.S. and Canada)	32	29.4	4	18.2
	Australia	17	15.6	1	4.5
Respondent company's equity share in joint venture	More than 50%	35	32.1	3	13.6
	Less than 50%	33	30.3	9	40.9
	Equal to 50%	41	37.6	10	45.5
Partner company nationality	UK	9	8.3	17	77.3
	Europe	43	39.4	—	—
	North America (U.S. and Canada)	13	11.9	4	18.2
	Australia	2	1.8	1	4.5
	Others	42	38.5	—	—
Industry of respondent company	Manufacturing	65	59.6	3	13.6
	Tertiary	44	40.4	19	86.4
Industry of joint venture company	Manufacturing	66	60.6	2	9.1
	Tertiary	43	39.4	20	90.9
Joint venture termination	Yes	24	22.0	4	18.2
	No	85	78.0	18	81.8
Joint venture age (years)	Mean	8.30		7.00	
	Standard Deviation	7.684		5.282	
		N = 109		N = 22	

the sample ranged between 1962 and 2007. At the time of data collection, a total of 21.4% of the IJVs had been terminated, with 78.6% of the IJVs continuing to operate. The sample characteristics for IJVs and DJVs are set out in Table 7.1.

Measures

Perception of Autonomy

Respondents were asked to assess the overall level of JV autonomy on a 5-point scale (1 = "no autonomy" to 5 = "complete autonomy"). This perceptual measure of autonomy across the JV system provides information regarding the extent to which the JV is viewed as autonomous by the parent firm.

Decision-Making Autonomy

Respondents were asked to assess the extent to which the JV was autonomous in its decision making across a range of 16 decision areas on a 5-point scale (1 = "no autonomy" to 5 = "complete autonomy"). The 16 decision areas were hiring and firing nontechnical personnel, hiring and firing technical personnel, pricing, distribution, marketing, day-to-day management, hiring and firing JV senior managers, cost control, manufacturing, patents and trademarks, technology and engineering of products, process technology, R&D, financing of the JV, deciding capital expenditures, and JV location.

Perceptions of Corporate Culture Differences

The respondents were asked the extent to which the corporate cultures differed between the respondent firm and the partner firm, measured on a 5-point scale (1 = "very small difference" to 5 = "very great difference"). Respondents were also asked how far they thought differences in corporate culture had contributed to different views between the respondent managers and their partner counterparts on the management of the joint ventures (1 = "not at all" to 5 = "a great deal").

Perception of Overall Trust

The respondents were asked to assess the overall level of trust on a 5-point scale (from 1 = "very low level of trust" to 5 = "very high level of trust") between the respondent manager and the main manager in the partner firm, between the middle-level managers in the partner firms, between the top management teams in the partner firms, and between the respondent company and the partner company. The factor analysis of the 4 items produced one underlying factor that makes good conceptual sense and explained a total of 74.8% of the observed variance for international joint ventures and 75.1% of the observed variance for domestic joint ventures. Cronbach alpha for the underlying factor was 0.887 for international joint ventures and for domestic joint ventures was 0.889, substantially over 0.70, which suggests a satisfactory level of construct reliability (Nunnally, 1978).

Perception of Performance

The subjective performance measure was broadly derived in the manner followed by Geringer and Hebert (1991). One *subjective measure* was obtained: the respondent company's subjective level of overall satisfaction with the JV's overall performance. The respondents were asked the extent to which they were satisfied with the JV performance on a 5-point scale (1 = "very dissatisfied" to 5 = "very satisfied").

FINDINGS AND DISCUSSION

Hypothesis 1

Hypothesis 1 maintains that the greater the corporate culture differences perceived by the parent firms then the greater the impact of corporate cultural differences on JV performance. The results relating to Hypothesis 1 are set out in Table 7.2, which shows the Spearman correlations between the perceptions of corporate culture differences and the impact of corporate culture differences on JV performance. For both IJVs ($p < 0.01$) and DJVs ($p < 0.1$), there is a significant correlation between the perceptions of corporate cultural differences and the impact of corporate cultural differences on JV performance. Hence, it may be argued that the greater the perceptions of the corporate cultural differences then the greater the impact of corporate cultural differences on JV performance. It is worth noting that the correlation coefficient and the significance of the correlation are greater for international joint ventures than domestic joint ventures, indicating that perceived corporate culture differences have a greater potential impact on JV performance for international joint ventures. These findings provide support for Hypothesis 1.

Hypothesis 2

Hypothesis 2 maintains that the greater the corporate cultural differences contributing to different views on the management of the JV then the less satisfied will be the parent firms with JV performance. Evidence relating to Hypothesis 2 is set out in Table 7.3, which shows the Spearman correlations between the corporate culture differences contributing to different views on JV management and the extent of satisfaction with JV performance. For both international joint ventures and domestic joint ventures, there is a significant negative correlation between the corporate cultural differences

TABLE 7.2 Correlations between the Perceptions of Corporate Culture Differences and the Impact of Corporate Culture Differences on JV Performance (Spearman's Rho)

	Impact of Corporate Culture Differences on JV Performance	
	International Joint Ventures	Domestic Joint Ventures
Perceptions of Corporate Cultural Differences	0.686^{***}	0.400^{*}

$^{***}p < 0.01$; $^{*}p < 0.1$

TABLE 7.3 Correlations between the Extent to which Corporate Culture Differences Contribute to Differing Views on JV Management and the Extent of Satisfaction with JV Performance (Spearman's Rho)

	Extent of Satisfaction with JV Performance	
	International Joint Ventures	Domestic Joint Ventures
Corporate culture differences contributing to differing views on the management of the joint venture	−0.301***	−0.558***

*** $p < 0.01$

contributing to different views on JV management and the extent of satisfaction with JV performance ($p < 0.01$). It is notable that the correlation coefficient is greater for domestic joint ventures than international joint ventures, indicating that corporate cultural differences influence the satisfaction of parent firms with JV performance to a greater extent for domestic joint ventures compared to international joint ventures. These findings provide support for Hypothesis 2.

Hypothesis 3

Hypothesis 3 maintains that the smaller the corporate culture differences contributing to differing views on JV management then the greater the autonomy granted to JV management. Respondents were asked to assess the overall level of IJV autonomy on a 5-point scale. For the sample of international joint ventures, the mean score measuring the level of IJV autonomy (Mean = 3.64; S.D. = 0.845) was above the median measure, indicating the perception of a fair (but certainly not a complete) degree of autonomy of decision making on the part of IJV managers. For the sample of respondent firms with domestic joint ventures, the mean score measuring the level of JV autonomy (Mean = 3.05; S.D. = 1.174) was above the median measure, indicating the perception of a fair (but certainly not a complete) degree of autonomy of decision making on the part of JV managers. The perceptions of autonomy granted (t-value = 2.268; $p < 0.05$) have marginally but significantly lower mean scores for domestic joint ventures compared to those of international joint ventures.

The results relating to Hypothesis 3 are set out in Table 7.4, which shows the Spearman correlations between the corporate culture differences contributing to differing views on JV management and the extent of decision-making autonomy granted. For international joint ventures, there is a significant negative correlation between corporate culture differences

TABLE 7.4 Correlations between the Extent to which Corporate Culture Differences Contribute to Differing Views on JV Management and Extent of Decision-Making Autonomy Granted to the JV

	Corporate culture differences contributing to differing views on JV management	
Extent of autonomy granted to the JV	**International Joint Ventures**	**Domestic Joint Ventures**
Autonomy granted	–0.184**	–0.412*
Hiring and firing nontechnical personnel	–0.016	–0.217
Hiring and firing technical personnel	–0.013	–0.445**
Pricing	–0.185**	–0.330
Distribution	–0.170*	–0.427*
Marketing	–0.236***	–0.334
Day-to-day management	–0.186**	–0.404*
Hiring and firing JV senior managers	–0.071	–0.190
Cost control	–0.207**	–0.297
Manufacturing	–0.094	–0.312
Patents and trademarks	–0.048	–0.353
Technology and engineering of products	–0.130	–0.480**
Process technology	–0.175*	–0.501**
R&D	–0.162	–0.368
Financing of the JV	–0.026	–0.071
Deciding capital expenditures	–0.199**	–0.103
Location of the JV	–0.045	0.070

***$p < 0.01$; **$p < 0.05$; *$p < 0.1$

contributing to differing views on JV management and degree of autonomy granted to JV management ($p < 0.05$). There are also several negative correlations across a number of dimensions of decision-making areas reported in Table 7.4. This is the case for pricing ($p < 0.05$), distribution ($p < 0.1$), marketing ($p < 0.01$), day-to-day management ($p < 0.05$), cost control ($p < 0.05$), process technology ($p < 0.1$), and deciding capital expenditures ($p < 0.05$).

For domestic joint ventures, there is a significant negative correlation between corporate culture differences contributing to differing views on JV management and degree of autonomy granted to JV management ($p < 0.1$). There are also several negative correlations across a number of dimensions of decision-making areas reported in Table 7.4. This is the case for hiring and firing technical personnel ($p < 0.05$), distribution ($p < 0.1$), day-to-day management ($p < 0.1$), technology and engineering of products ($p < 0.05$), and process technology ($p < 0.05$).

A key finding is that in general, greater IJV autonomy is negatively associated with the corporate culture differences contributing to differing views on JV management, providing some support for Hypothesis 3. It appears that the respondent firms allow JV management autonomy as long as fewer corporate culture differences contribute to differing views, but only in certain areas of decision making. In addition, corporate culture differences contributing to differing views on JV management are more significantly correlated with autonomy granted for international joint ventures compared to domestic joint ventures, with eight of the dimensions of autonomy evidencing significant correlations for IJVs, compared to six dimensions of autonomy evidencing significant correlations for DJVs. It is also notable that, whereas autonomy granted, distribution, day-to-day management, and process technology are significant for both IJVs and DJVs, pricing, marketing, cost control, and deciding capital expenditures are significant for IJVs, but not for DJVs; whereas hiring and firing technical personnel, and technology and engineering of products are significant for DJVs but not for IJVs. These findings indicate differences in the dimensions of autonomy afforded IJVs compared to DJVs.

Hypothesis 4

The results relating to Hypothesis 4, which maintains that the smaller the perceptions of corporate cultural differences between the JV partner firms, the greater the level of trust between the JV partner firms, are set out in Table 7.5. Table 7.5 shows the Spearman correlations between the perceptions of corporate cultural differences between the JV partner firms and the overall perception of trust. There are significant negative correlations between the perceptions of corporate cultural differences and the overall perception of trust ($p < 0.01$) for international joint ventures and domestic joint ventures. Consequently, the perceptions of corporate cultural differences influence the level of trust for both international joint ventures and domestic joint ventures. The correlations have the expected sign, showing the negative relationship between the perceptions of corporate cultural differences and trust.

TABLE 7.5 Correlations between Perceptions of Trust and (I) Perceptions of Corporate Cultural Differences, (II) Autonomy Granted, and (III) Satisfaction with Performance (Spearman's Rho)

	International Joint Ventures	Domestic Joint Ventures
(I) Perceptions of Corporate Cultural Differences	-0.494^{***}	-0.561^{***}
(II) Autonomy Granted	0.273^{***}	0.440^{*}
(III) Satisfaction with JV Performance	0.522^{***}	0.502^{**}

$^{***}p < 0.01$; $^{**}p < 0.05$; $^{*}p < 0.1$

Thus, the smaller the perceptions of corporate cultural differences between the JV partner firms, the greater the level of trust between the JV partner firms. This may be because IJV partners with dissimilar organizational cultures may spend more time and energy establishing mutual managerial practices and routines than partners with similar organizational cultures (Park & Ungson, 1997), which leads to lower trust between parent firms. The findings provide support for Hypothesis 4.

Hypothesis 5

The results relating to Hypothesis 5, which maintains that the greater the level of trust between the JV partner firms, the greater the degree of autonomy granted to the JV management, are set out in Table 7.5. Table 7.5 shows the Spearman correlations between the overall perception of trust and the degree of autonomy granted to the JV management. There are significant positive correlations between the perceptions of autonomy granted and the overall perception of trust for both international joint ventures and domestic joint ventures. It should be noted that the correlation is more significant for international joint ventures ($p < 0.01$) compared with domestic joint ventures ($p < 0.1$), although the coefficient is larger for DJVs. Consequently, the level of trust influences the degree of autonomy granted to a greater extent for international joint ventures compared to domestic joint ventures. The correlations have the expected sign, showing the positive relationship between trust and autonomy. Thus, the greater the level of trust between the JV partner firms, the greater the degree of autonomy granted to the JV management. These findings provide support for Hypothesis 5.

Hypothesis 6

Hypothesis 6 maintains that the JV autonomy will be positively associated with the perceived performance of the JV. A chi-square test was carried out between respondents' perceptions of performance and perceptions of autonomy. The null hypothesis is that satisfaction with JV performance and autonomy granted are independent. Therefore, the alternative hypothesis is that satisfaction with JV performance and autonomy granted are not independent. For the sample of respondents with domestic joint ventures, the chi-square test statistic between the satisfaction with performance and autonomy granted was significant ($\chi^2 = 3.521$; $p < 0.1$). For the sample of respondents with international joint ventures, the chi-square test statistic between the satisfaction with performance and autonomy granted was also significant ($\chi^2 = 4.867$; $p < 0.05$). As a result, the null hypothesis is rejected and the alternative hypothesis is accepted, implying that perceptions of performance and autonomy are not independent. The chi-square test provides reasonable support for the view that there is a relationship between the respondent company's satisfaction with performance and autonomy granted to the JV managers and provides reasonable support for Hypothesis 6.

To further examine this hypothesis, correlation between the perception of performance and perception of autonomy was calculated. For the sample of respondents with domestic joint ventures, the correlation between the satisfaction with performance and autonomy granted was significant ($\rho = 0.389$; $p < 0.1$). For the sample of respondents with international joint ventures, the correlation between the satisfaction with performance and autonomy granted was also significant ($\rho = 0.235$; $p < 0.05$). There is a positive significant but moderate level of correlation, providing support for Hypothesis 6 and support for the view that the better the JV performance, the greater the level of autonomy provided by the partners to the JV management. If the JV is performing well, then it may be assumed that the JV management will be afforded a greater level of autonomy; however, if the JV is performing poorly, then the autonomy of the JV management will be curtailed.

More detailed evidence relating to performance and autonomy is shown in Table 7.6, where correlations between the perception of satisfaction of performance and the perception of the extent of autonomy across a number of dimensions of decision making are reported. Significant positive correlations were expected between performance and the various areas relating to decision-making autonomy. For the sample of respondent firms with international joint ventures, significant positive correlations are found for hiring and firing nontechnical personnel ($p < 0.05$), hiring and firing technical personnel ($p < 0.01$), pricing ($p < 0.05$), distribution ($p < 0.1$), hiring and firing JV senior managers ($p < 0.1$), and cost control ($p < 0.01$). For the sample of respondent firms with domestic joint ventures, significant positive correlations are found for distribution ($p < 0.05$), marketing ($p < 0.1$), day-to-day management ($p < 0.01$), and hiring and firing JV senior managers ($p < 0.05$). Clearly, for the respondents as a whole, as IJV performance improves, there is an expectation of the granting of autonomy to the IJV managers in terms of hiring or dismissing the key personnel of the IJV.

The strongest positive and most significant correlations are in the most operational areas of activity, with the strength of correlation and level of significance increasing as the factor of autonomy becomes more operational. In clear contrast, the more strategic the factor is, the weaker the correlation, with none of the correlations significant. As anticipated, this implies that the better the perceived level of performance, the greater the level of autonomy granted to JV managers, however, this only applies to operational autonomy. The implication is that as the operational aspect of decision

TABLE 7.6 Correlation between Autonomy Granted and Satisfaction with Performance (Spearman's Rho)

	International Joint Ventures	Domestic Joint Ventures
Hiring and firing nontechnical personnel	0.207**	0.226
Hiring and firing technical personnel	0.270***	0.319
Pricing	0.214**	0.354
Distribution	0.185*	0.482**
Marketing	0.154	0.389*
Day-to-day management	–0.008	0.665***
Hiring and firing JV senior managers	0.174*	0.450**
Cost control	0.257***	0.282
Manufacturing	0.026	0.191
Patents and trademarks	0.081	0.101
Technology and engineering of products	0.080	0.299
Process technology	0.163	0.239
R&D	0.161	0.309
Financing of the JV	0.059	–0.075
Deciding capital expenditures	0.113	0.066
Location of the JV	0.064	–0.110

***$p < 0.01$; **$p < 0.05$; *$p < 0.1$

making increases, the greater the likelihood that autonomy is afforded to JV managers as performance improves. In contrast, as the strategic aspect of decision making increases, there is little likelihood of autonomy, even if performance improves.

As noted, however, there are a number of differences in the findings between IJVs and DJVs. For IJVs, the correlations between satisfaction of JV performance and hiring and firing nontechnical personnel, hiring and firing technical personnel, pricing, and cost control are significant, but are not significant for DJVs. In contrast, the correlations between satisfaction of JV performance and marketing and day-to-day management are significant for DJVs but not for IJVs.

A key finding from this study is that in general, greater JV autonomy is positively associated with perceived performance of the JV, but that the nature of this autonomy needs to be carefully specified. It appears that the respondent firms allow JV management autonomy as long as performance is acceptable to them, but only in certain areas of decision making. If performance deteriorates or is below what is expected, then there may be greater parent involvement and intervention in the operational running of the JV and in the JV decision-making processes. Overall, evidence from this study supports the view that the level of autonomy granted to JV managers and

JV performance are correlated, providing support for Hypothesis 6. This finding is in line with the views postulated in studies such as those of Killing (1983) and Newburry and Zeira (1999). A key finding from Glaister et al.'s (2003) study is that in general, greater IJV autonomy is positively associated with perceived performance of the IJV.

Hypothesis 7

The results relating to Hypothesis 7, which maintains there will be a positive significant correlation between the level of trust between the JV partner firms and the satisfaction with JV performance, are set out in Table 7.5. Table 7.5 shows the Spearman correlations between the respondent company's satisfaction with JV performance and the overall perception of trust. There are significant positive correlations between the satisfaction with JV performance and the perception of trust. It should be noted that the correlation is more significant for international joint ventures ($p < 0.01$) compared with domestic joint ventures ($p < 0.05$). Consequently, it may be argued that satisfaction with JV performance influences the level of trust to a greater extent for international joint ventures compared to domestic joint ventures. The correlations have the expected sign, showing the positive relationship between the satisfaction with JV performance and trust. Thus, the greater the respondent company's satisfaction with JV performance, the greater the level of trust between the JV partner firms. As previously noted, another way of viewing this relationship is to argue that the greater the level of trust between the JV partner firms, the greater the satisfaction with JV performance. Consequently, the greater the level of trust between the JV partner firms, the greater the satisfaction with JV performance. Overall, these findings provide support for Hypothesis 7.

A prevalent notion in the trust literature is that trust between organizations is an important independent variable of performance, because it facilitates enhanced cooperation, transaction cost savings, capability improvement, and increased strategic flexibility (Gulati, 1995; Mayer, Davis & Schoorman, 1995; McAllister, 1995; Smith, Carroll, & Ashford, 1995). The results confirmed the positive effect of trust as a driving force in sound JV performance. As such, for JV partners, trust-building as a social process should be viewed as a capital investment in a long-term asset that eventually manifests itself through greater returns (Madhok, 2006). Hence, this study provides support for previous findings of the importance of trust in explaining joint venture behavior and success (e.g., Ng, Lau, & Nyaw, 2007). The argument that performance leads to trust has merit as well. The findings confirmed that the greater the satisfaction with JV performance, the greater the level of trust between the parent firms. Poor performance may cause distrust between the partners, which leads to poor long-term JV performance (Killing, 1983).

Perceptions of Factors Influencing JV Performance

Respondents were asked the extent to which five factors influenced JV performance. The factors, ranked by the mean value of the response, are shown in Table 7.7. Of the five factors influencing JV performance, that of trust between partner firms is ranked first for both IJVs and DJVs, indicating the importance of this factor compared with the other factors. The literature suggests that one of the most critical factors determining alliance performance is the degree of trust between the partners (Das & Teng, 1998; Madhok, 1995). Baird, Lyles, and Wharton (1990) found trust to be ranked first among the factors that lead to successful joint ventures in a study of Chinese and U.S. middle-level managers. For IJVs, the level of joint venture autonomy is ranked second, and the level of joint venture control is ranked third. In contrast for DJVs, JV control is ranked second and corporate culture is ranked third. It may be noted that for both IJVs and DJVs, national culture compatibility is ranked fifth, indicating that this is perceived as a relatively less important factor compared with corporate culture compatibility. Ozorhon, Arditi, Dikmen, and Birgonul (2008) found that differences in organizational culture have a greater impact on IJV performance than differences in national and host country culture.

Although there are some differences in ranking between the relative importance of factors influencing JV performance, in only two instances are there significant differences in means. For IJVs, JV autonomy and national culture compatibility are relatively more influential on JV performance than for DJVs. For the national culture factor, this is hardly surprising, as the national culture will be the same in DJVs. The greater relative impor-

TABLE 7.7 Perception of Relative Importance of Factors Influencing JV Performance

	International Joint Ventures			Domestic Joint Ventures			
	Rank	Mean	S.D.	Rank	Mean	S.D.	*t*-value
JV Control	3	3.74	1.084	2	3.76	0.889	–0.075
JV Autonomy	2	3.93	1.007	4	3.05	1.284	3.497***
Trust between Partners	1	4.33	0.806	1	4.19	0.750	0.736
National Culture	5	3.27	1.068	5	2.00	1.500	3.350***
Corporate Culture	4	3.63	1.006	3	3.67	0.913	–0.142

*** $p < 0.01$

tance of JV autonomy on performance for IJVs compared to DJVs may be due to the fact that in IJVs, the partners have to rely on a more distant management of the JV than is the case of DJVs, where both partners are located in the same country.

CONCLUSIONS

This chapter provides new insights into the interrelationships between corporate culture differences, JV autonomy, trust, and the performance of JVs. A particular novelty of the chapter lies in assessing similarities and differences in these interrelationships between IJVs and DJVs. The chapter therefore makes a contribution to the literature as such a comparison between JV organizational forms has been relatively neglected in prior research. However, this is a preliminary study, and further research is required that considers the different aspects of IJVs and DJVs in order to enable better management, control, and performance of both organizational types.

Few prior studies have examined the relationship between autonomy and trust. The findings showed that the greater the level of trust between the JV partner firms, the greater the degree of autonomy granted to the JV management. With granting autonomy, partner firms delegate more responsibilities and decision-making authorities to the JV senior managers (Wong & Law, 1999). Partner firms and JV management can gain a better understanding of each other, which leads to familiarity and the grounds for trust development (Luhmann, 1988). In a reciprocal manner, the development of trust will enhance the granting of autonomy.

This study relied on a self-report questionnaire survey to collect data, and as such it cannot provide richer contextual information for the issues under consideration. Methodologically, using both interviews and questionnaire surveys would add value to the future research in IJVs. In addition, the study is cross-sectional and collects data for a particular point in time. As such, it has limitations in exploring the dynamics involved in the management of JVs. Longitudinal case studies may be more instrumental in disentangling the evolution of joint ventures rather than relying on cross-section data.

A limitation of the research method employed in this study is that it is conducted from the perspective of one JV parent, and it relies on data from a single respondent in each parent firm. A better data collection approach would involve obtaining data from multiple respondents within each of the parent firms. The findings of this study are based on JVs with parent firms from Europe, North America, and Australia. Future research may examine the current hypotheses in other national contexts in order to verify if the findings are generalizable.

The variables utilized in this study do not constitute an exhaustive list of the potential influences on the different perceptive measures of IJV performance. External factors related to industry attractiveness and environmental dynamism, as well as partner-specific factors related to international experience, absorptive capacity, and strategic goal alignment may provide additional insight in future studies. Another avenue worthy of further research would be to analyze how the use of performance indicators and the differences between partner firms change over time. There remains the need to know more about the relative differences between IJVs and DJVs regarding management, control, and performance, and how knowledge of these factors may enable each of these organizational forms to better attain their goals.

REFERENCES

Andaleeb, S. (1995). Dependence relations and the moderating role of trust: Implications for behavioral intentions in marketing channels. *International Journal of Research in Marketing, 12,* 157–172.

Anderson, E., & Gatignon, H. (1986). Modes of foreign entry: A transaction cost analysis and propositions. *Journal of International Business Studies, 17,* 1–26.

Aulakh, P. S., & Madhok, A. (2002). Co-operation and performance in international alliances: The critical role of flexibility. In F. J. Contractor & P. Lorange (Eds.), *Co-operative strategies and alliances* (pp. 25–48). Oxford, UK: Elsevier.

Baird, I. S., Lyles, M. A., & Wharton, R. (1990). Attitudinal differences between American and Chinese managers regarding joint venture management. *Management International Review, 30,* 53–68.

Balakrishnan, S., & Koza, M. P. (1993). Information asymmetry, adverse selection, and joint ventures. *Journal of Economic Behavior and Organization, 20,* 99–117.

Barkema, H. G., Bell, J. H. J., & Pennings, J. M. (1996). Foreign entry, cultural barriers, and learning. *Strategic Management Journal, 17,* 151–166.

Barkema, H. G., Shenkar, O., Vermeulen, F., & Ben, J. H. J. (1997). Working abroad, working with others: How firms learn to operate international joint ventures. *Academy of Management Journal, 40,* 426–442.

Beamish, P. W. (1988). *Multinational joint ventures in developing countries.* London: Routledge.

Beamish, P. W., & Banks, J. C. (1987). Equity joint ventures and the theory of the multinational enterprise. *Journal of International Business Studies, 18,* 1–15.

Beamish, P. W., & Kachra, A. (2004). Number of partners and JV performance. *Journal of World Business, 39,* 107–120.

Bleeke, J., & Ernst, D. (1993). *Collaborating to compete: Using strategic alliances and acquisitions in the global marketplace.* New York: Wiley.

Brown, L. T., Rugman, A. M., & Verbeke, A. (1989). Japanese joint ventures with western multinationals: Synthesising the economic and cultural explanations of failure. *Asia Pacific Journal of Management, 6,* 225–242.

Buckley, P. J., & Casson, M. (1988). A theory of cooperation in international business. In F. Contractor & P. Lorange (Eds.), *Cooperative strategies in international business* (pp. 31–53). Lexington, MA: Lexington Books.

Cartwright, S. & Cooper, C. L. (1993). The role of culture compatibility in successful organizational marriage. *Academy of Management Executive, 7*(2), 57–70.

Child J., & Mollering, G. (2003). Contextual confidence and active trust development in the Chinese business environment. *Organization Science, 14,* 69–80.

Choi, C-B., & Beamish, P. W. (2004). Split management control and international joint venture performance. *Journal of International Business Studies, 35,* 201–215.

Churchill, G. A. (1987). *Marketing research: Methodological foundations* (4th ed.). Chicago: Dryden Press.

Cycyota, C. S., & Harrison, D. A. (2006). Enhancing survey response rates at the executive level: Are employee- or consumer-level techniques effective? *Journal of Management, 28,* 151–176.

Das, T. K., & Teng, B. (1998). Between trust and control: Developing confidence in partner cooperation in alliances. *Academy of Management Review, 23,* 491–512.

Dhanaraj, C., Lyles, M. A., Steensma, H. K., & Tihanyi, L. (2004). Managing tacit and explicit knowledge transfer in IJVs: The role of relational embeddedness and the impact on performance. *Journal of International Business Studies, 35,* 428–442.

Dong, L., & Glaister, K. W. (2007a). National and corporate cultural differences in international strategic alliances: Perceptions of Chinese partners. *Asia Pacific Journal of Management, 24,* 191–205.

Dong, L., & Glaister, K. W. (2007b). The management of culture in Chinese international strategic alliances. *Asian Business and Management, 6,* 377–407.

Dyer, J. H. (1997). Effective interfirm collaboration: How firms minimize transaction costs and maximize transaction value. *Strategic Management Journal, 18,* 535–556.

Eisenhardt, K. M. (1989). Agency theory: An assessment and review. *Academy of Management Review, 14,* 57–74.

Fey, C. F., & Beamish, P. W. (2001). Organizational climate similarity and performance: International joint venture in Russia. *Organization Studies, 22,* 853–882.

Foddy, W. (1994). *Constructing questions for interviews and questionnaires: Theory and practice in social research.* London: Cambridge University Press.

Frayne, C. A., & Geringer, J. M. (1990). The strategic use of human resource management practices as control mechanisms in international joint ventures. *Research in Personnel and Human Resources Management, 2,* 53–69.

Geringer, J. M. (1991). Strategic determinants of partner selection criteria in international joint ventures. *Journal of International Business Studies, 22,* 41–62.

Geringer, J. M., & Hebert, L. (1991). Measuring performance of international joint ventures. *Journal of International Business Studies, 22,* 249–263.

Glaister, K. W., & Buckley, P. J. (1998). Measures of performance in the UK international alliances. *Organization Studies, 19,* 89–118.

Glaister, K. W., & Buckley, P. J. (1999). Performance relationships in U.K. international alliances. *Management International Review, 39*(2), 123–147.

Glaister, K. W., Husan, R., & Buckley, P. J. (2003). Decision-making autonomy in UK international equity joint ventures. *British Journal of Management, 14,* 305–322.

Goldenberg, S. (1988). *Hands across the ocean: Managing joint ventures with spotlight on China and Japan.* Boston: Harvard Business School Press.

Gulati, R. (1995). Does familiarity breed trust? The implications of repeated ties for contractual choice in alliances. *Academy of Management Journal, 38,* 85–112.

Harrigan, K. R. (1986). *Managing for joint venture success.* Lexington, MA: Lexington Books.

Harrigan, K. R. (1988). Joint ventures and competitive strategy. *Strategic Management Journal, 9,* 141–158.

Harzing, A. W. K. (1997). Response rates in international mail surveys: Results of a 22-country study. *International Business Review, 6,* 641–665.

Hill, R. C., & Hellriegel, D. (1994). Critical contingencies in joint venture management: Some lessons from managers. *Organization Science, 5,* 594–607.

Hofstede, G. (1980). *Culture's consequences: International differences in work-related values.* Beverly Hills, CA: Sage.

Hofstede, G., Neuijen, B., Ohavy, D. D., & Sanders, G. (1990). Measuring organizational cultures: A quantitative study across twenty cases. *Administrative Science Quarterly, 35,* 286–316.

Inkpen, A. (1995). *The management of international joint ventures: An organizational learning perspective.* London: Routledge.

Inkpen, A. C., & Currall, S. C. (1997). International joint venture trust: An empirical examination. In P. W. Beamish & J. P. Killing (Eds.), *Cooperative strategies: North American perspectives* (pp. 308–334). San Francisco: New Lexington Press.

Inkpen, A. C., & Currall, S. C. (2004). The coevolution of trust, control, and learning in joint ventures. *Organization Science, 15,* 586–599.

Jemison, D. B., & Sitkin, S. B. (1986). Corporate acquisitions: A process perspective. *Academy of Management Review, 11,* 145–163.

Jolly, D. R. (2005). The exogamic nature of Sino-foreign joint ventures. *Asia Pacific Journal of Management, 22,* 285–306.

Killing, J. P. (1983). *Strategies for joint venture success.* New York: Praeger.

Lane, H. W., & Beamish, P. W. (1990) Cross-cultural cooperative behavior in joint ventures in LDCs. *Management International Review, 30*(Special Issue), 87–102.

Li, J., & Guisinger, S. E. (1991). Comparative business failures of foreign-controlled firms in the United States. *Journal of International Business Studies, 22,* 209–224.

Li, J. J., Zhou, K. Z., Lam, S. S. K., & Tse, D. K. (2006). Active trust development of local senior managers in international subsidiaries. *Journal of Business Research, 59,* 73–80.

Lin, X., & Germain, R. (1998, First Quarter). Sustaining satisfactory joint venture relationships: The role of conflict resolution strategy. *Journal of International Business Studies, 29,* 179–196.

Luhmann, N. (1988). Familiarity, confidence, trust: Problems and alternatives. In D. Gambetta (Ed.), *Trust: Making and breaking cooperative relation* (pp. 94–107). Oxford, UK: Blackwell.

Luo, Y., Shenkar, O., & Nyaw, M. (2001). A dual parent perspective on control and performance in international joint ventures: Lessons from a developing economy. *Journal of International Business Studies, 32,* 41–58.

Lyles, M. A., & Reger, R. K. (1993). Managing for autonomy in joint ventures: A longitudinal study of upward influence. *Journal of Management Studies, 30,* 383–404.

Madhok, A. (1995). Revisiting multinational firms' tolerance for joint ventures: A trust-based approach. *Journal of International Business Studies, 26,* 117–138.

Madhok, A. (2006). How much does ownership really matter? Equity and trust relations in joint venture relationships. *Journal of International Business Studies, 37,* 4–11.

Mayer, R. C., Davis, J. H., & Schoorman, F. D. (1995). An integrative model of organizational trust. *Academy of Management Review, 20*(3), 709–734.

McAllister, D. J. (1995). Affect- and cognition-based trust as foundations for interpersonal cooperation in organizations. *Academy of Management Journal, 38,* 24–59.

Mohr, J., & Spekman, R. (1994). Characteristics of partnership success, partnership attributes, communication behavior, and conflict resolution techniques. *Strategic Management Journal, 15,* 135–152.

Newburry, W., & Zeira, Y. (1999). Autonomy and effectiveness of equity international joint ventures (EIJV's): An analysis based on EIJV's in Hungary and Britain. *Journal of Management Studies, 36,* 263–285.

Ng, P. W. K., Lau, C. M., & Nyaw, M. K. (2007). The effect of trust on international joint venture performance in China. *Journal of International Management, 13,* 430–448.

Nunnally, J. C. (1978). *Psychometric theory* (2nd ed.). New York: McGraw-Hill.

Oppenheim, A. N. (1992). *Questionnaire design, interviewing and attitude measurement.* New York: Pinter.

Ozorhon, B., Arditi, D., Dikmen, I., & Birgonul, M. T. (2008). Implications of culture in the performance of international construction joint ventures. *Journal of Construction Engineering and Management, 134,* 361–370.

Park, S. H., & Ungson, G. R. (1997). The effect of national culture, organizational complementarity, and economic motivation on joint venture dissolution. *Academy of Management Journal, 40,* 279–307.

Parkhe, A. (1993). Partner nationality and the structure-performance relationship in strategic alliances. *Organization Science, 4,* 301–324.

Pothukuchi, V., Damanpour, F., Choi, J., Chen, C., & Park, S. (2002). National and organizational culture differences and international joint venture performance. *Journal of International Business Studies, 33,* 243–265.

Roth, K., & Nigh, D. (1992). The effectiveness of headquarters-subsidiary relationships: The role of coordination, control, and conflict. *Journal of Business Research, 25,* 277– 301.

Saxton, T. (1997). The effects of partner and relationship characteristics on alliance outcomes. *Academy of Management Journal, 40,* 443–461.

Schaefer, D. R., & Dillman, D. A. (1998). Development of a standard e-mail methodology: Results of an experiment. *Public Opinion Quarterly, 62,* 378–397.

Schein, E. H. (1992). *Organizational culture and leadership* (2nd ed.). San Francisco: Jossey-Bass.

Seabright, M. A., Levinthal, D. A., & Fichman, M. (1992). Role of individual attachments in the dissolution of interorganizational relationships. *Academy of Management Journal, 35,* 122–160.

Shane, S. (1994). The effect of national culture on the choice between licensing and direct foreign investment. *Strategic Management Journal, 15,* 627–642.

Shenkar, O. (2001). Cultural distance revisited: Towards a more rigorous conceptualization and measurement of cultural differences. *Journal of International Business Studies, 32,* 519–535.

Shenkar, O., & Zeira, Y. (1992). Role conflict and role ambiguity of chief executive officers in international joint ventures. *Journal of International Business Studies, 23,* 55–75.

Sirmon, D. G., & Lane, P. J. (2004). A model of cultural differences and international alliance performance. *Journal of International Business Studies, 35,* 306–319.

Smith, J. B., & Barclay, D. W. (1997, January). The effects of organizational differences and trust on the effectiveness of selling partner relationships. *Journal of Marketing, 61,* 3–21.

Smith, K. G., Carroll, S. J., & Ashford, S. J. (1995). Intra- and interorganizational cooperation: Toward a research agenda. *Academy of Management Journal, 38,* 7–23.

Tallman, S. B., & Shenkar, O. (1994). A managerial decision model of international cooperative venture formation. *Journal of International Business Studies, 25,* 91–114.

Tatoglu, E., & Glaister, K. W. (1998a). Western MNCs' FDI in Turkey: An analysis of location specific factors. *Management International Review, 38*(2), 133–159.

Tatoglu, E., & Glaister, K. W. (1998b). Determinants of foreign direct investment in Turkey. *Thunderbird International Business Review, 40,* 279–314.

Tatoglu, E. & Glaister, K. W. (1998c). Performance of international joint ventures in Turkey: Perspectives of Western firms and Turkish firms. *International Business Review, 7,* 635–656.

Tsai, W., & Ghoshal, S. (1998). Social capital and value creation: The role of intrafirm networks. *Academy of Management Journal, 41,* 464–476.

United Nations Conference on Trade and Development (UNCTAD). (2004). *Prospects for FDI flows, transnational corporation strategies and promotion policies: 2004–2007.*

Wang, Y., & Nicholas, S. (2005). Knowledge transfer, knowledge replication, and learning in non-equity alliances: Operating contractual joint ventures in China. *Management International Review, 45,* 99–118.

Weber, Y., Shenkar, O. & Raveh, A. (1996). National and corporate culture fit in mergers/acquisitions: An exploratory study. *Management Science, 42,* 1215–1227.

Wilkof, M., Brown, D., & Selsky, J. (1995). When the stories are different: The influence of corporate culture mismatches on interorganizational relations. *Journal of Applied Behavioral Science, 31,* 373–388.

Wong, C. S., & Law, K. S. (1999). Managing localization of human resources in the PRC: A practical model. *Journal of World Business, 34,* 26–40.

Yan, A., & Gray, B. (1994). Bargaining power, management control, and performance in United States–Chinese joint ventures: A comparative case study. *Academy of Management Journal, 37,* 1478–1517.

Zeira, Y., & Parker, B. (1995). International joint ventures in the United States: An examination of factors related to their effectiveness. *International Executive, 37*(4), 373–393.

CHAPTER 8

THE USES AND ROLES OF INTERFIRM ACCOUNTING IN STRATEGIC ALLIANCES

Does Transparency Make a Difference?

Ariela Caglio
Angelo Ditillo

ABSTRACT

The aim of this chapter is twofold. On the one hand, we present a review of the most relevant contributions on the uses and functions of accounting information exchanges in partnerships and interfirm alliances. More specifically, we describe the accounting techniques and practices used in boundary-spanning contexts as well as the possible roles that accounting information may play within such forms of organizing, including supporting interfirm value-creation processes. On the other hand, we try to illustrate what the main unaddressed issues in this area are as a premise to exploring one possible way to advance research in this area. In doing so, we interpret transparency as a precise design choice that needs to take into consideration the interrelatedness of alliances' networked contexts as well as of their underlying processes of value creation. Our design approach underlines the influence of the

Strategic Alliances for Value Creation, pages 171–193

network architecture on interorganizational accounting and draws on some measures typical of Social Network Analysis that can be used to direct attention to the peculiar features of alliances and interfirm contexts and to their interorganizational accounting information flows.

INTRODUCTION

Despite a growing body of research on what has been labelled lateral processing of information or horizontal accounting, in the management accounting literature, the debate on the uses and functions of accounting information exchanges between partner firms is still open (Caglio & Ditillo, 2008a). The aim of this chapter is therefore twofold: on the one hand, we present a review of the most relevant contributions on this topic, to synthesize their many and varied results in an attempt to provide an overall picture of the field; on the other hand, we aim at defining what the main unaddressed issues for accounting information in interfirm alliances are, as well as at exploring one possible way to advance research in this area, that is related to the interpretation of transparency as a precise design choice that needs to take into consideration the interrelatedness of alliances' networked contexts as well as of their underlying processes of value creation.

With these objectives in mind, we develop the chapter in two directions: the first one, related to the accounting techniques and practices that can be used to foster transparency of interfirm relationships; the second one, concerning the definition of the possible roles that accounting information may play within such forms of organizing. More specifically, we describe the accounting techniques and practices used in boundary-spanning contexts, such as open-book accounting (OBA), the total cost of ownership (TCO), the value-chain analysis (VCA), target costing, and other interorganizational cost management (IOCM) techniques. To offer a more useful view of such practices, we propose a model that relates them to the stages of development of the alliance relationship, characterized by different information needs and different degrees of transparency. With reference to the roles of accounting in interfirm settings, we underline the fact that although it has quite unanimously been recognized that strategic alliances place new, challenging demands upon accounting, not only have variations in the theoretical and empirical underpinnings inhibited a coherent accumulation of findings, but also the initial doubts about the relevance of the role of accounting outside the borders of firms have for some time limited the kinds of questions that could be asked on its functionalities. Even in more recent times, when the accounting pervasiveness and significance in interorganizational relationships has been ultimately recognized, few contributions have also acknowledged the multifaceted role of accounting. Consequently, any attempt to present a comprehensive picture of its "multifunctionalities" can only be derived from a synthesis of the contributions existing so far in the literature. We try to provide such a picture by differentiating the roles of interfirm accounting into "functionalist" (e.g., for mapping value-creation processes, for coordinating tasks characterized by interdependence, for cooperatively taking interfirm decisions, for the establishment of the partners' responsibilities to each other, and performance measurement) and "nonfunctionalist" (e.g., a constitutional role in the formation and management of trusting relationships, accounting information as inscriptions that are used to represent certain aspects of the alliance's life on paper).

We will conclude by discussing one of the most critical flaws of the literature we mobilize in our chapter, i.e., the lack of specific accuracy on the way in which accounting information exchanges have been described with reference to interfirm alliances. In fact, even though most authors aim at identifying emerging accounting techniques and practices, suited to the "novel" interorganizational settings, the identification of features of interest for the design and functioning of interorganizational accounting information is underestimated or only superficially sketched. To overcome this limitation, we propose a design approach that emphasizes the influence of the network architecture on interorganizational accounting and that draws on a vast array of qualitative measures typical of social network analysis—centrality, density, connectivity, etc.—that can be used to direct attention to the peculiar features of interorganizational accounting information exchanges.

ACCOUNTING TECHNIQUES AND PRACTICES TO MAKE STRATEGIC ALLIANCES TRANSPARENT

Traditionally, accounting research has limited its scope to the boundaries of the firm (Hopwood, 1996). On the contrary, in recent developments within the management accounting literature, specific attempts to investigate the use of accounting in boundary-spanning contexts have been made by several contributors (i.e., Agndal & Nilsson, 2010; Dekker, 2003; Mouritsen, Hansen, & Hansen, 2001; Seal, Cullen, Dunlop, Berry, & Mirghani, 1999; Wouters, Anderson, & Wynstra, 2005). One of the seminal papers that focused on the exchanges of business information between partners in interorganizational relationships is the one by Tomkins (2001). This contribution puts forward fundamental concepts that relate to the need for information, including accounting information, and explores, among others, the roles that uncertainty, interdependence, and duration of the relationship have on the quantity and type of information communicated in different forms of corporate alliances and business networks.

Following this line of research, several management accounting contributors have focused their attention on information exchanges between firms and have used a specific label to indicate interorganizational accounting information flows, i.e., *open-book accounting* (OBA). This terms refers to the disclosure and use of information that is located in the sphere of influence of different companies within the value chain and is usually confidential. In particular, OBA is defined as the systematic exchange of management accounting information that would otherwise be kept secret between legally independent business partners beyond corporate borders (Hoffjan & Kruse, 2006; Kajuter & Kulmala, 2005; Mouritsen et al., 2001).

Some of the contributors to interorganizational accounting information exchanges have focused on OBA *per se,* concentrating on its features and on the enabling factors of successful OBA practices. Some others have seen the interorganizational exchanges of accounting information as a precondition for the implementation of cost management techniques—such as the total cost of ownership (TCO), the value-chain analysis (VCA), target costing, and other interorganizational cost management (IOCM) techniques—that might support interorganizational competitive and performance improvement initiatives for enhancing value-creation processes. The emphasis of these latter contributions has been on the additional opportunities for cost reductions that may arise in alliances and collaborative long-term relationships through these open exchanges compared to traditional cost management in single companies. These topics will be explored in turn in the following section.

Before the discussion of the aforementioned techniques, it is useful to anticipate a framework (see Figure 8.1) that can be employed to better understand the possible uses of such techniques in alliances and partnerships. The different methods that will be described in this chapter—through sharing the idea of enhancing joint value-creation processes by managing costs—can be leveraged at different stages of the alliance relationships life cycle (Caglio, 2008; Tomkins, 2001). These stages are characterized by a different emphasis on the objectives that can be achieved through interorganizational accounting information flows as well as by different information needs and degrees of interorganizational disclosure. In our view, this framework is not only useful to position interorganizational accounting techniques in a coherent theoretical framework, but also it can offer some practical hints on the appropriate matching of objectives, information needs, and stage of the alliance development, to increase the likelihood of success of value-improvement initiatives supported by interorganizational accounting.

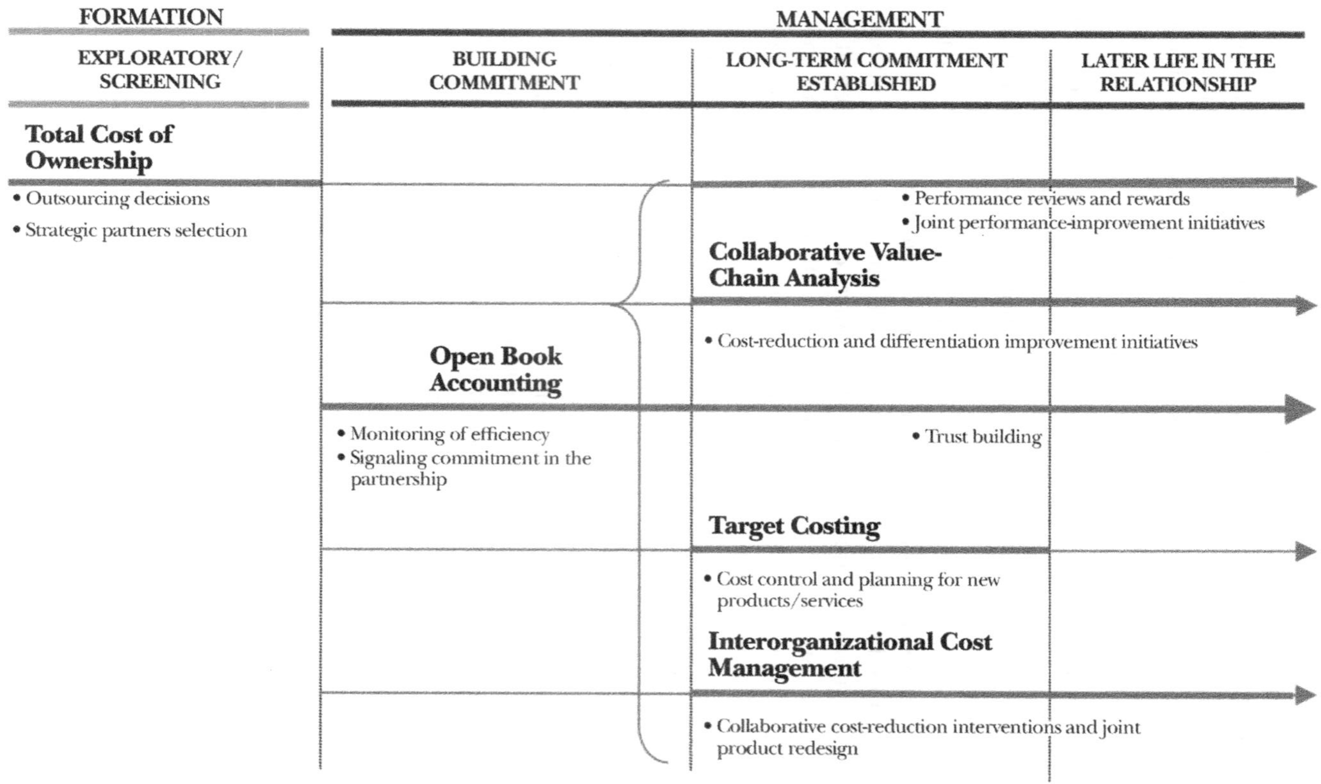

Figure 8.1 Accounting techniques and the development stages of partnerships and alliance relationships (adapted from Caglio, 2008, p. 52).

Open-Book Accounting and its Enabling Factors

When dealing with long-term collaborative partnerships and alliances, a quite common topic in the management accounting literature is the need for "accounting openness" between parties. This necessity translates into the use of *open-book accounting* practices that demand transparency on cost information, including data that would traditionally be kept secret by each partner for use in negotiations (Lamming, 1993, p. 214).

For example, Mouritsen et al. (2001) report how the sharing of accounting information made it possible to benchmark different supplier partners along the value chain and to redesign production and distribution activities, thus leading to cost reductions and improved value creation processes. Also Seal et al. (1999) describe the possibility of cost decreases related to the use of open book accounting practices with supplier partners.

Following this line of research, Kajüter and Kulmala (2005) observe the implementation and utilization of OBA practices in four different alliance networks. Starting from the observation of OBA failures, they apply a contingency framework to define the factors that may facilitate the successful use of OBA. In doing so, they classify the contextual factors determining the success or failure of management accounting data disclosure into exogenous environmental factors such as degree of competition and consequent pressures to cost reductions and economic trend; endogenous firm-specific contextual variables such as firm size, use of advanced cost accounting systems, competitive policy, and long-term commitment to the relationships; and network-specific factors such as type of network, type of product, existence of a specific infrastructure for the open-book process, trust, and social nature of the relationship (Carr & Ng, 1995; Dekker, 2003; Kulmala, 2004; Seal et al., 1999; Tomkins, 2001). This contingency framework is used to derive some common patterns regarding the relational context of open-book accounting emerging from the case analysis. More specifically, evidence showed that, regarding exogenous environmental factors, the disclosure of cost data is likely to occur in cases of intense competition and consequent pressures to cost reductions, as well as in environments characterized by economic growth trends. Concerning endogenous firm-specific contextual variables, the authors found evidence that large size, the use of advanced cost accounting systems, a cooperative approach to partnerships, and a firm's long-term commitment to the relationships may induce OBA. Finally, with reference to network-specific factors, Kajüter and Kulmala maintain that open-book accounting is most likely to work in long-term hierarchical networks that provide functional products, have in place some common infrastructures to support open-book practices, and comprise trust-based relationships.

Also, Hoffjan and Kruse (2006) use a contingency framework to study the effects of the characteristics of business relations—such as the degree of economic dependence, the duration of contract, and the number of contractual partners—on OBA and on OBA features. These latter refer to three different dimensions:

1. base data, comprising only actual data or both actual and planned ones;
2. direction of information flows;
3. degree of disclosure, ranging from
   a. complete: the information is disclosed exactly as it is used and available in the firm's own accounting system, and the data transfer is not delayed or modified in any way;
   b. to limited: an isolated nonsystematic sharing of cost information cannot be regarded as OBA.

The authors find that OBA is used most often in situations with a high degree of economic dependence, where there is a long duration of contract and generally comprises only a one-way exchange of cost information. Regarding the degree of economic dependence, the authors maintain that it influences the way in which OBA is applied: in situations of alliances characterized by unilateral dependence, it is mostly used as an instrument of control and communication. In cases of mutual dependence, OBA is used to foster optimization, as partners tend to pursue the same objectives. Economic dependence also influences the direction of information flows: when it is unilateral, information flows are just unidirectional. The duration of the contract impacts on the objectives that can be achieved through OBA: in relationships supported by short-term contracts, OBA practices can be used only to a limited extent to enhance the profitability of firms. Concerning the number of partners, OBA is easier to implement in bilateral contracts. In case of network agreements, OBA is more difficult to implement, unless there is a firm acting as a nodal point (a situation that is similar to multiple bilateral contracts).

Successful OBA practices lead to the disclosure of private data that can be elaborated through the use of interorganizational cost measurement and management techniques, which will be described in the following section. The common element of such techniques is that they are mainly used by alliance partners to support the implementation of performance-improvement initiatives with the aim of enhancing joint value-creation processes.

Total Cost of Ownership (TCO)

Partnerships and strategic alliances with suppliers have been said to represent an important solution to improve firms' performance, given that purchasing accounts for 60% to 70% of total expenditures in manufacturing and influences all the activities in a firm's value chain (Degraeve, Labro, & Roodhooft, 2004). Such issue has not received so far the attention it deserves from the Western firms. The most advanced examples in this field are referred to Japanese firms, which have been able to obtain large cost reductions as well as improving their competitive positions thanks to closer relationships with their most important suppliers. Some examples of the advantages derived from closer relationships with suppliers include (Ittner, Larcker, Nagar, & Rajan, 1999, p. 255) the reduction of product development costs; improved quality—and consequent decrease of costs due to low quality and defects—through closer and earlier controls of parts provided by suppliers; enhanced efficiency through the incorporation of supplier-originated innovations in products and shared processes (Carr & Ittner, 1992, pp. 48–50).

There can be several mechanisms that can support the involvement of suppliers into performance-improvement initiatives. In particular, there are three categories of supplier selection and monitoring practices that have been described in partnerships (Gietzmann, 1996; Ittner et al., 1999): frequent face-to-face contact and meetings that help decrease the inevitable information asymmetry between the parties; supplier certification, based on extensive investigation of suppliers' manufacturing operations, facilities, and personnel; non-price-selection criteria founded on a total-cost-of-ownership approach, including not only the quoted price but also all the costs of quality and delivery deficiencies, as well as administrative requirements, net of the additional benefits of suppliers collaboration in product development, and cost reduction initiatives (Carr & Ittner, 1992; Ellram & Siferd, 1998).

This last practice is slowly but steadily spreading among firms entertaining long-term, collaborative partnerships with their suppliers and is mainly used in strategic alliances, both as a selection and as a performance measurement and reward mechanism. More specifically, the TCO is a cost-accounting approach that calculates the cost associated with purchased goods and services along the entire supply chain, from the development of a new component (when done collaboratively with a supplier) until the possible warranty claims associated with that part when the product is used by the final customer. Therefore, the TCO approach takes into account a broader spectrum of acquisition costs, including also life-cycle costs associated with employing an item from a certain supplier, as well as the costs incurred once the item is in use by the buyer and by the final customer (Ellram, 1995).

In the management accounting literature, the emphasis has been put on the different possible uses of TCO analysis. Wouters et al. (2005) focus on TCO as an application and extension of activity-based costing logics at an interorganizational level to support decision makers in sourcing decisions. In effect, the authors suggest that purchasing managers may well use TCO techniques to quantify the costs involved in acquiring and using different offerings, such as transaction costs related to purchasing activities (e.g., ordering, freight, quality control) and the costs related to poor quality (e.g., rejection, rework, and warranties) (Carr & Ittner, 1992; Ellram, 1995). Nevertheless, since TCO in its most progressive form is a boundary-spanning concept that involves partners' cooperation and information sharing, the authors observe that the complexity and availability of cost data still represent the most important obstacle to the implementation and use of TCO analysis in strategic alliances.

Ellram (1993), similarly to Wouters et al. (2005), characterizes the TCO as a tool supporting purchasing decisions and, following this line of reasoning, she gives a comprehensive view on TCO items by relating the cost elements to the purchasing transaction. In this way, it is possible to distinguish pretransaction, transaction, and posttransaction costs (Ellram, 1993, p. 7). Pretransaction costs include all the costs incurred prior to placing the order, such as investigating alternative sources, adding suppliers to internal systems, and educating the firm to suppliers' operations. Transaction costs comprise all the costs related to order placement and receipt, and thus include price, order placement, delivery/transportation, tariffs/duties, billing/payment, inspection, returns, follow-up, and corrections. Finally, posttransaction costs (in practice, the least "recognized" costs among all the total cost of ownership items) include all the costs that occur while the supplied item is owned and used by the firm as well as by the firm's final customer (i.e., line fallout, defective goods rejected before sale, product repair in the field, maintenance costs, loss of customer goodwill/reputation of firm). Ellram also indicates four uses of the TCO, adding to the supplier selection, supplier evaluation and performance measurement, supplier motivation and reward, and finally, change processes/reengineering of interdependent activities along the supply chain. In this sense, she underlines that TCO techniques should be "embraced" by purchasing managers as a progressive way of doing business with suppliers and to build long-term commitment into their relationships. In fact, once the information is available and reliable, and the firms have some concrete success stories of using that information to obtain tangible benefits from improved sourcing decisions, the partners can begin to use such information to identify areas for potential development that would enhance their mutual profitability. Hence, the TCO approach is particularly suited to long-term strategic alliances between buyers and suppliers (Caglio, 2008).

Value-Chain Analysis (VCA)

In contrast with these views, Dekker (2003) underlines the limitations of TCO for supporting interfirm relationships when compared to value-chain analysis (VCA). In fact, while in its pure form, a TCO approach focuses only on the effects of buying from a supplier at the buyer's costs and no wider value-chain perspective is taken, a VCA takes into account the costs of all the firms in the value chain (i.e., suppliers and buyers), and recognizes the interdependencies of these activities and costs. Starting from such consideration, Dekker (2003) focuses on the use of VCA in buyer-supplier alliances for coordinating supply-chain interdependences. From an empirical point of view, he describes the new cost model—an ABC model—adopted by the firm under investigation as a response to its recognition of the need to manage the interdependence of activities along its supply chain with a specific group of suppliers. In this case study, VCA is examined jointly with other accounting practices such as benchmarking of collaborating partners, strategic what-if analysis, and monitoring of supply-chain cost trends.

Drawing on Shank and Govindarajan (1992, 1993), this chapter proposes a traditional definition of VCA as a structured method used to coordinate and optimize linkages between activities in the value chain and that suggests where costs can be reduced or differentiation can be improved. On the other hand, Dekker (2003) points out that the traditional view of VCA implies that the analysis is performed by one firm looking beyond its boundaries to its partners; while, in practice, to reap the full benefits of such analysis, VCA would need to be performed jointly and cooperatively by allied firms along the value chain. The author argues that in order to do so, allied firms need to share sensitive cost and performance information, suggesting that open-book accounting is an important constituent of collaborative VCA.[1]

In a similar vein, Dekker and Van Goor (2000) emphasize the usefulness of collaborative VCA for alliances by presenting a case study in the pharmaceutical industry. They show how activity-based costing can be used in shared business decisions about relocating and modifying logistics in order to increase the profits of alliance partners along the whole supply chain. Based on this experience, they conclude that organizations' performances can benefit from the strategic exploitation of value chains' reciprocal linkages, and that this can be done only by employing collaborative cost analysis.

However, there are two main challenges linked to applying collaborative VCA in practice. The first one is related to the potentially different advancement of the cost-accounting systems of value chain partners. In effect, it is quite common to find the coexistence of accounting systems with dissimilar degrees of sophistication. In addition, it is quite rare that firms have already in place a cost-accounting system that is designed to allocate costs to activities (Caglio & Ditillo, 2008b). A second difficulty can be related to potential opportunism and conflicts that may arise when partners decide to share sensitive cost and performance information. To face this challenge, partners need to be trustful that this information will not be used in an adversarial way. At early stages of the relationship, when likely trust is not high, oftentimes partners decide to use formal contractual agreements on profit and cost sharing, or confidentiality agreements for information exchanges before deciding to carry out a collaborative VCA (Dekker, 2003). An alternative way, which is practicable when the relationship is already consolidated, is the one chosen by the firm described by Dekker (2003). To increase the willingness of suppliers to participate in the collaborative VCA project, this firm declared that the disclosed information would not be used for direct comparisons between competitor suppliers. Obviously, if the firm had not respected this agreement, in turn, it would have damaged its reputation and would have compromised the possibility of implementing the cost-improvement initiative aimed at improving joint value creation.

Target Costing and Interorganizational Cost Management Techniques

If Dekker (2003), as previously illustrated, focused on the sharing of accounting information to support VCA to coordinate activities along the supply chain, some other authors have emphasized the use of open-book accounting as linked to the application of well-known approaches for cost reduction and planning, such as *target costing* and *functional analysis* (Carr & Ng, 1995; Cooper & Slagmulder, 1997, 1999; Mouritsen et al., 2001).

Carr and Ng (1995), for example, describe Nissan's method for total cost control, characterized by an approach based on OBA and target-costing principles. The authors illustrated, in particular, how such an approach was applied in the context of UK transplant operations and how it was extended to encompass local suppliers. In this respect, the main issues depicted in the paper are how Nissan was able to achieve total cost control through the whole supply chain (by means of peculiar techniques called "Total Cost Reduction Activity" and "Total Cost Achieving Activity") and how the firm used OBA to control the discrepancies of supplier partners from the target cost.

Mouritsen et al. (2001) analyzed the processes of developing interorganizational controls such as open-book accounting systems and target costing/functional analysis in an alarm systems manufacturer. The authors reported some control problems related to the outsourced development processes, which initiated a debate about which control strategies the firm needed to use interorganizationally. Target-cost management, through its functional analysis component, was suggested and thereafter implemented to reestablish control over the partnership. More specifically, functional analysis encouraged the firm and its partners to engage in a systematic discussion about the functionalities of the products and gained strategic importance as it allowed the firm to maintain a strong market position. Regarding open-book practices, the authors reported that the alarm systems manufacturer showed the overall purchasing budget to its suppliers as a way to emphasize the importance of cost efficiency.

While the contributions to target cost essentially look at the extended use of "intrafirm" costing approaches to a boundary spanning context, Cooper and Slagmulder (2004) take a step further by searching for peculiar "interfirm" costing solutions; i.e., for *interorganizational cost management (IOCM)* techniques. The authors maintain that target costing lies at the heart of IOCM. However, they suggest that target costing is an arm's-length cost-management technique as it does not actively involve the supplier in the buyer's cost-management program. The key extension of IOCM beyond intrafirm cost-management techniques is the active involvement of both the buyer's and supplier's design teams in the joint management of costs and in the collaborative identification of opportunities for joint value creation through cost reductions (Cooper & Slagmulder, 2004, p. 6). Focusing on product design in formalized buyer-supplier interactions, the authors aim to highlight the existence of a pattern of relationships between IOCM practices and the characteristics of the relational contexts associated with them.[2] More specifically, there are three IOCM techniques to support cost reduction interventions. The first one, "functionality-price-quality (FPQ) tradeoffs," can help in resolving minor cost overrun problems and involves only modest specification changes and hence limited interactions among the firms' design engineers. At the heart of a successful FPQ trade-off lies an effective value-engineering program. The second technique, "interorganizational cost investigations," is applied when FPQ trade-offs are unable to produce the desired level of cost reductions. There are two major differences with FPQ trade-offs: the ability to include design engineers from more than two firms in the supply chain, and the broader scope of the design changes contemplated, which include all of the steps from raw material to finished product. The final IOCM technique, "concurrent cost management," addresses cost problems that demand the most important cost reduction levels of all the three techniques. It requires the most intense interactions between the buyer's and supplier's design engineers and can lead to fundamental changes in both the buyer's product and the outsourced components. This is the technique that can have the higher impact in terms of improving value creation in buyer-supplier alliances.

In sum, in partnerships and alliances, IOCM techniques may be used to achieve the collaborative management of costs with the aim of improving the overall performance of each partner firm along the value chain. The outcomes associated with interorganizational cost-management systems include identifying ways of reducing costs and increasing revenues through activities such as joint product development and joint interorganizational cost investigations (Cooper & Slagmulder, 2004). Interorganizational cost-management techniques have a cooperative nature, because the underlying activities are undertaken with the common goal of creating value for all the involved partners through the revision of cost structures at an interorganizational level (Coad & Cullen, 2006; Mouritsen et al., 2001).

THE MULTIPLE ROLES OF INTERFIRM ACCOUNTING: WHY TO PURSUE TRANSPARENCY IN ALLIANCES

As evidenced in part by the techniques and practices described in the previous section, it has quite unanimously been recognized that interorganizational partnerships place new, challenging demands upon accounting. In contrast, many and varied views exist on the roles that accounting may play in interfirm contexts, ranging from hardly any role to very specific ones, given certain contextual settings.

Gietzmann (1996) and Gietzmann and Larsen (1998) are among the most critical commentators on the functions of accounting in supporting the development of interorganizational relationships. In fact, Gietzmann maintains that traditional accounting procedures are poorly suited to motivating cooperative working practices. Indeed, the reason for weak results of collaborative alliances in the West—when compared to Japanese initiatives—is in part due to continued reliance upon traditional accounting governance structures, such as the "make-or-buy" competitive bidding calculus. From a managerial accounting point of view, the subcontractor control problem is conventionally characterized as one of dichotomous competition between the firm and its suppliers; i.e., as a make-or-buy decision. However, the author argues that such vision conceals the full span of potential for managerial decision making and governance-structure design,[3] while the application of the habitual make-or-buy logics may even act as a major obstacle to the formation of close alliances with suppliers and to the exploitation of collaborative opportunities of joint value creation.

Baiman and Rajan (2002) interpret accounting information as one of the interorganizational design instruments that must be considered to stimulate cooperation between firms along the supply chain. In their view, the role of accounting in alliances is to mitigate incentive problems related to collaboration and joint value creation and to the division of surpluses derived from innovation. Anyhow, they maintain that different incentive systems, among which are accounting based, are substitutable so that the functions that accounting information may play are contingent upon the existence of other incentive systems. For example, the design of a supplier hierarchy can be seen as a substitute for accounting information about product quality and process performance.

Among those who clearly posited a distinct role for accounting in partnerships and alliances, there are some functionalist[4] contributors who explicitly linked such roles to *joint value-creation processes.* For example, Lambert, Stock, and Ellram (1998) maintain that partnerships are often activated to increase the value for the final customers and see accounting as fundamental to reach such an objective. They comment on this point: "Openness or transparency enabled via information exchange is seen as a vital element in creating a competitive interorganizational production system" (p. 48). The authors indicate that it is necessary that every element of the overall cost of the product or service offered to the market is visible to all the firms involved in its creation for any value-improvement initiative to succeed. Without the sharing of accounting data, each firm would just acknowledge its own internal costs and the price paid to other counterparts. The cost structure that the price information underlies would remain unknown, and no specific cost-reduction project would be jointly feasible. Transparency makes costs of all the alliance partners visible, thus jointly manageable.

According to Kulmala (2002), in theory, the sharing of sensitive accounting information would be useful for many different purposes, such as joint supply-chain planning and goal setting, for defining product-mix selections, for supporting product-development decisions, and for budgeting. However, the author comments that empirical observations have shown that OBA applications are focused almost exclusively on the improvement of the efficiency of partners' activities and on the initiation of process-development initiatives aimed at increasing the value generated by the partners.

Other contributors emphasized other important roles for accounting in interfirm alliances, going from the control of the relationship to more symbolic, nonfunctionalist roles.

Tomkins (2001) relates the use of information in interfirm alliances to two functions: the mastery of events and the development of trust. The author suggests that interfirm *coordination* is based on "Type II information," which is needed for the mastery of events by partner firms as if they form one single entity. He argues that Type II information consists of information that enables entities to plan and make decisions on collaborative futures and, more specifically, to make economic judgments on strategies, investments, and ongoing operations. On the other hand, Tomkins refers to information required to *warrant trust* as "Type I information," consisting of information on competence and on integrity of partners in both action and communication.

Similar to Tomkins (2001), drawing on the aforementioned distinction between Type I and Type II information, Dekker (2004) conceives information exchanges as an *ex post* (outcome) control mechanism used to *manage unresolved control problems deriving mainly from high levels of interdependencies.* For example, in order to manage tasks characterized by sequential interdependence, it is suggested that timely information about ordering quantities and expected demand as well as standard ordering procedures are needed. On the contrary, for the coordination of tasks characterized by reciprocal interdependence, a broader set of more complex mechanisms is necessary, including not only the aforementioned information exchanges but also task planning and specification, budgeting, progress evaluation, and performance measurement. Also, Dekker (2003) maintains that accounting is key to supporting interorganizational coordination between the allied firms. Accounting is essential to *cooperatively take decisions* at the level of the entire supply chain, such as whether to proceed with improvement projects or not, and to *define how to allocate the value created jointly by the partners.* The empirical evidence provided by the author reveals also a different use of the cost information for interorganizational coordination, which is in *joint communication, cooperation, and negotiation* between the partners.

Following this line of research, Angdal and Nilsson (2010) show how the sharing of accounting information can shape a purchasing partnership, leading it toward a more relational—versus transactional—orientation. Opening the books in alliances is said to be part of *trust building.* In fact, in relational contexts—where asset specificity is high, the counterparts are not easily substitutable, and the activities of the partners are highly interdependent—there are long-term incentives for the parties to disclose cost data through OBA practices. Such incentives are related to the benefits that are directly linked to the sharing of data in question and are, for example, the *increased chances of future collaboration,* better and *fairer profit sharing,* and, from the point of view of the suppliers, compensation for volume and factor cost fluctuations. The authors also observe that, in line with market-based controls, interorganizational accounting-information exchanges can also be used to contain behavioral uncertainties in arm's-length relationships. In addition, they show how knowledge about product costs can inspire an increasingly market-based approach to the management of interfirm relationships as cost data can be used to commoditize products to implement a more transactional purchasing strategy (Angdal & Nilsson, 2010, pp. 163–164).

Cost information is central for the *control of alliance relationships* also for Cooper and Slagmulder (2004). The authors observe that interfirm relational contexts are characterized by incomplete contracting, as it is neither possible nor practical to develop contracts that completely specify all of the potential outcomes of the interactions between both parties

(Baiman & Rajan, 2002). Consequently, interorganizational cost information exchanges may be used to *reduce the unavoidable information asymmetries* between the buyer and the supplier, especially regarding the relationship between the specifications for the outsourced item established by the buyer and the resulting costs to the supplier. Evidence showed that partner firms use accounting information to enable their design teams to coordinate and cooperate effectively with the aim of *identifying low-cost solutions* by either changing the specifications of the outsourced items or the end product itself.

Seal et al. (1999) discuss three important roles of management accounting information in interfirm relationships related to the use of such information: firstly, in the make-or-buy decision that can lead to the initiation of a partnership; secondly, in the actual management of the partnership; and finally, in the *establishment of the partners' responsibilities to each other*, which can also be seen in terms of *performance measurement*. According to the authors, the analogy between transfer pricing and negotiating over cost reductions in alliances is evident. In fact, agreements about transfer-pricing rules are important stabilizers within divisionalized companies sharing a common owner. The problem of stability is even more important in strategic partnerships, where the process of agreeing on costing issues and the sharing of benefits becomes an aid to collaboration in the absence of authority. Nonetheless, unlike with transfer pricing, equity and legitimacy must be granted in the interfirm agreement, not by means of authority. In such arrangements, there is no single owner of the accounting system and no central authority to lay down accounting rules. Therefore "technical solutions that merely demonstrate how the costs and benefits of a partnership are identified and measured are important but must also contribute towards the overriding issues of agreeing on an equitable distribution of the costs and benefits of co-operation" (Seal et al., 1999, p. 320). In this sense, the authors identify for accounting a *constitutional role* in the formation and management of trusting alliance relationships that may transcend the technical level to become more *symbolic*.[5]

It is interesting to notice that, independently from specific "accounting situations," openness has also been interpreted as a deliberated strategy to foster cooperative alliances between firms situated in a supply chain (Agndal & Nilsson, 2010; Caglio, 2008; Kulmala, 2002; Seal et al., 1999). With open-book agreements, a firm reveals its cost structure to another independent firm not only to conduct joint cost-reduction efforts and value improvement initiatives but also to *show commitment to the relationship* and to strengthen its position among competing firms in the supply chain through *mutual learning*. In this sense, accounting information can be seen also as a *stabilizer of alliances* and be interpreted as an actor supporting the shaping and consolidation of interorganizational alliances (Mouritsen & Thrane,

2006). However, while Seal et al. indicated that open-book accounting may even play a "constitutional role" in the establishment of cooperative and trusting alliances, Mouritsen et al. (2001) introduced trust as a prerequisite of such openness. In effect, quite in close proximity to this symbolic idea of accounting, Mouritsen (1999) and Mouritsen et al. observe that accounting information does not only have a role in enabling control of interorganizational processes at a distance but may also take part in the *re-presentation of phenomena* such as technology, organization, and strategy, thereby retranslating organizational power relations, identity, and core competencies of the firms involved into the interorganizational relationship. In this perspective, accounting information exchanges are inscriptions (Robson, 1992) that are used to represent certain aspects of the alliance's life on paper, including joint value-creation processes.

DESIGNING INTERFIRM ACCOUNTING THROUGH A NETWORK PERSPECTIVE

The analysis of the contributions on accounting in partnerships and alliances has revealed a certain variety in terms of theoretical approaches—among which are the theory of incomplete contracting applied to incentive problems (Baiman & Rajan, 2002; Gietzmann, 1996; Gietzmann & Larsen, 1998), the organizational theory and the transaction cost economics (Dekker, 2003, 2004), the Latourian framework (Mouritsen, 1999; Mouritsen et al., 2001), the structuration theory (Seal, Berry, & Cullen, 2004)—and empirical investigations, ranging from economic modelling on incentives design (Baiman & Rajan, 2002; Gietzmann & Larsen, 1998) to questionnaire surveys (Gietzmann, 1996), exploratory field-based research projects (Cooper & Slagmulder, 2004), in-depth case studies (Dekker, 2003, 2004; Seal et al., 1999), and interpretive case studies (Mouritsen, 1999; Mouritsen et al., 2001; Seal et al., 2004). For this reason, the body of knowledge generated so far is a bit fragmented and has not yet developed sufficient "critical mass" to confirm findings. Besides, the initial doubts about the relevance of the role of accounting outside firms' organizational boundaries (e.g., Gietzmann, 1996; Gietzmann & Larsen, 1998) have for some time limited the kinds of questions that could be asked on its role and functionalities, with expectations of it often couched in terms of its presence or absence in interorganizational settings.

Alongside with this point, it should be noted that though different forms of relational contexts have been observed—ranging from relationships in which the interactions are close to market driven, to strategic partnerships in which the firms have signalled their desire to work together closely over the long-term—the aforementioned contributions explore mainly one specific type of alliance relationships; i.e., buyer–supplier relations. Even though such concentration is beneficial for the accumulation of results in order to provide consistent findings, without accommodating other types of interfirm relationships into research, contributors are unlikely to address all the main pertinent issues for the understanding of accounting techniques and practices in interorganizational settings, especially referring to more "horizontal" relationships and downstream ones.

Yet one of the most important flaws that has emerged from the reviewed literature is related to the lack of specific accuracy on the way in which accounting-information exchanges in partnerships and alliances have been described. In fact, even though most authors aim at identifying emerging accounting techniques and practices, suited to the "novel" interorganizational settings, the identification of features of interest for the design and functioning of interorganizational accounting-information exchanges—such as which specific accounting information is being exchanged, with what frequency, in which way, whether it is actually used by partners and for which purposes, what are the relevant dimensions of this information (scope, timeliness, aggregation), etc.—is underestimated or only superficially sketched.

With reference to this issue, it should also be noted that the range and depth of characterizations of interorganizational accounting in alliances has been constrained by the unit of analysis chosen by previous contributors. For example, OBA has been mainly investigated in dyadic relationships (Kulmala, 2002; Mouritsen et al., 2001; Seal et al., 1999), though such an approach is usually applied to an entire set of collaborating firms. Also, interorganizational cost-accounting techniques, even when referred to many allied firms forming a network, have been analyzed only with reference to selected dyadic relationships (Cooper & Slagmulder, 2004). As observed also by Chua and Mahama (2007, p. 48), interfirm alliances are nested within broad networks, however most accounting contributors represent them as dyadic relationships, thus simplifying the multifaceted reality of such alliances. Consequently, researchers have been able neither to grasp the complete picture of accounting practices in alliances nor to propose some guiding principles for designing accounting-information exchanges that would take into account the heterogeneity of networked interorganizational contexts and of the underlying value-creation processes. In effect, each alliance is a peculiar combination of multiple and multifaceted relationships that can be fully understood not by describing each pair or different pairs of relationships at a time, but rather by considering all the relationships as a whole and at the same time. The more global and simultaneous the investigation of such a complex nexus of relationships is, the more the view becomes comprehensive and the design of such accounting information flows, uniquely specified and well-suited to reflect the peculiar joint processes of the value generation of each specific alliance.

One way of overcoming the limitation of extant literature would be to look at the entire set of accounting-information flows taking place between all the collaborating firms at the same time and looking at these information exchanges as a network. In this way only would it be possible to explore the impact that certain accounting information exchanges between two firms have on other firms and/or relationships, and their differential influence on the overall alliance as a starting point to fully discuss the corresponding design implications. This comprehensive set of accounting-information flows between collaborating firms could be defined as an Accounting Information Network (AIN). This latter can be characterized as a multilevel information system aiming at organizing, processing, and sharing accounting information in order to plan a collaborative future by setting down the objectives of the alliance and defining their feasibility as well as the partners' relative roles; control that the actions of the collaborative partners are in line with defined goals and expectations; and support multilayered decision making through the representation of joint value-creation processes (Amigoni, Caglio, & Ditillo, 2003; Caglio & Ditillo, 2008a, 2008b, 2010). The consideration of interorganizational accounting information as a network of accounting information exchanges would permit the investigation of their structural properties as a basis for developing some design principles that could be adapted to take into account the specificities of alliance contexts and of the value-creation processes that interorganizational accounting information flows map and make visible. One possible avenue to meaningfully mobilize future research in this direction is to incorporate, into the investigation of accounting in alliances, social network analysis (SNA), a methodology that is quite innovative for the accounting literature but which has already been applied in a large variety of settings, ranging from sociology and anthropology to social psychology, strategy, and organizational studies. SNA body of techniques and tools could be applied to map and measure the flows between different partner entities, unveiling patterns of interactions and exchanges of information and resources (Wasserman & Faust, 1994). Design implications and guidelines could be fruitfully explored by leveraging on the vast array of qualitative measures typical of SNA. Some of the key dimensions that would merit attention are (Wasserman & Faust, 1994) *centralization,* which refers to the extent to which a firm in the alliance is focal in the joint value-creation processes with remaining actors considerably less central; *density,* which describes the general level of linkage among the firms in an alliance as the number of connections among their value chains, expressed as a proportion of the maximum possible number of them; and *connectivity,* which is the minimum number of firms whose removal would not allow the partnership to remain connected and thus measures the level of cohesion of an alliance and of its joint value creation processes. These measures could be used to direct attention to interesting features of the alliance accounting-information networks. Through this approach, the role and configuration of interorganizational accounting information in partnerships and alliances would be not only described but also explained in the advantage of the state of our knowledge on how to design interfirm accounting information flows.

NOTES

1. Porter (1985) was rather skeptical about accounting usefulness in supporting VCA. In fact, he maintained that "While accounting systems do contain useful data for cost analysis, they often get in the way of strategic cost analysis" (p. 63). Porter's critique is referred to traditional management accounting practices that are based on an internally oriented concept of value-added disregarding the issue of managing interdependences between firms along the value chain. Also, Hergert and Morris (1989) identified three important limitations of traditional accounting systems for performing a VCA: first of all, they focus on responsibility centers and not on critical activities; secondly, they do not account for interdependencies between subunits and activities of such subunits; finally, they do not collect any information about the cost drivers providing insufficient clues about the economics of performing a certain activity. Several authors mention the use of activity-based costing analysis as a basis for performing VCA (Guilding, Cravens, & Tayles, 2000; Shank & Govindarajan, 1992, 1993) to solve the limitations outlined by Hergert and Morris. The cost-driver information derived from the analysis can be used, as suggested by Porter, to coordinate the performance of activities across the supply chain (Dekker, 2003).
2. Six attributes are of particular importance when determining the appropriate relational context for IOCM. Four of these attributes—design dependence, resource sharing, supplier participation, and bilateral commitment—relate to interaction characteristics of the buyer-supplier relationship. The final two—incentive and protective mechanism—pertain to the choices surrounding the governance structure of the buyer-supplier relationship.
3. In effect, the author observes that the traditional make-or-buy calculus is centered upon too restrictive a model of interorganizational interaction. This is due to the origins of such decision calculus, which are embedded within an ideology of dichotomous choice between market transactions and hierarchically controlled exchanges (Gietzmann, 1996, p. 612).
4. Chenhall (2003) proposes the distinction between "functionalist" approaches; i.e., those that consider the utility of accounting in achieving purposeful outcomes and assume that accounting assists managers in accomplishing organizational goals, and "nonfunctionalist" approaches; i.e., those that underline the fact that the roles that accounting may play are influenced also by factors other than the rational economic and technical, such as social, institutional, or political motivations. On this point see also Caglio and Ditillo (2008a).

5. In another paper, Seal et al (2004) conceive interorganizational accounting as "an expert system that is produced and re-produced through the interactions between supply chain actors and wider institutional influences" (p. 74) and interfirm accounting practices are interpreted as modalities (Giddens, 1991a, 1991b).

REFERENCES

Agndal, H., & Nilsson U. (2010). Different open book accounting practices for different purchasing strategies. *Management Accounting Research, 21,* 147–166.

Amigoni, F., Caglio, A., & Ditillo, A. (2003). Dis-integration through integration: The emergence of accounting information networks. In A. Bhimani (Ed.), *Management accounting in the digital economy* (pp. 17–35). New York: Oxford University Press.

Baiman, S., & Rajan, M. V. (2002). Incentive issues in interfirm relationships. *Accounting, Organizations and Society, 27,* 213–238.

Caglio, A. (2008). *Il costing oltre i confini d'impresa.* Milan, Italy: McGraw-Hill.

Caglio, A., & Ditillo, A. (2008a). A review and discussion of management control in interfirm relationships: Achievements and future directions. *Accounting, Organizations and Society, 33,* 865–898.

Caglio, A., & Ditillo, A. (2008b). *Controlling collaboration between firms. How to build and maintain successful relationships with external partners.* Oxford, UK: Elsevier.

Caglio, A., & Ditillo, A. (2010). Interdependence and accounting information exchanges in interfirm relationships. *Journal of Management and Governance.* doi: 10.1007/s10997-010-9136-3

Carr, C., & Ng, J. (1995). Total cost control: Nissan and its U.K. supplier partnerships. *Management Accounting Research, 6,* 347–365.

Carr, L.P., & Ittner, C. D. (1992, Fall). Measuring the cost of ownership. *Journal of Cost Management,* 42–51.

Chenhall, R. H. (2003). Management control systems design within its organizational context: Findings from contingency-based research and directions for the future. *Accounting, Organizations and Society, 28,* 127–168.

Chua, W. F., & Mahama, H. (2007). The effect of network ties on accounting controls in a supply alliance: Field study evidence. *Contemporary Accounting Research, 24,* 47–86.

Coad, A. F., & Cullen, J. (2006). Interorganizational cost management: Towards an evolutionary perspective. *Management Accounting Research, 17,* 342–369.

Cooper, R., & Slagmulder, R. (1997). *Target costing and value engineering.* Portland, OR: Productivity Press.

Cooper, R., & Slagmulder, R. (1999). *Supply chain development for the lean enterprise.* Portland, OR: Productivity Press.

Cooper, R., & Slagmulder, R. (2004). Interorganizational cost management and relational context. *Accounting, Organizations and Society, 29,* 1–26.

Degraeve, Z., Labro, E., & Roodhooft, F. (2004). An evaluation of vendor selection models from a total cost of ownership perspective. *European Journal of Operational Research, 125,* 34–58.

Dekker, H. C. (2003). Value chain analysis in interfirm relationships: A field study. *Management Accounting Research, 14,* 1–23.

Dekker, H. C. (2004). Control of interorganizational relationships: Evidence on appropriation concerns and coordination requirements. *Accounting, Organizations and Society, 29,* 27–49.

Dekker, H. C., & Van Goor, A. R. (2000). Supply chain management and management accounting: A case study of activity-based costing. *International Journal of Logistics, 3*(1), 41–52.

Ellram, L. M. (1993, Fall). Total cost of ownership: Elements and implementation. *International Journal of Purchasing and Materials Management,* 3–11.

Ellram, L. M. (1995, Winter). Activity-based costing and total cost of ownership: A critical linkage. *Journal of Cost Management,* 22–30.

Ellram, L. M., & Siferd, S. P. (1998). Total cost of ownership: A key concept in strategic cost management decisions. *Journal of Business Logistics, 19*(1), 55–84.

Giddens, A. (1991a). *The consequences of modernity.* Cambridge, UK: Polity Press.

Giddens, A. (1991b). *Modernity and self-identity.* Cambridge, UK: Polity Press.

Gietzmann, M. B. (1996). Incomplete contracts and the make-or-buy decision: Governance design and attainable flexibility. *Accounting, Organizations and Society, 21,* 611–626.

Gietzmann, M. B., & Larsen, J. G. (1998). Motivating subcontractors to perform development and design tasks. *Management Accounting Research, 9,* 285–309.

Guilding, C., Cravens, K. S., & Tayles, M. (2000). An international comparison of strategic management accounting practices. *Management Accounting Research, 11,* 113–135.

Hergert, M., & Morris, D. (1989). Accounting data for value chain analysis. *Strategic Management Journal, 10,* 175–188.

Hoffjan, A., & Kruse, H. (2006). Open book accounting in supply chains: When and how is it used in practice? *Cost Management, 20*(6), 40–47.

Hopwood, A. G. (1996). Looking across rather than up and down: On the need to explore the lateral processing of information. *Accounting, Organizations and Society, 21,* 589–590.

Ittner, C. D., Larcker, D. F., Nagar, V., & Rajan, M. V. (1999). Supplier selection, monitoring practices, and firm performance. *Journal of Accounting and Public Policy, 18,* 253–281.

Kajüter, P., & Kulmala, H. (2005). Open-book accounting in networks: Potential achievements and reasons for failures. *Management Accounting Research, 16,* 179–204.

Kulmala, H. (2004). Developing cost management in customer-supplier relationships: Three case studies. *Journal of Purchasing and Supply Management, 10,* 65–77.

Kulmala, H. I. (2002). Open-book accounting in networks. *Finnish Journal of Business Economics, 51,* 157–177.

Lambert, D., Stock, J., & Ellram, L. M. (1998) *Fundamentals of logistics management.* New York: McGraw-Hill.

Lamming, R. (1993). *Beyond partnership. Strategies for innovation and lean supply.* New York: Prentice Hall.

Mouritsen, J. (1999). The flexible firm: Strategies for a subcontractor's management control. *Accounting, Organizations and Society, 24,* 31–55.

Mouritsen, J., Hansen, A., & Hansen, C. Ø. (2001). Interorganizational controls and organizational competencies: Episodes around target cost management/functional analysis and open book accounting. *Management Accounting Research, 12,* 221–244.

Mouritsen, J., & Thrane, S. (2006). Accounting, network complementarities and the development of interorganizational relations. *Accounting, Organizations and Society, 31,* 241–275.

Porter, M. E. (1985). *Competitive advantage.* New York: Free Press.

Robson, K. (1992). Accounting numbers as "inscription": Action at a distance and the development of accounting. *Accounting, Organization and Society, 17,* 685–708.

Seal, W. B., Cullen, J., Dunlop, A., Berry, A., & Mirghani, A. (1999). Enacting a European supply chain: The role of management accounting. *Management Accounting Research, 10,* 303–322.

Seal, W., Berry, A., & Cullen, J. (2004). Disembedding the supply chain: Institutionalized reflexivity and inter-firm accounting. *Accounting, Organizations and Society, 29,* 73–92.

Shank, J. K., & Govindarajan, V. (1992). Strategic cost management: The value chain perspective. *Management Accounting Research, 4,* 177–197.

Shank, J. K., & Govindarajan, V. (1993). *Strategic cost management.* New York: Free Press.

Tomkins, C. (2001). Interdependencies, trust and information in relationships, alliances and networks. *Accounting, Organizations and Society, 26,* 161–191.

Wasserman, S., & Faust, K. (1994). *Social network analysis: Methods and applications.* Cambridge, UK: Cambridge University Press.

Wouters, M., Anderson, J. C., & Wynstra, F. (2005). The adoption of total cost of ownership for sourcing decisions—A structural equation analysis. *Accounting, Organizations and Society, 30,* 167–191.

CHAPTER 9

OUTCOMES OF WESTERN MANAGEMENT CONTROL IN INTERNATIONAL JOINT VENTURES

The Local Partner Perspective

Xiaohua Lin

ABSTRACT

In the context of U.S.–Chinese joint ventures, we revisit the issue of management control arrangement in international joint ventures by simultaneously considering local partners' performance and learning motives. We then examine the effect of U.S. management control on Chinese partners' acquisitions of managerial knowledge and joint venture performance. We developed our model by synthesizing field interview data and existing literature, which reflects the perspective of local partners. The subsequent tests of survey data reveal the dilemma Chinese joint venture partners face when dealing with U.S. management control: while the Chinese partners seek to learn about advanced managerial knowledge, and they generally favor such control, their emphasis on joint venture performance leads to objection to it. Our results

Strategic Alliances for Value Creation, pages 195–213

suggest that U.S. management control does not serve the purposes of Chinese management learning since it is detrimental to quality interactions. Joint venture performance also suffers under U.S. management control due to increased interpartner conflicts. These results offer an important implication for Western joint venture partners, that is, they should endeavor to improve the way control is exercised in order to build positive relationships and performance outcomes.

INTRODUCTION

In the volumes of international joint venture literature, there are at least two related and unsolved issues regarding management control. First, it is not altogether clear *how* the control structure is determined, particularly since equity position is necessarily associated with management control. Second, the control-performance link has not been fully established conceptually or empirically. Recent research has faced greater complexity with the realization that IJVs are a key venue for building organizational capabilities through the acquisition of knowledge between partners (Hamel, 1991; Kogut, 1988; Lin, 2005). This is an important departure from established models of IJV management, which have focused on the financial and operational performance of IJVs. The control implications of learning-oriented IJVs have been discussed only at the conceptual level (e.g., Hamel, 1991). Although research has begun to associate control with both IJV performance and learning (Cyr & Schneider, 1996; Makhija & Ganesh, 1987), scholars have rarely examined whether control impacts the two aspects of organizational outcomes in a consistent fashion. While it is generally recognized that learning will ultimately lead to enhanced organizational capabilities and competitive positions, there is the potential that learning and performance goals can conflict during the IJV operation, and this may be considered a managerial paradox (Inkpen, 1997). At this stage of conceptualization, however, there are issues that have not been considered or empirically established to a satisfactory degree. One of these issues is the tension between learning and performance in conventional terms. Third, within the context of IJVs formed between partners from developed and developing countries, the existing literature has suffered a Western-centric approach, rarely taking into account the perceptions of local partners (Hitt, Li, & Worthington, 2005; Tsang, 2001). This is unfortunate. For example, control structure must be a result of the bargaining process between local and foreign partners. Without knowing local the partners' perspective, foreign partners cannot effectively negotiate a control arrangement, and subsequently they will use the chosen control structure to serve its goals. With regard to local partner learning, the lack of attention to local partner perspective has led to a pervasive ignorance of indigenous interests in acquiring managerial knowledge and skills from Western partners. Increasingly, upgrading managerial knowledge has been recognized by both local and foreign partners as a key ingredient in managing a successful IJV (Inkpen, 1997; Li & Shenkar, 1996). While existing literature has largely built upon the perceptions of foreign partners from Western multinational companies, there is a growing realization that the "learning versus performance" paradox also faces local partners, and such a paradox may have implications for the continuing debate over relationships between control, conflicts, and performance in IJVs operating in less developed countries (Lyles & Salk, 1996).

The objective of the current study is to rectify this oversight by (a) simultaneously specifying the effect of both learning and performance motives of IJV partners on their choice of control structure and in turn the effect of a chosen control structure on actual learning and performance, (b) considering management control as a focal mechanism through which IJV performance and partner learning take place, and (c) examining these issues from the perspective of local partners, as opposed to foreign partners. In the rest of the study, we first review prior literature on IJV performance and learning, with a focus on the effect of control. We then introduce research methodology, including measurement development, sampling, and data collection that involved surveying 135 Chinese managers in Chinese–U.S. joint ventures. We subsequently report findings, discuss research and managerial implications, and consider limitations of the current study and future research directions.

CONCEPTUAL MODEL

The conceptual model (Figure 9.1) and hypotheses were developed by synthesizing findings from our fieldwork with Chinese JV partners and relevant research reflecting the perspective of Chinese IJV partners as well as local partners in other developing countries. Guided by the grounded-theory development principles (Danis & Parkhe, 2002; Hamel, 1991), we interviewed Chinese managers from 12 Sino–U.S. JVs. The JVs were selected from several manufacturing sectors, including transportation equipment, industrial equipment, computer and telecommunications equipment, and food processing. Most of the interviews were conducted during on-site visits and lasted about 1 to 2 hours each.

At one end of the conceptual model, local partners' choice of management control is linked to two motives for IJV formation: JV performance commitment and articulated learning intent. While local partners committed to JV performance generally have a straightforward objection to Western management control, they indirectly endorse such control through

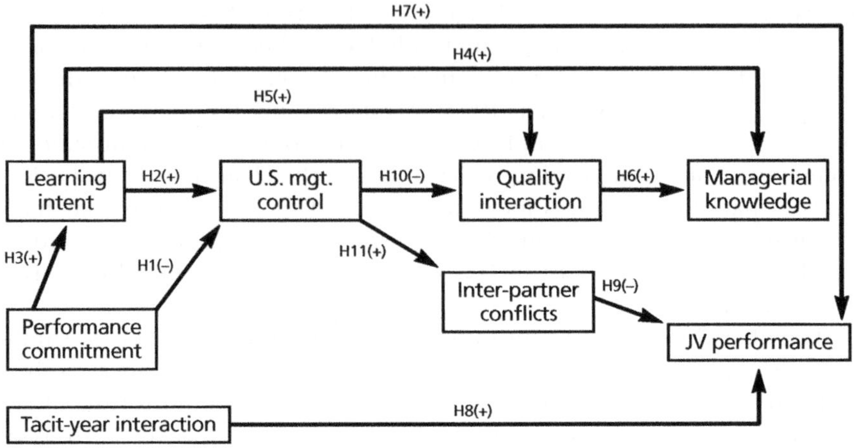

Figure 9.1 Conceptual model.

their desire to acquire managerial knowledge from their Western partners. At the other end of the conceptual model, we consider the factors that directly impact managerial knowledge acquisition and JV performance from the local partners' perspective. We propose that learning is positively affected by local partners' learning intent and quality interaction between JV partners. On the other hand, we propose that interpartner conflicts have a negative effect on JV performance, but managerial learning interacts with relationship age to positively affect JV performance. What then is the role of management control? In the context of Chinese–U.S. JVs, we do not see a direct effect of U.S. management control on either learning or performance; its effect is indirect through decreased interaction quality and increased interpartner conflicts. These effects, either confirmed or disconfirmed, will approve or disprove Chinese partners' approach toward U.S. management control and may carry implications for future changes in IJV dynamics in China.

Western Management Control and Local Partner Motives

Management control refers to "observable patterns of decision-making power" (Steensma & Lyles, 2000, p. 833). Much has been written on the distribution of decision making within IJVs in terms of shared versus dominant control (Beamish, 1993). However, despite the accumulated research efforts, why a partner prefers one control structure over another remains unknown. For example, empirical evidence on the equity ownership-control association are inconclusive and often contradictory (Choi & Beamish, 2004). According to Child and Yan (1999), management control may be categorized into strategic versus operational control.

Improving organizational performance is a key motive of IJV formation for partners in developing countries (Beamish, 1985; Tsang, 2001). By pooling resources, a party uses IJV as a remedy for its capability deficiencies, activates its idle resources in more productive direction, and thus improves its financial performance. It is well-documented that JV partners secure performance targets by exercising management control (Geringer & Hebert, 1989). In the context of Chinese–U.S. joint ventures, we suspect that as Chinese partners' commitment to the venture's successful JVs increases, their acceptance of Western partners' dominance in management will decrease proportionally. A higher level of commitment indicates a party's sense of responsibility for the JV. Unless one party can trust the other in delivering better performance, each party will strive to maintain control. Chinese partners, most of which are state-owned enterprises, often see IJVs with Western companies as a major venue for turnarounds and survival. For this reason, it is quite normal for a Chinese parent company to put its best portions of assets in an IJV (e.g., Cheng, 1999). With such a high stake, the Chinese partner wants to make sure that the JV is managed in its best interest. While "placing all its eggs in one basket," the Chinese may not see the same level of commitment in its Western counterpart. For large MNCs, a Chinese venture may be just one of its numerous overseas affiliates that serves its overall global strategy (Li & Wu, 2002). They may use the JV to tap a captive market, sourcing cheap parts or components, or filling a hole in its rationalized global manufacturing networks. In each of these cases, the Western partner would be oriented toward a direction that is not consistent with the performance goals set forth by the Chinese partner. For example, with management control, the Western partner will try to gain benefits at the expense of the JV through transfer pricing (Li & Guo, 2000). Organizational justice studies emphasize the importance of the equitable distribution of outcomes in a relationship and show that perceptions of unfairness lead to distrust (Lind, 1995). Thus, the more the Chinese partners attach importance to a JV's success, the more they will feel unfair when the U.S. counterparts are perceived as not committed to the JV's success, and the less likely they will allow its U.S. counterpart to dominate decision making. Stated formally, we consider the following hypothesis:

Hypothesis 1: *Chinese partners' JV performance commitment is inversely associated with their acceptance of U.S. management control.*

Like JV partners from other developing countries, Chinese partners entering a JV have motives beyond financial or economic performance such as acquiring advanced managerial knowledge from their Western partners (Hitt et al., 2005). Clearly and consistently, learning about Western managerial knowledge has been recognized as a key objective by the Chinese government in promoting IJVs as a major form of foreign direct investment (Gao, 1996; Li & Shenkar, 1996). In many cases, the Chinese majority partners volunteer chief executive positions to U.S. partners for the purpose of managerial learning. For example, the Chinese partner of Beijing Jeep Automotive Co., Ltd. allowed its U.S. partner to assign a general manager during the JV's initial 4-year period in order for these Americans to directly introduce Western managerial knowledge. During our fieldwork, one Chinese manager recalled how she endured "humiliated feelings" during her first year as a JV's deputy general manager: "Several times I cried and decided to quit after meeting with the U.S. general manager. I called my boss [at the Chinese parent company], but he always reminded me why I was here, why I should try my best to work with [the U.S. general manager]. It's very simple—we have to let them be the boss and that's how we can learn." In other words, although Western management control can be a painful reality for local partners, given their pride or fear, learning-oriented Chinese partners understand that U.S. management control offers an opportunity for them to observe, experience, and internalize advanced management knowledge and skills. Note that our argument may not be consistent with existing theorizing. For example, Lyles and Salk (1996) believe that a shared management structure is more likely to promote learning because of more frequent interaction under such management structure. Our alternative hypothesis is based on evidence from China. When Western partners hold a dominant position, they are better positioned to implement their management systems; the other side of the coin is the local partners' greater exposure to Western partners' total management skillset (Lin, 2005).

> **Hypothesis 2:** *Chinese partners' learning intent is positively associated with their acceptance of U.S. management control.*

Ironically, Chinese partners committed to JV performance are likely to give support to U.S. management control by also being committed to managerial learning. For local partners headquartered in less developed countries, improved performance may result for different reasons, including advanced technologies and more effective management (Tsang, 2001). In countries transitioning toward market-based economies, local firms must know how to manage in the unprecedented competitive environment (Child & Markoczy, 1993). For example, state-owned enterprises have difficulties when effectively responding to changes in customer needs, since their "task environment" has been regulated by government agents rather than by market forces prior to the economic transformation (Markoczy, 1994). While the initial focus might be on introducing Western technologies, these firms have increasingly realized that effective technology transfer must be accompanied by advanced managerial knowledge (Leonard-Barton, 1995) and that managerial learning often has a greater impact than technological learning on IJV performance (Lyles & Salk, 1996). We test the following hypothesis:

Hypothesis 3: *Chinese partners' commitment to JV performance is positively associated with their articulated learning intent.*

Antecedents of Managerial Learning

The learning literature has consistently confirmed that for effective learning to occur, an articulated learning intent must be in place. In a detailed study of nine international alliances, Hamel (1991) finds considerable variances in the learning actually achieved as a result of the degree to which the partners view the collaboration as a learning opportunity. Similarly, Simonin (1997) shows that learning intent is a strong and reliable predictor of knowledge transfer among international alliance partners. In IJVs operating in Hungary, Lyles and Salk (1996) show that articulated goals and plans are significant predictors of managerial knowledge acquisition because they help "focus IJV employees on acquiring potentially useful knowledge from the foreign parent." (p. 882). Importantly, an *abstract* learning intent is not sufficient for effective learning; the intent needs to be articulated against specific goals and plans. While Chinese JV partners tend to take the acquisition of Western management know-how as a main objective in forming an IJV, they do not necessarily have the objective articulated enough for action (Tsang, 2001). However, successful management learning always requires a partner to make its learning goals explicit so as to be acted upon (Si & Bruton, 1999).

Hypothesis 4: *Articulated learning intent is positively associated with managerial knowledge acquisition by Chinese JV partners.*

While proposing a direct link between learning intent and learning outcome, we also perceive an indirect link between the two via ongoing constructive interaction. Much has been written on the tacit nature of managerial knowledge. According to Nonaka (1994), tacit knowledge has a personal quality such that its transfer requires some kind of shared experience in order for parties to share and internalize personally embedded knowledge. However, not all interactions lead to effective knowledge acquisition.

As Lyles and Salk (1996) show, dysfunctional interaction creates conflicts and misunderstandings, which then impede learning. While often mentioned as *quality interaction*, Chinese managers in our fieldwork believed that such interaction begins with a quantity dimension. This requires sufficient numbers of expatriates at the JVs and adequate daily, interpersonal encounters (Tsang, 2001). To facilitate effective learning, a constructive and friendly atmosphere must be in place. In their study of JVs formed between Eastern and Western European firms, Cyr and Schneider (1996) find that interaction quality helps to create a new social reality that encourages local partners to learn about new behaviors and norms.

Hypothesis 5: *Articulated learning intent is positively associated with quality interaction.*

Hypothesis 6: *Quality interaction is positively associated with managerial knowledge acquisition by Chinese JV partners.*

Determinants of JV Performance

According to the knowledge-based view of the firm, acquiring knowledge allows a firm to build competitive advantage and ultimately to achieve superior performance (Kogut & Zander, 1992). When articulated, the intent to acquire management knowledge provides an indication of how the local partners intend to improve their performance (Lyles & Salk, 1994). With accelerated economic reforms and stiffened competition from Western firms, Chinese companies have an increasingly clear understanding of the weak points in their management knowledge that impede sound performance (Tsang, 2001). During our interviews, several Chinese managers attributed improved financial performance in their respective JVs to the conscious learning efforts of Chinese employees, who were guided through frequent communications with headquarters and memos. In a similar story, a JV's prosperity started when the partners put down on paper what they needed to know and included such a learning agenda as part of the JV's performance evaluation process (Si & Bruton, 1999).

We propose:

Hypothesis 7: *Chinese partners' learning intent is positively associated with their perceived JV performance.*

While acquired managerial knowledge will have a positive effect on JV performance, we believe that the effect must be materialized over time. As discussed earlier that managerial knowledge involves deep-rooted values and norms, and is developed over time as a result of interaction between cultural, organizational, and institutional contexts (Fink & Holden, 2005). As a result, partners operating in diverse contexts, such as Chinese and American business cultures, will need time to digest and integrate the acquired knowledge to get performance results. No matter how advantageous the acquired managerial knowledge is, time is also needed to integrate it into the existing practice and system. It is because of this long-term orientation that a Chinese JV partner is able to forego immediate financial returns (Si & Bruton, 1999). Summarizing the above discussion, we propose an interactive effect between management learning and relationship age on JV performance.

> **Hypothesis 8:** *Managerial knowledge acquisition by Chinese partners is positively associated with their perceived JV performance in long-lived JVs.*

The inevitability and effects of interpartner conflicts on JV performance are well documented. Conflicts are inevitable because of interdependency as well as differences in cultures and objectives among JV partners. Although conflicts may not always be dysfunctional, and their management could lead to constructive impact, frequent and intensive conflicts are detrimental to JV performance (Ding, 1997; Parkhe, 1991). Without repeating the numerous empirical studies, we simply propose:

> **Hypothesis 9:** *Interpartner conflicts are inversely associated with perceived JV performance.*

The Effects of U.S. Management Control

As shown in our conceptual model, we do not perceive any direct link from U.S. management control to either Chinese partner learning or JV performance. Instead, we see its effect through associations with quality interaction and interpartner conflicts. As shown in previous studies (e.g., Lyles & Salk, 1996), management control or the distribution of managerial responsibility is of importance to local partner learning. Choo and Drummond (2010) consider effective social interaction as the essential condition for productive learning to occur. Such interactions are based on norms and values such as care and trust, and help form a social environment conducive to knowledge creation, sharing, and use. According to Das and Teng (1998), trust between alliance partners and their respective staffs facilitates the acceptance of control especially when control is operated through close social interaction, which in turn is likely to enhance performance.

Overwhelmingly, the Chinese managers we interviewed in our fieldwork believed that U.S. management control does not bring about positive interaction, but rather it increases the likelihood of conflicts. Two explanations for this were given. First, they believed that U.S. managers tend to have little cultural understanding or, in other words, lack the necessary cross-cultural skills to carry out constructive interactions. Second, they blamed the U.S. managers' arrogant attitudes and styles toward Chinese partners. As Simon and Davies (1996) find in Hungary, when Western JV partners take a "colonialist" approach in management, Hungarian employees refused to learn about any new behavior or norms because of the perceived subordination and humiliation that may come with this kind of relationship. The above situations point to the cultural challenges inherent in global transfers of management knowledge. Without cross-cultural competence and respect for the local partner, an atmosphere conducive to local partner management learning cannot be created (Fink & Holden, 2005). Finally, foreign partner control could lead to conflicts for reasons beyond just a lack of cultural competence. In the context of Vietnam, Barden, Steensma, & Lyles (2005) showed that an imbalance of financial control by foreign parents, often the supplier of advanced skills to the IJVs, can lead to a sense of inequality, which is a likely source of conflicts. According to Das and Kumar (2009), control is necessary for coordination in JVs and could give rise to harmony instead of conflicts. However, if exercised inappropriately or unduly, control will become detrimental to productive interaction, and it will increase the likelihood of conflicts.

Hypothesis 10: *U.S. management control is inversely associated with quality interaction.*

Hypothesis 11: *U.S. management control is positively associated with interpartner conflict.*

MEASURES AND SAMPLE

We developed a survey questionnaire for testing the conceptual model and hypotheses based on our fieldwork, existing literature, and a pretest among JV managers and experts. We operationalized *JV performance commitment* with two questions regarding a Chinese parent's emphasis on JV's financial and market performance. A 3-item measure was developed for *Articulated Learning Intent.* We developed a 3-item measure in terms of agenda and plans for learning as well as JV managers' learning assignments. For *U.S. management control,* we asked the respondent to rate the extent to which the U.S. parent company exercised strategic and operational control. As mentioned in the prior section, quality interaction was found to possess the following characteristics: frequent, adequate, amiable, and constructive. Accordingly, we included four questions and asked the respondent about the degree to which interpartner interaction was considered as such. JV conflict is usually measured by enlisting the areas of potential conflicts and requesting the participants to indicate their frequency and intensity (Habib, 1987). Instead, we provided three broad conflict categories—personnel, strategic, and contractual—for the Chinese JV managers to rate their likelihood to occur. These three conflict categories were derived from a recent empirical investigation (Lin, 2007). For *managerial knowledge acquisition,* we used three statements to represent three knowledge domains; namely, managerial know-how, managerial perspective, and international knowledge. This is a theory-in-use approach, which summarizes what the Chinese managers say about management learning in our fieldwork. Managerial know-how and managerial perspective match the dichotomy discussed by Nonaka (1994), Leonard-Barton (1995), and Child and Markoczy (1993) using different terminologies. Chinese JV partners are eager to gain international managerial knowledge, such as knowledge about international markets, international business practice, and international alliance management know-how (Berdrow & Lane, 2003; Tsang, 1999; Yan & Child, 2002). The respondents also reported the number of years since a JV started operation; this is what we define as *relationship age.* In the empirical tests, we took the product of the two variables to create a new variable, named knowledge-time interaction. Finally, 3 items were used to measure *JV performance* in terms of financial performance, goal attainment, and overall satisfaction.

The questionnaire was developed in English (Table 9.1) and subsequently translated into Chinese following the conventional blind-translation method. With evidence of adequate reliability (Cronbach's alpha ranges from .80 to .93) through exploratory assessment, the total of 21 items was then subjected to a confirmatory factor analysis with LISREL 8.14, using covariance matrix as input. The X^2 value has been used historically as the initial estimator of model fit. However, because of the value's sensitivity to sample size and distribution, researchers have been looking for modified versions of the X^2, and the standardized X^2 (X^2/Degree of Freedom) is considered as a first alternative (Carmines & McIver, 1981). In our case, the *standardized* $X^2 = 2.71$ ($X^2 = 444.858$, df = 164) is within the accepted range of 2 to 3. This, in conjunction with CFI = .85, indicates adequate fit of the measurement model.

The questionnaire was administered using the interview method with a sample of 135 Chinese managers, each representing the Chinese partner in a U.S.–Chinese JV. A total of 139 interviews were conducted, but only 135 were usable and subsequently included in the analysis. The 135 Chinese managers—92 senior JV executives (general manager, deputy general

TABLE 9.1 Operational Measures and Scale Reliability

JV Performance Commitment

1. We are committed to the JV's financial success.
2. Enhancing the JV's efficiency deserves our maximum effort.

Articulated Learning Intent (α = .83)

1. Updating management skills is on our agenda for participating in the JV.
2. We have a clear intention to acquire useful managerial knowledge from the U.S. partner.
3. Chinese managers in the JV are conscious of our learning agenda concerning U.S. management know-how.

U.S. Management Control

1. The U.S. partner has controlled the JV's strategic planning and implementation.
2. The U.S. partner has controlled operational and daily decision making in this JV.

Quality Interaction (α = .93)

1. We have maintained frequent interaction with the U.S. partner in this JV.
2. In this JV, our interaction with U.S. partner is adequate.
3. We interact with the U.S. partner in an amiable climate.
4. In this JV, our interaction with U.S. partner carries a constructive mode.

Managerial Knowledge Acquisition (α = .80)

We have been successful in acquiring managerial knowledge from the U.S. partner in terms of:

1. Management skills
2. Philosophy or rationales underlying management skills
3. Knowledge about managing internationally.

Relationship Age

Number of years since the JV started operation

Interpartner Conflicts (α = .84)

Rate the extent to which the partners had to deal with conflicts on following issues:

1. Personnel
2. Strategic
3. Contractual

JV Performance (α = .89)

1. The joint venture's financial performance is satisfactory.
2. The joint venture has realized the goals we set out to achieve.
3. Overall, we were satisfied with the performance of the joint venture.

Note: α = Cronbach's alpha for scales with three or more items.
All 5-point scales except Relationship Age; "low"/"high" endpoints.

managers, or equivalents) and 43 divisional managers (e.g., HR manager)—represented U.S.–Chinese JVs from a wide range of manufacturing sectors including petroleum, industrial machinery, paper, food, and transportation equipment. These JVs had an average of 9.1 years in operation and $6.3 million in registered investment. U.S. and Chinese partners had equal equity ownership in 44 (32.6%) of the sample JVs, whereas U.S. partners held ma-

TABLE 9.2 Correlation Matrix and Summary Statistics

	x1	x2	y1	y2	y3	y4	y5	y6	Mean	sd
x1									3.86	.57
x2	.06								34.02	15.37
y1	.54[a]	.05							3.89	.60
y2	–.06	.22[b]	.15						2.99	.63
y3	.61[a]	.04	.42[a]	–.10					3.83	.67
y4	–.22[b]	–.00	–.09	.14	–.31[a]				1.23	.91
y5	.51[a]	.09	.51[a]	.07	.59[a]	–.23[a]			3.80	.54
y6	.49[a]	.19[b]	.62[a]	.06	.41[a]	–.20[b]	.37[a]		3.68	.60

Note: **x1** = performance commitment; **x2** = knowledge-age interaction; **y1** = learning intent; **y2** = U.S. management control; **y3** = quality interaction; **y4** = interpartner conflict; **y5** = Chinese knowledge acquisition; **y6** = JV performance

[a] $p < .01$; [b] $p < .05$; (two-tailed tests).

jority ownership in 69 (51.1%) and minority in 22 (16.3%). No significant differences were found in organization characteristics (e.g., investment size, duration, and foreign ownership) between the 135 JVs and other JVs in the database. Table 9.2 provides variable correlations and descriptive statistics.

RESULTS

The empirical model (Figure 9.2) was tested through LISREL 8.14, suggesting an adequate model fit with *standardized* $X^2 = 2.69$ ($X^2 = 485$, df = 180) and CFI = .84. For each structural path, Table 9.3 presents the completely standardized estimate and t-value. Details of model fit, which is adequate, are also presented. The squared multiple correlation for the individual structural equations, interpreted similar to an R^2, are .578 for managerial knowledge acquisition and .555 for JV performance. Using one-tailed testing at .05 level, all our hypotheses are supported. Going back to our overarching research questions, we also found a significant, negative total effect from JV performance commitment to U.S. management control (we already know the direct link from learning intent to U.S. management control). In other words, despite their endorsement of learning that in turn support U.S. management control, Chinese partners with a strong concern about JV performance will ultimately reject a U.S. dominant control. On the other hand, the total negative effect of U.S. management control is significant for Chinese acquisition of managerial knowledge, but insignificant for JV performance.

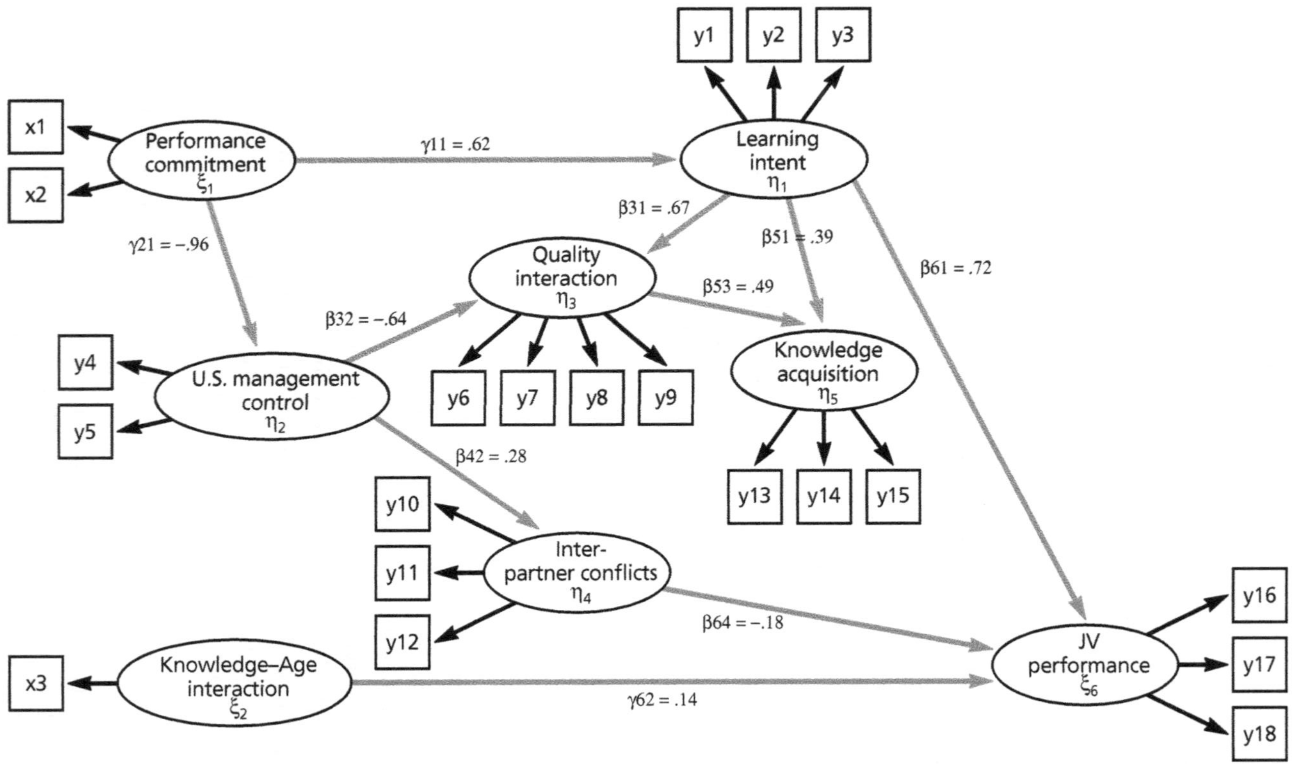

Figure 9.2 Empirical model. Note: Measurement model test results: $\chi^2 = 444.86$, df = 164; $p < .01$; CFI = .85. Estimates are completely standardized.

TABLE 9.3 LISREL Model Results

Path	Hypothesis	Estimate	*t*-value
JV performance commitment → U.S. control	H1	–.960	–2.89*
Learning intent → U.S. control	H2	.875	2.72*
JV performance commitment → Learning intent	H3	.618	5.68*
Learning intent → Knowledge acquisition	H4	.392	3.81*
Learning intent → Quality interaction	H5	.669	4.00*
Quality interaction → Knowledge acquisition	H6	.487	4.18*
Learning intent → JV performance	H7	.720	2.36*
Knowledge acquisition × Relationship age → JV performance	H8	.140	1.98*
Interpartner conflicts → JV performance	H9	–.175	–2.57*
U.S. control → Quality interaction	H10	–.640	–2.48*
U.S. control → Interpartner conflicts	H11	.278	2.14*

Empirical model test results: **p* < .05 (one-tailed tests). χ^2 = 485, df = 180; *p* < .000; CFI = .84. Estimates are completely standardized.

DISCUSSIONS AND CONCLUSION

Control is arguably the most debated issue in the IJV and alliance literature, particularly for its effect on organizational performance. However, the control-performance link has not been established conclusively (Choi & Beamish, 2004), especially taking into consideration partner learning as a key performance outcome (Makhija & Ganesh, 1997). It is not surprising that research has rarely considered how control by Western partners effects local learning, since control is usually viewed as one of mechanisms used by a partner to facilitate its own learning, and prior investigations have largely been conducted from the point of view of Western partners for which learning is seldom an objective when forming an alliance with a partner based in a developing country. However, the current study has shown that control exercised by the Western partner will have a significant impact on how effectively the local partner can learn, which should be in the interest of the Western partner as knowledge upgrading of the local partners will contribute to the alliance's bottom-line performance (Child & Markoczy, 1993).

In the context of IJVs based in China, our study calls for greater attention to managerial learning as a key motive for local partners entering IJVs with Western firms. Logically, acquiring managerial knowledge through international collaboration, a motive likely found in IJVs operating in Western countries (Hamel, 1991), should be a more pressing objective among local partners. There are several reasons for this omission in the literature.

First, local partners are not necessarily looking for learning or to the degree they may appear. Many local companies, which tend to be state-owned, deal with poor performance and pressure for quick turnaround in times of economic transitions. These companies participate in IJVs in a survivalist state of mind. Unlike under proreform communist regimes, management in these local companies bears a strong performance imperative, yet they tend to have a short trajectory (Hu, 2003; Tsang, 2001). Second, local partner learning may be prevailing, but it is not receiving its due attention among researchers whose perspective is implicitly Western. Touching upon the phenomenon, their focus is not so much on how local partners learn as how local partners need to change in order to meet the standards of Western management (Child & Markoczy, 1993). However, the above assumptions may be questioned, as recent evidence shows signs of not only performance imperatives but openness among Chinese state-owned enterprises (Woetzel, 2008).

In conjunction with their concern about JV performance, local partners' motives for managerial learning better explains their preference for management control structure. To a large extent, balancing the two concerns is reflected in their quest for Western management involvement as well as insistence on local majority ownership (Shenkar, 1990). Ultimately, this may be the reason why JV has been the preferred FDI arrangement along with shared management; while never clearly defined or unambiguously promoted, it has been the favored JV management structure by the Chinese government (Gao, 1996). However, learning and performance objectives may be inconsistent. For example, learning by ceding management control may harm the chance of the partnership's survival. As we have shown, only long-lived JVs may allow the Chinese partners to benefit from managerial learning, thus preventing U.S. partners from dominating. This makes sense if it assures the Chinese a better chance of survival. However, dominant control by the Chinese will certainly defeat the purpose of learning, particularly because the majority of Chinese JV partners carry residual state enterprise "baggage," maintaining that their old way of managing is not an ideal way of achieving sound performance. On the other hand, as our results show, U.S. management control is not an ideal option either. By being detrimental to quality interaction and causing interpartner conflicts, such control has a negative effect on Chinese-partner learning and on JV performance. Is shared management therefore a better option from either the Western partners' perspective (Beamish, 1993) or the local partners' perspective (Lyles & Salk, 1996)?

We cannot offer a convincing answer to such questions in the current study. Ideally, we should have modeled and allowed for comparing U.S. management control versus shared management control. In other words, the current study has shown why dominant control by Western partners is not in the best interest of Chinese JV partners, but is unable to identify a better alternative. Further, answers to such questions will need to take into account both foreign and local partners' perspectives. While we started this study with a critique of a Western-centric approach, our current study is a one-sided story as well. Not only is managerial learning in IJVs often a two-way street involving Western and local partners (Si & Bruton, 1999), but performance objectives must be constituted and acted on in a congruent manner by the parent companies (Beamish & Lupton, 2009). By linking learning and performance objectives and taking both parties' concerns into consideration, we can move toward a better understanding of control issues in IJVs.

The findings of the current study bear important messages for U.S. firms doing business in China, not necessarily as JV partners. In the years since China started using IJVs to attract foreign direct investment, there has been wide criticism about Chinese partners' passivity, especially their attitude toward learning. Evidence, including our own, has shown however, that a learning orientation may be gradually germinating within Chinese partner firms. Conversely, should the U.S. managers reconsider their approach to control as they are often given the opportunity to manage Chinese IJVs? Specifically, is control exercised in a way that is construed to be constructive and nonthreatening by the Chinese? This is a sensible question since many U.S. managers know from experience that Chinese partners sometimes perceive things differently, and that what is right for the Americans may not be right for the Chinese.

REFERENCES

Barden, J. Q., Steensma, H. K., & Lyles, M. A. (2005). The influence of parent control structure on parent conflict in Vietnamese international joint ventures: An organizational justice-based contingency approach. *Journal of International Business Studies, 36,* 156–174.

Beamish, P. W. (1985). The characteristics of joint ventures in developed and developing countries. *Columbia Journal of World Business, 20,* 13–19.

Beamish, P. W. (1993). The characteristics of joint ventures in the People's Republic of China. *Journal of International Marketing, 1*(2), 29–48.

Beamish, P. W., & Lupton, N. C. (2009). Managing joint ventures. *Academy of Management Perspectives, 23*(2), 75–94.

Berdrow, I., & Lane, H. W. (2003). International joint ventures: Creating value through successful knowledge management. *Journal of World Business, 38,* 15–30.

Carmines, E., & McIver, J. (1981). Analyzing models with unobserved variables: Analysis of covariance structures. In G. W. Bohrnstedt & E. F. Borgatta (Eds.), *Social measurement: Current issues* (pp. 65–115). Beverly Hills, CA: Sage.

Cheng, Z. M. (1999). The dissolution of a Chinese–U.S. joint venture: Nanjing A.O. Smith Hot Water Co., Ltd. *Management World* (in Chinese), *4,* 189–196.
Child, J., & Markoczy, L. (1993). Host-country managerial behavior and learning in Chinese and Hungarian joint ventures. *Journal of Management Studies, 30,* 611–631.
Child, J., & Yan, Y. (1999). Investment and control in international joint ventures: The case of China. *Journal of World Business, 34,* 3–15.
Choi, C. B., & Beamish, P. W. (2004). Split management control and international joint venture performance. *Journal of International Business Studies, 35,* 201–215.
Choo, C. W., & Drummond, A. N. (2010). Beyond the BA: Managing enabling contexts in knowledge organizations. *Journal of Knowledge Management, 14,* 592–610.
Cyr, D. J., & Schneider, S. C. (1996). Implications for learning: Human resource management in East-West joint ventures. *Organization Studies, 17,* 207–226.
Danis, W. M., & Parkhe, A. (2002). Hungarian-Western partnerships: A grounded theoretical model of integration processes and outcomes. *Journal of International Business Studies, 33,* 423–455.
Das, T. K., & Kumar, R. (2009). Interpartner harmony in strategic alliances: Managing commitment and forbearance. *International Journal of Strategic Business Alliances, 1,* 24–52.
Das, T. K., & Teng, B. (1998). Between trust and control: Developing confidence in partner cooperation in alliances. *Academy of Management Review, 23,* 491–512.
Ding, D. Z. (1997). Control, conflict, and performance: A study of U.S.–Chinese joint ventures. *Journal of International Marketing, 5*(3), 31–45.
Fink, G., & Holden, N. (2005). Introduction: The global transfer of management knowledge. *Academy of Management Executive, 19*(2), 5–8.
Gao, S. (1996). *China's economic reform.* New York: St Martin's Press.
Geringer, J. M., & Hebert, L. (1989). Control and performance of international joint ventures. *Journal of International Business Studies, 20,* 235–254.
Habib, G. M. (1987). Measures of manifest conflict in international joint ventures. *Academy of Management Journal, 30,* 808–816.
Hamel, G. (1991). Competition for competence and inter-partner learning within international strategic alliances. *Strategic Management Journal, 12,* 83–103.
Hitt, M. A., Li, H., & Worthington, W. J., IV (2005). Emerging markets as learning laboratories: Learning behaviors of local firms and foreign entrants in different institutional contexts. *Management and Organization Review, 1,* 353–380.
Hu, F. (2003). The economics explanation on the stock right structure change of business cooperation with Chinese and foreign investment. *Taxation and Economy* (in Chinese), *2*(127), 21–24.
Inkpen, A. C. (1997). An examination of knowledge management in international joint ventures. In P. Beamish & P. Killing (Eds.), *Cooperative strategies: North American perspectives* (pp. 337–369), San Francisco: New Lexington Press.
Kogut, B. (1988). Joint ventures: Theoretical and empirical perspectives. *Strategic Management Journal, 9,* 319–332.
Kogut, B., & Zander, U. (1992). Knowledge of the firm, combinative capabilities, and the replication of technology. *Organization Science, 3,* 383–397.
Leonard-Barton, D. (1995). *Wellsprings of knowledge: Building and sustaining the sources of innovation.* Boston: Harvard Business School Press.

Li, J., & Shenkar, O. (1996). In search of complementary assets: Co-operative strategies and knowledge seeking by prospective Chinese partners. In J. Child & Y. Lu (Eds.), *Management issues in China: Volume II: International enterprises* (pp. 52–56). New York: Routledge.

Li, S., & Guo, F. (2000). The role of Chinese ownership in Chinese-foreign joint ventures. *Journal of Northeastern University* (in Chinese), *2*(4), 236–238.

Li, W. A., & Wu, X. M. (2002). Governance in parent-controlled Chinese-foreign JVs. *World Economy & Politics* (in Chinese), *5*, 52–56.

Lin, X. (2005). Local partner acquisition of managerial knowledge in international joint ventures: Focusing on foreign management control. *Management International Review, 45*, 219–237.

Lin, X. (2007). Appointing a general manager in international joint ventures: Partner competence and organizational consequences. *International Journal of Organizational Analysis, 15*, 152–165.

Lind, E. A. (1995). *Social conflict and social justice: Some lessons from the social psychology of justice.* Leiden, The Netherlands: Leiden University Press.

Lyles, M. A., & Salk, J. (1996). Knowledge acquisition from foreign parents in international joint ventures: An empirical examination in the Hungarian context. *Journal of International Business Studies, 27*(Special Issue 5), 877–903.

Makhija, M. V., & Ganesh, U. (1997). The relationship between control and partner learning in learning-related joint ventures. *Organization Science, 8*, 508–527.

Markoczy, L. (1994). Modes of organizational learning. *International Studies of Management & Organization, 2*(4), 5–30.

Nonaka, I. (1994). A dynamic theory of organizational knowledge creation. *Organization Science, 5*, 14–37.

Parkhe, A. (1991). Interfirm diversity, organizational learning, and longevity in global strategic alliances. *Journal of International Business Studies, 22*, 579–601.

Shenkar, O. (1990). International joint ventures' problems in China: Risks and remedies. *Long Range Planning, 23*(2), 82–90.

Si, S. X., & Bruton, G. D. (1999). Knowledge transfer in international joint ventures in transitional economies: The China experience. *Academy of Management Executive, 13*(1), 83–90.

Simon, L., & Davies, G. (1996). A contextual approach to management learning: The Hungarian case. *Organization Studies, 17*, 269–289.

Simonin, B. L. (1997). The importance of collaborative know-how: An empirical test of the learning organization. *Academy of Management Journal, 40*, 1150–1174.

Steensma, H. K., & Lyles, M. (2000). Explaining IJV survival in a transitional economy through social exchange and knowledge-based perspective. *Strategic Management Journal, 21*, 831–848.

Tsang, E. W. K. (1999). A preliminary typology of learning in international strategic alliances. *Journal of World Business, 34*, 211–229.

Tsang, E. W. K. (2001). Managerial learning in foreign-invested enterprises of China. *Management International Review, 41*, 29–51.

Woetzel, J. R. (2008). Reassessing China's state-owned enterprises. *McKinsey Quarterly, 3*, 59–65.

Yan, Y., & Child, J. (2002). An analysis of strategic determinants, learning and decision-making in Sino-British joint ventures. *British Journal of Management, 13*, 109–122.

CHAPTER 10

THE DYNAMIC FIT OF ALLIANCE PORTFOLIO CHARACTERISTICS WITH COMPETITIVE STRATEGY AND INDUSTRY DYNAMISM

Don Goeltz

ABSTRACT

Alliances are used for a number of purposes, including market access, strategic positioning, and organizational learning. Most alliances are opportunistic and focused on a single objective, such as introduction of a new product or an R&D milestone. However, the value of a firm's alliances is enhanced if they are viewed as a portfolio that can be managed to reflect the generic competitive strategy of the firm and the dynamic nature of the firm's industry. This chapter develops a model relating firm performance to the fit of alliance portfolio characteristics with generic strategies and industry dynamism. The value of an alliance portfolio is enhanced if managers dynamically adjust the fit of alliance governance choices and the mix of exploration and exploitation alliances to changes in strategies and the external environment. Two portfolio characteristics are associated here with learning in alliances: the ratio of exploration to exploitation and the balance between equity and nonequity

Strategic Alliances for Value Creation, pages 215–236

alliances. The hypotheses associate enhanced firm performance with the fit of these alliance portfolio characteristics with the firm's strategy and external environment. After developing theoretical support for these hypotheses, an approach to empirically testing the hypotheses is described, followed by a discussion of areas for further study.

INTRODUCTION

In dynamic environments, alliances are often used for organizational learning, as a bridge to fast-moving technologies and markets (Eisenhardt & Martin, 2000). From an organizational learning perspective, the learning objective of an alliance is either exploitative of the current knowledge base or exploration of new areas of knowledge. Organizational learning in an alliance is also affected by the governance structure chosen for the alliance, either nonequity alliances or equity-based joint ventures (Teng & Das, 2008). This chapter develops the theoretical support for managing the fit between learning and governance characteristics of an alliance portfolio with generic industry strategy and industry dynamism.

Several distinct perspectives are taken in developing this theory of alliance portfolio characteristics and firm performance. The first perspective is an organizational learning perspective, where the primary purpose of an alliance is to access and acquire new knowledge. Secondly, a portfolio perspective is taken, where the firm's alliance portfolio is defined as current and prior direct alliances (Wassmer, 2008). Alliances here are also viewed from the resource-based view (RBV) perspective as a unique and valuable source of a long-term competitive advantage (Das & Teng, 2000). As part of the RBV, alliances are also viewed as one way of attaining a strategic "fit" between internal resources and capabilities, and the external environment. The final perspective is a longitudinal, dynamic view of fitting the portfolio characteristics with changes in the firm's strategy and with changes in the external environment. The hypotheses developed here associate this dynamic fit with above-average long-term firm performance.

Organizational learning is closely linked with the objective of improving firm performance through new knowledge acquisition (Simon, 1960), and learning assists in interpretation of the environment (Daft & Weick, 1984). Levinthal and March (1993) state that learning "generally increases average performance" as well as generally increases reliability (p. 106). In an empirical evaluation of learning, Goh and Ryan (2008) define a set of learning companies and compare the performance of those companies to their direct competitors over a 22-year period, finding superior performance on financial and market measures for learning companies. This chapter addresses managing a portfolio of alliances in order to enhance organizational learning and concomitant firm performance.

Organizational learning is one of the primary purposes of an alliance (Inkpen, 1998; Kogut, 1988). Alliances are defined as collaborative arrangements between two or more independent organizations directed at pooling, trading, or sharing resources and knowledge, and directed at gaining competitive advantage (Das & Teng, 2000; Gulati, 1998). Alliances present unique learning opportunities (Inkpen, 1998), with learning across technological as well as organizational boundaries (Rosenkopf & Nerkar, 2001). In an alliance, learning is addressed as interfirm learning, where partners learn from participation in the alliance from formal routines and informal individual interactions.

The characteristics of an alliance that affect organizational learning include the learning objective of the alliance and the governance structure of the alliance. From an organizational learning perspective, alliances are either exploitative or exploratory (March, 1991). Organization learning from an alliance is also affected by whether it is an equity alliance or a nonequity alliance (Sampson, 2007). These characteristics of alliances are developed further in this chapter, as are the fit of the characteristics with industry strategy and with industry dynamism.

An emerging subject in the literature on alliances is the study of a firm's alliances as a group, or a portfolio (Wassmer, 2008). The alliance portfolio has been studied in terms of the management of the portfolio (Hoffmann, 2007), the characteristics of the portfolio (George, Zahra, Wheatley, & Raihan, 2001; Goeltz, 2010), and the interaction of the alliances in the portfolio as members of a network (Gulati, 1998). Authors addressing the second area, the characteristics of the portfolio, typically include the association of particular characteristics with some measure of performance, such as return on equity (Yamakawa, Yang, & Lin, 2011) or patenting (Sampson, 2007; Wuyts, Dutta, & Stremersch, 2004). This chapter furthers the literature on portfolio characteristics and performance by developing the concept of strategic fit between alliance portfolio characteristics and firm strategy, and the fit between portfolio characteristics and industry dynamism.

Strategic fit has a long history in strategy literature as a normative model, where strategic fit or congruence between the firm and its external environment is viewed as having a positive effect on firm performance (Miles, Snow, Meyer, & Coleman, 1978). This concept has been applied to contingency concepts of fit between technology and structure (Woodward, 1965) and organization-environment alignment (Thompson, 1967). With strategic fit comes superior performance (Venkatraman & Camillus, 1984).

The concept of fit that is applied here is one of domain of fit (Venkatraman & Camillus, 1984), in particular the fit between internal variables and strategic conduct variables and the external environment. Following this model of fit, the internal variables in this study are the alliance portfolio characteristics, while the strategic conduct variable is the firm's industry strategy. The level of industry dynamism, as it is often associated with the need for organizational learning (Brown & Eisenhardt, 1997), is used to characterize the external environment.

The hypotheses developed here associate firm performance with this fit of alliance portfolio characteristics with firm strategy and the external environment. The link between portfolio fit and performance is established from the association of learning with performance and the association of strategic fit with performance, as discussed above. As we are concerned with the long-term effects of both exploratory and exploitative learning, a longitudinal study is proposed to evaluate the hypotheses developed in this chapter.

Several authors address parts of the approach that is used in this chapter. For example, Wu, Wu, and Lin (2004) use the learning perspective in evaluating governance mechanisms and performance. Most recently, Yamakawa et al. (2011) took a portfolio perspective in examining the effect on performance of internal and external factors in light of the mix of exploration and exploitation alliances. No studies to date have combined the approaches described above in a longitudinal study of dynamic fit.

In developing a portfolio of alliances, management has the opportunity to choose both the learning focus and the governance structure of the alliances. These choices should be made in light of the firm's competitive strategy and the dynamism of the firm's industry. In addition, management can address the level of fit between these choices over time as the level of industry dynamism changes and as the firm's generic strategy adapts to the external environment.

ALLIANCE CHARACTERISTICS

From an organizational learning perspective, alliances are classified by the learning objective of the alliance and the governance structure of the alliance. This discussion reviews learning objectives—exploitative and exploratory—and the governance structures of alliances.

Exploration and Exploitation

Exploration and exploitation are often positioned as two very different types of learning activities. As defined by March (1991, p. 71), "Exploration includes things captured by terms such as search, variation, risk taking, experimentation, play, flexibility, discovery, innovation." Levinthal and March (1993) add to this broad definition of exploration by stating that it involves "a pursuit of new knowledge" (p. 105). On the other hand, exploitation includes such things as "refinement, choice, production, efficiency, selection, implementation, and execution" (March, 1991, p. 71).

Several studies have classified alliances as exploitation or exploration. Lavie and Rosenkopf (2006), in studying exploration and exploitation, code alliances as knowledge-leveraging (exploitation) or knowledge-generating (exploration), finding that firms tend to balance the categories of alliances over time. Rothaermel and Deeds (2004) categorize biotechnology alliances as exploitation alliance for products in development and existing products, finding support for a product development path that starts with exploration and continues with exploitation alliances. Lin, Yang, and Demirkan (2007) classify alliances by the number of the new partners, with exploitative alliances associated with existing partners and exploratory alliances associated with new partners.

Equity and Nonequity Alliances

The governance structure of an alliance can be classified as an equity-based joint venture, a minority equity arrangement, or a nonequity agreement (Powell, Koput, & Smith-Doerr, 1996; Teng & Das, 2008). Joint ventures are typically new legal entities with joint equity by the alliance partners, while minority-equity alliances can cover a wide range of alliance types, such as R&D alliances. Nonequity alliances can be a preliminary step to a more formal, equity-based arrangement, or they can be downstream agreements such as marketing or distribution alliances (Teng & Das, 2008).

The choice of alliance governance structure has been studied in terms of the effect on innovation in external venturing (Keil, Maula, Schildt, & Zahra, 2008), the effect of governance structure on knowledge exchange in international R&D alliances (Oxley & Sampson, 2004), and the effect of alliance structure and technological diversity of the partners on innovation (Sampson, 2007). Alliance governance has also been studied as a choice that is affected by alliance objectives (Teng & Das, 2008) and by the knowledge base of the partners (Sampson, 2007).

The choice of a learning focus for an alliance and of a governance structure is dependent on the alliance opportunity and purpose, but should also reflect the fit with the firm's generic competitive strategy and the level of industry dynamism. These two variables are addressed next, followed by a review of the concept of strategic fit.

COMPETITIVE STRATEGY AND INDUSTRY DYNAMISM

Alliance portfolios are intended to supplant and support the way a firm deploys resources in its competitive strategies and as a way of coping with dynamic external environments. Prior to discussing aligning the alliance portfolio with competitive strategy and industry dynamism, the background of these two constructs are reviewed.

Generic Competitive Strategy

Several authors have postulated that corporations follow generic competitive strategies that lead to superior performance. Miles et al. (1978) suggested that there are four general strategic types of organizations: prospector, defender, analyzer, and reactor organizations. Other classifications include Rumelt (1974) on diversification strategies and Lieberman and Montgomery (1998) with the strategy of first-mover advantage. Porter (1985) develops three generic strategies that can be used to create a defendable competitive position—cost leadership, differentiation, and focus. Porter theorizes that failure to choose between cost leadership and differentiation will result in below-average performance. According to Porter (p. 18), "a firm will ultimately reach the point where further cost reduction requires a sacrifice in differentiation. It is at this point that generic strategies become inconsistent and a firm must make a choice."

Porter's (1985) model has gained wide acceptance and has been extensively empirically tested (Campbell-Hunt, 2000). A cost leadership strategy relies on efficiency and low cost relative to competitors. The cost leadership strategy gives direction to mangers in all aspects of the value chain and in organizational structure, including alliances. The differentiation strategy relies on one or more unique aspects of the product/service for a competitive advantage—such as style, quality, branding, or freshness—for which the firm can charge a premium price. Internal strengths associated with a differentiation strategy might include R&D, design, or branding capabilities.

Empirical support in the strategic management literature for a positive association of Porter's generic strategies with superior performance includes Baum, Locke, and Smith (2001) and Dess and Davis (1984). The literature on generic competitive strategy and alliances includes a framework of joint ventures (Harrigan, 1988) that addresses adapting the number and type of alliances to the competitive strategy. A second study by Rosenkranz (2007) finds that alliances in larger markets tend more toward differentiation, and that the mix of cost and differentiation alliances changes with industry evolution.

Industry Dynamism

Dynamism is defined generally as the rate of change and the degree of instability in the external environment (Dess & Beard, 1984). With the broad rise in the rate and amount of change brought about by technological advances and by globalization, an increase in research into these environments has also occurred (Inkpen, 1998).

In a dynamic environment, organizational learning, and in particular, external exploration through alliances, becomes a critical capability for survival and competitive success (Hitt, Keats, & DeMarie, 1998). Brown and Eisenhardt (1997) find that in dynamic environments, successful firms rely on a wide variety of low-cost probes into the future, including strategic partnerships and experimental products. As the rate of change increases, exploration increases in importance (McGrath, 2001). In a technology-intensive environment, dynamism can result in a replacement of the underlying technological base (Benner & Tushman, 2002), making the core competencies of a firm into core rigidities (Leonard-Barton, 1992). Alliances can be an important learning investment to avoid core rigidities in dynamic environments.

In most studies, dynamism in the external environment is captured as industry dynamism. Industry dynamism is a common moderating variable in studies associating alliance characteristics with firm performance (Bierly & Daly, 2007; Uotila, Maula, Keil, & Zahra, 2009). In this study, the fit of alliance portfolio characteristics with competitive strategy and with industry dynamism is proposed to be associated with firm performance.

In summary, the value of an alliance portfolio is enhanced and associated with firm performance if the characteristics of exploration and exploitation focus and alliance governance are managed to fit with the firm's generic competitive strategy and with the level of industry dynamism. The hypotheses concerning this fit are developed after a review of the concept of strategic fit.

HYPOTHESES: STRATEGIC FIT

The concept of strategic fit is one of the earliest tenets of the management literature. The external environment dictates fit with internal resources (Van de Ven, 1976), and the firm's strategy drives the organizational structure (Chandler, 1962). Strategy serves the purpose of matching and aligning organizational resources with the opportunities and threats of the external environment (Andrews, 1971; Porter, 1980).

The concept of fit extends to multiple elements of both the internal and external environments. All of the internal elements of the organization must be in congruence (Randolf & Dess, 1984), and multiple elements form a "gestalt" (Miller, 1981; Miller & Frisen, 1978). The concept of fit is also extended from a static view to a dynamic view (Venkatraman & Camillus, 1984) with the recognition that a longitudinal perspective was required. Zajac, Kraatz, and Bresser (2000) developed a dynamic model of strategic fit of organizational and external environmental contingencies that imply both strategy changes and performance.

Fit is applied here by matching multiple elements of the alliance portfolio to the firm's competitive strategy and industry dynamism. Several studies (Oxley, 1997; Pisano, 1989) have addressed the concept of governance from a transaction cost perspective, where control over the knowledge flow and contract costs are the primary criteria for fit. Here, organizational learning is the primary criteria of fit; for example, does a nonequity alliance provide a better learning environment for a cost strategy than an equity alliance? With fit comes enhanced firm performance associated with organizational learning that is aligned with firm strategy and external environment. The fit of the portfolio characteristics is examined first from a static perspective and then from a dynamic perspective.

Fit of Governance Structure with Competitive Strategy

One of the most critical decisions in developing an alliance is the choice of a governance structure (Parkhe, 1993; Teng & Das, 2008). Although there are many possible structural configurations and variations, they are generally divided into three classes based on the level of equity participation in the alliance (Teng & Das, 2008). The level of equity, and the attendant control and support mechanisms of the alliance, influence the alliance's learning characteristics and therefore determine the fit of the governance structure with the firm's competitive strategy and external environment.

Equity alliances most closely approximate the structure of the firm, as there is generally a board of directors and a definitive reporting structure (Pisano, 1989). In some ways, the structure of an equity alliance is more controlled than a firm, as the partners agree *a priori* on budgets, contributions, and ownership of the projected results of the alliance (Oxley & Sampson, 2004). The control mechanisms of an equity alliance that are established for contributions and management reporting also apply to the flow of information and knowledge. In minority-equity alliances, there is less formal control, and nonequity alliances are generally regarded as one step above a market-based, contractual arrangement. Here we are focused on the two extremes of governance—equity and nonequity alliances.

The structure of an alliance affects the transfer of knowledge in an alliance. Knowledge in an alliance can be either tacit or explicit (Nonaka, 1994). For an alliance, tacit knowledge resides in the members of the alliance as well as with the partner employees, while explicit knowledge is transferred by the reporting structure and by the activities of the alliance.

The flow of explicit knowledge in an alliance is governed by the structure and control mechanisms, with increasing control provided by escalating levels of equity participation and formal structure. The control structure of an equity alliance provides a preset path for knowledge transfer through joint management routines and through reporting against alliance milestones. Equity alliances also share tacit knowledge, but through informal interaction of the individuals within the alliance. In an equity alliance, the partners' employees most often staff the new entity, and those employees often rotate jobs back and forth from the alliance to the home company (Sampson, 2007), providing an efficient means of transferring tacit knowledge. Nonequity alliances have much less structure and do not have informal employee channels for the exchange of tacit knowledge.

Therefore, from a learning perspective, equity alliances provide the best structure for transfer of both tacit and explicit knowledge, while nonequity alliances are better suited for the transfer of explicit knowledge. Several authors agree with this conclusion (Grant & Baden-Fuller, 2004; Inkpen,1998; Sampson, 2007; Schoenmakers & Duysters, 2006), although others have argued that the rigid structure of the equity alliance results in transferring only the knowledge that is specified by the agreements (Pangarkar & Klein, 2001). Also, contracts can limit the flexibility in pursuing new knowledge (Wu et al., 2004) and limit the potential for combining knowledge (Grant & Baden-Fuller, 2004). Managers of equity alliances have overcome these learning issues by using adaptable contracts (Oxley & Sampson, 2004) and through the informal sharing of knowledge by equity alliance employees.

Porter (1980) states, "The generic strategies imply different organizational arrangements, control procedure, and inventive systems." Alliances are an extension of the corporate structure and strategy. Differentiation strategies are more likely associated with R&D and the development of knowledge that is more distant from the individual partners' knowledge base (Sampson, 2007). Cost improvement strategies are more associated with refinement of the current value chain (Porter, 1980) and are therefore more likely to be associated with manufacturing and distribution alliances. Thus, companies following cost strategies are generally focused on alliances directed at manufacturing improvements and at reducing the costs of distribution and customer support. Alliances in support of differentiation strategies are generally directed at exploring new knowledge through R&D or marketing partnerships.

R&D and marketing alliances involve more tacit information, and there is general agreement that the best structure for R&D and marketing alliances is an equity alliance (Kogut, 1988; Teng & Das, 2008). An equity alliance is also superior when the technical diversity of the partners is high (Sampson, 2007). Manufacturing alliances and distribution alliances are usually less knowledge intensive than R& D alliances, requiring less structure and less knowledge transfer.

In summary, the learning aspects of equity alliances are a better fit with differentiation strategies, and nonequity alliances are a better fit with cost strategies. From an organizational learning perspective and strategy perspective, this fit is associated with firm performance. At the portfolio level of analysis, managers should make governance choices so that the long-term fit is consonant with the choice of generic competitive strategy, leading to above-average long-term performance. Hence,

Hypothesis 1a: *For a firm pursuing a generic cost strategy, an alliance portfolio composed primarily of nonequity alliances is associated with above-average firm performance.*

Hypothesis 1b: *For a firm pursuing a generic differentiation strategy, an alliance portfolio composed primarily of equity alliances is associated with above-average firm performance.*

Fit of Governance Structure with Industry Dynamism

As described above, equity alliances are generally regarded as superior structures for transferring complex knowledge, both tacit and explicit, between alliance partners. Nonequity alliances are better suited for the transfer of less complex, primarily explicit knowledge. Hence, equity alliances are often chosen as the governance structure for R&D and marketing alliances, while nonequity alliances are a better fit for manufacturing and distribution alliances. Here we address the fit between these alliance structure choices and different levels of industry dynamism.

A dynamic industry environment is characterized by rapid changes in the underlying technologies (Harrigan, 1988) as well as changes in economic, cultural, and competitive factors (Suarez & Lanzolla, 2007). In this environment, organizational learning is closely associated with firm performance (Brown & Eisenhardt, 1997; Teece, Pisano, & Shuen, 1997), and alliances are a primary source of external learning (Hoffmann, 2007).

Environmental dynamism, i.e., the pace and nature of external change, has been described by a number of different authors and labels including turbulence (Siggelkow & Rivkin, 2005), uncertainty (Hoffmann, 2007), dynamism (Dess & Beard, 1984), velocity (Eisenhardt, 1989), and hypercompetition (Ilinitch, D'Aveni, & Lewin, 1996). In all cases, the breadth and depth of knowledge required to manage in these environments has increased, plus the connection among knowledge, action, and performance becomes less certain (Bourgeois & Eisenhardt, 1988). In addition, the external environment has become more complex and interdependent (Siggelkow & Rivkin, 2005).

In dynamic industries, the knowledge base of the partners is likely to be farther apart than in more stable environments, as the alliance is directed at reducing the complexity and uncertainty of the environment. The knowledge is also more likely to be tacit, as the complexity and rate of change makes explicit knowledge less valuable.

In order to effectively support learning in this environment, alliance partners rely on equity forms with structural coordination mechanisms, as well as the informal flow of information and knowledge among employees. If partners have developed technological expertise in the same fields, mutual learning will be easier with all else being equal, as firms are better able to absorb each other's knowledge. Under these circumstances, the need for sophisticated coordination mechanisms and the amount of the associated relation-specific investments are considerably reduced, as is the likelihood of resorting to equity modes.

Equity alliances allow firms to deal more effectively with rapid change in technological knowledge (Columbo, 2003). A number of empirical studies generally lend support to such predictions (Garcia-Canal, 1996; Gulati & Singh, 1998; Osborn & Baughn, 1990; Oxley, 1997).

In summary, the learning aspects of equity alliances are a better fit with dynamic environments and dynamic industries, and nonequity alliances are a better fit with less dynamic industries. From an organizational learning perspective and strategy perspective, this fit is associated with firm performance. At the portfolio level of analysis, managers should make governance choices so that the long-term fit is consonant with the choice of industry and associated dynamism, leading to above-average long-term performance. Thus,

> **Hypothesis 1c:** *For a firm in an industry with lower industry dynamism, an alliance portfolio composed primarily of nonequity alliances is associated with above-average firm performance.*

> **Hypothesis 1d:** *For a firm in an industry with higher industry dynamism, an alliance portfolio composed primarily of equity alliances is associated with above-average firm performance.*

Fit of Exploitation/Exploration with Competitive Strategy and Industry Dynamism

In addition to the choice of governance structure, managers can also enhance the value of an alliance portfolio by tailoring the fit of the learning mix of exploration/exploitation of the portfolio to the firm's generic strategy and to the dynamism of the industry. As with the discussion on governance structure, the fit is determined from an organizational learning perspective.

Initial scholars posed that the firm should try for a balance between exploration and exploitation, since too much exploration will lead to aimless churning, and excessive exploitation will cause strategic stagnation (March, 1991). A balance between exploration and exploitation is required for effective learning and performance improvement (Gupta, Smith, & Shalley, 2006; March, 1991). However, later researchers recognized that the proper mix of exploration and exploitation is contingent upon a number of factors, including the strategy and the external environment.

Exploration is concerned with knowledge that is distant from the focal company's base, while exploitation focuses on knowledge that is close or that is a refinement of existing knowledge. An increase in variation and search breadth is associated with exploration, while exploitation is directed at local search and search depth. Exploration is riskier and has a longer time frame than exploitation (March, 1991).

In examining the generic knowledge strategies in the pharmaceutical industry, Bierly and Chakrabarti (1996) distinguish between internal versus external learning, and radical versus incremental learning. A similar distinction between internal versus external and familiar versus new is made by Rosenkopf and Nerkar (2001), who define four types of exploration from a technology boundary and organizational boundary perspective.

Exploratory alliances cross both technology and organizational boundaries, while exploitation alliances just cross the organizational boundaries with external partners. The knowledge base of exploratory alliance partners has an inverse-U-shaped relationship with alliance learning and performance; in other words, the partners should have related knowledge bases, but not too related (Sampson, 2007).

Determining the fit between the exploration/exploitation balance of an alliance portfolio and the firm strategy of cost or differentiation is quite straightforward. The majority of alliances for a company with a cost strategy are focused on improving the existing value chain or lowering cost by altering the value chain. The partner knowledge of these alliances is close to the existing knowledge base of the focal firm—it is local search from a learning perspective—and the partners can specify a desired goal for the alliance. These alliances are usually associated with distribution or manufacturing and are exploitation alliances.

Therefore, an alliance portfolio for a firm with a differentiation strategy should primarily be exploratory alliances, focused on new products and markets or a shift in the firm's technology base (Hoffmann, 2007; Rosenkopf & Nerkar, 2001; Schildt, Maula, & Keil, 2005). These alliances are usually associated with R&D and marketing, and are exploratory alliances.

The interaction between a dynamic external environment and exploration has been extensively studied. Several studies have found an association between external exploration and increased learning, and performance in dynamic environments (Brown & Eisenhardt, 1997; Hitt et al., 1998). Miller and Friesen (1980), in a study of Canadian and U.S. firms, find that the external environment moderates the relationship between innovation and performance, and that successful firms increase the rate of innovation when environmental dynamism increases. Bierly and Daly (2007) examine the moderating effect of the external environment on both exploitation and exploration, finding that exploration has a higher impact on performance in high-tech dynamic environments than in stable, low-tech environments.

Therefore, an alliance portfolio for a firm in a dynamic external environment should primarily be exploratory alliances, and that fit with the external environment is associated with firm perfromance. Hence,

> **Hypothesis 2a:** *For a firm pursuing a generic cost strategy, an alliance portfolio composed primarily of exploitation alliances is associated with above-average firm performance.*

> **Hypothesis 2b:** *For a firm pursuing a generic differentiation strategy, an alliance portfolio composed primarily of exploration alliances is associated with above-average firm performance.*

> **Hypothesis 2c:** *For a firm in an industry with lower environmental dynamism, an alliance portfolio composed primarily of exploitation alliances is associated with above-average firm performance.*

> **Hypothesis 2d:** *For a firm in an industry with higher environmental dynamism, an alliance portfolio composed primarily of exploration alliances is associated with above-average firm performance.*

Dynamic Strategic Fit

As discussed above, the concept of fit has been one of the most widely ascribed and enduring concepts in strategic management (Venkatraman & Camillus, 1984) and is associated with performance improvements (Miles et al., 1978). The concept and its applications originally implied fit or alignment at a point in time; that is, a matching of internal capabilities and resources to external environment as a static model of strategy. As strategy has become a more dynamic concept, the application of fit has been adapted to the concept of strategic change (Rajagopalan & Spreitzer, 1997). Strategic fit is also studied as a dynamic fit over time, involving multiple environmental factors and multiple organizational contingencies (Zajac et al., 2000).

Allied with dynamic fit is the theory of dynamic capabilities, the ability to reconfigure assets in response to shifts in the dynamic external environment (Eisenhardt & Martin, 2000). Dynamic capabilities assist the firm in adapting over time and may include the ability to rebalance the ambidextrous capability of exploring new opportunities and exploiting existing businesses (O'Reilly & Tushman, 2008).

Dynamic fit is defined as the change in internal assets and capabilities in the proper amounts and when they are needed; and organizations that apply dynamic fit are associated with above-average long-term performance (Zajac et al., 2000). A study of alliance portfolios over time (Columbo, 2003) confirms the association with performance for partner diversity, but concluded that a focused set of approaches to alliance governance is superior to a balance between equity and nonequity alliances.

Therefore, firms should be concerned with dynamic fit among alliance portfolio characteristics, generic competitive strategy, and industry dynamism. The ability to change the alliance portfolio fit by adjusting the mix of governance and learning objectives to match changes in strategy and industry dynamism is a dynamic capability that is associated with long-term performance. Hence,

> **Hypothesis 3:** *The adaptation of an alliance portfolio fit to changes over time in the firm strategy and changes in industry dynamism is associated with above-average long-term performance.*

The relationships in Hypotheses 1, 2, and 3 are shown in the conceptual model in Figure 10.1.

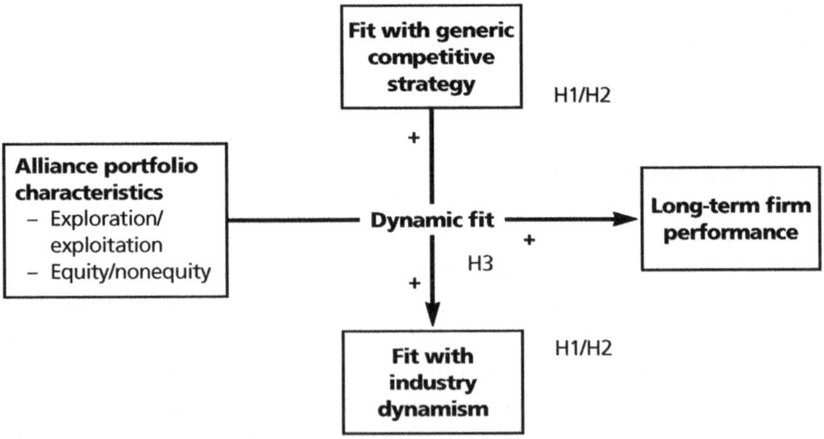

Figure 10.1 The dynamic fit of alliance portfolio characteristics—conceptual model.

PROPOSED EMPIRICAL EVALUATION

The model summarized in Figure 10.1 relates the governance and learning characteristics of a portfolio of alliances to the firm's generic strategy and industry dynamism. The potential empirical evaluation of the model is described by defining the industries and the longitudinal nature of the study approach, describing the variables in the study and the data sources, explaining the analysis techniques, and providing an overview of the expected study results.

Industries, Sample, and Study Period

Five different dynamic industry sectors will be used for this study: telecommunications equipment manufacturing, biotechnology, business software services, chemical products, and pharmaceuticals. These industries have experienced varying amounts of global competition and technological changes, and have varying levels of technology intensiveness. The industries also represent a sample of industry age and industry type, acting as a control for these factors. In all of the industries, only public U.S. firms are included in the study sample. For each of these five industries, medium and larger firms—those over $100 million in revenues by the end of the study period—will be sampled, as they are more likely to be the initiator of long and costly exploratory activities (March, 1991).

In order to capture the dynamic adaption of the alliance portfolio characteristics, a longitudinal study is planned. Several studies of alliances have been longitudinal. Rothaermel and Deeds (2004) used a sample of exploration and exploitation alliances over a 25-year period in their study of the new product development cycle. Schildt et al. (2005) examined external technological learning, including alliances, based on the patent filings of 110 communications technology firms from 1992 to 2000. Therefore, a longitudinal study is planned, using data for the years 1990 to 2009—a 20-year study period.

Variables and Measurements

Independent Variables

The SDC Platinum database provides data for the measurement of alliance governance and the purpose of the alliance. The SDC data is coded for each alliance as equity joint venture or nonequity alliance, and it also has fields for the alliance purpose. Alliances focused on R&D and marketing will be coded as exploratory, and alliances focused on manufacturing or distribution will be coded as exploitation alliances.

Diversity of exploration/exploitation and equity/nonequity is calculated using a measure called the Blau index, sometimes called the Herfindal-Hirschman index of homogeneity. For any given diversity variable, $D = 1 - \Sigma\ (Pi^2)$, where P is the proportion for any given category. The Blau index results in a measure between 0 (no diversity) and 1 for a perfectly heterogeneous group.

Industry dynamism is commonly measured as the R&D intensity, the ratio of R&D to industry revenues. The National Science Foundation reports R&D intensity annually. A rolling 3-year average of the variable is computed to smooth out yearly revenue variations.

The firm's competitive strategy—differentiation versus cost—is measured by the relative annual expenditures on R&D, and marketing versus sales, general and administrative expenditures (Yamakawa et al., 2001).

Control Variables

Firm size, firm slack, and firm age will be used as control variables, as these variables have been shown to affect organizational learning and firm performance. Firm size, age, and slack are associated with firm resources—resources that are required to support a strategy that includes both exploration and exploitation (March, 1991). Firm size will be measured here by calculating the average number of employees in the last 5 years of the study period. Slack will be measured as the current ratio of current assets to current liabilities. Firm age will be measured from the date that the firm was founded to the end of the study period.

Dependent Variable

The dependent variable is in annual return on assets (ROA), with a 3-year rolling average of the variable as the measurement. This data is available from the CompuStat database. Superior performance is defined here as relative to the industry average of ROA. For the dependent variable, the firm data is compared to the industry average, and the variable is measured as a percentage difference from the industry average.

Analysis Techniques and Expected Results

To test the hypotheses, two separate analyses will be required. For Hypotheses 1 and 2, an overall Blau index is calculated for the portfolio for the 20-year period. A 20-year average of the dominant generic strategy, the industry dynamism, and ROA is also used. To test Hypothesis 3, a year-by-year calculation of all of the variables is required.

In both analytical tests, hierarchical regression analyses are run for ROA and the independent variables. For each analysis, company performance is regressed with the study control variables in a hierarchical model. In a second step, the independent variables are added to the model, and finally, the control variables are added. Using hierarchical regression, the most variance in the dependent variable can be seen for each successive set of independent variables.

These analyses are expected to confirm Hypotheses 1 and 2 that the fit of the alliance portfolio characteristics with firm competitive strategy and industry dynamism is positively associated with above-average performance. The second analysis is expected to confirm that adjusting the fit with changes in strategy and dynamism is associated with above-average long-term performance.

SUMMARY AND DISCUSSION

This chapter develops a model relating firm performance to the fit of alliance portfolio characteristics with generic strategies and industry dynamism. The value of an alliance portfolio is enhanced if managers dynamically adjust the fit of alliance governance choices and the mix of exploration/exploitation alliances to changes in strategies and the external environment.

An organizational learning perspective is taken at the portfolio level to evaluate the issues of fit. The governance structures of equity and nonequity alliances are compared in terms of their relative treatment of knowledge flows and learning between alliance partners. Likewise, the characteristics of exploitation and exploration alliances differ in terms of learning objective, scope, and knowledge bases of the partners. These characteristics determine best fit between alliance governance choices and generic strategies, and between governance and the level of industry dynamism. Similarly, the best fit is evaluated between exploration and exploitation alliances with generic strategies and dynamism.

The resulting model hypothesizes eight relationships regarding fit:

- nonequity alliances are a superior fit with cost strategy
- equity alliances are a superior fit with differentiation strategy
- nonequity alliances are a superior fit with lower dynamism
- equity alliances are a superior fit with higher dynamism
- exploitation alliances are a superior fit with cost strategy
- exploration alliances are a superior fit with differentiation strategy
- exploitation alliances are a superior fit with lower dynamism
- exploration alliances are a superior fit with higher dynamism

For each hypothesis, the predominance of the portfolio fit between characteristics and generic strategy and industry dynamism is associated with above-average long-term performance. A final hypothesis associates firm performance with dynamic fit—the adaptation over time of the fit in the hypotheses above to changes in the firm's strategy and to changes in industry dynamism.

This chapter has the potential to be of assistance to managers in evaluating alliances in a systematic manner as part of an alliance portfolio instead of as one-by-one opportunities. Managers can view each alliance opportunity not only in terms of alliance objective and partnering potential, but also in terms of how the overall portfolio fits with the firm's generic competitive strategy and with the level of the firm's industry dynamism. For example, the model indicates that firms pursuing a differentiation strategy in a dynamic industry would benefit from a portfolio of predominantly equity alliances and exploratory alliances.

Areas that potentially could be strengthened in this model include broadening the scope of alliance characteristics, evaluating other generic strategy models, and adding other external factors. For example, the balance of domestic versus international alliances in a portfolio, the explorer and defender strategies, and level of industry competition could be evaluated as variables. This model shares a common issue in most alliance studies—the complexity of the field of study. For example, by taking the portfolio perspective of the mix of exploration and exploitation, the study ignores the evolution of an alliance over time at the dyad level. Finally, other aspects of a portfolio of alliance that affect learning, such as partner characteristics, were not included in this study. The author welcomes comments on these areas, as well as any other aspect of this chapter.

REFERENCES

Andrews, K. R. (1971). *The concept of corporate strategy.* New York: Dow Jones-Irwin.

Baum, J. R., Locke, E. A., & Smith, K. G. (2001). A multidimensional model of venture growth. *Academy of Management Journal, 44,* 292–403.

Benner, M., & Tushman, M. (2002). Process management and technological innovation: A longitudinal study of the photography and paint industries. *Administrative Science Quarterly, 47,* 676–706.

Bierly, P., & Chakrabarti, A. (1996). Generic knowledge strategies in the U.S. pharmaceutical industry. *Strategic Management Journal, 17,* 123–135.

Bierly, P., & Daly, P. S. (2007). Alternative knowledge strategies, competitive environment, and organizational performance in small manufacturing firms. *Entrepreneurship Theory and Practice, 31,* 493–516.

Bourgeois, L. J., & Eisenhardt, K. M. (1988). Strategic decision processes in high velocity environments. *Management Science, 34,* 816–835.

Brown, S. L., & Eisenhardt, K. M. (1997). The art of continuous change: Linking complexity theory and time-paced evolution in relentlessly shifting organizations. *Administrative Science Quarterly, 42,* 1–34.

Campbell-Hunt, C. (2000). What have we learned about generic competitive strategy? A meta-analysis. *Strategic Management Journal, 21,* 127–154.

Chandler, A. D. (1962). *Strategy and structure.* Cambridge, MA: MIT Press.

Colombo, M. G. (2003). Alliance form: A test of the contractual and competence perspectives. *Strategic Management Journal, 24,* 1209–1229.

Daft, R., & Weick, K. (1984). Toward a model of organizations as interpretation systems. *Academy of Management Review, 9,* 284–295.

Das, T. K., & Teng, B. (2000). A resource-based theory of strategic alliances. *Journal of Management, 26,* 31–61.

Dess, G. G., & Beard, D. (1984). Dimensions of organizational task environments. *Administrative Science Quarterly, 29,* 52–75.

Dess, G. G., & Davis, P. S. (1984). Porter's (1980) generic strategies as determinants of strategic group membership and organizational performance. *Academy of Management Journal, 27,* 467–498.

Eisenhardt, K. M. (1989). Making fast strategic decisions in high-velocity environments. *Academy of Management Journal, 32,* 543–576.

Eisenhardt, K. M., & Martin, J. A. (2000). Dynamic capabilities: What are they? *Strategic Management Journal, 21*(10), 1105–1121.

Garcia-Canal, E. (1996). Contractual form in domestic and international strategic alliances. *Organization Studies, 17,* 773–794.

George, G., Zahra, S. A., Wheatley, K., & Raihan, K. (2001). The effects of alliance portfolio characteristics and absorptive capacity on performance: A study of biotechnology firms. *Journal of High Technology Management Research, 12,* 205–226.

Goeltz, D. (2010). Alliance portfolio characteristics and organizational learning. In T. K. Das (Ed.), *Researching strategic alliances: Emerging perspectives.* Charlotte, NC: Information Age Publishing.

Goh, S. C., & Ryan, P. J. (2008). The organizational performance of learning companies. *Learning Organization, 10,* 225–239.

Grant, R. M., & Baden-Fuller, C. (2004). A knowledge assessing theory of strategic alliances. *Journal of Management Studies, 41,* 61–84.

Gulati, R. (1998). Alliances and networks. *Strategic Management Journal, 19,* 293–317.

Gulati, R., & Singh, H. (1998). The architecture of cooperation: Managing coordination costs and appropriation concerns in strategic alliances. *Administrative Science Quarterly, 43,* 781–814.

Gupta, A. K., Smith, K. G., & Shalley, C. E. (2006). The interplay between exploration and exploitation. *Academy of Management Journal, 49,* 693–706.

Harrigan, K. R. (1988). Joint ventures and competitive strategy. *Strategic Management Journal, 9,* 141–158.

Hitt, M. A., Keats, B. W., & DeMarie, S. M. (1998). Navigating in the new competitive landscape: Building strategic flexibility and competitive advantage in the 21st century. *Academy of Management Perspectives, 12*(4), 22–42.

Hoffmann, W. H. (2007). Strategies for managing a portfolio of alliances. *Strategic Management Journal, 28,* 827–856.

Ilinitch, A. Y., D'Aveni, R. A., & Lewin, A. Y. (1996). New organizational forms and strategies for managing in hypercompetitive environments. *Organization Science, 7,* 211–220.

Inkpen, A. C. (1998). Learning and knowledge acquisition through international strategic alliances. *Academy of Management Executive, 12*(4), 69–80.

Keil, T., Maula, M., Schildt, H., & Zahra, S. A. (2008). The effect of governance modes and relatedness of external business development activities on innovative performance. *Strategic Management Journal, 29,* 895–907.

Kogut, B. (1988). Joint ventures: Theoretical and empirical perspectives. *Strategic Management Journal, 9,* 319–332.

Lavie, D., & Rosenkopf, L. (2006). Balancing exploration and exploitation in alliance formation. *Academy of Management Journal, 49,* 797–818.

Leonard-Barton, D. (1992). Core capabilities and core rigidities: A paradox in managing new product development. *Strategic Management Journal, 13,* 111–125.

Levinthal, D. A., & March, J. G. (1993). The myopia of learning. *Strategic Management Journal, 14,* 95–112.

Lieberman, M. B., & Montgomery, D. B. (1998). First-mover (dis)advantages: Retrospective and link with the resource-based view. *Strategic Management Journal, 19,* 1111–1125.

Lin, Z., Yang, H., & Demirkan, I. (2007). The performance consequences of ambidexterity in strategic alliance formations: Empirical investigation and computational theorizing. *Management Science, 53,* 1645–1658.

March, J. G. (1991). Exploration and exploitation in organizational learning. *Organization Science, 2,* 71–87.

McGrath, R. G. (2001). Exploratory learning, innovative capacity, and managerial oversight. *Academy of Management Journal, 44,* 118–131.

Miles, R. E., Snow, C. C., Meyer, A. D., & Coleman, H. J., Jr. (1978). Organizational strategy, structure, and process. *Academy of Management Review, 3,* 546–562.

Miller, D. (1981). Toward a new contingency approach: The search for organizational gestalts. *Journal of Management Studies, 18,* 1–26.

Miller, D., & Friesen, P. H. (1978). Archetypes of strategy formulation. *Management Science, 24,* 921–933.

Nonaka, I. (1994). A dynamic theory of organizational knowledge creation. *Organization Science, 5,* 14–37.

O'Reilly, C. A., & Tushman, M. L. (2008). Ambidexterity as a dynamic capability: Resolving the innovator's dilemma. *Research in Organizational Behavior, 28,* 185–206.

Osborn, R. N., & Baughn, C. C. (1990). Forms of interorganizational governance for multinational alliances. *Academy of Management Journal, 33,* 503–519.

Oxley, J. E. (1997). Appropriability hazards and governance in strategic alliances: A transaction cost approach. *Journal of Economic Behavior & Organization, 13,* 387–409.

Oxley, J. E., & Sampson, R. C. (2004). The scope and governance of international R&D alliances. *Strategic Management Journal, 25,* 723–749.

Pangarkar, N., & Klein, S. (2001). The impacts of alliance purpose and partner similarity on alliance government. *British Journal of Management, 12,* 341–353.

Parkhe, A. (1993). Strategic alliance structuring: A game theoretic and transaction cost examination of interfirm cooperation. *Academy of Management Journal, 36,* 794–829.

Pisano, G. P. (1989). Using equity participation to support exchange: Evidence from the biotechnology industry. *Journal of Law, Economics, and Organization, 5,* 109–126.

Porter, M. (1980). *Competitive strategy.* New York: Free Press.

Porter, M. (1985). *Competitive advantage.* New York: Free Press.

Powell, W. W., Koput, K. W., & Smith-Doerr, L. (1996). Interorganizational collaboration and the locus of innovation: Networks of learning in biotechnology. *Administrative Science Quarterly, 41,* 116–145.

Rajagopalan, N., & Spreitzer, G. (1997). Toward a theory of strategic change: A multi-lens perspective and integrative framework. *Academy of Management Review, 22,* 48–79.

Randolph, W. A., & Dess, G. G. (1984). The congruence perspective of organization design: A conceptual model and multivariate research approach. *Academy of Management Review, 9,* 114–127.

Rosenkopf, L., & Nerkar, A. (2001). Beyond local search: Boundary-spanning, exploration, and impact in the optical disk industry. *Strategic Management Journal, 22,* 287–306.

Rosenkranz, S. (2007). Strategic positioning of alliances. *International Journal of the Economics of Business, 14*(1), 135–149.

Rothaermel, F. T., & Deeds, D. L. (2004). Exploration and exploitation alliances in biotechnology: A system of new product development. *Strategic Management Journal, 25,* 201–224.

Rumelt, R. P. (1974). *Strategy, structure, and economic performance.* Boston: Harvard Business School Press.

Sampson, R. C. (2007). R&D alliances and firm performance: The impact of technological diversity and alliance organization on innovation. *Academy of Management Journal, 50,* 364–386.

Schildt, H., Maula, M., & Keil, T. (2005). Explorative and exploitative learning from external corporate ventures. *Entrepreneurship Theory and Practice, 29,* 493–515.

Schoenmakers, W., & Duysters, G. (2006). Learning in strategic technology alliances. *Technology Analysis & Strategic Management, 18,* 245–264.

Siggelkow, N., & Rivkin, J. W. (2005). Speed and search: Designing organizations for turbulence and complexity. *Organization Science, 16,* 101.

Simon, H. A. (1960). *The new science of management decision.* New York: Harper & Brothers.

Suarez, F. F., & Lanzolla, G. (2007). The role of environmental dynamics in building a first mover advantage theory. *Academy of Management Review, 32,* 377–392.

Teece, D. J., Pisano, G., & Shuen, A. (1997). Dynamic capabilities and strategic management. *Strategic Management Journal, 18,* 509–533.

Teng, B., & Das, T. K. (2008). Governance structure choice in strategic alliances: The roles of alliance objectives, alliance management experience, and international partners. *Management Decision, 46,* 725–742.

Thompson, J. D. (1967). *Organizations in action: Social sciences base of administrative theory.* New York: McGraw-Hill.

Uotila, J., Maula, M., Keil, T., & Zahra, S. A. (2009). Exploration, exploitation, and financial performance: Analysis of S&P 500 corporations. *Strategic Management Journal, 30,* 221–231.

Van de Ven, A. H. (1976). On the nature, formation, and maintenance of relations among organizations. *Academy of Management Review, 1,* 24–36.

Venkatraman, N., & Camillus, J. C. (1984). Exploring the concept of "fit" in strategic management. *Academy of Management Review, 9,* 513–525.

Wassmer, U. (2008). Alliance portfolios: A review and research agenda. *Journal of Management, 36,* 141–171.

Woodward, J. (1965). *Industrial organization: Theory and practice.* London: Oxford University Press.

Wu, W., Wu, Y., & Lin, Z. (2004). The impact of governance mechanisms on interfirm learning and relationship performance. *Proceedings of the Asia-Pacific Management Conference,* 447–462.

Wuyts, S., Dutta, S., & Stremersch, S. (2004, April). Portfolios of interfirm agreements in technology-intensive markets: Consequences for innovation and profitability. *Journal of Marketing, 68,* 88–100.

Yamakawa, Y., Yang, H., & Lin, Z. J. (2011). Exploration versus exploitation in alliance portfolio: Performance implications of organizational, strategic, and environmental fit. *Research Policy, 40,* 287–296.

Zajac, E. J., Kraatz, M. S., & Bresser, R. K. F. (2000). Modeling the dynamics of strategic fit: A normative approach to strategic change. *Strategic Management Journal, 21,* 429–453.

CHAPTER 11

COMPLEMENTARITY BETWEEN INTERNAL AND EXTERNAL KNOWLEDGE IN INTRADISTRICT NETWORKS

César Camisón

ABSTRACT

No firm can rely entirely on its internal knowledge capacities and sources to create competitive innovation advantages. Firms would be proactively asking for the complementarity between the activities of internal knowledge creation and the assimilation of external knowledge from different sources, forming strategic alliances between them. Specifically, innovation can be regarded as resulting from research opportunities focused on how knowledge creation and diffusion processes would benefit from localized knowledge spillovers between firms colocated within industrial clusters, defined as a network of personnel, or an interorganizational and institutional network. However, the literature has not yet well understood how these processes benefit from both these localized knowledge spillovers and networks within the cluster or whether their effects are consistently positive. This chapter, grounded in the resource-based view, the Scandinavian Approach to the industrial district, and the social capital perspective, and with a multilevel analysis, presents a synthesis of the existing theory on the knowledge creation and transfer pro-

Strategic Alliances for Value Creation, pages 237–277

cesses within industrial districts, and proposes a theoretical framework by studying in depth the relationships between district-level and firm-specific capacities, as well as the effects of the intracluster networks on both the firm's knowledge-generative and absorptive capacities, and its skill in facing both incremental and radical technological innovation. This understanding of the topic allows the proposition of firm-specific strategies for value creation and value appropriation in intracluster networks and alliances by increasing the company's exploration and knowledge-absorption capacities.

EXTERNAL AND INTERNAL KNOWLEDGE PROCESSES

Knowledge is accumulated by two processes: the internal creation of knowledge and the absorption of external knowledge (Chakravarthy, McEvily, Doz, & Devaki, 2003). Although different in nature, these two processes are interrelated: a company's innovative assets exist as a consequence of the complementarity between the creation of internal knowledge and the assimilation of external knowledge (Cassiman & Veugelers, 2006; Cohen & Levinthal, 1990; Teece, Pisano, & Shuen, 1997; Zahra & George, 2002).

We understand a firm's *internal knowledge creation capacity* to mean "all the competences associated with the creation of an internal system of continuous learning in the firm" (Camisón & Forés, 2011, p. 68). A firm's internal knowledge creation is, fundamentally, generated by research and development (R&D) investment and internal problem solving (Prieto, Revilla, & Rodríguez-Prado, 2009). Chandler's (1990) paradigm counsels firms to obtain competitive advantages through scale and scope economies, to develop these advantages as large diversified corporations do, along with vertical integration and the creation of industrial R&D labs. The antecedents of a firm's internal knowledge creation are the employees' abilities, level of education, experience, training, and skills, which they acquire in the workplace through their interaction with other agents having different knowledge bases (Nonaka & Takeuchi, 1995). This variety of knowledge gives us a diversity of perspectives to process the newly acquired knowledge by driving to new associations and to innovation. The firm's directors can collaborate with the knowledge creation by creating the structural and cultural conditions for this, making the internal generation of knowledge feasible. This organizational environment matches the definition of a mission that stimulates the sense of identity of a firm's employees (Davenport, De Long, & Beers, 1998; De Long & Fahey, 2000); an appropriate structure (Nonaka & Takeuchi, 1995), which includes the formation of self-management teams and informal social networks (Mahnke, Pedersen, & Venzin, 2005; Staples, Greenaway, & McKeen, 2001); as well as an organizational culture and leadership focused on knowledge obtainment and learning objectives by including values as a greater autonomy. These values allow employees to achieve more complex learning by creating new ideas and mental models (Nonaka & Takeuchi, 1995).

The Chandlerian view requires that firms be able to internally develop the knowledge they need. Some environmental changes have reduced this need for vertical integration and for internal knowledge development. Between the drivers of an evolution toward new practices in knowledge development, we include the rapid technological changes and increased competition in a globalized economy (Gassman, 2006; Mowery, 2009), increasing interfirm modularity and labor division (Langlois, 2003a, 2003b), increased mobility of knowledge (through labor mobility), and availability of venture capital to create new firms to capitalize on such knowledge (Chesbrough, 2003a). Together, new ways of conceptualizing innovation based on absorptive capacity (Cohen & Levinthal, 1990) or open innovation (Chesbrough, 2003a, 2003b, 2006 ; von Hippel & von Krogh, 2003) have relaxed many of the assumptions in the Chandlerian model. This literature has established some well-known, empirically tested propositions that are robust points of departure for building an explanatory model for the knowledge-development process.

Two points are of particular note. It is generally accepted that no firm can rely exclusively on its internal knowledge capacities and sources to create competitive advantages with respect to innovation (Camisón & Forés, 2011, p. 66). External sources of innovation have gained relevance. The flows of knowledge that come from a firm's environment are opportunities for companies to obtain a wider base of knowledge and to be on top of technological advances by making up the internal knowledge shortages common to all firms today and by developing the internal creativity and problem-solving capabilities (Soo, Devinney, & Midgley, 2007). The acquisition of knowledge also offers more possibilities for a company to recombine its stock of this asset with the newly acquired knowledge to transform it into useful ideas more quickly than rivals (Teece & Pisano, 1994). The external acquisition increases the flexibility of the firm, flexibility being a critical aspect for competitiveness in a dynamic and innovative environment (Almeida, Phene, & Grant, 2003; Grant, 1996). Therefore, it hardly seems likely that a company's innovative capacity is solely an increasing function of its own knowledge-creation effort. Firms should combine purposive inflows and outflows of knowledge to accelerate internal innovation (Chesbrough, 2003b, p. 38; Teece et al., 1997). The open-innovation paradigm assumes that firms can and should combine external and internal ideas into their architecture and systems having requirements defined by a business model to create value. Further, it identifies successful firms as those making the best simultaneous use of internal and external ideas.

Unlike the internal development of knowledge within a company, the absorption of external knowledge implies the utilization of mechanisms by which outside knowledge can be assimilated, transformed, and applied. Cohen and Levinthal (1990) define *absorptive capacity* as a firm's capacity to value, assimilate, and apply knowledge derived from external sources for commercial ends. This definition of absorptive capacity, in the context of technological knowledge, has proven fundamental for the conceptualization of the construct and helpful to an extent that very few subsequent studies have revised or expanded it.

We follow the line of authors who defend the need to study absorptive capacity from a dynamic or process-oriented perspective. Specially, Zahra and George (2002) link the construct to a set of organizational routines and strategic processes through which firms identify, acquire, assimilate, transform, and exploit knowledge, with the aim of creating a dynamic organizational capacity. This definition by Zahra and George reformulates the traditional three-dimensional model introduced by Cohen and Levinthal (1989, 1990), as it identifies four different complementary dimensions: acquisition, assimilation, transformation, and application. The concept of each of these processes is described in Table 11.1. Zahra and George suggest that these dimensions can be integrated into two complementary components: (a) potential absorptive capacity, which comprises external knowledge-acquisition and assimilation capacities; and (b) realized absorptive capacity, which includes both knowledge-transformation capacity and the capacity to exploit newly developed knowledge.

TABLE 11.1 Dimensions of Firm's Absorptive Capacity by Zahra and George (2002)

- Acquisition capacity is defined as the firm's ability to locate, identify, value, and acquire external knowledge that is critical to its operations (Lane & Lubatkin, 1998; Zahra & George, 2002).
- Assimilation capacity refers to the firm's capacity to absorb external knowledge. This capacity can also be defined as the processes and routines that allow the new information or knowledge acquired to be analyzed, processed, interpreted, understood, internalized, and classified (Szulanski, 1996; Zahra & George, 2002).
- Transformation capacity is the firm's capacity to develop and refine the internal routines that facilitate the transfer and combination of previous knowledge with the newly acquired or assimilated knowledge. Its main objective is to establish how to adapt the new knowledge to the reality and needs of the organization (Zahra & George, 2002).
- Finally, application or exploitation capacity refers to the firm's ability to use new knowledge, for commercial ends, to achieve its objectives (Lane & Lubatkin, 1998). This capacity can also be defined as the organizational capacity based on routines that enable firms to incorporate acquired, assimilated and transformed knowledge into their operations and routines not only to refine, perfect, expand, and leverage existing routines, processes, competences, and knowledge, but also to create new operations, competences, and routines (Zahra & George, 2002).

Nevertheless, firms vary in their ability to access and leverage external sources of knowledge, and it is quite likely that this variability of firms in their ability to learn and profit from these external knowledge sources is largely dominated by their internal organization. Acquiring external knowledge requires internal effort and R&D investment by the recipient firm for developing a specific knowledge base (Cockburn & Henderson, 1998; Cohen & Levinthal, 1990; Lane & Lubatkin, 1998; Leany & Neary, 2007). Therefore, a second starting point is the capacity of a firm to absorb new external knowledge, which capability depends on how the organization adjusts its internal structures (Caloghirou, Kastelli, & Tsakanikas, 2004; Fosfuri & Tribó, 2008; Zahra, Filatotchev, & Wright, 2009). This internal reorganization is necessary to support the formation and sustenance of other organizational capabilities, which are essential to the absorption of external knowledge, such as corporate venturing and intrapreneurship (Zahra et al., 2009); the development of qualified specialist technicians, scientists, and engineers (Rothwell & Dodgson, 1991); and the development of cultural patterns and an open and dynamic communication system. The effective management of this externally acquired knowledge will then likely require the development of complementary internal networks (Hansen, 1999, 2002; Hansen & Nohria, 2004) for internal learning (Arora & Gambardella, 1994; Cassiman & Veugelers, 2002, 2006). The cumulative and path-dependent process of capability accumulation is therefore highly specific to each firm, so that even if the same amount of time has passed and firms operate in the same macroenvironment and industry, they may end up with different levels of technological capabilities (Figueiredo, 2002). The widespread use of external knowledge from open innovation sources does not change the nature nor reduce the relevance of a firm's core competences. Although firms become skilled at incorporating each other's specialized technologies or ideas, rather than necessarily developing their own, that practice provides a much broader market for a firm's core competences, enabling these capabilities to then support other organizations' business and technologies (West, Vanhaverbeke, & Chesbrough, 2006).

These two propositions point to a third basic point: firms would proactively request the complementarity between the activities of internal knowledge creation and the assimilation of external knowledge from different sources (Cohen & Levinthal, 1990; Fosfuri & Tribó, 2008; Teece et al., 1997; Veugelers, 1997; Volberda, Foss, & Lyles, 2010; Zahra & George, 2002). Firms must be able to see external knowledge flows as opportunities for acquiring information from their environments and to complement such acquisition with the internal knowledge stock, transforming it into useful knowledge more quickly than their rivals (Escribano, Fosfuri, & Tribo, 2009; Teece & Pisano, 1994).

ABSORPTIVE CAPACITY AND INTERORGANIZATIONAL NETWORKS

Firms are increasingly using various methods as external knowledge sources to complement their internal knowledge creation. These sources include the hiring of qualified researchers with valuable knowledge (Cockburn & Henderson, 1998); the formation of informal social relationships among members of different organizations (Gulati, 1988; Oliver & Liebeskind, 1998); and strategic alliances rooted in social and commercial relationships with customers, suppliers, competitors, consultants, public agencies, and trade and professional associations (Anderson, Forsgren, & Holm, 2002; Chen, 2004; Gulati, Nohria, & Zaheer, 2000; Koka & Prescott, 2002; Uzzi & Lancaster, 2003).

Innovation and learning must be regarded as resulting from distributed *interorganizational networks and strategic alliances* (Das, 2010; Das & Kumar, 2007), rather than from single firms (Coombs, Harvey, & Tether, 2003; Douglas & Ryman, 2003; Dyer & Singh, 1998). Hamel (1991) defines the acquisition of new specialized knowledge as motivation to develop interorganizational cooperation. Firms establish a variety of interorganizational ties and alliances, such as technology licences (Atuahene-Gima, 1992), R&D alliances (Hagedoorn, Link, & Vonortas, 2000), innovation-centered collaboration along the supply chain (Harabi, 1998), business alliances (Kumar & Nti, 1998), and cooperative agreements with both public and private research centers (Meyer-Krahmer & Schmoch, 1998).

This insight is convergent with the studies disclosing the nonlinear, interactive, and multiagent character of innovation processes (Kline, 1985; Lundvall, 1988; von Hippel, 1987). Some papers (e.g., Chesbrough, 2003a; Fabrizio, 2006; Perkmann & Walsh, 2007) postulate that open innovation cannot be conceived without considering the networking between innovating firms, on the one hand, and universities and research labs, on the other hand. West and Gallagher (2006) explore how communities of practitioners and firms create a symbiotic relationship that leads to the explosive growth of open-source software.

Firms can also access knowledge resulting from spillovers that circulate freely in their environment without explicit permission from the innovators of this knowledge. Spillover effects are externalities of economic activity or processes upon those who are not directly involved in it. Knowledge spillover is a nonrival knowledge-market externality that has an effect on the exchange of ideas, and that stimulates technological improvements in a neighbor company through one's own innovation. The literature on knowledge spillovers postulates that knowledge created within organizations can be used by other firms when pieces of that knowledge can be codified and transferred, thus generating positive externalities. This method is particularly attractive for small and medium-sized firms (SME) that have fewer economic and technological resources with which to establish external links (Rothwell & Dodgson, 1991). In general, the new absorption, versus open-based innovation models, have been presented as suitable for large multinational firms. Nevertheless, the application of these models also offers advantages to understanding the case of a firm's (basically SMEs) working cluster.

LOCALIZED KNOWLEDGE SPILLOVERS IN INDUSTRIAL DISTRICTS

Within the literature on interorganizational innovation networks, there are already other research opportunities focused on how knowledge creation and diffusion processes would benefit from localized knowledge spillovers between firms in the same industry (e.g., Verspagen & Schoenmakers, 2004). So, Breschi and Lissoni (2001) define localized knowledge spillovers as knowledge externalities bounded in space, which allow companies located in close proximity of one another to get information and knowledge from neighboring organizations without cost. It remains a broad opportunity for research on how geography affects innovation activities between firms (West et al., 2006).

The more interesting case of firms' spatial colocation is the *industrial district,* or cluster, concept. Industrial districts are models of industrial development that have been observed, from the 1970s onwards, in different countries and industries (principally with the profile of traditional manufacturing like furniture, ceramics, clothes, shoes, and toys). Industrial districts are especially evident in Italy, particularly in some small and medium-sized cities in the center and northeast of the country, like Prato, Modena, and Carpi. Since the initial studies by Becattini (1979) and Brusco (1982), a very broad body of economics and sociological literature has been generated, closely examining the Italian experience (e.g., Becattini, 1987, 1989, 1990b; Bellandi, 1989, 1992; Brusco, 1990). Similar industrial areas have been identified in many other countries (Sengerberger, Loweman, & Piore, 1990). Spain also has a significant number of such districts for various industries and in various geographical areas (e.g., Camisón, 2004).

The first studies on industrial districts, essentially based on the work of Marshall (1919) and his theory of external economies, highlight the importance of cooperative behavior among the firms embedded in a specific geographical area as a way of stimulating growth and facing the challenges of international competition. Industrial districts were defined canonically in Becattini's seminal work (1979), which took up Marshall's definition of industrial district and profiled its stylized features. Becattini's canonical concept defined an industrial district as a socioeconomic entity characterized by the active presence of a population of firms (basically SMEs specializing in certain activities) in a limited territorial and historically bounded area, linked with a dense structure of cooperation networks, knowledge transfer, and supplier-purchaser relationships. This productive system is embedded in a community of people who share a feeling of belonging, trust, and common identity, as well as in a community with a relatively homogeneous system of values and ideas, which sustain collective and individual learning processes, minimize the threat of opportunism (Dei Ottati, 1994) inherent in temporal strategic alliances (Das, 2006; Das & Rahman, 2010), and enable transactional relationships to be established at a lower cost than the internal coordination costs that derive from a hierarchical form of organization—or vertical integration (D'Aveni & Illinich, 1992). By considering a community of people and firms, other more intangible, sophisticated resources and relationships are taken into account, thus going beyond Marshall's agglomeration economies. The perspective of the embeddedness (Granovetter, 1985) further enriches this vision with the perception of the industrial district as a dense social network of links among firms. Other aspects that have been considered are the existence of a specific labor market and of support programs, institutions, and infrastructures developed by public bodies.

The local learning and innovation processes are habitually based more on collective actions by interconnected agents within networks than on individual strategies. This concept of knowledge spillovers as a key agglomeration factor supports the idea that tacit knowledge flows are better when organizations are located in the same area (Malipiero, Munari, & Sobrero, 2005). The concept of localized knowledge spillovers has developed to describe the spatial boundaries of knowledge flows in which knowledge is free of charge (Boari & Lipparini, 1999), "in the air" (e.g., Audretsch & Feldman, 1996), or public goods bounded in space (Krugman, 1991). The strong interdependence among people and firms within a common space, and the shared competences circulating freely, would promote the internal homogeneity of the district (Becattini, 1979, 1990a; Brusco, 1990), in terms of firms' capacities to identify, value, acquire, assimilate, transform, and apply external knowledge for the purposes of innovation.

The fruitful experiences described above have formed the basis for a fertile line of research that views industrial districts as an effective industrial model in the face of the changes being experienced by traditional industrial organizations, due to the technological dynamism, adaptation to the economic crises, growing international presence, capacity for innovation, and flexible specialization of the firms integrated into these territorial agglomerations. In particular, from strategic and management research, industrial districts have increasingly been recognized as an organizational model that enables small and medium-sized enterprises to compete internationally (Batteyri, 1988; Becattini, 1979, 1987; Brusco, 1982; Krugman, 1991; Lazerson, 1995; Miles & Snow, 1986; Powell, 1990; Wiklund & Karlsson, 1994). These studies view an industrial district as a system, and its nuclear hypothesis can be expressed as follows (Figure 11.1):

> **Hypothesis 1:** *There is a positive relationship between the organization of the industrial model as a district and its competitiveness.*

Some empirical studies have provided evidence that firms belonging to an industrial district perform better (Becchetti & Rossi, 2000; Karlsson & Klaesson, 2000; Paniccia, 1998, 1999; Signori, 1994), and they are associated with superior learning and innovative performance (Audretsch, 1998; Audretsch & Feldman, 1996). However, another line of papers (e.g., Camisón, 1992; Camisón, Roig, & Torcal, 1992) does not confirm the hypothesis that the industrial district is a superior organizational model in general. Industrial districts are heterogeneous, their proximity to the canonical model varies, and we can observe internationally competitive clusters, together with clusters in decline or with a poor level of international competitiveness.

These contradictions, originating from the economic contributions to the industrial districts research, have some relevant weaknesses that require careful consideration of the results. Two such weak points are particularly noteworthy: (a) the methodological and conceptual problems in theoretical and empirical studies (Paniccia, 1998; Parr, 2002), and (b) the lack of a theoretical model to guide research into the sources of industrial districts' success (Foss, 1996a).

The methodological deficiencies stem from research based on industrial district case studies selected idiosyncratically by the researcher (Paniccia, 1998). A further important methodological problem is the difficulty in measuring basic concepts, beginning with the very definition of agglomeration economies (Malmberg & Maskell, 2002; Parr, 2002) and of an industrial district; these difficulties being a consequence of putting the attention on different territorial agglomeration-based models (Brenner, 2000). Becattini (1990a, p. 51) has already noted the need to conceptualize the industrial district to enable "the precision and conclusions derived from empirical studies to be improved."

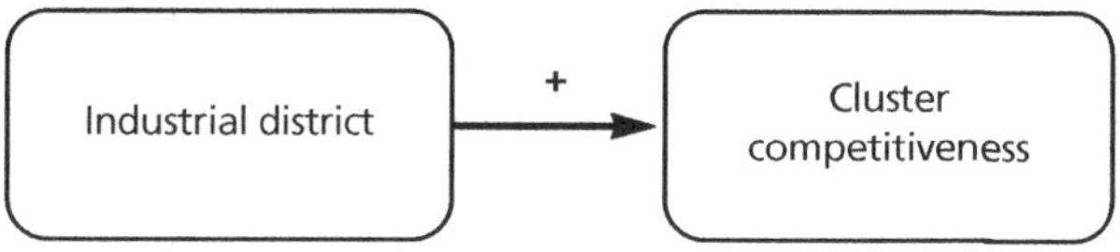

Figure 11.1 The canonical approach to the industrial district competitiveness.

Conceptual controversy surrounding the industrial district concept has two fundamental dimensions. First, the distinctive notes of their content, with parallel approaches centered exclusively on economic variables (e.g., Bellandi, 1989, 1992) or on those enriched with cultural and social variables (Becattini, 1979, 1990a; Lazerson & Lorenzoni, 1999). It is therefore typical (particularly in American research, e.g., DeCarolis & Deeds, 1999) that the cluster is only partially conceptualized, focusing above all on regional R&D institutions. Second, the setting of its geographical boundaries, with a good number of studies—most typical in American research—marks out districts at the regional level (DeCarolis & Deeds, 1999; Enright, 1995, 1998; Porter, 1990, 1998, 2000; Porter & Sölvell, 1998; Saxenian, 1991, 1994), because they are thinking specially in regional clusters; on the contrary, canonical, Marshallian definition maintains that the most appropriate level is the local scope. The concept of an industrial district not only as a spatial system, but instead as a homogenous historical, social, and cultural area, is an important difference from regional clusters: these boundaries are more limited (local versus regional dimension), and collective R&D processes typical of industrial districts would be better defined by intensive practices for disseminating innovation. In regional clusters, by contrast, companies develop extensive practices to protect innovation (patents and other legal safeguards).

With respect to the second problem, Foss (1996a) pointed out the absence of a firm theory in the studies on territorial agglomerations. The strategic analysis of industrial districts is of notable interest because of its emphasis on the factors determining the achievement of a sustained competitive advantage and steady economic rents. To generalize the conclusions, with a stronger theoretical and statistical basis, it is necessary to approach the study of industrial districts from theories that are based on the contribution of the intradistrict shared competences and firm-specific resources and capabilities. The resource-based view (RBV) is an appropriate perspective for this purpose. This theoretical model supports the view that superior business performance is only achieved when the firm has valuable resources and capabilities available as a source of sustainable competitive advantages (Barney, 1986, 1991; Peteraf, 1993; Wernerfelt, 1984). RBV is a plural approach, with different and complementary perspectives for analyzing the firm's resources and capabilities. Within the RBV dynamic perspective (Nelson & Winter, 1982; Teece et al., 1997; Zollo & Winter, 2002), the competences-based view (CBV) (Foss, 1997; Foss & Knudsen, 1996; Grant, 1996; Kogut & Zander, 1992; Sánchez, Heene, & Thomas, 1996) is of particular interest. CBV is a firm-level theory that identifies tacit knowledge and intangible assets as the basic source of competitive advantage and explains the firm's knowledge-acquisition process as a consequence of interfirm variability in the learning process that leads to the reconfiguration and transformation of existing capabilities and innovation.

CBV can be applied to the knowledge-creation and absorption processes in an industrial district. The CBV extension to industrial districts is mainly grounded in the Scandinavian approach. The first works to use this approach were those by Foss and Eriksen (1995) and Foss (1996b), which engendered a stream of fruitful literature (e.g., Karlsson & Klaesson, 2000; Lawson, 1999; Lawson & Lorenz, 1999; Lorenzen, 1998, 2003; Lorenzen & Foss, 2003; Lorenzen & Maskell, 2004; Malmberg, Malmberg, & Lundequist, 2000; Malmberg & Maskell, 2002; Maskell, 2001a, 2001b; Maskell & Lorenzen, 2004; Maskell & Malmberg, 1999).

SHARED COMPETENCES AND DISTRICT COMPETITIVENESS

The developments as to the concepts and drivers of knowledge-based capabilities flowing within a cluster have been stopped by the ambiguous definition of the resources and capacities accumulated in the industrial district and shared by all firms located within it.

Research inspired by the RBV has been applied to strategic alliances (e.g., Das & Teng, 2000), with some papers (Camisón, 2001, 2004; Douglas & Ryman, 2003; Dyer & Singh, 1998) mentioning the shared competences by networked organizations. Additionally, Arikan (2008) has developed the concept of a cluster's knowledge-creation capability, which is also based on the conditions that stimulate interfirm knowledge exchanges within industrial districts. Shared competences by firms located in an industrial district, such as the concepts by Camisón (2004), Foss (1996a), Foss and Eriksen (1995), and Lorenzen (1998, p. 143), are a higher order of knowledge than are firm-specific capabilities. Shared competences are a measure of the structural attractiveness of knowledge spillovers from the industrial district into which the organization is inserted. This attractiveness determines the endowment of knowledge that may be deposited in it, which is then accessible to the intradistrict firms, and it is the first source of cluster heterogeneity.

By integrating the Social Capital Approach and Scandinavian Approach, we define "shared competences as consisting of social capital that stimulates the wealth of intradistrict knowledge flows and complementary assets as an institutional framework facilitating support services and organizations" (Camisón & Forés, 2011, p. 70). Lorenzen (2007) also shares this concept and defines social capital as a matrix of various social relations, combined with particular normative and cognitive social institutions that facilitate cooperation and reciprocity, growing the density of matrix with spatial proximity.

From this theoretical definition, we define intradistrict shared competences in industrial districts from two dimensions: the external capacity for knowledge creation and transfer, and the coordination of collective effort.

External Capacity of Knowledge Creation and Transfer

This dimension integrates the knowledge spillovers emerging from both a collective, localized learning curve (Lawson & Lorenz, 1999; Lorenzen, 1998, 2003, 2007), the fast transfer of information and innovations with few restrictions among intradistrict firms, and benchmarking processes by which companies access the knowledge and successful experiences (on innovation, strategy, and the internal organization models) of their neighbor companies (Camisón, 2004). The first driver of this capacity is the availability of a rich local pool of qualified human capital—consultants, subcontractors, and equipment manufacturers—who have acquired the specialized education and experience in technologies and processes in institutions and firms located in a cluster. The second driver is knowledge spillovers resulting from dynamism in the information and knowledge flows about products, processes, technologies, consumers, and markets, which circulate informally within the system (Lorenzen & Maskell, 2004). These knowledge spillovers include explicit knowledge about customers or suppliers available through extra-nets, business-to-business webs, or sector webs; alongside tacit knowledge about R&D projects developed by intradistrict firms in cooperation with technological institutes or universities. These flows are intensified by the intensity of cooperation relationships, one of the most important defining elements of an industrial district. The diffusion of knowledge derives basically from direct, personal contacts between people employed in local organizations (Audretsch & Felman, 1996; Dahl & Pedersen, 2004; Maskell & Malmberg, 1999; Saxenian, 1994) that operate side-by-side in a geographical environment with a highly permeable and flexible social structure, processes of "cross-pollination" favored by the high turnover of local labor among intradistrict companies, and local spin-offs.

The rich, local diffusion of knowledge is not a simple consequence of geographical proximity. It also needs a relationship pattern for the informal transfer of ideas and technology within the local territorial environment. The literature on open innovation concludes that the relevance of interpersonal and interorganizational networks for knowledge-diffusion processes is rooted in the nature of knowledge creation and transfer as a socially embedded process (e.g., Brown & Duguid, 1991). Therefore, the intradistrict collaborative model depends upon the existence of a people community

(Crewe, 1996; Grandori, 1999; Harrison, 1991; Paniccia, 1998) characterized by the concept of embeddedness from Granovetter (1985). This social context produces strong social links, the mutual knowledge and widely agreed-upon standards on the desired behavior (Becattini, 1979, 1990a; Lazerson & Lorenzoni, 1999; Nahapiet & Ghoshal, 1998), which are deeply embedded in the local traditions (Malmberg & Maskell, 2002) by way of a cognitive community (Lorenzen & Foss, 2003). Intradistrict relationships are cohesive networks that facilitate trust and cooperative exchanges (Coleman, 1988). This highly permeable and flexible social structure facilitates the limitation of the risk of opportunistic behaviors and enables intradistrict firms to extend their skills in exchanging quality knowledge (Dei Ottati, 1994; Foss & Koch, 1996; Lorenz, 1992; Yli-Renko, Autio, & Sapienza, 2001); but at the same time, these social mechanisms are difficult for the district-specific knowledge transfer outside.

Coordination of Collective Effort

This dimension reflects the presence of local institutions (universities, vocational training centers, technological institutes, R&D centers, industrial policy agencies, business and professional associations, competitors clubs) that provide a host of collective support mechanisms for collective learning processes driven by sector leaders or business networks. Local institutions have been recognized as relevant actors in industrial districts (McEvily & Zaheer, 1999). You and Wilkinson (1994) indicate that this institutional structure serves four functions: to create an environment for cooperation, provide procedures for resolving conflicts, impose sanctions on offenders, and provide appropriate support for companies to align themselves with environmental changes. First, these locally oriented organizations can act as intermediaries that play a relevant role in providing intradistrict firms with new information and knowledge, and in supporting business innovation (Breschi & Lissoni, 2001; Camisón, 2004; Saxenian, 1991). Local institutions also provide training and services to coordinate cooperative relationships (Newlands, 2003; Oughton & Whittam, 1997). The existence of local institutions is especially valuable, as they collaborate in the creation and maintenance of an environment in which constructive types of cooperation and competence—particularly innovative competence—predominate over destructive ways of operating based on price competition (Dei Ottati, 1994; Mistri & Solari, 2001). Collective strategy also includes public institutions (Henry & Pinch, 2001), which coordinate the agents located within the industrial district, support business development, and promote the design of a local strategic orientation in the cluster. Finally, there is a process of the institutional creation of a collective reputation based on the communication activities carried out cooperatively by competitor groups, business associations, or public institutions, which can be clearly differentiated from those of competitors outside the agglomeration.

Shared competences accumulated in a district are accessible to the intradistrict firms, but not available to firms located beyond its boundaries. The literature (e.g., Hall, 1993) has repeatedly emphasized the special value of intangible assets as a source of sustainable competitive advantages due to the barriers raised to duplication (Barney, 1991; Dierickx & Cool, 1989; Grant, 1991) and to substitution by similar strategic assets (Barney, 1986, 1991; Dierickx & Cool, 1989; Peteraf, 1993). The barriers for the imitation, appropriation, or substitution of shared competences are even greater because they are largely district specific, idiosyncratic, path dependent, complex, and based on tacit knowledge accumulated in a district (Enright, 1998: Maillat, 1998). Porter and Sölvell (1998) state that this type of knowledge is based on traditional routines, business practices, unique institutions, and multiple links between actors, which cannot be reproduced outside the area, and thus, its mobility is greatly restricted. In addition, Sölvell and Zander (1998) use the concept of the isolating mechanism in local innovation systems to underline the strategic nature of these collective capabilities. The knowledge spillovers in an industrial district are strongly dependent on an economic, social atmosphere that includes a pattern of human-capital development, and learning and knowledge flows are either not easy to come by outside the district, or cannot be reproduced outside the area. Together, the agents that coordinate the collective effort will offer more opportunities to provide that knowledge to firms located inside the district than to competitors located outside it.

A growing number of empirical studies provide evidence that industrial districts are a rich common space of learning and knowledge spillovers bounded in space with the profile of shared competences we have described. For example, from a study of 952 firms and 35 clusters in Spain, Camisón (2004) and Camisón and Forés (2011) reported that industrial districts are environments defined by localized knowledge spillovers, which intracluster firms can access, and which include strong, stable, long-term interpersonnel and interorganizational relationships, density in networks of information and knowledge exchange, coordination of collective effort by local institutions that provide a host of supports, a stock of human capital with a high turnover interfirm, and a social structure that shares a value system and supports a trusting environment.

Therefore, industrial clusters are heterogeneous in shared competences stock, and this variability in shared competences can explain their competitiveness as a system. The simple relocation into an industrial district does not necessarily lead to superior competitiveness, because the key drivers to obtaining an advantage over outsider firms are based on the wealth of

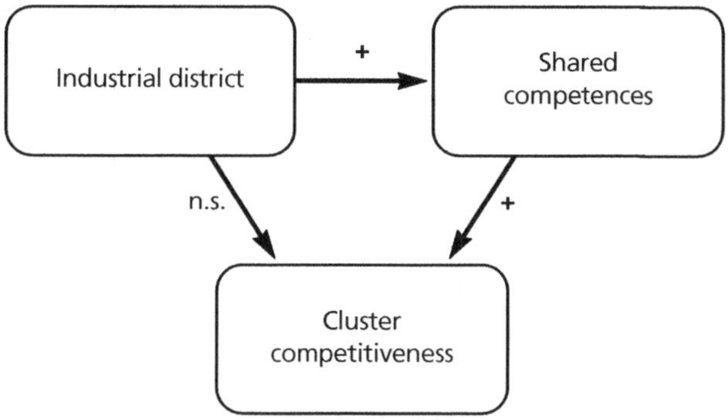

Figure 11.2 The shared competences approach to the industrial district competitiveness.

resources and the capabilities associated with the intradistrict networks and institutions. A second proposition may be outlined (Figure 11.2):

> **Hypothesis 2:** *There is a positive relationship between the shared competences accessible within an industrial district and the cluster competitiveness.*

THE MULTILEVEL NATURE OF KNOWLEDGE-BASED CAPABILITIES

Given that the definition of the resources and capacities accumulated and shared in the industrial district, and the explanation of their differences from firm-specific, knowledge-based capabilities have advanced thanks to previous studies, we can now extend the distinction of Camisón (2002) between personal and corporate capabilities, to aggregate the shared competences. Camisón (2004) differentiates *three levels of competences.* The personal capabilities are equivalent to what many authors call skills and are defined as competences possessed by an individual or a group of individuals inside the organization as the leadership or the experience. The corporate capabilities consist of combinations of knowledge and skills that are a firm's property. In contrast to the potentially migratory character of the tacit individual knowledge, corporate knowledge tends to be independent of individuals and to persist in the organization when individuals leave, because such knowledge is embedded in the organizational activities and structures. We define industrial districts as an external space containing shared capabilities to which intracluster firms could have access. But companies could not appropriate these capabilities because they are embedded in the processes, networks, and institutions existing within the district (Camisón, 2001, 2004; Keeble & Wilkinson, 1999).

The multilevel nature of the concept capabilities (Peteraf, 2005) has become more evident. But this progress has developed other methodological lags: specifically, the lack of a specified level of analysis. The research on a multilevel construct-as-capabilities demands a multilevel study (Klein, Dansereau, & Hall, 1994; Mossholder & Bedeian, 1983).

The problem of lack of specification of the analysis level is labeled in levels literature as committing a fallacy of the wrong level (e.g., Glick, 1988; Glick & Roberts, 1984). Following Klein et al. (1994), the level issue refers to a specific organizational context described as "individuals within groups." The term "group" is used broadly and can be interpreted to mean any higher-level organizational entity—the industrial district in our case (or a strategic alliance). Similarly, the term "individuals" may be interpreted to refer to members of higher-level entities, in our case, firms located or not within an industrial district. Failing to specify a theory level can produce problems, because the researcher does not describe the target for which theoretical generalizations are made or because the methodological and/or statistical analyses are incongruent with the level of theory, in which case, the results may misrepresent the theoretical relationship, a fact the research would have uncovered. Klein et al. (1994) highlight the primacy of theory in addressing the levels issue. Therefore, the first step in addressing this issue is the specification of the level of one's theory, which describes the target (e.g., individual, group, firm, interorganizational network, industry, or industrial district) that researchers aim to explain and from which generalizations can be made.

The relevance and meaning of the level-of-analysis issue within industrial districts literature have not been explored, despite the fact that new theoretical developments about the knowledge process in firms and industrial districts have highlighted these issues. A multilevel construct as knowledge-based capabilities may be conceptualized from different theoretical approaches with alternative assumptions that specify a theory at diverse levels. By making this decision, the researcher (implicitly or explicitly) predicts that members located in an industrial district are homogeneous, independent, or heterogeneous in relation to the constructs of the theory (knowledge-based capabilities), and consequently, the relationships among different categories of capabilities (firm-specific versus shared competences) are a consequence of differences among clusters, among independent firms located in clusters, or among firms within clusters.

In specifying that the level of a theory is a group, a researcher predicts that group members are homogeneous with respect to a theoretical construct, and that these individuals' values are identical, and they may be characterized as a whole, and consequently, the proposed relationships should focus on the variation between groups. The canonical approach to industrial districts (Becattini, 1979; Brusco, 1982) is a good example of this view. This theoretical approach considers the industrial district as a homogeneous space with rich resource and capability stocks, which firms can access. This definition comes close to that of Porter (2000, p. 16), who conceptualizes the cluster as a "geographically proximate group of interconnected companies and associated institutions in a particular field linked by commonalities and complementarities."

The intense interdependence among people and firms derived from stable, long-term, direct relationships between the agents in the local environment, within a relatively homogeneous community that shares a value system, should also play a key role in supporting intradistrict symmetry. The free and spontaneous transmission of knowledge, and the model of reference within the specific industrial atmosphere of the district, should also act as a force to foster shared behaviors. In that case, a canonical approach would study industrial districts as a homogeneous group, by which the target unit is conceptualized as a single and whole unit and described by a single value.

At the opposite extreme, much of the organizational and strategy literature has adopted an independence approach, and studies firms in relation to a group, such as the potential cluster in which they are located. From this perspective, researchers have specified the level of theory as the independent firm, and they predict that individual firms (even when they are located within a cluster) will be independent of that group's influence. Because cluster membership would be irrelevant to the theory's constructs, the distinction of within-cluster and between-cluster variation is viewed as irrelevant. Variation in the constructs is conceptualized only as a between-firms variation. The main line of this level of theory is RBV.

It should be recognized that many of the studies included in the canonical approach and CBV have noted that the research into the behaviors and performance of firms located within an industrial district is a cross-level study, and logically, higher-level district properties should homogeneously influence lower-level organizational properties. However, the theories differ and can be placed in the industrial district (as a group) or firms (as individuals).

Specifically, beyond the study of the two classical alternatives (homogeneity versus independence; e.g., Glick, 1988), the recognition of a third alternative of heterogeneity (Glick & Roberts, 1984; Klein et al., 1994) is relevant, because in discussing the meaning and implications of heterogeneity, we discover a fruitful avenue for theory building regarding knowledge-based capabilities. When the researcher adopts a cross-level theory, the focus is not just upon the firm (individuals) or the cluster (group), but rather the firms within clusters (individuals within the group), and therefore, it is necessary to combine the study of the individual attributes of intradistrict firms and the cluster average for evaluating this attribute. Further, it is asserted that firms located in an industrial district (group members) are neither homogeneous nor independent of the cluster, but instead heterogeneous, and that they vary within intradistricts with respect to the construct of interest. So, preceding works have pointed out the specificities of knowledge flows within industrial districts and competitive asymmetries between firms within the same industrial district derived from their different patterns of appropriation of shared competences (Arikan, 2008; Camisón, 2004; DeCarolis & Deeds, 1999; Lazerson & Lorenzoni, 1999; McEvily & Zaheer, 1999; Rabellotti, 1993; Rabellotti & Schmitz, 1999), which are in turn connected with their heterogeneous firm-specific capacities. Camisón and Forés (2011) developed the first theoretical approach to the topic from a multilevel perspective. Their cross-level approach is an interesting contribution to the understanding of knowledge creation and diffusion flows by firms located within an industrial district, regarding the multilevel nature of the concept capabilities. Following Camisón and Forés, a firm's knowledge-based capabilities stock can be explained using suprafirm-level variables in the theoretical discussion, as the Social Capital Approach and Scandinavian Approach propose.

Due to the growing external relationships and sources of knowledge that firms use to represent social capital, through interaction with other agents, they are channels for the exchange of a variety of capital, information, and knowledge (Inkpen & Tsang, 2005; Koka & Prescott, 2002; Tsai, 2000; Tsai & Ghoshal, 1998), by creating learning opportunities for firms, and by fostering obligations and expectations that are based on reciprocity and equity. *Social capital* can be defined as "the sum of resources that accrue to a firm by virtue of possessing a durable network of interfirm relationships" (Bourdieu & Wacquant, 1992, p. 199). The depth, extent, and efficiency of the mutual exchange is determined by the use the firm makes of its external relationships for acquiring and exploiting knowledge, and it is regulated by the amount of social capital embedded in these networks (Yli-Renko et al., 2001).

The Social Capital Approach can be integrated into the CBV in two ways. First, its propositions are consistent with the Relational-based View (Lane & Lubatkin, 1998), which suggests that a firm's competitive advantages derive both from the resources the firm itself owns and from the resources embedded in the dyadic and network relationships with the environment. Second, the Social Capital Approach is also aligned with the knowledge-based view that considers knowledge to be the basic source of competitive advantage (Grant, 1996; Kogut & Zander, 1992). In both cases, knowledge that is accessible through the firm's social network can be viewed as a strategic asset in itself, because the network is path-dependent and, as a result, is idiosyncratic and difficult to imitate or to substitute. Social capital is a matrix of various social relationships, combined with particular normative and cognitive social institutions that facilitate cooperation and reciprocity, and in which the density of matrices increases with the proximity (Lorenzen, 2007). Therefore, this concept can be applied to the cases of firms with knowledge resulting from spillovers that circulate in industrial districts in which they are located.

The CBV extension to industrial districts, grounded in the Scandinavian Approach, can also be a suitable approach to taking a theoretical assumption of heterogeneity of intradistrict firms within a higher-level unit (the cluster) in studying the effects on the knowledge-creation and absorption processes of a firm's integration into an industrial district (Grant, 1991, p. 548). This extension stems from the suggestion by Peteraf (2005) that RBV is a useful approach to exploring multilevel linkages and the multilevel nature of capabilities. A CBV of competitive advantage naturally links the firm to its market environment and the other players within that environment.

From this perspective, the cluster is deemed to be a meaningful level. Knowledge of cluster context is necessary to interpret an individual firm's placement within the district. An industrial district can be an external space containing shared competences that are common assets and not exclusive to one single firm inside the cluster. All intracluster firms have access to these assets, but any can appropriate them because shared competences are embedded into the processes, networks, and institutions existing within the district. This common space is a promoting factor for internal homogeneity within the district (Becattini, 1990a; Brusco, 1990), as it conditions the behavior of firms located within it. The strong interdependence between people and firms within a relatively homogenous community having a shared value system works in favor of symmetry. The transmission of knowledge and reference models within the particular industrial atmosphere of the district is another force in favor of common behavior patterns (Camisón, 2004, p. 2231).

But this literature also highlights the cluster dependence of a firm's knowledge process. The knowledge-based competitive advantage is a function of the capabilities of a specific company, relative to its competitors. Heterogeneity, as to capabilities, implies that some firms have capabilities that can generate more economic value than those of other firms (Peteraf & Barney, 2003). In this vein, for example, a single firm may be a superior performer relative to its extracluster competitors and an inferior performer relative to its intradistrict competitors.

From this multilevel study, clusters are heterogeneous between them, and this variability can explain their competitiveness as a system. But the intradistrict firms' competitiveness cannot be explained solely by shared competences within the district because they are also heterogeneous. The competitive asymmetries between firms located in an industrial district derive from the specific firm capability stock. A cross-level approach demands

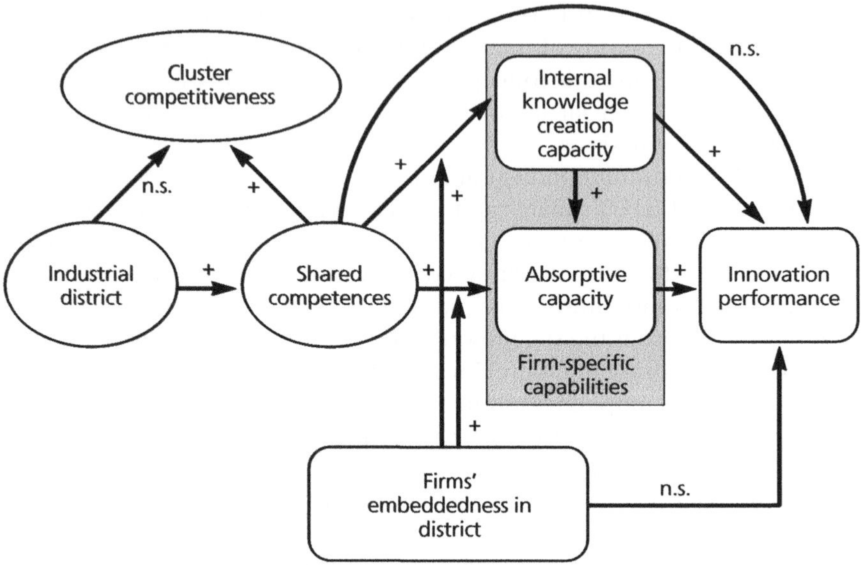

Figure 11.3 A theoretical and multilevel model of intracluster firms competitiveness based on knowledge capabilities.

that the focus be put upon, not only the firm or the cluster, but rather the firms within a cluster, and therefore it is necessary to combine the study of the individual knowledge-based capabilities of intradistrict firms with the cluster-shared competences. The competitiveness and performance of a firm located within an industrial cluster would derive from their different patterns of appropriation of shared competences, which are, in turn, connected with their heterogeneous firm-specific capacities. Figure 11.3 schematically represents the theoretical framework in studying competitiveness and the results of intradistrict firms from this multilevel approach.

A FIRM'S CLUSTER EMBEDDEDNESS, INTRADISTRICT SHARED COMPETENCES, AND FIRM-SPECIFIC KNOWLEDGE CAPABILITIES

Intradistrict Shared Competences and a Firm's Knowledge-Absorption Capacity

Shared competences are external knowledge accessible within the industrial district due to the knowledge flows and an institutional infrastructure. But they are different from absorptive capacity, which describes a firm's capability to acquire, assimilate, transform, or apply that external knowledge. Although they are capabilities at different levels, they are correlated, and postulating that shared competences are drivers for a firm's absorptive capacity is feasible.

Explicit knowledge may be relatively easy for a firm to absorb through passive efforts, such as attending conferences; or more active methods, such as benchmarking (Lane & Lubatkin, 1998). But intracluster knowledge spillovers comprise a large portion of district-specific tacit knowledge flows, which are difficult to codify and can only be transferred through face-to-face interactions, which are frequent within industrial districts. The existence of a large number of interpersonal links (Foss & Pedersen, 2002; Tsai & Ghoshal, 1998), the strength or degree of closeness of these links (Brown & Konrad, 2001), the intensity and repetition of interactions (Maskell & Malmberg, 1999; Triglia, 2001; Yli-Renko et al., 2001) that an organization carries out with other agents in its environment, and the mutual trust and reciprocity among organizations within a cluster (Levin, Cross & Abrams, 2003) increase their ability to evaluate, acquire, and assimilate quality knowledge, particularly knowledge with a certain tacit component (Cohen & Levinthal, 1990; Dyer & Singh, 1998; Lane & Lubatkin, 1998). Due to the mutual trust among intradistrict agents, thanks to restraints, the lack of the threat of opportunism (Dei Ottati, 1994; Foss & Koch, 1996; Yli-Renko et al., 2001) produces savings in surveillance mechanisms, thus freeing up resources that can be used for more extensive communication (Zaheer, McEvily, & Perrone, 1998). The large number of interactions that take place among firms physically located in a close space, and the speed with which knowledge resources flow, also lead to a reduction in the costs of searches, transactions, and communication among the parties located within this space (Maskell, 2001a).

The existence of a series of intermediary agents, such as the local institutions that are specialists in acquiring information and knowledge (Brusco, 1990) as well as leading firms, connected by diverse external networks and knowledge communities, collaborate for intradistrict firms to develop their absorptive capacity as well. These gatekeepers help district firms to access information and knowledge from inside, as well as outside, the industrial district, and to reduce the costs of searches and access they face for exploration and analysis of external information and knowledge (Maskell, 2001a; McEvily & Zaheer, 1999).

Considering the above, we put forward the following hypothesis:

Hypothesis 3: *Ceteris paribus: the greater the shared competences in an industrial district, the higher the firm's capacity to absorb external knowledge.*

The existence of localized knowledge spillovers within an industrial district will not be sufficient to ensure that intracluster firms internalize them satisfactorily (Pennings & Harrianto, 1992). Perhaps explicit external knowledge can be absorbed by intradistrict firms directly and easily without the presence of other internal knowledge. But although the complex and tacit knowledge that flows within localized knowledge spillovers is not protected, this does not mean that this knowledge will be automatically acquired by intracluster firms. The identification, acquisition, and above all, implementation of external knowledge are by no means simple processes (Veugelers, 1997), nor are they cost-free (Harabi, 1995). The existence of social interaction and supportive local institutions plays a key role in knowledge transfer, particularly for tacit knowledge, but does not guarantee that the recipient firm will be able to internalize that external knowledge.

The absorption of this knowledge requires that it be accompanied by the development and availability of internal knowledge that both supports the acquisition and assimilation of external knowledge and can be combined for transformation, and finally application, for commercial ends. This is the complementarity hypothesis between the activities of internal knowledge creation and the assimilation of external knowledge enunciated for all external sources (e.g., Cohen & Levinthal, 1990; Escribano et al., 2009; Fosfuri & Tribó, 2008; Teece et al., 1997; Volberda et al., 2010; Zahra & George, 2002). This condition has two steps: the shared competences require a simultaneous effort by intracluster firms to develop internal knowledge that capacitates it to acquire and assimilate the knowledge spillovers; only when this previous internal knowledge base is available, can the external and internal knowledge be combined, transformed, and applied. Therefore, rather than a direct relationship between shared competences and absorptive capacity, there is an indirect relationship, which is mediated by the internal knowledge-creation capacity. We theoretically justify this new relationship in two steps.

Intradistrict Shared Competences and Firms' Internal Knowledge-Creation Capacity

The individual firms located in industrial districts are still free agents that play the leading role in their own development (DeCarolis & Deeds, 1999; Lazerson & Lorenzoni, 1999; McEvily & Zaheer, 1999). Therefore they can act in different ways when faced with the opportunities the intracluster environment offers.

Intracluster companies could have the temptation of limiting their knowledge availability to the knowledge absorbed from the cluster. When this scenario occurs, external knowledge can substitute for or diminish internal investment for R&D (e.g., Harabi, 1995; Levin & Reiss, 1988; Veugelers, 1997; Veugelers & Cassiman, 1999). Together, the possibility of a firm's internally generated knowledge being exploited by its closest competitors may also lead it to reduce investment in R&D and training (Bernstein & Nadiri, 1989; Spence, 1984). Another potential barrier to a positive relationship between external knowledge and internal knowledge creation stems from the diversity argument. Literature on creativity postulates that diversity within a context is what matters to innovation, and therefore, the more knowledge-sharing, the less diversity and less innovation (Henderson & Cockburn, 1996). Industrial districts are local productive systems with localized knowledge spillovers, which are rich and rarely varied, and have a dense supply by spatial closest competitors. Furthermore, the stock of shared competences and knowledge may be detrimental to the internal generation of knowledge. Although these ideas are correct, location in an industrial district would encourage firms to cut back on their efforts to create knowledge internally and to instead concentrate on capitalizing on the knowledge spillovers that circulate in their environment.

Of course, all firms located in industrial districts enjoy access to a common stock of shared competences and knowledge within their immediate environment. But when an intradistrict firm cuts back on its efforts to create knowledge internally and instead concentrates on exploiting the localized knowledge spillovers that circulate within the cluster, it ignores the need to supplement this exploitation with the exploration of new sources of ideas and technologies. Firms that do not want to lose their competitive position in the district and aspire to accessing the knowledge opportunities in their environment must also work to develop new routines and structures and a culture that fosters internal knowledge generation. The relationships of competition and cooperation between firms within the cluster (You & Wilkinson, 1994), explained by their physical proximity and the similarity in the products they offer, stimulate the continuous internal generation of knowledge and new technologies in firms striving to hold on to their competitive advantage in the market (Camisón & Forés, 2011, p. 72). Additionally, industrial clusters are environments with rich, localized knowledge spillovers, within which firms could access knowledge exchanges. In this way, the district acts as a "cognitive laboratory" (Bellandi, 1989) or a collective R&D laboratory, in which innovation continuously flourishes (Camisón, 2004).

In light of the above, we consider that the existence of shared competences acts as an incentive for the development of internal knowledge-creation capacity. Our fourth hypothesis is therefore,

Hypothesis 4: *Ceteris paribus: the higher the level of shared competences in an industrial district, the higher the firm's internal knowledge-creation capacity.*

Firms' Internal Knowledge-Creation Capacity and Absorptive Capacity

As we have explained previously, although the external knowledge is not easy to protect, this does not mean it will be automatically acquired by other firms. These external knowledge opportunities can only be absorbed if the firm has previously generated a critical internal mass of knowledge through R&D investment (e.g., Cohen & Levinthal, 1990; Leany & Neary, 2007), and has developed complementary capabilities that allow this new external knowledge to be valued, understood, and related to the previous knowledge base, and finally, applied (e.g., Caloghirou et al., 2004; Fosfuri & Tribo, 2008; Hansen & Nohria, 2004; Zahra et al., 2009). Likewise, a firm immersed in an environment with freely circulating knowledge flows will only be able to take advantage of the pool of knowledge spillovers when it is complemented with internal knowledge creation (Fabrizio, 2009; Nieto & Quevedo, 2005).

Therefore, for acquiring the external tacit knowledge flowing within an industrial intracluster, firms must be combined with certain firm-specific capacities and practices to absorb those external competences (Camisón, 2004; Foss, 1996a; Lawson, 1999; Malmberg & Maskell, 2002). The cumulative and path-dependent process of capability accumulation is therefore highly specific to each firm, so that even if the same amount of time has passed, and firms operate within the same macroenvironment and industry, they may end up with different levels of technological capabilities (Figueiredo, 2002). Without this previously related knowledge base, intradistrict firms will not be able to identify the innovativeness potential of external knowledge for the creation of competitive advantages, and may even be unaware of the existence of the cooperative knowledge networks. But an intradistrict firm's knowledge base is constrained to certain scientific and technological domains (Lane & Lubatkin, 1998). Therefore, it is logical to assume that the effect of shared competences on the development of a firm's absorptive capacity is also limited and mediated by its internal knowledge stock. Intracluster firms need, in order to access and exploit external knowledge flowing within the cluster, qualified and specialized human and intellectual capital in the knowledge domains district, embedded cultural patterns fitted to the social community, and a communication system open to change and learning.

Specifically, following De Clercq and Dimov (2008), we suggest a variety of mechanisms to explain why a firm's internal knowledge-creation capacity in a particular domain will lead it to develop domain-specific absorptive capacity. First, the diversity and depth of the firm's internal knowledge base provide it with different frames of reference, standards, languages, and codes. These advantages give the firm a more comprehensive understanding of the new information it receives, increasing its ability to scan and identify valuable tacit knowledge in the environment. Internal knowledge-creation capacity generates the ability to discover additional and superior ideas (Chesbrough, 2003a), and to access and select external opportunities more efficiently (Chatterji, 1996) and faster (Cohen & Levinthal, 1990). At the same time, internally developed knowledge and technologies increase operational flexibility, also facilitating the external acquisition of technology (Gans & Stern, 2000). Moreover, through the process of interacting with other employees, new knowledge, which increases the capacity to access knowledge from external firms (Liao, Fei, & Chen, 2007), can be acquired.

Secondly, a larger prior-knowledge base facilitates more abstract mapping of the domain of the firm's activity and allows for a higher level of articulation and codification of its knowledge base. These abstract representations lead to improved assimilation and integration of the new information into the existing knowledge base (Zollo & Winter, 2002).

Thirdly, according to Cohen and Levinthal (1990), the diversity of the knowledge base will augment the organization's capacity for making new linkages and associations between new external knowledge and preexisting concepts. Knowledge developed internally therefore enhances the firm's ability to incorporate additional knowledge into its internal processes (Arora & Gambardella, 1994) and to apply it for commercial ends through its incorporation into the firm's operations (Van den Bosch, Volberda, & de Boer, 1999).

In light of the above, we can state that the firm's internal knowledge-creation capacity is required to acquire, assimilate, and transform knowledge from outside its boundaries and to apply it to innovative strategies (Cohen & Levinthal, 1990). In light of the above, we can state that the firm's internal knowledge-creation capacity is required to acquire, assimilate, and transform knowledge from outside its boundaries and to apply it to innovation. Accordingly, our fifth hypothesis is as follows:

> **Hypothesis 5:** *The greater the firm's internal knowledge-creation capacity, the higher its capacity to absorb external knowledge.*

CLOSED-SPATIAL NETWORKS AND ALLIANCES: EFFECTS IN EXPLORATION AND EXPLOITATION

Organizational learning requires both the *exploration* of new paths and the *exploitation* of what is already known (Gupta, Smith, & Shalley, 2006; He & Wong, 2004). Therefore, learning and the generation of new knowledge exist in exploration activities related to searching, experimentation, and risk taking, as well as in exploitation processes consisting of the leveraging of and expanding upon existing competences and technologies, and also focusing on gaining efficiency (March, 1991). The way firms reach a balance between explorative and exploitative activities is complex, since as March indicated, the two processes can require routines of a very different nature to develop. A balance between the explorative and the exploitative processes requires an organizational design that comes close to the ambidexterity model (Benner & Tushman, 2003).

The strong interdependence among people and firms within a common space, and the localized knowledge spillovers, constitute pressure for the internal homogeneity of the district (Becattini, 1979; Brusco, 1990), in terms of firms' capacities to acquire, assimilate, transform, and apply external knowledge for the purposes of innovation. The intradistrict knowledge transfer is also stimulated by the sharing and joint development of experience by intradistrict agents (suppliers, competitors, customers, public institutions) through a dense network of non-production-related cooperation agreements. Territorial clusters are characterized by a dense network of strong connections that have a positive impact through the promotion of social norms and sanctions that promote trust and cooperation among members (Uzzi, 1996, 1997).

Some previous literature has distinguished between different outcomes, according to the existence of a large number of links (Tsai & Ghoshal, 1998) and the strength of the ties among individuals and companies (Brown & Konrad, 2001). Some studies (e.g., Uzzi, 1996) associate strong ties with exchanges of high-quality information and tacit knowledge (bonded capital). Others (e.g., Granovetter, 1973) extend the benefits to weak ties. Strong bonds increase the capability to profit from existing opportunities and facilitate the continuous improvement or incremental innovation of existing technologies. The positive association between social interaction and knowledge acquisition and assimilation capacities is consistent with the assumptions that learning, particularly learning involving information that is difficult to transfer (i.e., tacit information), is facilitated by intensive, repeated interactions (Kogut & Zander, 1992). Knowledge spillovers might consist of a large proportion of district-specific tacit knowledge flows, which are difficult to codify and can only be transferred through face-to-face interactions, which occur frequently within industrial districts.

However, there is empirical evidence that the informational advantages have less to do with the intensity of ties than with the degree of closeness or repetition of interactions (Maskell & Malmberg, 1999; Triglia, 2001; Yli-Renko et al., 2001) between an organization and other agents in its environment; in other words, network structural holes from which firms obtain access to information and knowledge of nonredundant sources (Krackhardt, 1992). The literature on creativity (Milliken & Martins, 1996; Paulus, 2000; Sethi & Park, 2001; Woodman, Sawyer, & Griffin, 1993) postulates that diversity in skills, knowledge, and experience among individuals within a context is what matters to innovation, because a heterogeneous population will draw on the most varied sources of information and may lead to a wider variety of interpretations, a greater number of alternatives, and a superior capacity to solve disparate problems. The assumption of homogeneity prevailing in the canonical view could lead to the belief that, within the cluster, there is little variety in shared ideas and approaches and fewer opportunities to learn about different perspectives, leading therefore to a diversity-reduced probability of finding more innovative solutions. Closed-spatial, interorganizational networks have the disadvantage of potential redundancies in the relationships between their members, which limits access to new knowledge and restricts the benefits of the diversity of information and of the availability of infrequent commercial associations (bridging capital) (McEvily & Zaheer, 1999).

The local institutions could act as an intermediary that plays a relevant role in providing intradistrict firms with new information and knowledge, including the ones associated with sparse networks strewn with structural holes (Burt, 1992, 1997). Consequently, they can help individual firms avoid the disadvantages that stem from being redundantly connected with other participants in an industrial district. Therefore, they extend the benefits derived from access to diverse information and knowledge and from brokerage opportunities related to the maintenance of nonredundant relationships.

The intradistrict heterogeneity is also stimulated by the variety of networks of interfirm relationships. The variety in social capital embedded in the networks in which every intradistrict firm is involved is another explanatory factor of the positive encouragement of location in a cluster on both the exploitation of existing knowledge and the development of incremental improvements upon it, and the exploration of new knowledge or the development of radical innovations.

CONCLUSIONS

The dynamism and complexity of the current economic environment forces firms to be aware of the importance of knowledge in holding on to their competitive advantages and creating value. They must therefore develop an understanding of the degree of ideal complementarity between their internal knowledge-creation activities and their absorption of external knowledge. The influence of different methods for accessing external knowledge, based on interorganizational cooperation and strategic alliances on firms' capacities to acquire and assimilate knowledge, has been noted in the literature (e.g., Douglas & Ryman, 2003; Dyer & Singh, 1998;

Zahra & George, 2002). In contrast, research on the effect of location in an industrial district and the stock of shared competences as triggers of the knowledge-accumulation process in the firms based in the district is scarce. This chapter, grounded in the RBV, the Scandinavian Approach to the industrial district, and the Social Capital perspective, and with a multilevel analysis, presents a synthesis of the existing theory on the knowledge-creation and transfer processes within industrial districts and extends the previous theoretical framework by studying in depth the relationships between district-level and firm-specific capacities that have been explored by very few studies (e.g., Camisón, 2004; Camisón & Forés, 2011; Lawson, 1999; Malmberg & Maskell, 2002). The research concludes that there is ample opportunity for amplifying the accumulated knowledge on the topic in the strategic management and industrial districts literature by adding a better understanding of the effects of the intracluster networks in both the firm's knowledge-generative and absorptive capacities, as well as its skill in facing incremental and radical technological innovation. This understanding of the topic allows the proposition of firm-specific strategies for value creation and value appropriation in intracluster networks and alliances by raising a company's exploration and absorptive capacities.

Following Camisón (2004) and Camisón and Forés (2011), this chapter postulates that knowledge-based capabilities is a multilevel construct, and that we can distinguish two levels of strategic assets: shared competences accumulated in industrial districts and firm-specific, knowledge-based capabilities. These competences are accessible and shared by all firms embedded in this local community, thanks largely to the coordination of collective efforts by local institutions that provide a host of supports to intradistrict firms for the dissemination of specialist knowledge and information, and for developing innovative strategies.

Based on empirical evidence from previous literature (e.g., Camisón, 2004; Camisón & Forés, 2011), our theoretical model postulates that there is no direct correlation between the location in an industrial district and either the cluster competitiveness or the firm-specific knowledge-based capabilities. Simply being located inside an industrial district, however rich its knowledge flows or dense its network of contacts and support institutions, might not help the assimilation of this shared knowledge.

However, there are empirical tests for a positive and significant relationship between the configuration of a local productive system, as a canonical concept of an industrial district, and their shared competences stock, i.e., intracluster firms are embedded in a space with localized learning and knowledge spillovers and other shared advantages. The wealth of these shared competences within an industrial district is a driver for cluster competitiveness, and therefore, shared competences are a mediating variable in the relationship between organizations as an industrial district and cluster competitiveness.

Shared competences within a cluster are also a mediating factor between shared competences accumulated within an industrial district and firm-specific knowledge capabilities within an intradistrict organization. Firms must strive to reinforce their internal learning capacity by taking advantage of the opportunities that this common space offers on an exclusive basis. Only when this critical mass of knowledge has been accumulated will an intradistrict firm take maximum advantage of the external knowledge circulating inside the district. A firm's absorptive capacity grows when it combines intradistrict and firm-specific capabilities. Camisón and Forés (2011) reported empirical evidence about the complementarity between a favorable environment for learning in the industrial district and internal knowledge-creation capacity in order to develop the capacity to absorb external knowledge. A firm's capacity for internal knowledge creation and its capacity to absorb external knowledge are complementary, and an exceptional wealth of potential for assimilating external knowledge should not detract firms from investing internally in R&D and from striving to build a culture, structure, and human and intellectual capital aligned with the social and institutional environment dominant within the cluster.

Intradistrict firms are heterogeneous in their resources and capabilities stock. The absorption of the knowledge derived from the spillovers localized within industrial districts, to create competitive advantages and value, depends on this stock, which determines the emergence of a learning microenvironment better capable of absorbing the external knowledge flows. Together, intradistrict firms are not all integrated with the same networks, and their personnel, social, and institutional links are different. Therefore, intradistrict firms are also heterogeneous in their relational competences derived from their idiosyncratic embeddedness within a cluster. Some previous studies (e.g., Camisón, 2004) found empirical evidence that a firm's embeddedness in an industrial district moderates the complementarity between external and internal learning in industrial districts. Specifically, the greater the degree of a firm's embeddedness in a cluster, the greater the effect of its shared competences on firm-specific, knowledge-based capabilities. Therefore, a firm can develop its embeddedness by becoming part of the greater number of intradistrict networks and strategic alliances, because this way, an organization can access a greater amount and variety of localized knowledge spillovers.

ACKNOWLEDGEMENTS

This research was financially supported by two research funds from the National Plan for R&D&i 2009–2012 of the Spanish Science and Innovation Department (ref. ECO2009-12522), and Generalitat Valenciana (ACOMP/2010/233, ACOMP/2011/042).

REFERENCES

Almeida, P., Phene, A., & Grant, R. (2003). Innovation and knowledge management: Scanning, sourcing and integration. In M. Easterby-Smith & M. A. Lyles (Eds.), *Handbook of organizational learning and knowledge management* (pp. 356–371). London: Blackwell.

Anderson, U., Forsgren, M., & Holm, U. (2002). The strategic impact of external networks: Subsidiary performance and competence development in the multinational corporation. *Strategic Management Journal, 23,* 979–996.

Arikan, A. T. (2008). Interfirm knowledge exchanges and the knowledge creation capability of clusters. *Academy of Management Review, 34,* 658–676.

Arora, A., & Gambardella, A. (1994). Evaluating technological information and utilizing it: Scientific knowledge, technological capability, and external linkages in biotechnology. *Journal of Economic Behavior and Organization, 24,* 91–114.

Atuahene-Gima, K. (1992). Inward technology licensing as an alternative to internal R&D in new product development: A conceptual framework. *Journal of Product Innovation Management, 9*(2), 156–167.

Audretsch, D. B. (1998). Agglomeration and the location of innovation activity. *Oxford Review of Economic Policy, 14*(2), 18–29.

Audretsch, D. B., & Feldman, M. (1996). R&D spillovers and the geography of innovation and production. *American Economic Review, 86,* 630–640.

Barney J. B. (1986). Strategic factor markets: Expectations, luck and business strategy. *Management Science, 32,* 1231–1241.

Barney J. B. (1991). Firm resources and sustained competitive advantage. *Journal of Management, 17,* 99–120.

Batteyri, P. Y. (1988). The concept of impartition policies: A different approach to vertical integration strategies. *Strategic Management Journal, 9,* 507–520.

Becattini, G. (1979). Dal settore industriale al distretto industrial [From industrial sector to industrial district]. *Rivista di Economia e Politica Indu*striale, *1,* 1–8.

Becattini G. (Ed.). 1987. *Mercato e forze locali: Il distretto industrial* [Market and local power: The industrial district]. Bolonia, Italy: Il Mulino.

Becattini G. (1989). Sectors and/or districts: Some remarks on the conceptual foundation on industrial economics. In E. Goodman & J. Bamford (Eds.), *Small firms and industrial districts in Italy* (pp. 123–135). London: Routledge.

Becattini G. (1990a). The Marshallian industrial district as a socio-economic notion. In F. Pyke, G. Becattini, & W. Sengenberger (Eds.), *Industrial districts and interfirm cooperation in Italy* (pp. 37–51). Geneva, Italy: International Institute for Labour Studies.

Becattini, G. (1990b). Italia. In W. Sengenberger, G. Loweman, & M. J. Piore (Eds.), *The re-emergence of small enterprises: Industrial restructuring in industrialized countries* (pp. 187–219). Geneva, Italy: International Institute for Labour Studies.

Becchetti, L., & Rossi, S. (2000). The positive effect of industrial district on the export performance of Italian firms. *Review of Industrial Organization, 16,* 53–68.

Bellandi, M. (1989). The industrial district in Marshall. In E. Goodman & J. Bamford (Eds.), *Small firms and industrial districts in Italy* (pp. 136–152). New York: Routledge.

Bellandi, M. (1992). The incentives to decentralized industrial creativity in local systems of small firms. *Revue d'Economie Industrielle, 59,* 99–110.

Benner, M. J., & Tushman, M. L. (2003). Exploitation, exploration, and process management: The productivity dilemma revisited. *Academy of Management Review, 28,* 238–256.

Bernstein, J. I., & Nadiri, M. I. (1989). Research and development and intra-industry spillovers: An empirical application of dynamic duality. *Review of Economic Studies, 56,* 249–267.

Boari, C., & Lipparini, A. (1999). Networks within industrial districts: Organizing knowledge creation and transfer by means moderate hierarchies. *Journal of Management and Governance, 3,* 339–360.

Bourdieu, P., & Wacquant, L. (1992). *An invitation to reflexive sociology.* Chicago: University of Chicago Press.

Brenner, T. (2000, June 15–17). *Industrial districts: A typology from an evolutionary perspective.* DRUID Conference 2000, Rebild, Denmark.

Breschi, S., & Lissoni, F. (2001). Knowledge spillovers and local innovation systems: A critical survey. *Industrial and Corporate Change, 10*(4), 975–1005.

Brown, D. W., & Konrad, A. M. (2001). Granovetter was right: The importance of weak ties to a contemporary job search. *Group & Organization Management, 26,* 434–462.

Brown, J. S., & Duguid, P. (1991). Organizational learning and communities-of-practice: Toward a unified view of working, learning and innovation. *Organization Science, 2,* 40–57.

Brusco, S. (1982). The Emilian model: Productive decentralization and social integration. *Cambridge Journal of Economics, 6,* 167–184.

Brusco, S. (1990). The idea of the industrial district: Its genesis. In F. Pyke, G. Becattini, & W. Sengenberger (Eds.), *Industrial districts and interfirm cooperation in Italy* (pp. 10–19). Geneva, Italy: International Institute for Labour Studies.

Burt, R. S. (1992). The social structure of competition. In N. Nohria & R. G. Eccles (Eds.), *Networks and organizations: Structure, form, and action* (pp. 57–91). Boston: Harvard Business School Press.

Burt, R. S. (1997). Contingent value of the social capital. *Administrative Science Quarterly, 42,* 339–364.

Caloghirou, Y., Kastelli, I., & Tsakanikas, A. (2004). Internal capabilities and external knowledge sources: Complements or substitutes for innovative performance. *Technovation, 24*(1), 29–39.

Camisón, C. (1992, July-August). Experiencias de cooperación en la industria valenciana: Evidencias empíricas [Cooperation experiences in Valencian industry: Empirical evidences]. *Economía Industrial, nº 286,* 49–57.

Camisón, C. (2001). *La competitividad de la empresa industrial de la Comunidad Valenciana: Análisis del efecto del atractivo del entorno, los distritos industriales y las estrategias empresariales* [The industrial firm competitiveness from Valencian Community: Analysis of the effect from environment attractive, industrial districts, and firm strategies]. Valencia, Spain: Tirant lo Blanch.

Camisón, C. (2002). Las competencias distintivas basadas en activos intangibles [The distinctive competences based on intangible assets]. In P. Morcillo & J. Fernández-Aguado (Coords.), *Nuevas claves para la dirección estratégica* [New keys for strategic management] (pp. 117–151). Barcelona, Spain: Ariel.

Camisón, C. (2004). Shared, competitive, and comparative advantages: A competence-based view of industrial-district competitiveness. *Environment and Planning A, 36,* 2227–2256.

Camisón, C., & Forés, B. (2011). Knowledge creation and absorptive capacity: The effect of intradistrict shared competences. *Scandinavian Journal of Management, 27,* 66–86.

Camisón, C., Roig, S., & Torcal, V. R. (1992). *Análisis sectorial del mueble y la madera: Cambio tecnológico y descentralización productiva en l'Horta Sud* [Furniture and wood sector analysis: Technological change and productive decentralization in Horta Sud]. Torrente, Spain: IDECO/CAM.

Cassiman, B., & Veugelers, R. (2002). R&D cooperation and spillovers: Some empirical evidence from Belgium. *American Economic Review, 92,* 1169–1184.

Cassiman, B., & Veugelers, R. (2006). In search of complementarity in innovation strategy: Internal R&D and external knowledge acquisition. *Management Science, 52,* 68–82.

Chandler, A. D. (1990). *Scale and scope: The dynamics of industrial capitalism.* Cambridge, MA: Belknap Press.

Chakravarthy, B., McEvily, S., Doz, Y., & Devaki, R. (2003). Knowledge management and competitive advantage. In M. Easterby-Smith & M. A. Lyles (Eds.), *Handbook of organizational learning and knowledge management* (pp. 305–323). London: Blackwell.

Chatterji, D. (1996). Accessing external sources of technology. *Research Technology Management, 39*(2), 48–56.

Chen, C. (2004). The determinants of knowledge transfer through strategic alliances. *Academy of Management Proceedings,* H1–H6.

Chesbrough, H. W. (2003a). *Open innovation: The new imperative for creating and profiting from technology.* Boston: Harvard Business School Publishing.

Chesbrough, H. W. (2003b). The era of open innovation. *MIT Sloan Management* Review, *44*(3), 35–41.

Chesbrough, H. W. (2006). Open innovation: A new paradigm for understanding industrial innovation. In H. W. Chesbrough, W. Vanhaverbeke, & J. West (Eds.), *Open innovation: Researching a new paradigm* (pp. 1–12). Oxford, UK: Oxford University Press.

Cockburn, I., & Henderson, R. (1998). Absorptive capacity, coauthoring behavior, and the organization of research in drug discovery. *Journal of Industrial Economics, 46*(2), 157–182.

Cohen, W. M., & Levinthal, D. A. (1989). Innovation and learning: The two faces of R&D. *Economic Journal, 99,* 569–596.

Cohen, W. M., & Levinthal, D. A. (1990). Absorptive capacity: A new perspective on learning and innovation. *Administrative Science Quarterly, 35,* 128–152.

Coleman, J. S. (1988). Social capital in the creation of human capital. *American Journal of Sociology, 94,* 95–120.

Coombs, R., Harvey, M., & Tether, B. S. (2003). Analysing distributed processes of provision and innovation. *Industrial & Corporate Change, 12,* 1125–1155.

Crewe, L. (1996). Material culture: Embedded firms, organizational networks and local economic development of a fashion quarter. *Regional Studies, 30,* 257–272.

Dahl, M. S., & Pedersen, C. O. R. (2004). Knowledge flows through informal contacts in industrial clusters: Myth or reality? *Research Policy, 33,* 1673–1686.

Das, T. K. (2006). Strategic alliance temporalities and partner opportunism. *British Journal of Management, 17,* 1–21.

Das, T. K. (Ed.). (2010). *Researching strategic alliances: Emerging perspectives.* Charlotte, NC: Information Age Publishing.

Das, T. K., & Kumar, R. (2007). Learning dynamics in the alliance development process. *Management Decision, 45,* 684–707.

Das, T. K., & Rahman, N. (2010). Determinants of partner opportunism in strategic alliances: A conceptual framework. *Journal of Business and Psychology, 25,* 55–74.

Das, T. K., & Teng, B. (2000). A resource-based theory of strategic alliances. *Journal of Management, 26,* 31–61.

D'Aveni, R., & Illinich, A. (1992). Complex patterns of vertical integration in the forest products industry. *Academy of Management Journal, 35,* 596–625.

Davenport, T. H., De Long, D. W., & Beers, M. C. (1998, Winter). Successful knowledge management projects. *Sloan Management Review,* 43–57.

De Clercq, D., & Dimov, D. (2008). Internal knowledge development and external knowledge access in venture capital investment performance. *Journal of Management Studies, 45,* 585–612.

DeCarolis, D. M., & Deeds, D. L. (1999). The impact of stocks and flows of organizational knowledge on firm performance: An empirical investigation of the biotechnology industry. *Strategic Management Journal, 20,* 953–968.

Dei Ottati, G. (1994). Co-operation and competition in the industrial district as an organizational model. *European Planning Studies, 2*(4), 35–53.

De Long, D., & Fahey, L. (2000). Diagnosing cultural barriers to knowledge management. *Academy of Management Executive, 14,* 113–128.

Dierickx, I., & Cool, K. (1989). Asset stock accumulation and sustainability of competitive advantage. *Management Science, 35,* 1504–1513.

Douglas, T. J., & Ryman, J. A. (2003). Understanding competitive advantage in the general hospital industry: Evaluating strategic competencies. *Strategic Management Journal, 24,* 333–347.

Dyer, J. H., & Singh, H. (1998). The relational view: Cooperative strategy and sources of interorganizational competitive advantage. *Academy of Management Review, 23,* 660–679.

Enright, M. J. (1995). Organization and coordination in geographically concentrated industries. In R. L. Naomi & D. M. G. Raff. (Eds.), *Coordination and information* (pp. 103–146). Chicago: University of Chicago Press.

Enright, M. J. (1998). Regional clusters and firm strategy. In A. D. Chandler, P. Hagström, & O. Sölvell (Eds.), *The dynamic firm* (pp. 318–342). New York: Oxford University Press.

Escribano, A., Fosfuri, A., & Tribó, J. A. (2009). Managing external knowledge flows: The moderating role of absorptive capacity. *Research Policy, 38,* 96–105.

Fabrizio, K. R. (2006). The use of university research in firm innovation. In H. W. Chesbrough, W. Vanhaverbeke, & J. West (Eds.), *Open innovation: Researching a new paradigm* (pp. 134–160). Oxford, UK: Oxford University Press.

Fabrizio, K. R. (2009). Absorptive capacity and the search for innovation. *Research Policy, 38,* 255–267.

Figueiredo, P. N. (2002). Does technological learning pay off?: Interfirm differences in technological capability-accumulation paths and operation performance improvement. *Research Policy, 31,* 73–94.

Fosfuri, A., & Tribó, J. A. (2008). Exploring the antecedents of potential absorptive capacity and its impact on innovation performance. *Omega, 36,* 173–187.

Foss, N. J. (1996a). Introduction: The emerging competence perspective. In N. J. Foss & C. Knudsen (Eds.), *Towards a competence theory of the firm* (pp. 1–12). London: Routledge.

Foss, N. J. (1996b). Higher-order industrial capabilities and competitive advantage: Some analytical suggestions. *Journal of Industry Studies, 3,* 1–20.

Foss, N. J. (1997). Resources and strategy: Problems, open issues, and ways ahead. In N. J. Foss (Ed.), *Resources, firms, and strategies. A reader in the resource-based perspective* (pp. 345–365). New York: Oxford University Press.

Foss, N. J., & Eriksen, B. (1995). Industry capabilities and competitive advantage. In C. A. Montgomery (Ed.), *Evolutionary and resource-based approaches to strategy* (pp. 43–69). Boston: Kluwer.

Foss, N. J., & Knudsen, C. (Eds.). (1996). *Towards a competence theory of the firm.* Boston: Routledge.

Foss, N. J., & Koch, C. A. (1996). Opportunism, organizational economics, and the network approach. *Scandinavian Journal of Management, 12,* 189–205.

Foss, N. J., & Pedersen, T. (2002). Transferring knowledge in MNCs: The role of sources of subsidiary knowledge and organizational context. *Journal of International Management, 8,* 49–67.

Gans, J. S., & Stern, S. (2000). Incumbency and R&D incentives: Licensing the gale of creativity destruction. *Journal of Economics and Management Strategy, 9,* 485–511.

Gassmann, O. (2006). Open innovation: An agenda. *R&D Management, 36,* 229–236.

Glick, W. H. (1988). Organizations are not central tendencies: Shadowboxing in the dark, round 2. *Academy of Management Review, 13,* 133–137.

Glick, W. H., & Roberts, K. (1984). Hypothesized interdependence, assumed independence. *Academy of Management Review, 9,* 722–735.

Grandori, A. (Ed.). (1999). *Interfirm networks.* London: Routledge.

Granovetter, M. (1973). The strength of weak ties. *American Journal of Sociology, 78,* 1360–1380.

Granovetter, M. (1985). Economic action and social structure: The problem of embeddedness. *American Journal of Sociology, 91,* 481–510.

Grant, R. M. (1991). The resource-based theory of competitive advantages: Implications for strategy formulation. *California Management Review, 33*(3), 114–135.

Grant, R. M. (1996, Summer). Toward a knowledge-based theory of the firm. *Strategic Management Journal, 17*(Special Issue), 109–122.

Gulati, R. (1988). Alliances and networks. *Strategic Management Journal, 19,* 293–317

Gulati, R., Nohria, N., & Zaheer, A. (2000). Strategic networks. *Strategic Management Journal, 21,* 203–215.

Gupta, A. K., Smith, K. G., & Shalley, C. E. (2006). The interplay between exploration and exploitation. *Academy of Management Journal, 49,* 693–706.

Hagedoorn, J., Link, A. N., & Vonortas, N. S. (2000). Research partnerships. *Research Policy, 29,* 567–586.

Hall, R. H. (1993). A framework linking intangible resources and capabilities to sustainable competitive advantage. *Strategic Management Journal, 14,* 607–618.

Hamel, G. (1991). Competition for competence and inter-partner learning within international strategic alliances. *Strategic Management Journal, 12*(Special Issue), 83–103.

Hansen, M. T. (1999). The search-transfer problem: The role of weak ties in integrating knowledge across subunits. *Administrative Science Quarterly, 44,* 82–111.

Hansen, M. T. (2002). Knowledge networks: Explaining effective knowledge sharing in multiunit companies. *Organization Science, 13,* 232–248.

Hansen, M. T., & Nohria, N. (2004). How to build collaborative advantage. *Sloan Management Review, 46*(1), 22–30.

Harabi, N. (1995). Appropriability of technical innovations an empirical analysis. *Research Policy, 24*(6), 981–992.

Harabi, N. (1998). Innovation through vertical relations between firms, suppliers and customers: A study of German firms. *Industry and Innovation, 5*(2), 157–181.

Harrison, B. (1991). Industrial districts: Old wine in new bottles? *Regional Studies, 26,* 469–483.

He, Z. L., & Wong, P. K. (2004). Exploration vs. exploitation: An empirical test of the ambidexterity hypothesis. *Organization Science, 15,* 481–494.

Henderson, R., & Cockburn, I. (1996). Scale, scope and spillover: The determinants of research productivity in drug discovery. *RAND Journal of Economics, 27*(11), 32–59.

Henry, N., & Pinch, S. (2001). Neo-Marshallian nodes, institutional thickness and Britain's "Motor Sport Valley": Thick or thin?. *Environment and Planning A, 33,* 1169–1183.

Inkpen, A., & Tsang, E. (2005). Social capital, networks, and knowledge transfer. *Academy of Management Review, 30,* 146–165.

Karlsson C., & Klaesson, J. (2000). Success in manufacturing employment in an industrial district: Higher productivity or lower wages? *Investigaciones Europeas de Dirección y Economía de la Empresa [European Research in Firm Management and Economics], 6*(2), 65–90.

Keeble, D., & Wilkinson, F. (1999). Collective learning and knowledge development in the evolution of regional cluster of high technology SMEs in Europe. *Regional Studies, 33,* 295–303.

Klein, K. J., Dansereau, F., & Hall, R. L. (1994). Levels issues in theory development, data collection, and analysis. *Academy of Management Review, 19,* 195–229.

Kline, S. J. (1985). Innovation is not a linear process. *Research Management, 28*(4), 36–45.

Kogut, B., & Zander, U. (1992). Knowledge of the firm, combinative capabilities, and the replication of technology. *Organization Science, 3,* 383–397.

Koka, B. R., & Prescott, J. E. (2002). Strategic alliances as social capital: A multidimensional view. *Strategic Management Journal, 23,* 795–816.

Krackhardt, D. (1992). The strength of strong ties: The importance of *philos* in organizations. In N. Nohria & R. G. Eccles (Eds.), *Networks and organizations: Structure, form, and action* (pp. 216–239). Boston: Harvard Business School Press.

Krugman, P. (1991). Increasing returns and economic geography. *Journal of Political Economy, 99,* 483–499.

Kumar, R., & Nti, K. (1998). Differential learning and interaction in alliance dynamics: A process and outcome discrepancy model. *Organization Science, 9,* 356–367.

Lane, P. J., & Lubatkin, M. (1998). Relative absorptive capacity and interorganizational learning. *Strategic Management Journal, 19,* 461–477.

Langlois, R. N. (2003a). The vanishing hand: The changing dynamics of industrial capitalism. *Industrial and Corporate Change, 12,* 351–385.

Langlois, R. N. (2003b). Modularity in technology and organization. *Journal of Economic Behavior and Organization, 49*(1), 19–37.

Lawson, C. (1999). Towards a competence theory of the region. *Cambridge Journal of Economics, 23,* 151–166.

Lawson, C., & Lorenz, E. (1999). Collective learning, tacit knowledge and regional innovative capacity. *Regional Studies, 33,* 305–317.

Lazerson, M. H. (1995). A new Phoenix?: Modern putting-out in the Modena knitwear industry. *Administrative Science Quarterly, 40,* 34–59.

Lazerson, M. H., & Lorenzoni, G. (1999). The firms that feed industrial districts: A return to the Italian source. *Industrial and Corporate Change, 8,* 238–266.

Leany, D., & Neary, J. P. (2007). Absorptive capacity, R&D spillovers, and public policy. *International Journal of Industrial Organization, 25,* 1089–1108.

Levin, D. Z., Cross, R., & Abrams, L. C. (2003). Trust and knowledge sharing: A critical combination. In L. Prusak & E. L. Lesser (Eds.), *Creating value with knowledge* (pp. 36–43). Oxford, UK: Oxford University Press.

Levin, R. C., & Reiss, P. C. (1988). Cost-reducing and demand-creating R&D with spillovers. *RAND Journal of Economics, 19,* 538–556.

Liao, S. H., Fei, W. C., & Chen, C. C. (2007). Knowledge sharing, absorptive capacity, and innovation capability: An empirical study of Taiwan's knowledge-intensive industries. *Journal of Information Science, 20,* 1–20.

Lorenz, E. H. (1992). Trust, community, and cooperation: Toward a theory of industrial districts. In M. Storper & A. J. Scott (Eds.), *Pathways to industrialization and regional development.* London: Routledge.

Lorenzen, M. (Ed.). (1998). *Specialisation and localised learning. Six studies on the European furniture industry.* Copenhagen, Denmark: Copenhagen Business School Press.

Lorenzen, M. (2003). *Localised learning and cluster capabilities.* Cheltenham, UK: Edward Elgar.

Lorenzen, M. (2007). Social capital and localised learning: Proximity and place in technological and institutional dynamics. *Urban Studies, 44,* 799–817.

Lorenzen, M., & Foss, N. J. (2003). Cognitive coordination, institutions and clusters: An exploratory discussion. In D. Fornahe & T. Brenner (Eds.), *Cooperation, networks and institutions in regional innovation systems* (pp. 82–104). Cheltenham, UK: Edward Elgar.

Lorenzen, M., & Maskell, P. (2004). The cluster as a nexus of knowledge creation. In P. Cooke & A. Piccaluga (Eds.), *Regional economics as knowledge laboratories* (pp. 77–92). Cheltenham, UK: Edward Elgar.

Lundvall, B. A. (1988). Innovation as an interactive process: From user-producer interaction to the national system of innovation. In G. Dosi, C. Freeman, G. Silverberg, & L. Soete (Eds.), *Technical change and economic theory*. London: Pinter.

Malipiero, A., Munari, F., & Sobrero, M. (2005). *Focal firms as technological gatekeepers within industrial districts: Knowledge creation and dissemination in the Italian packaging machinery industry*. (DRUID Working Paper No. 05-05). Danish Research Unit for Industrial Dynamics.

Malmberg, A., Malmberg, B., & Lundequist, P. (2000). Agglomeration and firm performance: Economies of scale, localisation, and urbanisation among Swedish export firms. *Environment and Planning A, 32,* 305–321.

Malmberg, A., & Maskell, P. (2002). The elusive concept of localization economies: Towards a knowledge-based theory of spatial clustering. *Environment and Planning* A, *34,* 429–449.

Mahnke, V., Pedersen, T., & Venzin, M. (2005). The impact of knowledge management on MNC subsidiary performance: The role of absorptive capacity. *Management International Review, 45,* 101–119.

Maillat, D. (1998). From the industrial district to the innovative milieu: Contribution to an analysis of territorized productive organisations. *Recherches Economiques de Louvain, 64,* 111–129.

March, J. G. (1991). Exploration and exploitation in organizational learning. *Organization Science, 2,* 71–87.

Marshall, A. (1919). *Industry and trade.* London, UK: MacMillan.

Maskell, P. (2001a). Knowledge creation and diffusion in geographic clusters. *International Journal of Innovation Management, 5,* 213–237.

Maskell, P. (2001b). Towards a knowledge-based theory of the geographical cluster. *Industrial and Corporate Change, 10,* 921–944.

Maskell, P., & Lorenzen, M. (2004). The cluster as market organisation. *Urban Studies, 41,* 991–1009.

Maskell, P., & Malmberg, A. (1999). Localised learning and industrial competitiveness. *Cambridge Journal of Economics, 23,* 167–185.

McEvily, B., & Zaheer, A. (1999). Bridging ties: A source of firm heterogeneity in competitive capabilities. *Strategic Management Journal, 20,* 1133–1158.

Meyer-Krahmer, F., & Schmoch, U. (1998). Science-based technologies: University-industry interactions in four fields. *Research Policy, 27,* 835–851.

Miles, R. E., & Snow, C. C. (1986). Network organization: New concepts for new forms. *California Management Review, 28*(3), 62–73.

Milliken, F. J., & Martins, L. L. (1996). Searching for common threads: Understanding the multiple effects of diversity in organizational groups. *Academy of Management Review, 21,* 402–434.

Mistri, M., & Solari, S. (2001). Social networks and productive connectance: Modeling the organizational form of the industrial district. *Human Systems Management, 20,* 223–236.

Mossholder, K. W., & Bedeian, A. G. (1983). Cross-level inference and organizational research: Perspectives on interpretation and application. *Academy of Management Review, 8,* 547–558.

Mowery, D. C. (2009). Industrial R&D in the third industrial revolution. *Industrial and Corporate Change, 18*(1), 1–50.

Nahapiet, J., & Ghoshal, S. (1998). Social capital, intellectual capital and organizational advantage. *Academy of Management Review, 23,* 242–266.

Nelson, R. R., & Winter, S. (1982). *An evolutionary theory of economic change.* Cambridge, MA: Harvard University Press.

Newlands, D. (2003). Competition and cooperation in industrial clusters: The implications for public policy. *European Planning Studies, 11,* 521–532.

Nieto, M., & Quevedo, P. (2005). Absorptive capacity, technological opportunity, knowledge spillovers, and innovative effort. *Technovation, 25,* 1141–1157.

Nonaka, I., & Takeuchi, H. (1995). *The knowledge-creating company: How Japanese companies create the dynamics of innovations.* New York: Oxford University Press.

Oliver, A. L., & Liebeskind, J. P. (1998). Three levels of networking for sourcing intellectual capital in biotechnology: Implications for studying interorganizational networks. *International Studies of Management and Organization, 27*(4), 76–103.

Oughton, C., & Whittam, G. (1997). Competition and cooperation in the small firm sector. *Scottish Journal of Political Economy, 44*(1), 1–30.

Paniccia, I. (1998). One, a hundred, thousands of industrial districts: Organizational variety of local networks in small and medium-sized enterprises. *Organization Studies, 19,* 667–669.

Paniccia, I. (1999). The performance of industrial districts: Some insights from the Italian case. *Human Systems Management, 18,* 141–159.

Parr, J. B. (2002). Agglomeration economies: Ambiguities and confusions. *Environment and Planning A, 34,* 717–731.

Paulus, P. (2000). Groups, teams, and creativity: The creative potential of idea-generating groups. *Applied Psychology, 49,* 237–263.

Pennings, J. M., & Harrianto, F. (1992). Technological networking and innovation implementation. *Organization Science, 3,* 356–382.

Perkmann, M., & Walsh, K. (2007). University-industry relationships and open innovation: Towards a research agenda. *International Journal of Management Reviews, 9,* 259–280.

Peteraf, M. A. (1993). The cornerstone of competitive advantage: A resource-based view. *Strategic Management Journal, 14,* 179–191.

Peteraf, M. A. (2005). A resource-based lens on value creation, competitive advantage, and multilevel issues in strategic management research. In F. Dansereau & F. J. Yammarino (Eds.), *Multilevel issues in strategy and methods: Research in multilevel issues* (Vol. 4, pp. 177–188). London: Emerald Group Publishing.

Peteraf, M. A., & Barney, J. (2003). Unraveling the resource-based tangle. *Managerial and Decision Economics, 24,* 309–323.

Porter, M. E. (1990). *The competitive advantage of nations.* New York: Free Press.

Porter, M. E. (1998). Clusters and the new economics of competition. *Harvard Business Review, 76*(6), 77–90.

Porter, M. E. (2000). Location, competition, and economic development: Local clusters in a global economy. *Economic Development Quarterly, 14*(1), 15–34.

Porter M. E., & Sölvell, P. (1998). The role of geography in the process of innovation and the sustainable advantage of firms. In A. D. Chandler, P. Hagström, & O. Sölvell (Eds.), *The dynamic firm* (pp. 440–457). New York: Oxford University Press.

Powell, W. W. (1990). Neither market nor hierarchy: Network forms of organization. *Research in Organizational Behavior, 12,* 295–336.

Prieto, I. M., Revilla, E. & Rodríguez-Prado, B. (2009). Building dynamic capabilities in product development: How do contextual antecedents matter? *Scandinavian Journal of Management, 25,* 313–326.

Rabellotti, R. (1993). Is there and industrial district model?: Footwear district in Italy and Mexico compared. *World Development, 23,* 29–41.

Rabellotti, R., & Schmitz, H. (1999). The internal heterogeneity of industrial districts in Italy, Brazil and Mexico. *Regional Studies, 33,* 97–108.

Rothwell, R., & Dodgson, M. (1991). External linkages and innovation in small and medium-sized enterprises. *R&D Management, 21,* 125–137.

Sánchez, R., Heene, A., & Thomas, H. (Eds.). (1996). *Dynamics of competence-based competition: Theory and practice in the new strategic management.* Oxford, UK: Elsevier Science.

Saxenian, A. (1991). The origins and dynamics of production networks in Silicon Valley. *Research Policy, 20,* 423–437.

Saxenian, A. (1994). *Regional advantage: Culture and competition in Silicon Valley and Route 128.* Cambridge, MA: Harvard University Press.

Sengenberger, W., Loweman, G., & Piore, M. J. (Eds.). (1990). *The re-emergence of small enterprises: Industrial restructuring in industrialized countries.* Geneva, Italy: International Institute for Labour Studies.

Sethi, R. S., & Park, C. W. (2001). Cross-functional product development teams, creativity, and the innovativeness of new consumer products. *Journal of Marketing Research, 38,* 73–85.

Signori, L. F. (1994). The price of Prato, or measuring the ID effect. *Papers in Regional Science, 73,* 369–392.

Sölvell, P., & Zander, I. (1998). International diffusion of knowledge: Isolating mechanisms and the role of the MNE. In A. D. Chandler, P. Hagström, & O. Sölvell (Eds.), *The dynamic firm* (pp. 402–416). New York: Oxford University Press.

Soo, C. W., Devinney, T. M, & Midgley, D. F. (2007). External knowledge acquisition, creativity and learning in organisational problem solving. *International Journal of Technology Management, 38,* 137–159.

Spence, M. (1984). Cost reduction, competition, and industry performance. *Econometrica, 52*(1), 101–121.

Staples, D. S., Greenaway, K., & McKeen, J. (2001). Opportunities for research about managing the knowledge-based enterprise. *International Journal of Management Reviews, 3,* 1–20.

Szulanski, G. (1996). Exploring internal stickiness: Impediments to the transfer of best practice within the firm. *Strategic Management Journal, 17,* 27–43.

Teece, D. J., & Pisano, G. (1994). The dynamic capabilities of firms: An introduction. *Industrial and Corporate Change, 3,* 537–556.

Teece, D., Pisano, G., & Shuen, A. (1997). Dynamic capabilities and strategic management. *Strategic Management Journal, 18,* 509–533.

Triglia, C. (2001). Social capital and local development. *European Journal of Social Theory, 4,* 427–442.

Tsai, W. (2000). Social capital, strategic relatedness and the formation of intraorganizational linkages. *Strategic Management Journal, 21,* 925–939.

Tsai, W., & Ghoshal, S. (1998). Social capital and value creation: The role of intrafirm networks. *Academy of Management Journal, 41,* 464–476.

Uzzi, B. (1996). The sources and consequences of embeddedness for economic performance of organizations: The network effect. *American Sociological Review, 61,* 674–698.

Uzzi, B. (1997). Social structure and competition in interfirm networks: The paradox of embeddedness. *Administrative Science Quarterly, 42,* 35–67.

Uzzi, B., & Lancaster, R. (2003). Relational embeddedness and learning: The case of bank loan managers and their clients. *Management Science, 49,* 383–399.

Van den Bosch, F. A. J., Volberda, H. W., & de Boer, M. (1999). Coevolution of firm absorptive capacity and knowledge environment: Organizational forms and combinative capabilities. *Organization Science, 10,* 551–568.

Verspagen, B., & Schoenmakers, W. (2004). The spatial dimension of patenting by multinational firms in Europe. *Journal of Economic Geography, 4*(1), 23–42.

Veugelers, R. (1997). Internal R&D expenditures and external technology sourcing. *Research Policy, 26,* 303–315.

Veugelers, R., & Cassiman, B. (1999). Make and buy in innovation strategies: Evidence from Belgian manufacturing firms. *Research Policy, 28,* 63–80.

Volberda, H. W., Foss, N., & Lyles, M. A. (2010). Absorbing the concept of absorptive capacity: How to realize its potential in the organization field. *Organization Science, 21,* 931–951.

Von Hippel, E. (1987). *The sources of innovation.* New York: Oxford University Press.

Von Hippel, E., & von Krogh, G. (2003). Open source software and the "private-collective" innovation model: Issues for organization science. *Organization Science, 14,* 209–223.

Wernerfelt, B. (1984). A resource-based view of the firm. *Strategic Management Journal, 5,* 171–180.

West, J., & Gallagher, S. (2006). Patterns of open innovation in open source software. In H. W. Chesbrough, W. Vanhaverbeke, & J. West (Eds.), *Open innovation: Researching a new paradigm* (pp. 82–106). Oxford, UK: Oxford University Press.

West, J., Vanhaverbeke, W., & Chesborugh, H. (2006). Open innovation: A research agenda. In H. W. Chesbrough, W. Vanhaverbeke, & J. West (Eds.), *Open innovation: Researching a new paradigm* (pp. 285–307). Oxford, UK: Oxford University Press.

Wiklund, J., & Karlsson, C. (1994). Flexible companies in an industrial district: The case of the Gnosjö region in Sweden. In J. M. Veciana (Ed.), *SMEs: Internationalization, networks and strategy* (pp. 103–128). Aldershot, UK: Avebury Ashgate Publishing.

Woodman, R. W., Sawyer, J. E., & Griffin, R. W. (1993). Toward a theory of organizational creativity. *Academy of Management Review, 18,* 293–322.

Yli-Renko, H., Autio, E., & Sapienza, H. J. (2001). Social capital, knowledge acquisition, and knowledge exploitation in young technology-based firms. *Strategic Management Journal, 22,* 587–613.

You, J., & Wilkinson, F. (1994). Competition and cooperation: Toward understanding industrial districts. *Review of Political Economy, 6,* 259–278.

Zaheer, A., McEvily, B., & Perrone, V. (1998). Does trust matter?: Exploring the effects of interorganizational and interpersonal trust on performance. *Organization Science, 9,* 141–159.

Zahra, S. A., & George, G. (2002). Absorptive capacity: A review, reconceptualization, and extension. *Academy of Management Review, 27,* 185–203.

Zahra, S. A., Filatotchev, I., & Wright, M. (2009). How do threshold firms sustain corporate entrepreneurship?: The role of boards and absorptive capacity. *Journal of Business Venturing, 24,* 248–260.

Zollo, M., & Winter, S. G. (2002). Deliberate learning and the evolution of dynamic capabilities. *Organization Science, 13,* 339–351.

CHAPTER 12

OPEN INNOVATION THROUGH A COLLABORATIVE COMMUNITY OF FIRMS

An Emerging Organization Design

Charles C. Snow
Refik Culpan

ABSTRACT

We develop a model of the multifirm collaborative innovation process using data on Blade.org, a collaborative community of more than 200 firms in the computer server industry. We argue that a collaborative community is a new way of organizing for open innovation, following the three established approaches of alliances, static networks, and outsourcing. A collaborative community of firms is a powerful organizational form for firms wanting to pursue product/service and market opportunities in environments where knowledge is complex and widely distributed. We expect this organizational form to be used increasingly in knowledge-intensive industries where continuous innovation is a strategic objective.

Strategic Alliances for Value Creation, pages 279–300

INTRODUCTION

Firms today understand that they cannot be continuously innovative by going it alone. Increasingly, firms are involving their customers, suppliers, and other external parties in product and technological innovation, a phenomenon referred to as "open innovation" (Chesbrough, 2003, 2006; Chesbrough & Appleyard, 2007). An open innovation philosophy and process can help firms innovate by reducing the cost of product development and process improvement, accelerating time to market for new products, improving product quality, and accessing customer, supplier, and other external knowledge and expertise. Until recently, the open innovation process has taken three main forms: alliances, static networks, and outsourcing. For example, firms in a particular industry may form a consortium or other type of alliance in order to pool their R&D resources (Culpan, 2002). Alternatively, a firm may construct a fixed network of outside specialists that they can rely on to enhance the innovation process. Procter & Gamble's "Connect and Develop" program (Huston & Sakkab, 2006) is one such effort. Last, firms may turn to outside resources for help when their own internal innovation initiatives become stalled. For example, many firms have outsourced their intractable problems to Innocentive, a company that provides a market in which independent scientists and hobbyists act as external problem solvers for those companies.

A new form of open innovation is emerging, and given its initial success, it may grow rapidly in the coming years. We call this form a *collaborative community of firms* (Miles, Miles, & Snow, 2005; Snow, Fjeldstad, Lettl, & Miles, 2011; Snow, Strauss, & Culpan, 2009; Snow, Strauss, & Lettl, 2009). A collaborative community innovates differently from an alliance, external network, or outsourcing partner. Essentially, this organizational approach assembles a group of complementary firms (Stieglitz & Heine, 2007) in which community values and collaborative capabilities and processes enable firms to work with one another temporarily on innovation projects. Based on data on Blade.org, a prominent example of a collaborative community of firms in the computer server industry, we develop and support empirically a model of the multifirm collaborative innovation process and assess the ability of the collaborative community of firms organizational model to create value for those firms that adopt it.

Our chapter is structured as follows. First, we describe the new strategic orientation of large-scale multifirm collaboration and its associated community values and organizational structures by identifying and describing the factors that have led to this emerging organizational form. Second, we describe our method and data, which involve an in-depth, longitudinal study of Blade.org, including the collection of online survey data from Blade.org's member firms. Third, we build a model of collaborative strategy, structure, and process. Last, we make an overall assessment of multifirm collaborative innovation. We denote innovation outcomes by pointing out the benefits that accrue to community members in the form of new products, access to collaboration partners, and capability development. Our chapter contributes to the innovation management literature in two main ways. First, we identify a new and growing form of open innovation—a collaborative community of firms—by describing its properties, strengths, and limitations. Second, based on the Blade.org case, we build a model of the multifirm collaborative innovation process that both researchers and managers can benefit from as an important new way of pursuing continuous innovation.

COLLABORATIVE STRATEGY AND A COMMUNITY OF FIRMS

In order for firms to compete effectively in a complex, dynamic, and highly interconnected global business environment, they have to innovate continuously. Traditionally, firms have relied on their own resources and capabilities to do so. Today, however, in many fields, relevant knowledge for innovation is dispersed across firms, industries, and countries. Few firms possess all of the required knowledge and capabilities to single-handedly develop new products and apply new technologies. Moreover, in knowledge-intensive industries, the ability to both create and apply knowledge is of vital importance for firm competitiveness and sustainable advantage. According to Chesbrough (2003, p. 177), "In many industries today, the logic supporting an internally oriented, centralized approach to R&D has become obsolete. Useful knowledge is widespread in many industries, and ideas must be used with alacrity if they are not to be lost. These factors create the new logic of Open Innovation, which embraces external ideas and knowledge in conjunction with internal R&D."

Drawing on the logic of open innovation, we develop a conceptual model of the multifirm collaborative innovation process. Two streams of theoretical thought underlie our model. The first is the knowledge-based view of the firm (Grant, 1996; Nickerson & Zenger, 2004; Nonaka & Takeuchi, 1995; Nonaka, Toyama, & Hirata, 2008). This view says that a firm is a learning, knowledge-creating entity, and it argues that knowledge and the capability to create and utilize knowledge are the most important sources of a firm's sustainable competitive advantage. The second research stream is strategic alliances between and among firms, suggesting that firms can create value in the form of new products and technologies by sharing knowledge and other resources (Culpan, 2009; Dyer & Hatch, 2006; Grant & Baden-Fuller, 2004; Inkpen, 1996; Inkpen & Tsang, 2005; Mesquita, Anand,

& Brush, 2008). Building on these two theoretical streams, we argue that in knowledge-intensive industries, firms are moving beyond the traditional open innovation approaches of alliances, external networks, and outsourcing. The emerging collaborative community of firms organizational model has received research attention because it has demonstrated its ability to create value in the form of innovative products and technologies that is both faster and more effective than alliances, static networks, and outsourcing. Pisano and Verganti (2008) call this approach an "innovation community," referring to a dynamic network where anybody can propose problems, offer solutions, and decide which solutions to use. They further argue that "It is no longer just a matter of hiring the most talented and creative people or establishing the right internal environment for innovation. The new leaders in innovation will be those who can understand how to design collaborative networks and how to tap their potential" (p. 80).This signifies a major strategic change from a sole-player approach—or even a small number of players in an alliance—to large sets of multiple players working together dynamically and collaboratively. It also signifies a change in the managerial mindset, moving from a "closed" business model to a "collaborative" business model with "multiple partners." Of course, not every organization is ready for or capable of handling such a paradigm shift. Organizations can undertake such ventures only when they realize their own capabilities and limitations but also foresee the benefits of collaborating with others.

Shifting from firm-based innovation to community-based innovation, Lee and Cole (2003) built a model of knowledge creation in purposeful, loosely coordinated, distributed systems as an alternative to a firm-based approach. Specifically, by citing the case of the Linux kernel development project, they demonstrated an evolutionary knowledge creation process in which thousands of talented volunteers, dispersed across organizational and geographical boundaries, collaborate via the Internet to produce an innovative product of high quality. Their community-based model suggests that the product development process can be effectively organized as an evolutionary process of learning driven by criticism and error correction.

Along the same lines, but focusing on commercial organizations, Snow, Strauss, & Lettl (2009) view a community of firms as a form of organizing in which independent member firms network temporarily with one another and also commit to a set of shared values and norms, and where there are mechanisms to exert moral suasion and to extract compliance from members. Further, Snow et al. (2011) argue that the broad emergence of community-like structures across strategy types, industries, and geographies leads to the proposition that the community model of organizing is a strong complement to the network model of organizing. In order to understand how firms that form and/or participate in communities achieve long-term competitive success, one needs to know (a) the various forms communities may assume and (b) the different ways firms can use communities to leverage their innovation efforts. Last, Miles, Snow, Fjeldstad, Miles, & Lettl (2010) assert that collaborative communities are a powerful means for firms to pursue opportunities in the global marketplace, and collaborative values and capabilities offer a promising approach for addressing the many challenges that the global economy poses. They describe two types of situations in which large-scale multiparty collaboration is required in order to successfully pursue global opportunities or to resolve global problems: (a) situations in which a large number of actors depend on and contribute to a resource commons and (b) situations in which a large number of actors share a common goal, and each actor provides its complementary contribution to the larger system in a coordinated manner. In the next section, we develop a community-based model for innovation based on data from Blade.org, where a large group of complementary firms work collaboratively and share common goals and values.

METHOD AND DATA

Blades, the fastest-growing segment of the computer server market, reached sales of more than $1 billion in 2007 (Datacenterknowledge.com, 2007). As firms look to grow their data centers or replace aging infrastructures, many are employing blades to save space, increase density, and decrease power consumption while lowering total cost and improving infrastructure flexibility. Blade.org was established in 2006 by IBM, Intel, and six other founding firms to promote the development and innovation of blade technology to help customers meet the growing demands on their information technology (IT) systems. We and our colleagues have been studying Blade.org since 2007. Members of the research team have conducted multiple interviews with leaders in Blade.org's principal office and with various executives and technical specialists in five member firms, including two of the founding firms and one international member firm. We have also attended, and gathered data at, two all-member meetings of Blade.org, which are held three times a year. In May 2008, we conducted an online survey of Blade.org member firms that focused specifically on community-of-firms organizational issues and processes, and these data are reported here. We remain in contact with the executives in Blade.org's principal office in order to monitor and analyze developments as they occur.

Origin and Purpose of Blade.org

The origin of Blade.org can be traced to August 2004 when IBM announced that it was opening the specifications to its BladeCenter server chassis (Clabby Analytics, 2007). IBM stated that its goal was to build a developer community that would focus on expanding the number of solutions that could be made available from its promising blade architecture. IBM also noted that it could not drive all innovation on blade applications itself; it expected its partners to play a major role in creating future blade-based solutions. In February 2006, IBM announced the formation of an independent organization (Blade.org) that would serve as the facilitator for a community of blade developers, and it invited relevant vendor and user firms to provide feedback and develop solutions (products) specifically for BladeCenter.

The economic purpose of Blade.org is to foster and accelerate the growth of solutions based on the blade processor technology. The specific purposes for which Blade.org is organized include enabling the ongoing development of blade-based solutions, helping to bring solutions to the market in a timely fashion, increasing the adoption and number of solutions in both existing and new markets, and increasing customer confidence in blade-based solutions. The Blade.org community undertakes a wide variety of activities to achieve these purposes, including the provision of guidelines to member firms for designing their solutions, developing independent compliance testing procedures that member firms may use, hosting industrywide SolutionFests and other marketing events, educating the marketplace on blade platform solutions, and incorporating member concerns and preferences into strategic initiatives that expand and improve the community.

Membership and Governance Structure

Blade.org has three membership categories: Governing Members, Sponsoring Members, and General Members. Governing Member firms, each of whom has a representative who sits on Blade.org's Board of Directors, are limited by the organization's bylaws to 11 in number and include the original eight founding firms (Brocade, Citrix, IBM, Intel, Network Appliance, Nortel, Novell, and VMWare). Governing Member firms pay annual membership dues (as do all member firms except customers), entitling them to certain rights (see www.Blade.org Membership Benefits, 2008; Bylaws of Blade.org, 2006):

- Opportunities to collaborate with other Blade.org solution providers
- Influence the direction of the blade server market
- Networking opportunities with industry leaders at trade shows and other industry events
- Increased visibility within the marketplace

- Ability to leverage Blade.org's marketing activities including use of the Blade.org logo in promotional literature
- Use of independent compliance testing arranged by Blade.org
- Increased media coverage through access to Blade.org's public relations firm
- Speaking opportunities at Blade.org events
- Free banner advertising on the Blade.org Web site and various discounts
- Ability to appoint a member of the Board of Directors
- Eligibility for their employees to serve as Chair of a technical committee or subcommittee and to participate in the activities of any committee or subcommittee
- Influence the agenda of all-member meetings.

Of these various rights, the core rights that accrue from membership in Blade.org are opportunities to collaborate with other member firms and eligibility for participation in the work of technical committees and subcommittees.

Sponsoring Member firms are of three types: (a) They are currently distributing or developing hardware, software, or services offerings for the blade platform; (b) they provide consulting or distribution support for blade-based solutions or products; or (c) they currently use blade platform solutions. Sponsoring Members have the same rights as Governing Members except for the right to appoint a representative to the Board of Directors. Last, a firm can become a General Member of Blade.org if it has a legitimate business interest in participating in the community and is willing to publicly support Blade.org and its mission by being listed on the organization's Web site and in press releases. A General Member must be approved by a majority vote of the Board of Directors.

In early 2008, Blade.org began to offer free membership to its corporate customers (called end users). End user membership benefits include invitations to participate in a variety of technical and marketing activities; an opportunity to join any Blade.org committee or subcommittee; access to a forum where they can voice concerns and suggestions directly to Blade.org vendors; and an opportunity to network with other firms, which allows customers to share best practices within the blade community. Overall, such benefits allow customers to influence the overall direction of the blade market as well as solution development.

Blade.org operates as a "program" under the auspices of the Industry Standards and Technology Organization (ISTO). ISTO, whose parent organization is the long-established Institute of Electrical and Electronics Engineers (IEEE), was started in 1999 as a not-for-profit corporation that offers industry groups (e.g., consortia, special interest groups, alliances, forums, working groups) support for technology and standards development. The IEEE-ISTO serves as an umbrella organization to provide a legal forum for industry groups to operate without the need to incorporate. Programs of the IEEE-ISTO enjoy the legal protections and insurance benefits of operating within an incorporated, fully insured, nonprofit organization. The IEEE-ISTO provides a complete menu of administrative and operational support, leaving Blade.org's member firms free to focus on the community's mission and activities.

Blade.org has a principal office located in Research Triangle Park, North Carolina (contiguous to the cities of Raleigh, Durham, and Chapel Hill). The principal office houses the strategic leadership of Blade.org, and its executives plan and organize strategic initiatives designed to expand and enrich the community. Initiatives are developed using feedback from Blade.org's member firms. In addition, Blade.org has nine technical committees staffed by volunteers from the member firms. These committees are organized by function and include committees on technology, solutions architecture, hosted client work group, power and cooling, compliance and interoperability, marketing, small and medium businesses, membership benefits, and bylaws and membership. The Blade.org volunteer committees perform a dual function for the community of firms: They do work that is useful to the community as a whole, and they serve as a repository of knowledge that member firms can tap into when needed. Thus, the committees are keepers and developers of the community's knowledge commons.

Collaborative Innovation Processes

The key to understanding Blade.org's organization design is to focus on the strategic role it is playing. IBM is the inventor of the blade technology, and it holds a number of patents related to that technology. Given IBM's size and capabilities, creating one or more dedicated blade business units which, in turn, would partner with select suppliers and lead users would be the taken-for-granted approach to developing commercial applications for the blade technology. However, rather than attempting to exploit the blade IP through its own business units or through specific technology alliances with other firms, IBM, along with its fellow founding firms, chose to form a collaborative community of firms focused on accelerating the development and adoption of blade server solutions. Thus, the founding firms created an organizational system (or "platform") that enables the member firms to develop their own solutions.

Solutions are developed through interfirm collaborations that can take one of four main forms: (a) bilateral collaboration (a Blade.org member firm collaborates with its customer on a new solution, perhaps using consulting advice from IBM as the inventor of the blade technology); (b) direct collaboration (a small temporary network of member firms work together on the development of a new solution); (c) pooled collaboration (Blade.org member firms supply ideas, information, and experiences to a central database called Bladeuser.org, which is accessible by member firms wanting to pursue innovation projects); and (d) external collaboration (a Blade.org member firm works with a non-Blade.org firm on a one-off blade-based innovation project).

Findings from the Online Survey

In 2007, an online survey was conducted with the member firms of Blade.org to determine their motives for joining the community as well as their attitudes and opinions regarding Blade.org's processes and benefits. A total of 50 of the 61 member firms at the time replied to the survey, resulting in a response rate of 82%. The membership types of responding firms are 27% Governing Members, 22% Sponsoring Members, and 51% General Members. The types of firms are shown in Figure 12.1. As the data show, most Blade.org participants are hardware providers followed by end users (customers), software providers, developers, distribution partners, and resellers. (Currently, end users outnumber all other types as customers were offered free membership beginning in January 2008.)

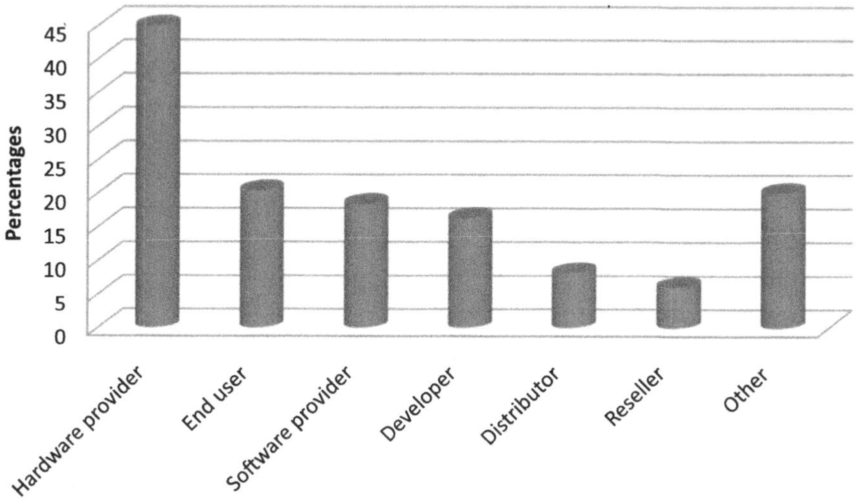

Figure 12.1 Types of member firms.

The members of Blade.org are highly motivated to be involved in the community as the data in Figure 12.2 indicate. The primary motivation for joining is to keep up with technical and market developments, and this is closely followed by the perceived opportunity to collaborate with the founding firms and with other member firms. Member firms perceive the community as an ecosystem of collaborative learning and innovation. By joining the community, member firms seek primarily the benefits of identifying potential collaboration partners and obtaining new knowledge (see Figure 12.3).

Regarding collaborative relationships, member firms expressed favorable opinions (agree and strongly agree) in the following areas: identify and evaluate new collaboration partners, access to collaboration partners, willingness to collaborate with other member firms, improve ability to innovate, acquire new technical capabilities, and improve existing technical capabilities (see Figure 12.4).

In terms of community identity and interfirm trust, both of which are considered to be essential for the success of collaborative innovation, the data show that the majority of member firms agree or strongly agree with the following factors: identifying with Blade.org values (openness, sharing,

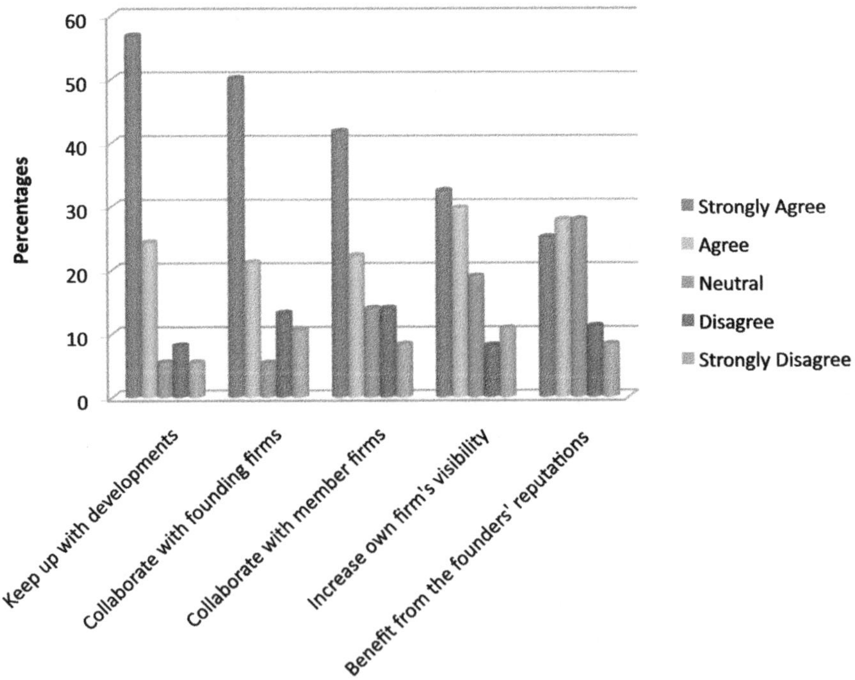

Figure 12.2 Reasons for joining.

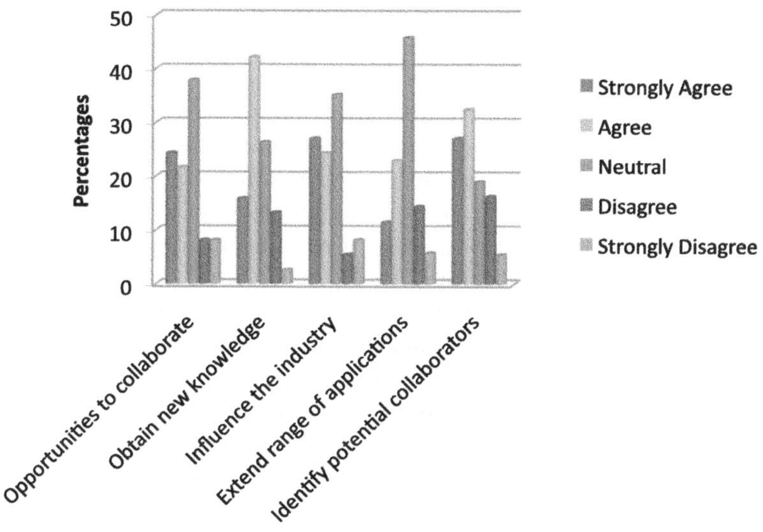

Figure 12.3 Perceived benefits of membership.

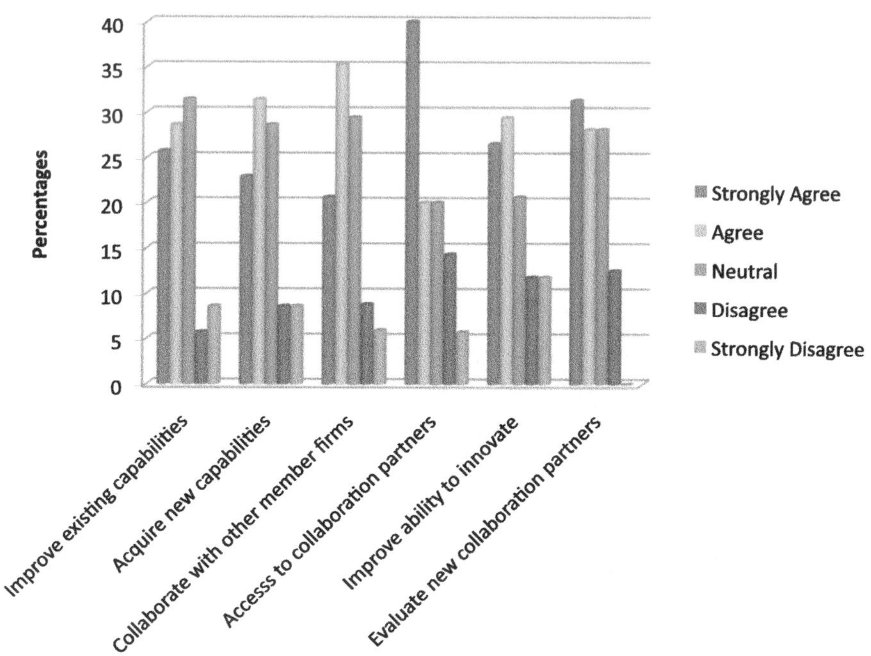

Figure 12.4 Collaborative relationships.

volunteerism, etc.), expecting that other firms in the community will carry out the activities that they have agreed to, believing that the firms in the community have the abilities to do what they say they will do, considering Blade.org membership to be important to their identity, believing in the importance of supporting the Blade.org community by contributing ideas and knowledge even if they do not directly benefit, and perceiving that firms in the community act in mutually beneficial ways. All of these perceptions and beliefs reflect a strong sense of community identity and the existence of trust among the member firms (see Figure 12.5).

The responses of the member firms regarding community leadership are shown in Figure 12.6. The data indicate that in all areas (albeit less in helping form linkages among member firms and recruiting new members), member firms think that Blade.org leaders play an effective facilitating role. These areas include helping members and prospective members understand the benefits of collaboration within the community; being ef-

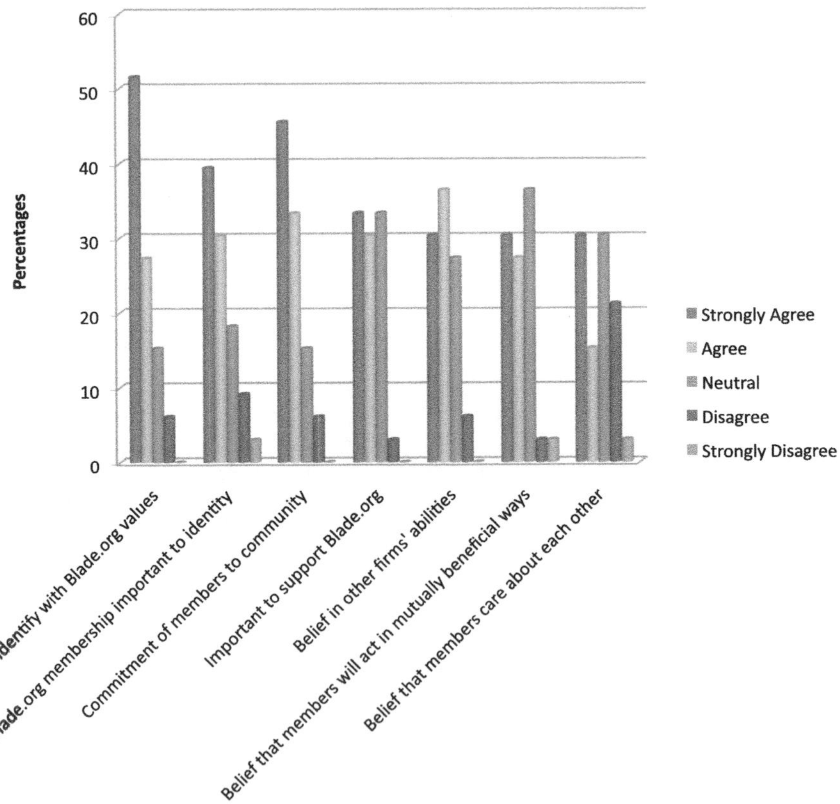

Figure 12.5 Community identity and interfirm trust.

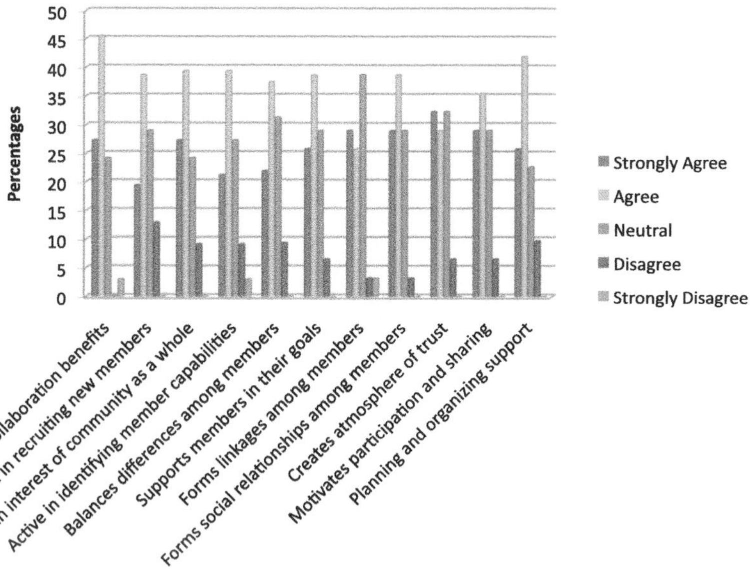

Figure 12.6 Community leadership.

fective in planning and organizing strategic initiatives that help the community as a whole; contributing to the formation of social relationships among the members; acting in the interests of the community as a whole; supporting member firms in the creation and pursuit of common goals; motivating member firms to participate and openly share valuable knowledge; creating an atmosphere of trust within the community; being active in identifying roles, capabilities, and goals of individual member firms; and balancing differences in goals and interests among member firms. Overall, the data indicate that the leadership of Blade.org is largely effective in the eyes of member firms.

The data displayed in Figure 12.7 delineate the types of investments made by the member firms. Investments in the community include the provision of collaborative software, testing equipment, and conference facilities. These resources were largely provided by the founding firms, and member firms' investments in these areas are small. The major investment made by member firms is time—time to learn about the blade processor technology, the products and business practices of other member firms, how to transfer knowledge to other firms, and how to collaborate. Overall, member firm time investments are significant while capital and financial investments are small.

At bottom, every business strategy and organization design is judged by its outcomes and performance. The survey results in this regard are shown

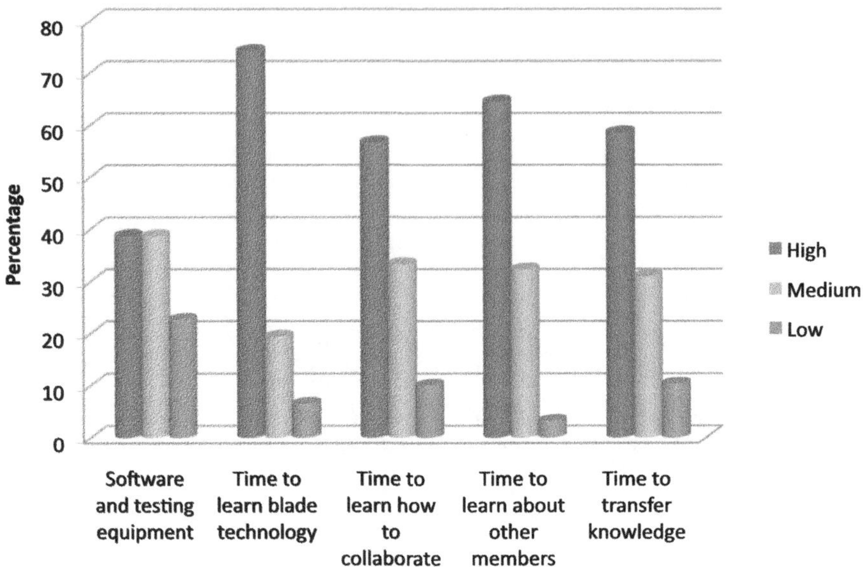

Figure 12.7 Investments in the community made by member firms.

in Figure 12.8. Member firms agree or strongly agree that the Blade org. community is achieving the following results: lowering the costs of bringing innovations to market; reducing the time required to bring innovations to market; creating innovations that are effective in the marketplace; increasing end user satisfaction with products and services; strengthening relationships with existing customers; developing new customer relationships; working with customers who are on the leading edge of market or technological trends; strengthening relationships with existing suppliers; developing new supplier relationships; working with suppliers that are on the leading edge of market or technological trends; developing innovations that could not have been done alone; developing novel or "nonobvious" solutions (as opposed to incremental solutions); ensuring that products and services are compatible with industry standards; increasing the ability to create new products and services on a continuous basis; and increasing the ability to act entrepreneurially (i.e., to identify and develop business opportunities beyond a member firm's current domain). Thus, the data show that the Blade.org organizational model is producing numerous benefits for member firms and that these benefits far outweigh costs and investments.

Lastly, the survey asked member firms to assess their overall satisfaction with their experiences in Blade.org. They answered that they were satisfied as follows: 37% strongly agree, 41% agree, 18% neutral, 4% disagree, and 0% strongly disagree (see Figure 12.9). These responses, along with

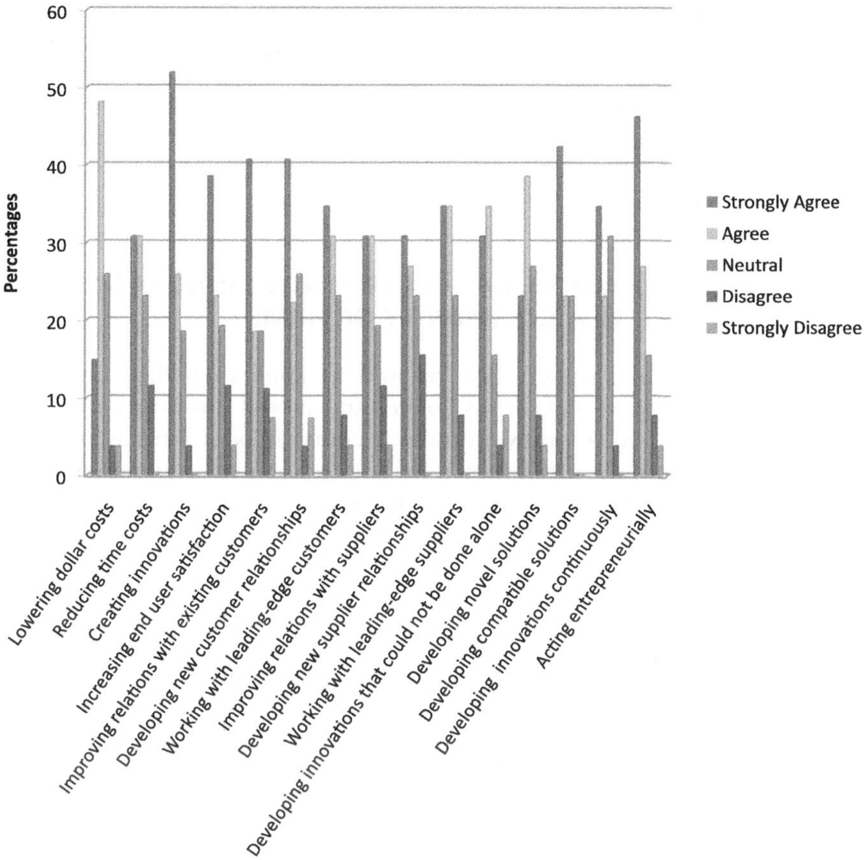

Figure 12.8 Community outcomes and member firm benefits.

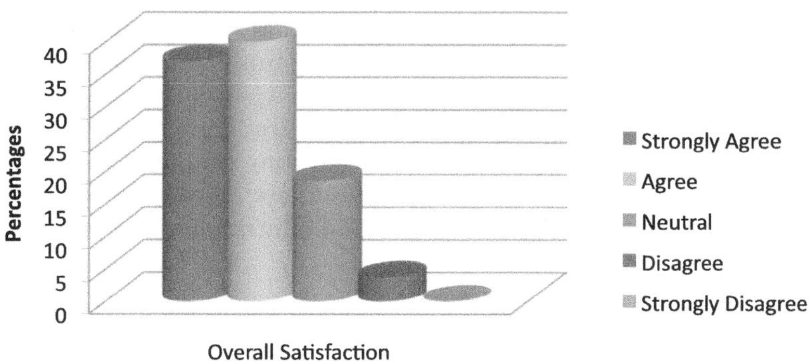

Figure 12.9 Overall satisfaction of member firms.

those shown in Figure 12.8, suggest that the member firms have generally benefitted from their involvement in Blade.org and are satisfied with their experiences to date. Coupled with the fact that Blade.org member firms developed more than 60 solutions (new products) during the first 18 months of the community's existence, it appears that the community of firms organizational model is effective both in generating innovations and in facilitating member firms' collaborative efforts.

CONCEPTUAL MODEL OF COLLABORATIVE INNOVATION IN A COMMUNITY OF FIRMS

Based on the online survey data, as well as contextual data obtained through interviews, we develop a conceptual model consisting of three main components: collaborative strategy, a community of firms as an organization design, and the innovation outcomes of such an arrangement (see Table 12.1). The model is summarized below.

Perceived Benefits

From a management perspective, each member firm is driven by incentives, expectations, and perceived rewards. As shown in Table 12.1, the members of a well-designed community of firms perceive the main benefits to be the opportunity to work collaboratively and to identify potential collaboration partners.

Community Creation

A key characteristic of an effective community of firms is how it was created. Of foremost importance is the reputation of the founding firms. Also, the process can be enhanced by (a) developing mission and vision statements that describe the community's technical and economic purposes and (b) using the business networks of the founding firms and effective communication (e.g., a well-designed Web site) to attract desirable firms into the community. Last, it is important to invite "relevant" firms to join the community. In the case of Blade.org, this meant inviting complementors—firms whose complementary knowledge and skillsets are required to develop the computer server industry in a systematic and effective manner.

Community Development

A community of firms cannot grow and develop without an appropriate organization structure. In the case of Blade.org, the structure involved

TABLE 12.1 A Model of Collaborative Innovation in a Community of Firms

Collaborative Strategy	Organization Design: Community of Firms					Outcomes
Multifirm Collaboration	**Perceived Benefits**	**Community Creation**	**Community Development**	**Identity and Trust**	**Investments**	**Innovations and Member Firm Benefits**
In environments where knowledge is complex, growing, and widely distributed, firms seek alliances with others, and the locus of innovation is a community of firms	Access to new business opportunities Opportunities to collaborate with founding firms and other member firms Obtain new knowledge and ideas Ability to influence development of blade processor market	IBM's reputation used to attract relevant firms Mission and vision statements that describe the community's technical and economic purpose Business networks of the founding firms used to invite complementary firms into the community	Legally binding bylaws support the governance system Administrative services provided by IEEE-ISTO Infrastructure and strategic initiatives provided by the Principal Office Maintenance and development of the knowledge commons by the technical committees	Member firms identify with collaborative values of Blade.org Belief that fellow member firms are competent and dependable Belief that fellow member firms will act in mutually beneficial ways Belief that member firms care about each others' welfare	Capital Assets: Collaboration software, testing equipment, and facilities Intangible Assets: Time to learn about blade technology Time to learn about products and business practices of other member firms Time to learn how to collaborate with other member firms	Continuous solution development Development of solutions that could not be accomplished alone Achievement of solution compatibility Lower costs and reduced development times Better relationships with existing customers and creation of new customers Better relationships with existing suppliers and creation of new suppliers

legally binding bylaws, administrative services provided by IEEE-ISTO, a facilitator (Principal Office) that provides infrastructure and strategic initiatives, and knowledge commons maintained and developed by technical committees staffed with representatives from member firms.

Identity and Trust

An important ingredient of collaborative communities is the member firms' identification with community values and their trust of fellow members. It is important for members to identify themselves with Blade.org and to value their membership. It is also vital for members to support the organization in an open and voluntary manner and to make commitments to it. Equally important is the degree of trust the members have in the deeds and abilities of other members as well as the belief that member firms care about the welfare of their collaboration partners.

Investments

A community of firms requires initial investments to be made by both the founding firms and the member firms. In the case of Blade.org, the founding firms (primarily IBM) invested in physical assets such as collaboration software and testing equipment as well as the executive staff in the Principal Office. Investments made by the member firms primarily involved time—time to learn about the blade processor technology, the products and business practices of other community members, and how to transfer knowledge to other firms via collaboration on innovation projects.

Outcomes and Benefits

Collaborative innovation among the member firms of a community yields numerous outcomes and benefits. In the case of Blade.org, the primary outcome is the ability to conduct open and continuous innovation. At the level of the individual firm, there are numerous benefits, including increased capacity to innovate, lower costs of innovation, faster innovation times, and the opportunity to learn and grow.

ORGANIZATIONAL AND MANAGERIAL ASSESSMENT OF COLLABORATIVE INNOVATION

Based on the case of Blade.org and the related online survey findings, we believe that the collaborative community of firms organizational model appears to be a valuable means of conducting continuous innovation. Nevertheless, there are many important questions that can be raised about this evolving approach. For example, why did a capable and powerful company such as IBM (and its fellow founding firms) choose to form a collaborative community of firms instead of competing in the computer server market by itself? Can other firms form communities that are equally successful? Will the collaborative community of firms model work in other industries and contexts?

We believe that most firms would struggle to form a collaborative community of firms, certainly more than IBM and its fellow founding firms did. IBM had participated in the open-source software movement in the 1990s and had been a generous financial supporter of the worldwide Linux community in its early years. IBM had built up a large stock of goodwill and experience in community-based organizations. It had also developed an early version of a collaborative community in a large project called Eclipse, and it learned from that experience that a community of firms was a better vehicle for developing products and markets than going it alone (or via a series of alliances). When IBM, Intel, and the other founding firms invited relevant and complementary firms in the computer server industry to join a collaborative community, virtually all of them readily accepted the invitation. Without the capabilities and reputation of IBM as a solid collaboration partner, other large firms probably would not be able to form a collaborative community of firms as quickly or as effectively. When the next large collaborative community appears, it is likely to be in a knowledge-intensive industry such as computers or nanotechnology, and we expect it to be formed by a capable, reputable firm whose business philosophy embraces community values and principles.

The creation of a community of firms for collaborative innovation means a new strategic orientation and organizational arrangement for firms. It is a result of the dispersion of knowledge across companies and countries and the direct interdependency of collaborating firms to develop product, market, and technological innovations (Powell, Koput, & Smith-Doerr, 1996). Multifirm collaboration entails some strategic and organizational requirements that may contradict the traditional managerial philosophies and approaches of hierarchical and centralized organizations. Thus, companies interested in this new breed of organization will need to make changes in two major areas. First, as noted above, strategists and managers of such organizations will need to change their mindset of self-reliance and the sole developer of innovation as well as the appropriation of excessive returns from innovation. They must be willing to work with numerous other capable parties to develop new ideas and products/services. The idea of collective generation of innovation lays the foundation for large-scale, multiparty collaboration. Second, in addition to having diverse skills and knowledge, firms wishing to form and participate in collaborative communities must be willing and able to play a facilitator role. From an organizational perspective, the purpose of Blade.org—heavily manifested in the activities of its principal office—is to enable the member firms to identify, connect with, and collaborate with other member firms. Blade.org is not a hierarchical organization; it is a community in which the member firms self-organize using the protocols and infrastructures provided by a facilitator (Bøllingtoft, Müller, Ulhøi, & Snow, 2012).

Despite the advantages of achieving innovations through a collaborative community of firms as opposed to hierarchical organization structures, collaborative designs present challenges as well. IBM, for example, believed that it would be better off by sharing its blade technology with others and by inviting them to develop product applications and to contribute to the technology's further development. According to Culpan (2002), the starting point in strategic alliance decisions to increase innovation capacity is resource and competence sharing as the means of building competitive advantage. This can be accomplished by exploiting symmetrical competencies, deploying asymmetrical competencies, or creating new competencies. IBM and the other founding firms, as well as the member firms of Blade.org, have openly shared valuable resources within a commercial framework that permits each firm to pursue both its individual and collective interests. In their study, Ozcan and Eisenhardt (2009) found that executives are more likely to assemble high-performing portfolios when they visualize those portfolios in the context of the entire industry as opposed to a series of single ties.

As the number of members increases, the governance mechanism of a community of firms must accommodate. There is a need for a well-defined governance mechanism in defining the roles of members, the rules of governance, and in facilitating the activities of members and resolving conflicts if they arise. In alliance governance, especially with a multiparty alliance, the large number of contractual and relational interactions and transactions make governance complex. Recognizing this fact, Fjeldstad, Snow, Miles, & Lettl (in press) have offered a governance framework for multiparty collaboration that is scalable and allows the actors to self-organize. The framework is built on (a) commons where the actors accumulate and share resources and (b) protocols, processes, and infrastructures that enable peer-to-peer collaboration.

Leaders of communities of firms need to support member firms in the creation and pursuit of common goals by designing an incentive system such that member firms commit their assets, resources, and time to learn and share knowledge created as a result of their collaborative interactions. When a firm joins a community of firms, it has certain expectations and goals. It is vital for a community of firms to meet member expectations and objectives by providing a trusting and collaborative environment that is conducive to innovation. The main incentives for accomplishing this are opportunities to collaborate with other firms to create value in the form of new products, markets, and knowledge, and to appropriate that value based on recognized contributions.

CONCLUSION

A collaborative community of firms such as Blade.org has emerged as a result of circumstances where knowledge is complex, growing, and widely distributed, thus stimulating the need for multiparty collaboration. Such circumstances cause the locus of innovation to shift from within a single firm to groups and communities of firms. We do not suggest that open innovation conducted by means of alliances, static networks, and outsourcing will decline, but rather that innovation conducted according to a collaborative community of firms model offers a valuable alternative in certain situations. Open innovation strategy implemented through a collaborative community of firms marks a reversal of the traditional philosophy and approach that has dominated organization theory and practice for many years.

REFERENCES

Bøllingtoft, A., Müller, S., Ulhøi, J. P., & Snow, C. C. (2012). Collaborative innovation communities: Role of the shared services provider. In A. Bøllingtoft, L. Donaldson, G. Huber, D. D. Håkonsson, & C. C. Snow (Eds.), *Collaborative communities: Purpose, process, and design.* New York: Springer.

Chesbrough, H. W. (2003). *Open innovation: The new imperative for creating and profiting from technology.* Boston: Harvard Business School Press.

Chesbrough, H. W. (2006). *Open business models: How to thrive in the new innovative landscape.* Boston: Harvard Business School Press.

Chesbrough, H. W., & Appleyard, M. M. (2007). Open innovation and strategy. *California Management Review, 50*(1), 57–76.

Clabby Analytics. (2007). *Blade.org: The snowball effect.* Retrieved from http://clabbyanalytics.com/uploads/Blade.org_-_The_Snowball_Effect_Final_Final.pdf.

Culpan, R. (2002). *Global business alliances: Theory and practice.* Westport, CT: Quorum Books.

Culpan, R. (2009). A fresh look at strategic alliances: Research issues and future directions. *International Journal of Strategic Business Alliances, 1*(1), 4–23.

Datacenterknowledge.com. (2007). *Quarterly Tracker.* Retrieved from: http://www.datacenterknowledge.com/archives/2007/12/04/idc-sales-of-blades-hit-1-billion-in-3q07

Dyer, J. H., & Hatch, N. W. (2006). Relation-specific capabilities and barriers to knowledge transfers: Creating advantage through network relationships. *Strategic Management Journal, 27,* 701–719.

Fjeldstad, Ø. D., Snow, C. C., Miles, R. E., & Lettl, C. (in press). The architecture of collaboration: Organizing resources among large sets of actors. *Strategic Management Journal.*

Grant, R. M. (1996). Toward a knowledge-based theory of the firm. *Strategic Management Journal, 17,* 109–122.

Grant, R. M., & Baden-Fuller, C. (2004). A knowledge accessing theory of strategic alliances. *Journal of Management Studies, 41,* 61–84.

Huston, L., & Sakkab, N. (2006). Connect and develop: Inside Procter & Gamble's new model for innovation. *Harvard Business Review, 84*(3), 58–66.

Inkpen, A. C. (1996). Creating knowledge through collaboration. *California Management Review, 39*(1), 123–140.

Inkpen, A. C., & Tsang, E. (2005). Social capital, networks, and knowledge transfer. *Academy of Management Review, 30,* 146–165.

Lee, G. K., & Cole, R. E. (2003). From a firm-based to a community-based model of knowledge creation: The case of the Linux kernel development. *Organization Science, 14,* 633–649.

Mesquita, L. F., Anand, J., & Brush, T. E. (2008). Comparing the resource-based and relational views: Knowledge transfer and spillover in vertical alliances. *Strategic Management Journal, 29*(9), 913–941.

Miles, R. E., Snow, C. C., Fjeldstad, Ø. D., Miles, G., & Lettl, C. (2010). Designing organizations to meet 21st-century opportunities and challenges. *Organizational Dynamics, 39*(2), 93–103.

Miles, R. E., Miles, G., & Snow, C. C. (2005). *Collaborative entrepreneurship: How communities of networked firms use continuous innovation to create economic wealth.* Stanford, CA: Stanford University Press.

Nickerson, J. A., & Zenger, T. R. (2004). A knowledge-based theory of the firm: The problem-solving perspective. *Organization Science, 15,* 617–632.

Nonaka, I., & Takeuchi, H. (1995). *The knowledge-creating company: How Japanese companies create the dynamics of innovation.* Oxford, UK: Oxford University Press.

Nonaka, I., Toyama, R., & Hirata, T. (2008). *Managing flow: A process theory of the knowledge-based firm.* London: Palgrave Macmillan.

Ozcan, P., & Eisenhardt, K. M. (2009). Origin of alliance portfolios: Entrepreneurs, network strategies, and firm performance. *Academy of Management Journal, 52,* 246–279.

Pisano, G. P., & Verganti, R. (2008). Which kind of collaboration is right for you? *Harvard Business Review, 86*(12), 78–86.

Powell, W. W., Koput, K. W., & Smith-Doerr, L. (1996). Interorganizational collaboration and the locus of innovation: Networks of learning in biotechnology. *Administrative Science Quarterly, 41,* 116–145.

Snow, C. C., Fjeldstad, Ø. D., Lettl, C., & Miles, R. E. (2011). Organizing continuous product development and commercialization: The collaborative community of firms model. *Journal of Product Innovation Management, 28*(1), 3–16.

Snow, C. C., Strauss, D. R., & Culpan, R. (2009). Community of firms: A new paradigm for open innovation and an analysis of Blade.org. *International Journal of Strategic Business Alliances, 1,* 53–72.

Snow, C. C., Strauss, D. R., & Lettl, C. (2009). Blade.org: A collaborative community of firms. In A. Bøllingtoft, D. D. Håkonsson, J. F. Nielsen, C. C. Snow, & J. Ulhoi (Eds.), *New approaches to organization design* (pp. 3–21). New York: Springer.

Stieglitz, N. & Heine, K. (2007). Innovations and the role of complementarities in a strategic theory of the firm. *Strategic Management Journal, 28,* 1–15.

CHAPTER 13

STRATEGIC PACING OF ACQUISITIONS AND ALLIANCES

A Temporal View

Weilei (Stone) Shi
John E. Prescott

ABSTRACT

For small and medium size firms (SMEs), little is known regarding the relationship between the strategic pacing of acquisitions and alliances, their performance effects, and the moderating role of key contingencies. Building on learning theory, we begin to bridge this gap by investigating pacing of alliance and acquisition initiatives. We propose an inverted-U relationship between pacing and performance. Our contingency approach reasons that the nonlinear relationship is stronger for alliances than acquisitions and for cross-border than domestic alliances. We also suggest a Red Queen effect for the pacing of acquisitions. Drawing on a sample of SMEs in the specialty pharmaceutical industry, we find considerable support for our propositions. Temporal theorizing assists SMEs' managers in effectively incorporating a time dimension in the mobilization and allocation of scarce organizational resources.

Strategic Alliances for Value Creation, pages 301–320

INTRODUCTION

Research on the pacing of acquisitions and alliances enriches our understanding by directly addressing the temporal nature of firms' acquisition and alliance experience and resulting performance outcomes (Hayward, 2002; Kusewitt, 1985; Laamanen & Keil, 2008; Nadolska & Barkema, 2007; Vermeulen & Barkema, 2002). Firms having the same level of acquisition and alliance experience does not imply that they pace these strategic initiatives in a similar way. Pacing is defined as how frequently a firm conducts a series of corporate-level initiatives over its life course (Barkema, Baum, & Mannix, 2002; Laamanen & Keil, 2008; Prescott & Shi, 2008). A pacing approach complements the count-based experience perspective in that pacing adds a time dimension regarding *when* a firm conducts it strategic initiatives (Finkelstein & Haleblian, 2002; Haleblian & Finkelstein, 1999; Schreiner, Kale, & Corsten, 2009; Zollo & Singh, 2004). The incorporation of a time dimension explicitly acknowledges that the impact of experience is fundamentally related to *when* experience occurs.

The emerging pacing research strand leverages learning, unlearning, and routine development mechanisms to explain the pacing-performance relationship over a firm's life course (Shi & Prescott, 2011). Pacing activities are particularly relevant and represent unique challenges for small and medium size firms (SMEs). SMEs are increasingly engaging in multiple acquisition and alliance initiatives to achieve growth objectives since they often do not possess internal capabilities or resources for organic growth (Lu & Beamish, 2006; Malo & Norus, 2009; Shi & Prescott, 2011). Thus, how to temporally pace acquisition programs and alliance portfolios is a critical area of concern given that commits to acquisitions and alliances require a substantial investment of resources and managerial time (Fernhaber & Li, 2010). SMEs are regarded as a driving force for industrial renewal and innovation (Audretsch, 1995). Their survival environment is extremely dynamic, and competitive advantage often accrues to firms that can manage the temporal pace of their collaborative activities (Barkema et al., 2002).

While empirical evidence regarding the performance implication of pacing has been found in the context of large organizations (Hayward, 2002; Laamanen & Keil, 2008; Vermeulen & Barkema, 2002), we focus on bringing clarity to two additional areas central to SMEs. First, prior studies have examined strategic initiatives individually, focusing on either acquisitions (Hayward, 2002; Laamanen & Keil, 2008) or foreign subsidiary expansion (Vermeulen & Barkema, 2002). Firms are increasingly engaged in strategic initiatives that are characterized by low levels of exclusivity such as when acquisition and alliance initiatives occur simultaneously (Ofori-Dankwa & Julian, 2001). Since acquisition and alliance initiatives compete for resources, have important interdependencies, and are likely to have distinctive temporal paces (Ancona & Chong, 1996), it is fruitful to investigate these initiatives together as well as examine their differential pacing impact on firm performance.

Second, firms' strategic initiatives are embedded in an environment where there is competition for alliance partners and acquisition targets. As a result, a firm's pacing strategy needs to consider their competitors' pacing activity. We incorporate a Red Queen competition effect that views competitive dynamics as a coevolving arms race embedded in a learning context (Barnett & Pontikes, 2008). As evolutionary scholars stress, SMEs are generally more responsive to Red Queen competition than their larger counterparts (Barnett & McKendrick, 2004; Derfus, Maggitti, Grimm, & Smith, 2008) due to tighter linkages between internal processes and external pressures (Hickson, Pugh, & Pheysey, 1969) and their less complex internal cooperation requirements since they have a smaller number of managers (Barnett & McKendrick, 2004).

We make three important contributions to the strategy literature. First, we contribute to the emerging pacing stream of research by articulating the performance impact of SMEs' pacing of acquisitions and alliances simultaneously and individually. Second, we begin to integrate the pacing and competitive dynamic literatures. Adopting multiple theoretical lenses enrich our understanding of pacing strategy from both a firm and firm-environment interactive perspective. Lastly, given the fact that pacing is an effective mechanism for the management of time, we resonate with the call for a temporal lens in management research (Ancona, Okhuysen, & Perlow, 2001; Bluedorn & Denhardt, 1988) and further open the window for organizational strategists to theorize how SMEs' managers should leverage their limited time in mobilizing and allocating scarce organizational resources.

Our chapter is structured as follows: First, we discuss the theoretical arguments underlying the pacing phenomena. Specifically, we draw on both behavioral theory and the learning perspective to discuss how each view affects the relationship between pacing and performance. The behavioral approach provides rationales as to why pacing should not proceed too quickly, while an organizational learning perspective provides rationales for why pacing should not proceed too slowly. Some of the key concepts we draw on from each perspective include bounded rationality, absorptive capacity (Argote & Greve, 2007), limited cognitive scope (Pouder & St. John, 1996), time compression diseconomy (Dierickx & Cool, 1989), and organizational forgetting (Argote, Beckman, & Epple, 1990; Benkard, 2000; Darr & Argote, 1995). Next, we discuss the contingent effects. Our main rationale for developing contingencies for our strategic pacing thesis is largely based on the conjecture that different strategic initiatives have fundamentally different temporal maps (Ancona & Chong, 1996). Key contingency includes acquisition versus alliance and cross-border alliance versus domestic alliance. Strategic alliances are dissimilar from acquisitions in terms of subsequent independence and mutual interdependence (Parkhe, 1993), both of which contribute to creating a distinctive temporal nature. We also suggest that the complexity of learning is different in cross-border alliances as compared to domestic alliances. Rivals' strategic actions influence the pacing of the focal firm's strategic initiatives and subsequent performance. Drawing on competitive dynamics and co-evolution literature, we discuss the performance implication of the Red Queen effect for focal firms' pacing initiatives. We next discuss our empirical context and share a set of results. Lastly, discuss theoretical and managerial implications of and identify some useful venues for future research.

PACING, BEHAVIORAL THEORY, AND LEARNING MECHANISMS

Consistent with recent studies, we define pacing as how frequently a firm conducts a series of strategic activities over a period of time (Laamanen & Keil, 2008; Vermeulen & Barkema, 2002). In the acquisition literature, the concept of pacing is equivalent to acquisition rate (Laamanen & Keil, 2008) or average temporal distance between two consecutive acquisitions (Hayward, 2002). We draw on the behavioral and organizational learning perspectives to bracket our inverted-U pacing-performance hypotheses. The behavioral learning approach provides rationales as to why pacing should not proceed too quickly, while the organizational learning perspective provides rationales for why pacing should not proceed too slowly.

Drawing on the well-accepted tenets of bounded rationality and absorptive capacity (Argote & Greve, 2007), behavioral-based pacing studies emphasize the downside of a fast pace (Laamanen & Keil, 2008; Vermeulen & Barkema, 2002), i.e., firms should not pace their activities too quickly due to individuals' bounded rationality (March, 1991; Simon, 1955) and limited cognitive scope (Pouder & St. John, 1996). If a firm conducts too many acquisitions or alliances in a short period of time, managers will strain their cognitive capacity and limit their search to well-known and limited domains. Behavioral scholars have applied the concepts of time compression diseconomy (Dierickx & Cool, 1989) to convincingly demonstrate that "diseconomies emerge when firms do not allocate appropriate time to learn from prior experiences and apply them throughout the organization" (Vermeulen & Barkema, 2002, p. 640). A fast pace does not provide sufficient time for managers to draw inferences from their strategic initiatives or to accumulate knowledge regarding the development of alliance/acquisition capabilities. As a result, behavioral researchers postulate either a negative moderating effect (Vermeulen & Barkema, 2002) or a direct negative effect of pacing (Kusewitt, 1985; Laamanen & Keil, 2008) on performance. However, behavioral scholars' emphasis on absorptive capacity and time-compression diseconomies have paid less attention to other complementary pacing mechanisms such as organizational forgetting.

While behavioral theorists state that a fast pace has negative performance outcomes, organizational learning scholars assert that an infrequent pace hurts organizational performance as well. Hayward (2002, p. 25), for instance, contends that "very long intervals between a focal acquisition and the one before it magnify the inaccessibility of learning." Infrequent pacing of acquisitions or alliances tends to increase organizational forgetfulness (Benkard, 2000) preventing firms from accessing and leveraging prior learning experience. According to scholars of organizational forgetting (Argote et al., 1990; Darr & Argote, 1995), if firms do not learn before, during, or after undertaking strategic initiatives, their processes and knowledge structures will get rusty and become inefficient. When the pacing of acquisitions and alliances is too infrequent, knowledge simply will not accumulate because organizations and their managers cannot remember what they did and how they did it (Carley, 1992; Hayward, 2002). Eisenhardt and Martin (2000) demonstrated the forgetting hypothesis within the context of acquisitions. Firms may also forget when key personnel who took part in previous strategic activities leave, retire, or move on to other positions within the firm (Laamanen & Keil, 2008).

In the context of alliances, experience from prior alliances such as knowledge transfer processes between partners decays over time, especially in high-velocity environments (Henderson & Cool, 2003; Sampson, 2005). Similarly, in the context of acquisitions, acquisition experience differs significantly across economic cycles. In a boom economy, business development teams usually focus on targets that are in financial trouble. The best opportunities in a downturn, as suggested by business practitioners, however, are often good pieces of a distressed portfolio forced into a fire sale (Capaldo, Cogman, & Suonio, 2009). This suggests that experiential learning obtained in a boom is different from learning in a downturn.

The notion of forgetfulness is particularly important in our global specialty pharmaceutical empirical context where young firms are more likely to forget critical knowledge obtained from previous organizational learning processes (Keh, Nguyen, & Ng, 2007; Mohan-Neill, 1995). Although firms can establish routines that store relevant knowledge, unless these routines are recurringly utilized, knowledge decays or become antiquated (Barkema & Schijven, 2008; Bercovitz & Mitchell, 2007). In our high-technology context, even in the presence of routines, the stock of firm knowledge is subject to obsolescence due to significant changes in the external market (Powell & Grodal, 2005).

Decay rates vary across environments (Henderson & Cool, 2003). Many organizational forgetfulness studies have been conducted in high-frequency contexts, i.e., product production or years of operating experience in shipbuilding (Argote et al., 1990), auto parts (Arthur & Huntley, 2005), semiconductor manufacturing (Hatch & Dyer, 2004), and airplane manufacturing (Argote & Epple, 1990). Acquisitions and alliances occur relatively less frequently in the global specialty pharmaceutical industry, and learning outcomes may not depreciate as rapidly. However, as Haunschild and Sullivan (2002) assert, even in the context of rare and low-frequency events, it is unlikely that temporally distant events are more relevant to current events than those that occurred recently. In our context, due to resource constraints, young firms are unlikely to devote resources to corporate development offices resulting in the underdevelopment of explicit learning routines.

Drawing on both behavioral theory and organizational learning/forgetfulness perspectives, we suggest the following hypothesis:

> **Hypothesis 1:** *The strategic pacing of acquisitions and alliances exhibits an inverted-U relationship with performance, i.e., a moderate level of pacing generates the highest level of performance.*

A CONTINGENCY VIEW OF STRAEGIC PACING

We adopt a contingency perspective to hypothesize why the form of the inverted-U differs across acquisitions and alliances, cross-border versus domestic alliances, and Red Queen effects.

Acquisitions vs. Alliances

Our rationale to develop and test contingencies for our strategic pacing hypotheses is based on the conjecture that different strategic initiatives have fundamentally different temporal maps (Ancona & Chong, 1996). As Barkema and his associates (2002) posit, the "research" and "development" sides of R&D require distinctive temporal maps. While there are many similarities, alliances and acquisitions differ in terms of subsequent independence and mutual interdependence (Parkhe, 1993). Both characteristics contribute to the distinctive temporal nature and the form and strength of the pacing-performance relationship for acquisitions versus alliances.

Under subsequent independence, partner firms remain independent after the formation of an alliance. This is clearly not the case in acquisitions, where target firms discontinue their legal and independent operation. Mutual interdependence indicates that alliance partners rely on each other in terms of shared control and coordination (Inkpen, 2002), whereas in an acquisition, the firms are more tightly integrated. Mutual interdependence and subsequent independence create different learning contexts for partners in alliances from those for acquirers.

Three types of learning have been identified by alliance scholars, (Dussauge, Garrette, & Mitchell, 2004; Inkpen, 2002), including (a) joint learning, defined as skill familiarity that supports the alliance partners' ability to jointly create value; (b) learning from partner or interpartner learning, defined as firms' attempt to learn the practices, strategies, knowledge, and technology possessed by other organizations; and (c) learning by doing, or experiential learning (also called learning to learn from alliances; Anand & Khanna, 2000), defined as learning from strategic alliance experience (Dussauge et al., 2004). These types of learning exist irrespective of the motivation of the strategic alliance. In contrast, in the case of acquisitions, the majority of knowledge transfer occurs in the form of experiential learning, similar to the third type of learning in strategic alliance (Haleblian & Finkelstein, 1999). The absence of mutual interdependence and subsequent independence mitigate incentives for acquirers (targets) to concentrate on the other two types of learning. To a greater extent, experiential learning is under the control of firms in acquisitions than in alliances due to mutual interdependence.

In multiple types of learning settings, both the volume and complexity of information acquisition and knowledge transfer are significantly increased. As a result, learning capability requirements are significantly enlarged. At the individual level, capacity constraints result from the fact that managers are indivisible and can only appear in one place at a time (Carlstein, 1982). At the firm level, firms overcome individual capacity constraints through recruiting additional staff and division of labor. Even in this case, time-demanding activities within the firm will increase since individuals place demand on one another's time due to division of labor and associated coordination or integration mechanisms. Staffing and structural changes often do not create increased time capacity at the firm level.

Therefore, when firms pace their alliances, as opposed to acquisitions, they will more quickly reach an inflection point with respect to their positive impact, after which performance begins to decrease. Since firms have to simultaneously manage three types of learning for an alliance, an accelerated pace will inevitably increase time-demanding activities. Frequent pacing of alliances results in time competition among the various types of alliance learning.

In alliances, multiple types of learning involve different learning objectives, content, and processes, which may not be mutually compatible. For instance, learning by doing involves implementing technology transfer and

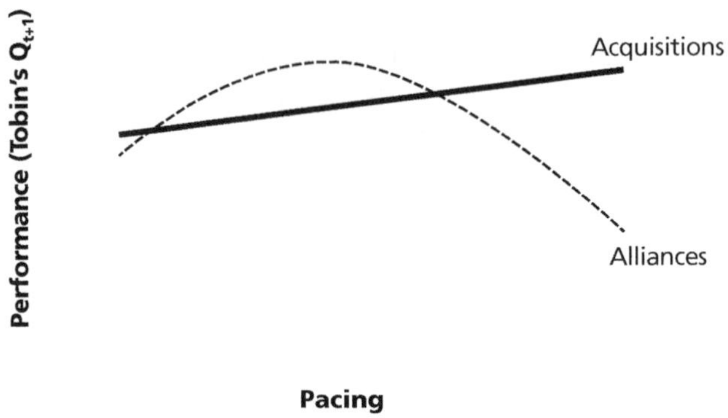

Figure 13.1 Interaction between strategic pacing and type of strategy predicting firm performance (Hypothesis 2).

managing the strategic alliance per se, which requires an experiential learning process, while learning from partners involves internalizing partners' skills, know-how, and capabilities, which entails a vicarious learning process often leading to private benefits (Dussauge et al., 2004). Fast pacing of alliances, compared with acquisitions, will therefore generate greater managerial time-capacity constraints due to increased information processing needs related to the multiple forms of learning. Managers need more time between alliances to internalize the benefits as well as mitigate their costs.

In sum, firm performance is more sensitive to the pacing of strategic alliances than acquisitions, i.e., a small increase in the pacing of alliances will have a disproportional impact on performance compared to the same level of increase in the pacing of acquisitions. As illustrated in Figure 13.1, an inflection point is more quickly reached in the pacing of alliances.

Hypothesis 2: *The inverted-U relationship between strategic pacing and performance will be stronger*[1] *for the pacing of alliances than for the pacing of acquisitions.*

Cross-Border Alliances vs. Domestic Alliances

While the distinctive characteristics of mutual interdependence and subsequent independence distinguish alliances from acquisitions in terms of the forms of learning, cross-border and domestic alliances differ in their learning mechanisms. Within the strategic alliance literature, scholars view cross-border alliance as a way to exploit knowledge, information, and resources in new markets or previously undefined domains (Kenis & Knoke, 2002; Koka & Prescott, 2002). This same view is shared by international management scholars who regard cross-border alliances as a strategic tool for seeking new resources and strategic assets (Dunning, 1993). One key distinction in cross-border alliances that is not encountered in domestic alliances is the added complexity due to different cultural, normative, and regulatory regimes resulting in increased learning complexity.

Learning about partners and joint learning of one's institutional context is imperative in cross-boarder alliances. For instance, a mutual understanding of cultural nuances increases relative absorptive capacity (Lane & Lubatkin, 1998) that leads to skill familiarity and contributes to an enhanced partners' ability to jointly create value. Similarly, learning by doing in a cross-border alliance requires firms to apply their experiences in different international contexts and make operating adjustments that conform to regulatory policies and social norms.

The increased complexity creates challenges for firms in managing the pacing of their cross-border alliances. We contend that these learning mechanisms will have a similar effect on performance as stated in Hypothesis 2. Essentially, firm performance will be more sensitive to the pacing of cross-border alliances than the pacing of domestic ones due to enlarged time-demanding activities, its associated capacity constraints, and the challenge of increased coordination and integrations costs. An increase in the pace of cross-border alliances will reach an inflection point more quickly than the same increase in the pace of domestic alliances.

> **Hypothesis 3:** *The inverted-U relationship between strategic pacing and performance will be stronger for the pacing of cross-border alliances than for the pacing of domestic alliances.*

Pacing and Coevolution

Rivals' actions influence the pacing of a firm's strategic initiatives and subsequent performance. Competitive dynamics researchers incorporate contingent competition as part of an organization's learning process (Barnett & Hansen, 1996; Smith, Ferrier, & Grimm, 2001). Both the coevolution and competitive dynamics perspectives acknowledge firm interdependence and shared learning. According to this view, "competition triggers a self-reinforcing process, equilibrium is continually upset and responses to competition are the deliberate acts of top managers" (Barnett & Hansen, 1996, p. 141). The result of these processes is commonly known as the Red Queen effect, which refers to the self-reinforcing process as an "arms race" (Dawkins, 1982), triggered by both competition and organizational learning (Barnett & Pontikes, 2008).

Firms that engage in Red Queen competition are expected to enhance their organizational performance through two underlying mechanisms (Barnett & Pontikes, 2008). First, over time, firms become more capable at exploiting their existing context due to an upwardly adjusted aspiration level (Lant, 1992). This occurs when a firm's ability to search for targets, alliance partners, and the coordination of multiple completed acquisitions and alliances becomes increasingly efficient, which further challenges their rivals to become equally, if not more, efficient. Rivals' subsequent improvement poses a threat to the firm, which in turn stimulates another cycle of upward adjustment. Second, firm performance increases due to a "selection effect," i.e., weaker competitors will be selected out. When the least competitive members are weeded out by increased competitive pressure (Sorenson, 2000), the survival bar within the population will be raised. In the acquisition and alliance context, this suggests that the pressure to search for targets or alliance partners forces the weakest firms out of the game due to their insufficient abilities to search and coordinate multiple deals or alliances. The performance of the remaining firms is consequently enhanced.

The aforementioned arguments imply that performance will increase when firms match their pacing of acquisition and alliance initiatives with their competitors. This view has been echoed by Volberda and Lewin (2003), who argued that organizations must maintain requisite variety (i.e., their internal rate of changes must match the coevolution rate of the system within which firms are embedded). *The McKinsey Quarterly* (Foster & Kaplan, 2001) also suggests increasing the rate of creative destruction to the level of the market as a prescription to firms operating in industries characterized by hypercompetition (D'Aveni, 1994). Matching the pace of strategic initiatives with U of competitors is a dynamic form of strategic fit (Zajac, Kraatz, & Bresser, 2000). The traditional view of strategic fit literature has mainly dealt with "what" (such as resources) or "how" (such as process and structures) to match (Miller & Snow, 1978; Miller, Wiseman, & Gomez-Mejia, 2002). The matching of pace view focuses on "when" and "at what frequency" to temporally match, and is a form of organizational adaptation that involves repetitive adjustments to an ongoing environmental pacer (Pérez-Nordtvedt, Payne, Short, & Kedia, 2008).

An alternative explanation for a focal firms' matching or imitation behavior can be derived from information-based theorizing, where "firms match/follow others that are perceived as having superior information" instead of "maintaining competitive parity or limit rivalry" (Lieberman & Asaba, 2006, p. 368). Based on Lieberman and Asaba's three criteria that differentiate information-based imitation from rivalry-based imitation behaviors, we argue that the competitive arena in our context is dominated by rivalry-based imitation processes for two important reasons. First, although our sample firms occupy different product niches, competition does not hinge at the product level, but rather at the resource level, i.e., they are competing for investors' confidence and attention in an attempt to secure financial resources. Second, firms in our sample have similar resources and share similar origins and history. As Lieberman and Asaba argued, when firms are rivals and when they share similar resources, rivalry-based motives are likely to be the dominant rationale for imitation.

Hypothesis 4: *Firms that match the pacing of their acquisitions and alliances with the industry average will achieve higher performance.*

INDUSTRY CONTEXT

We conduct our research on a sample of 58 publically traded SMEs in the global specialty pharmaceuticals industry (SP). We define SP as firms that deal with expensive medications that treat rare, chronic diseases inflicting a small proportion of people (Maas, 2005). Special diseases include but are not limited to hemophilia, hepatitis C, oncology, HIV/AIDs, and transplant, which are classified as orphan diseases. The time period spans the years 1985 to the end of 2003. Prior to this period, two important events occurred that shaped the evolution of the SP industry. The enactment of the Orphan Drug Act in 1984 created incentives to develop products for diseases affecting relatively small numbers of patients. The U.S Drug Price Competition and Patent Term Restoration Act of 1984 standardized U.S. procedures for recognition of generic drugs.

The SP sector is a rapidly growing market with annual sales increases of 43% from 2002 to 2005, a much faster pace than the 10.2% average increase in drug spending (Catton, 2006). It is estimated to double in size, reaching $99 billion by 2010 (Mantone, 2008). Firms in this sector are relatively younger and smaller compared with traditional giant pharmaceutical firms.

We select this industry for several reasons consistent with our theoretical logic. First, for small and young SP firms, their growth strategies are largely driven by acquisition and alliance activity. The acquisition and alliance growth-driven strategy provides an ideal context for firms to pace their strategic initiatives and allows firms to develop skills to facilitate and institutionalize a temporal map for their multiple acquisition and alliance activity. Second, SP firms often do not possess the requisite complementary resources and knowledge for in-house development activities; instead they rely on partner firms for important resources such as finance, marketing, and manufacturing (Lee, Lee, & Pennings, 2001). The lack of internal capabilities to develop downstream resources suggests that they are more likely to proactively search for targets or partners. Third, small, young, and specialized firms are regarded as a driving force for industrial renewal and innovation (Audretsch, 1995). Their survival environment is extremely dynamic, and competitive advantage often accrues to firms that can manage the temporality of their collaborative activities (Barkema et al., 2002). Fourth, our context is appropriate for examining the Red Queen effect since SMEs are more responsive to Red Queen competition than their larger counterparts (Barnett & McKendrick, 2004; Derfus et al., 2008).

We unpack our data to understand the individual features of our sample firms' initiatives. On average, our sample firms conduct 0.32 acquisitions and 0.15 alliances (noncumulative) a year, which is low compared with giant pharmaceutical firms (for instance, Abbott conducted 10 acquisitions in 2006). The low-frequency context is consistent with our approach to studying pacing strategy that allows firms to track temporal features of their pacing strategy.

We obtained alliance and acquisition data from Thomson Financial Security Data Company's (SDC) database, financial data from COMPSTAT, and supplemented company information through Web sites, trade journals, and industry experts. Our measures for pacing, Red Queen competition, performance, and controls are consistent with those in the literature. Our estimates employ panel data using a feasible generalized least square (FGLS) regression. Details of our sample, operationalizations, and analytical methods are available from the authors.

DISCUSSION OF FINDINGS

Combining the behavioral and organizational learning approaches, we proposed an inverted-U relationship between pacing and performance for SMEs. To this end, our approach builds on and complements emerging research on the pacing of corporate strategic initiatives such as acquisition and foreign expansion.

Existing studies on pacing tend to focus on the negative consequence of a fast pace, suggesting that frequent acquirers or foreign expansion will suffer significantly from time-compression diseconomies, hence affecting firms' accumulation and assimilation of acquisition ability (Kusewitt, 1985; Laamanen & Keil, 2008) or foreign expansion capability (Vermeulen & Barkema, 2002). Our study, to some extent, shares theoretical underpinnings proposed by Hayward (2002) who stresses that neither a fast nor slow pace is beneficial for performance. According to this logic, infrequent acquirers suffer due to their inability to remember what had been learned earlier. Previous learning can be forgotten (Argote et al., 1990; Darr & Argote, 1995) and decays over time (Sampson, 2005). This is especially true for SMEs where knowledge and market information routines are underdeveloped. In other words, SMEs are more likely to forget what they learn if they pace their strategic initiatives too slowly.

Based on our preliminary findings, we did not validate prior scholars' empirical findings for acquisitions. Although we found an inverted-U relationship between pacing of overall strategic initiative (including both acquisition and alliance) and performance, our contingency analysis shows that this relationship is largely driven by alliances. Thus, while evidence was found in support of Hypothesis 1, the results suggest that in future research, separate hypotheses should be developed for acquisitions and alliances. For acquisitions, Figure 13.1 shows that the pacing of acquisition has a positive relationship with performance up to the inflection point, which predicts a decline in performance at acquisition rates of over approximately three per year. (This lies outside of our data range.) The results support Hypothesis 2. This is in contrast to Kusewitt (1985), who found an inflection point around one per year. One possible explanation is that strategic momentum differs across the two study's context, which includes but is not limited to an average acquisition rate (0.32 versus 2.55 per year), time period (1985 to 2003 versus 1967 to 1976), and size of the acquirers (SME SP firms versus larger U.S. manufacturing firms).

The differential performance impact between alliances and acquisitions (and between cross-border and domestic alliances supporting Hypothesis 3; see Figure 13.2) corroborates the notion that different activities have fundamentally different temporal pacing (Ancona & Chong, 1996). Alliances and acquisitions differ on two important dimensions: subsequent independence and mutual interdependence. These two dimensions matter because they create different learning contexts. Alliances are associated with a more complex and higher volume of knowledge transfer than acquisitions, creating time constraints at both the individual and firm level. To

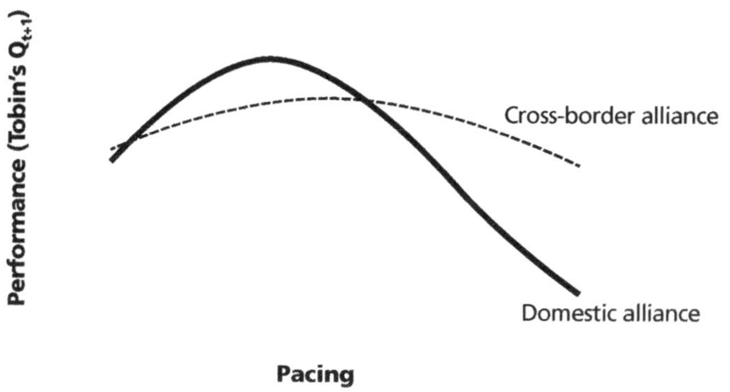

Figure 13.2 Interaction between strategic pacing and nature of strategic alliance predicting firm performance (Hypothesis 3).

some extent, this suggests a boundary condition for pacing strategy (Dubin, 1978). This boundary condition demonstrates a challenge for SMEs who lack sufficient resources (managerial and financial) to conduct alliance and acquisition simultaneously (Fernhaber & Li, 2010). In this vein, SMEs may benefit from leveraging intratemporal economies of scope (Helfat & Eisenhardt, 2004) or internal temporal entrainment (Khavul, Pérez-Nordtvedt, & Wood, 2010; Pérez-Nordtvedt et al., 2008; Standifer & Bluedorn, 2006) that achieve workflow coordination (Eisenhardt & Brown, 1998).

We also posit that SMEs' learning ability and the development of their alliance/acquisition capability are contingent upon their competitive landscape. On one hand, they need to strike a balance internally between learning and forgetfulness by maintaining a moderate temporal pace. On the other hand, they need to pay attention to their external learning environment, which is largely driven by their competitor's learning behaviors. In our view, SMEs are particularly responsive to Red Queen competition (Barnett & McKendrick, 2004; Derfus et al., 2008) due to tighter linkages between internal processes and external pressures (Hickson et al., 1969) and their less complex cooperation requirements due to a smaller number of managers (Barnett & McKendrick, 2004). Our interviews indicated that SME SP firms compete extensively with each other for public investors' attention and confidence in the hope that investors will provide sufficient financial resources; demonstrating a Red Queen phenomena (Barnett & McKendrick, 2004). Our theoretical lens is based on traditional organizational theory, which emphasizes the importance of interaction between firms and their environment (Thompson, 1967). The central theme of this view is that firms need to achieve strategic fit with their respective environment (Miller & Snow, 1978; Miller et al., 2002). We extend the notion of strategic fit by incorporating a dynamic nature (Zajac et al., 2000), i.e., firms need to continuously adjust their pace to the ongoing competitive environment over a period of time (Pérez-Nordtvedt et al., 2008).

Our preliminary analysis indicated that Red Queen competition generated a positive performance impact for acquisitions, but not for alliances. One possible explanation might be that acquisition targets are limited in a competitive space (this is especially true in the SP sector), while the supply of alliance partners is significantly larger since multiple specialty drug companies can ally with multiple giant pharmaceutical firms. Investors tend to value firms that can effectively match their acquisition pace with their rivals.

FUTURE RESEARCH

Our preliminary results provide some puzzles that require further clarification. For instance, if the relationship between pacing and performance is an inverted-U, why would corporate-level managers continue to engage in new acquisitions and alliances when their performance benefits begin to decline? Our capacity constraint hypothesis (H1) could be one explanation. However, if Hypothesis 4 (Red Queen effect) is correct, then why do firms not adjust their pacing level to the "industry average?" We speculate that firms fail to adjust their pacing due to three important reasons.

First, industry average pacing is a retrospective and dynamic concept, i.e., researchers can objectively measure it on a retrospective base, but firms have a difficult task perceiving and measuring it on a concurrent base since an industry average is a function of simultaneous actions of a focal firm and its competitors. As such, the industry average is changing over time, weakening a firm's ability to adjust their pace. Alternatively, firms can predict an industry average proactively. However, a firm's predictive ability may be attenuated by uncertainty and the lack of a sophisticated competitive intelligence system (Prescott & Miller, 2001).

Second, pacing is a path-dependent concept. Firms may well realize that they are far behind their competitors. However, they cannot easily make adjustments because pacing is a strategic pattern that emerges through a series of prior decisions. Changing a firm's current pace requires a related set of changes in resource allocation and interaction patterns. Previous pacing generates inertia that restricts further adjustment. Future research that aims to empirically test these issues will aid in our understanding of the pacing-performance relationship.

Third, managers may attempt to match their industry average. However, if the degree of firm and competitor temporal-pace misfit is too great, then adjustments may not be sufficient to overcome past misfits (Pérez-Nordtvedt et al., 2008). Given this possibility, future research could examine how a misfit gap serves as an obstacle to a firm changing their pacing strategy.

A potential limitation is that our publically traded companies may not represent the entire population. Our focus on a single context (specialists in one industry), while offering advantages in terms of reducing several confounding effects, poses limits to generalizing our finding to generalist firms who have a wide variety of product lines, manufacturing processes, and other value chain activities. An interesting extension could focus on how specialists compete with generalists by manipulating their pacing strategically across different stages of the resource partitioning processes.

An intriguing extension would be to examine how managers assess the pacing strategy of their competitors. In a recent interview,[2] Junxia Ma, a former Olympic gold medal winner in the 5,000m, contends that experienced distance runners can tell the pace of their opponents based on the frequency of their exhaling and inhaling, and they can then adjust their own pace accordingly. In the corporate world, how do managers judge their competitors' "exhaling and inhaling?" To stimulate discussion, we suggest focusing on competitive analysis.

At the firm level, companies can reverse-engineer the sequence of actions of their competitors (Shi & Prescott, 2011) and make predictions about what they are likely to do next. Understanding competitors starts with having insights regarding their resources, processes, and values. Resources, processes, and values matter because they facilitate and constrain available options for the strategic pacing of corporate initiatives. Competitors are likely to develop their pacing strategy based on a strategic fit between their resource endowments and external environment. When competitors have similar resources profiles, the likelihood of them pursuing a similar pacing strategy will significantly increase. At the individual level, firms need to profile their competitors' decision makers. Profiling key decision makers involves understanding their intentions, personalities, interests, preferences, motivations, and past decisions.

There is evidence of a growing interest in a temporal perspective of strategy and how it contributes to competitive advantage (Pérez-Nordtvedt et al., 2008). Our study is a small step in demonstrating how the pacing of acquisitions and alliances contributes to performance outcomes.

NOTES

1. A stronger inverted-U relationship is the one that has a steeper curve and smaller "open mouth." Mathematically, we argue that the moderation effects are for both the linear and quadratic term. In other words, a stronger effect makes the linear term "more positive" and the quadratic term "more negative." A graphic demonstration can be found in Barkema and Vermeulen, 1998 and Shaw, Duffy, Johnson, and Lockhart, 2005.
2. Information accessible at http://www.dragontv.cn/export/sites/default/dragontv/channel/fcjy/textnews/2008031401.html

REFERENCES

Anand, B. N., & Khanna, T. (2000). Do firms learn to create value? The case of alliances. *Strategic Management Journal, 21,* 295–315.

Ancona, D. G., & Chong, C. (1996). Entrainment: Pace, cycle, and rhythm in organizational behavior. *Research in Organizational Behavior, 18,* 251–284.

Ancona, D. G., Okhuysen, G. A., & Perlow, L. A. (2001). Taking time to integrate temporal research. *Academy of Management Review, 26,* 512–529.

Argote, L., Beckman, S. L., & Epple, D. (1990). The persistence and transfer of learning in industrial setting. *Management Science, 36,* 140–154.

Argote, L., & Epple, D. (1990). Learning curves in manufacturing. *Science, 23,* 920–924.

Argote, L., & Greve, H. R. (2007). A behavioral theory of the firm—40 years and counting: Introduction and impact. *Organization Science, 18,* 337–349.

Arthur, J. B., & Huntley, C. L. (2005). Ramping up the organizational learning curve: Accessing the impact of deliberate learning on organizational performance under gainsharing. *Academy of Management Journal, 48,* 1159–1170.

Audretsch, D. B. (1995). Innovation, growth and survival. *International Journal of Industrial Organization, 13,* 441–457.

Barkema, H. G., Baum, J. A. C., & Mannix, E. A. (2002). Management challenges in a new time. *Academy of Management Journal, 45,* 916–930.

Barkema, H. G., & Schijven, M. (2008). How do firms learn to make acquisitions? A review of past research and an agenda for the future. *Journal of Management, 34,* 594–634.

Barkema, H. G., & Vermeulen, F. (1998). International expansion through start-up acquisition: A learning perspective. *Academy of Management Journal, 41,* 7–26.

Barnett, W. P., & Hansen, M. T. (1996). The red queen in organizational evolution. *Strategic Management Journal, 17*(Special Issue), 139–157.

Barnett, W. P., & McKendrick, D. G. (2004). Why are some organizations more competitive than others? *Administrative Science Quarterly, 49,* 535–571.

Barnett, W. P., & Pontikes, E. G. (2008). The red queen, success bias, and organizational inertia. *Management Science, 54,* 1237–1251.

Benkard, C. L. (2000). Learning and forgetting: The dynamics of aircraft production. *American Economic Review, 90,* 1034–1055.

Bercovitz, J., & Mitchell, W. (2007). When is more better? The impact of business scale and scope on long-term business survival, while controlling for profitability. *Strategic Management Journal, 28,* 61–79.

Bluedorn, A. C., & Denhardt, R. B. (1988). Time and organizations. *Journal of Management, 14,* 299–320.

Capaldo, A., Cogman, D., & Suonio, H. (2009, January). What's different about M&A in this downturn. *The McKinsey Quarterly.*

Carley, K. (1992). Organizational learning and personnel turnover. *Organization Science, 3,* 20–46.

Carlstein, T. (1982). *Time resources, society and ecology.* London: George Allen and Unwin.

Catton, G.. (2006, September 25). Specialty pharma takeout valuations rise. *Mergers & Acquisitions Report, 19*(36), 1.

Darr, E. D., & Argote, L. (1995). The acquisition, transfer, and depreciation of knowledge in service organizations: Productivity in franchises. *Management Science, 41,* 1750–1763.

D'Aveni, R. A. (1994). *Hypercompetition: Managing the dynamics of strategic maneuvering.* New York: Free Press.

Dawkins, R. (1982). *The extended phenotype.* New York: Oxford University Press.

Derfus, P. J., Maggitti, P. G., Grimm, C. M., & Smith, K. G. (2008). The red queen effect: Competitive actions and firm performance. *Academy of Management Journal, 51,* 61–80.

Dierickx, I., & Cool, K. (1989). Asset stock accumulation and sustainability of competitive advantage. *Management Science, 35,* 1504–1513.

Dubin, R. (1978). *Theory building* (Rev. ed.). New York: Free Press.

Dunning, J. H. (1993). Multinational enterprises and the global economy. Reading, MA: Addison-Wesley.

Dussauge, P., Garrette, B., & Mitchell, W. (2004). Asymmetric performance: The market share impact of scale and link alliances in the global auto industry. *Strategic Management Journal, 25,* 701–711.

Eisenhardt, K. M., & Brown, S. L. (1998). Time pacing: Competing in markets that won't stand still. *Harvard Business* Review, *76*(2), 59–69.

Eisenhardt, K. M., & Martin, J. A. (2000). Dynamic capabilities: What are they? *Strategic Management Journal, 21*(Special Issue), 1105–1121.

Fernhaber, S. A., & Li, D. (2010). The impact of interorganizational imitation on new venture international entry and performance. *Entrepreneurship: Theory & Practice, 34*(1), 1–30.

Finkelstein, S., & Haleblian, J. (2002). Understanding acquisition performance: The role of transfer effects. *Organization Science, 13,* 36–47.

Foster, R. N., & Kaplan, S. (2001). Creative destruction. *McKinsey Quarterly, 3,* 41–51.

Haleblian, J., & Finkelstein, S. (1999). The influence of organizational acquisition experience on acquisition performance: A behavioral learning perspective. *Administrative Science Quarterly, 44,* 29–56.

Hatch, N. W., & Dyer, J. H. (2004). Human capital and learning as a source of sustainable competitive advantage. *Strategic Management Journal, 25,* 1155–1178.

Haunschild, P. R., & Sullivan, N. (2002). Learning from complexity: Effects of prior accidents and incidents on airlines' learning. *Administrative Science Quarterly, 47,* 609–643.

Hayward, M. L. A. (2002). When do firms learn from their acquisition experience? Evidence from 1985–1995. *Strategic Management Journal, 23,* 21–39.

Helfat, C. E., & Eisenhardt, K. M. (2004). Inter-temporal economies of scope, organizational modularity, and the dynamics of diversification. *Strategic Management Journal, 25,* 1217–1232.

Henderson, J., & Cool, K. (2003). Learning to time capacity expansions: An empirical analysis of the worldwide petrochemical industry, 1975–95. *Strategic Management Journal, 24,* 393–413.

Hickson, D. J., Pugh, D. S., & Pheysey, D. C. (1969). Operations technology and organization structure: An empirical reappraisal. *Administrative Science Quarterly, 14,* 378–397.

Inkpen, A. (2002, July/August). From the prune capital of America to Silicon Valley: Knowledge flows, networks, and innovation. *Thunderbird International Business Review, 44,* 557–563.

Keh, H. T., Nguyen, T. T. M., & Ng, H. P. (2007). The effects of entrepreneurial orientation and marketing information on the performance of SMEs. *Journal of Business Venturing, 22,* 592–611.

Kenis, P., & Knoke, D. (2002). How organizational field networks shape interorganizational tie-formation rates. *Academy of Management Review, 27,* 275–294.

Koka, B. R., & Prescott, J. E. (2002). Strategic alliances as social capital: A multidimensional view. *Strategic Management Journal, 23,* 795–816.

Khavul, S., Pérez-Nordtvedt, L., & Wood, E. (2010). Organizational entrainment and international new ventures from emerging markets. *Journal of Business Venturing, 25,* 104–119.

Kusewitt, J. B. (1985). An exploratory study of strategic acquisition factors relating to performance. *Strategic Management Journal, 6,* 151–169.

Laamanen, T., & Keil, T. (2008). Performance of serial acquirers: An acquisition program perspective. *Strategic Management Journal, 29,* 663–672.

Lane, P. J., & Lubatkin, M. (1998). Relative absorptive capacity and interorganizational learning. *Strategic Management Journal, 19,* 461–477.

Lant, T. K. (1992). Aspiration level adaptation: An empirical exploration. *Management Science, 38,* 623–644.

Lee, C., Lee, K., & Pennings, J. M. (2001). Internal capabilities, external networks and performance: A study on technology-based ventures. *Strategic Management Journal, 22,* 615–640.

Lieberman, M. B., & Asaba, S. (2006). Why do firms imitate each other? *Academy of Management Review, 31,* 366–385.

Lu, J. W., & Beamish, P. W. (2006). Partnering strategies and performance of SMEs' international joint ventures. *Journal of Business Venturing, 21,* 461–486.

Maas, E. (2005, January). Specialty pharmacy carve-out can yield savings. *Employee Benefit News, 19*(1), 32.

Malo, S., & Norus, J. (2009). Growth dynamics of dedicated biotechnology firms in transition economies. Evidence from the Baltic countries and Poland. *Entrepreneurship & Regional Development, 21,* 481–502.

Mantone, J. (2008, March 20). Rising spending on specialty drugs leads to pushback. *The Wall Street Journal.* Retrieved from http://blogs.wsj.com/health/2008/03/20/rising-spending-on-specialty-drugs-leads-to-pushback/

March, J. G. (1991). Exploration and exploitation in organizational learning. *Organization Science, 2,* 71–87.

Miller, J. S., Wiseman, R. M., & Gomez-Mejia, L. R. (2002). The fit between CEO compensation design and firm risk. *Academy of Management Journal, 45,* 745–756.

Miller, R. E., & Snow, C. C. (1978). *Organizational strategy, structure, and process.* New York: McGraw-Hill.

Mohan-Neill, S. I. (1995). The influence of firm's age and size on its environmental scanning activities. *Journal of Small Business Management, 33*(4), 10–21.

Nadolska, A., & Barkema, H. G. (2007). Learning to internationalize: The pace and success of foreign acquisitions. *Journal of International Business Studies, 38,* 1170–1186.

Ofori-Dankwa. J., & Julian, S. D. (2001). Complexifying organizational theory: Illustrations using time research. *Academy Management Review, 26,* 415–430.

Parkhe, A. (1993). Strategic alliance structuring: A game theoretic and transaction cost examination of interfirm cooperation. *Academy of Management Journal, 36,* 794–829.

Pérez-Nordtvedt, L., Payne, G. T., Short, J. C., & Kedia, B. L. (2008). An entrainment-based model of temporal organizational fit, misfit, and performance. *Organization Science, 19,* 785–801.

Pouder, R., & St. John, C. H. (1996). Hot spots and blind spots: Geographical clusters of firms and innovation. *Academy of Management Review, 21,* 1192–1225.

Powell, W. W., & Grodal, S. (2005). Networks of innovators. In J. Fagerberg, D. C. Mowery, & R. R. Nelson (Eds.), *The Oxford handbook of innovation* (pp. 56–85). Oxford, UK: Oxford University Press.

Prescott, J. E., & Miller, S. (2001). *Proven strategies in competitive intelligence: Lessons from the trenches.* New York: Wiley.

Prescott, J. E., & Shi, W. (2008). A temporal perspective of corporate M&A and alliance portfolios. In S. Finkelstein & C. Cooper (Eds.), *Advances in M&As* (pp. 1–27). Bingley, UK: JAI Press.

Sampson, R. C. (2005). Experience effects and collaborative returns in R&D alliances. *Strategic Management Journal, 26,* 1009–1031.

Schreiner, M., Kale, P., & Corsten, D. (2009). What really is alliance management capability and how does it impact alliance outcomes and success? *Strategic Management Journal, 30,* 1395–1419.

Shaw, J. D., Duffy, M. K., Johnson, J. L., & Lockhart, D. E. (2005). Turnover, social capital losses, and performance. *Academy of Management Journal, 48,* 594–606.

Shi, W., & Prescott, J. E. (2011). Sequence patterns of firms' acquisition and alliance behavior and their performance implications. *Journal of Management Studies, 48,* 1044–1070.

Simon, H. A. (1955). A behavioral model of rational choice. *Quarterly Journal of Economics, 69,* 99–118.

Smith, K., Ferrier, W. J., & Grimm, C. (2001). King of the hill: Dethroning the industry leader. *Academy of Management Executive, 15,* 59–70.

Sorenson, O. (2000). The effect of population level learning on market entry: The American automobile industry. *Social Science Research, 29,* 307–326.

Standifer, R., & Bluedorn, A. C. (2006). Alliance management teams and entrainment: Sharing temporal mental models. *Human Relations, 59,* 903–927.

Thompson, J. D. (1967). *Organizations in action: Social science bases of administrative theory.* New York: McGraw-Hill.

Vermeulen, F., & Barkema, H. (2002). Pace, rhythm, and scope: Process dependence in building a profitable multinational corporation. *Strategic Management Journal, 23,* 637–653.

Volberda, H. W., & Lewin, A. Y. (2003). Co-evolutionary dynamics within and between firms: From evolution to co-evolution. *Journal of Management Studies, 40,* 2111–2136.

Zajac, E. J., Kraatz, M. S., & Bresser, R. K. F. (2000). Modeling the dynamics of strategic fit: A normative approach to strategic change. *Strategic Management Journal, 21,* 429–453.

Zollo, M., & Singh, H. (2004). Deliberate learning in corporate acquisitions: Post-acquisition strategies and integration capability in U.S. bank mergers. *Strategic Management Journal, 25,* 1233–1256.

CHAPTER 14

ENTREPRENEURIAL FIRMS IN SEARCH OF ALLIANCE PARTNERS

T. K. Das
Irene Y. He

ABSTRACT

How can entrepreneurial firms succeed in strategic alliances, especially with established firms? Although alliance partner selection criteria have received a great deal of attention in the literature, extant research has focused primarily on established firms, to the relative neglect of the unique interests of entrepreneurial firms. In this chapter, we review the alliance partner selection criteria research in order to shed light on how entrepreneurial firms should choose established firms as alliance partners. We identify 15 intrinsic and alliancing factors that differ between entrepreneurial and established firms. Critical differences between entrepreneurial and established firms are presented to emphasize the special risks in alliances between these two types of firms. Illustrative cases are presented of both successful and unsuccessful cases of strategic alliances between entrepreneurial and established firms. A list of recommendations is developed for entrepreneurial firms in their choice of established firms as alliance partners. In short, our attempt has been to fill a gap in the two literatures on entrepreneurship and strategic alliances regarding research-based guidance available for entrepreneurial firms in the selection of established firms as partners in strategic alliances.

Strategic Alliances for Value Creation, pages 321–359

INTRODUCTION

Research on strategic alliances has been mostly focused on large companies. This focus is perhaps the result of the ready availability of relevant secondary data, which tend to ignore entrepreneurial and relatively unknown companies engaged in strategic alliances. There is now a rising interest in small and entrepreneurial firms engaging in strategic alliances, many of which are in the biotechnology, semiconductor, and computer industries. However, most researchers do not adequately distinguish between entrepreneurial and large firms, while others observe that strategic alliances between these two types of firms are especially problematic.

Strategic alliances between entrepreneurial and established firms are different from traditional ones (i.e., alliances between large firms) because the partners differ in terms of bargaining power, learning ability, organizational compatibility, attention given to the alliances, and so on. They are also different from alliances in which both partners are small firms. Although alliances between entrepreneurial firms and established firms with compatible resources and strategic objectives have potential to prosper, the sharp inequality in bargaining power often puts such alliances in peril. Also, entrepreneurial firms become less attractive as a partner after established firms absorb the innovations or expertise of their entrepreneurial partners. In such cases, lacking the valuable complementary resources (Das & Teng, 2000a, 2003), entrepreneurial firms are left underfinanced and even become vulnerable to premature acquisition.

How can entrepreneurial firms succeed in strategic alliances with established firms? To better respond to this issue, we first look at how entrepreneurial firms differ from established firms in terms of several factors: resources, innovativeness, status in competition, legitimacy, history/track record, economic/political power, organizational characteristics, business focus, planning horizon, control over technology, confidence in the technology, interorganizational interface, criticality of alliancing, strategic purpose, and consistency of commitment. The literature on partner selection, which is mostly focused on alliances between large established firms, does not adequately reflect these differences between entrepreneurial and established firms. Based on these difference factors, we will propose a set of partner selection criteria suited specifically to entrepreneurial firms when they consider forming alliances with established firms.

DIFFERENCES BETWEEN ENTREPRENEURIAL AND ESTABLISHED FIRMS

Strategic alliances have been forming at an increasing rate in the last few decades, especially in technology-intensive industries. In particular, alliances between entrepreneurial and established firms have been growing significantly in recent years in the telecommunications, pharmaceutical, Internet, electronics, and oil and gas industries. In Table 14.1, we have summarized the studies on strategic alliances involving entrepreneurial firms.

Large companies have generally been considered the main source of innovation because of their capability to invest heavily in R&D. However, although large firms consistently have been found to spend more in R&D, small firms have been found to have higher rates of innovation compared to their share of sales or number of employees, especially in the early stages of major new technologies (Freeman & Soete, 1997; Powell & Brantley, 1992; Shefer & Frenkel, 2005). Specifically, Dougherty and Hardy (1996) found that very few large, mature firms have sustained product innovation, because they are not organized to facilitate innovation, and innovators lack the power to connect occasional innovation with organizational resources, processes, and strategy. In fact, Larson (1992) defines entrepreneurial as adaptive and innovative, and characterizes entrepreneurial firms as small, successful, and high-growth.

There has been some effort to address the lack of innovativeness in established firms, leading to the emergence of so-called intrapreneurship research in the entrepreneurship field. However, both anecdotal and statistical evidence shows that large corporations have been unsuccessful in creating intrapreneurs or an entrepreneurial climate (Dougherty & Hardy, 1996), and many managers involved in intrapreneurial ventures have had to leave large companies in frustration to start their own ventures.

Entrepreneurship research has long been intertwined with research on small business (e.g., Busenitz, West, Shepherd, Nelson, Chandler, & Zacharakis, 2003) and new technology-based firms (e.g., Hindle & Yencken, 2004). In general, we do not find explicit definitions of entrepreneurial firms in the published studies that deal with strategic alliances by such firms. These studies generally use “start-ups” and “small start-ups” and “entrepreneurial firms” interchangeably, and use data collected from young and small firms in high tech industries to address entrepreneurial issues (e.g., Deeds & Hill, 1999; Hull et al., 1988; Shan et al., 1994; Stuart et al., 1999). In keeping with this tradition in the entrepreneurship field, we define entrepreneurial firms as generally young, small, and highly innovative firms in industries with rapidly developing technologies.

Being new and small, entrepreneurial firms are associated with many characteristics that are essentially different from established firms, including limited internal resources and external relations, a lack of legitimacy, and unfamiliarity with new roles and norms created within itself. These disadvantages have contributed to a “liability of newness” (Stinchcombe, 1965). Doz (1988) looked at disappointing partnerships between smaller and larger firms, and identified three sets of critical issues: conver-

TABLE 14.1 Alliance Studies Involving Entrepreneurial Firms

Study	Research Question	Data	Findings / Propositions
Almeida, Dokko, & Rosenkopf (2003)	This study examines the patent citation patterns of semiconductor startups as external learning (p. 302).	Secondary data were collected on 71 startup semiconductor firms between 1980 and 1995 (pp. 308–309).	The startups that entered into alliances cited patents more (p. 310). But there is no evidence that the likelihood of a start-up learning (measured by the number of patent citations) from an alliance varies with firms size, while the start-up learns less from hiring an inventor or from colocation in a region as it grows (p. 311).
Alvarez, & Barney (2001)	"This article offers some suggestions for managers in entrepreneurial firms to help them appropriate more of the economic value created by their alliances with large firms" (p. 140).	Interviews were conducted on 128 alliances between large and entrepreneurial firms in three industries: biotechnology, IT, and oil and gas (p. 139).	"In almost 80 percent of these alliances, managers from entrepreneurial firms felt unfairly exploited by their large firm partners" (p. 140). The research shows that "the ability of large firms to learn about an entrepreneurial firm's new technology faster than an entrepreneurial partner can imitate a large firm's organizational resources puts the entrepreneurial firm at risk" (p. 142). The authors give five alternatives for entrepreneurial firms: going it alone, slowing the large firm's learning rate, using detailed and elaborate contracts to define the alliance relationship, building a relationship of trust, and bringing other resources to the alliance besides a single technology (p. 143).
BarNir & Smith (2002)	"What are the characteristics of a manager's network that are particularly supportive of creating interfirm alliances" for small business? (p. 220).	Survey data were collected on 149 small and midsized manufacturing firms in electronic components and medical instruments and supplies industries (pp. 223–224).	"Our findings indicate that the overall number of alliances a firm engages in is explained by three network properties: propensity to network, strength of ties, and prestige of network members" (p. 228). Different network properties are associated with different types of alliances: technology/manufacturing alliances were explained by prestige of network members, while support alliances were explained by propensity to network and the strength of ties (p. 229). Moreover, scope of networking activity was negatively associated with support alliances (p. 229).

Barley, Freeman, & Hybels (1992)	This is a tentative and descriptive study on the structure of the biotechnology community and its alliances (p. 319).	Data were compiled from *Bioscan* (1988) and other directories on alliances by U.S.-based organizations that contributed to the commercialization of biotechnology through 1987 (p. 319).	"A majority of the organizations that form alliances with dedicated biotechnology firms (DBFs) are large diversified corporations. Many are among the most powerful actors in the pharmaceutical, chemical, food, energy, and agricultural industries" (p. 343). "Strategic alliances in biotechnology generally involve the exchange of knowledge for money. Often the exchange requires a smaller firm to sacrifice some degree of autonomy (for instance, over determining its goals for research and development) to gain access to markets with high barriers to entry. For many biotechnology firms, the compromise may forestall bankruptcy, merger, or acquisition" (pp. 343–344). Only 6% of the freestanding dedicated biotechnology firms ceased operating since 1975, which demonstrates an exceptionally low mortality rate that can be attributed to the large number of alliances (p. 324). For diversified corporations, alliancing with small biotechnology provides "access to and leverage over a broad range of research" (p. 343). "Since the early 1980s there has been a significant shift away from forming freestanding firms toward founding organizations with direct corporate sponsorship," i.e., subsidiaries and joint ventures (p. 324).
Baum, Calabrese, & Silverman (2000)	This study investigates the early performance outcomes of alliance networks that start-ups configure at the time of their founding (p. 267).	Secondary data were collected on 142 start-up biotechnology firms (BFs) founded between 1991 and 1996, and 471 incumbent BFs founded prior to 1991 in Canada.	"Startup biotechnology firms (BFs) that, at the time of their founding, formed upstream and downstream alliances (H1) and configured them to provide access to more diverse information and capabilities per alliance (H2) generally exhibited stronger initial performance. In contrast, startups that initially formed alliances with established potential rivals tended to experience weaker performance, on average (H3)" (p. 287). "Startups with broader market domains than potential rival BFs with which they are allied are less likely to experience harmful effects of strong partner learning incentives" (pp. 283–285). "Startups with highly innovative potential rival partner BFs always have higher patenting rates than startups without partner BFs—even when they face a severe scope disadvantage (p. 285).

(continued)

TABLE 14.1 (continued) Alliance Studies Involving Entrepreneurial Firms

Study	Research Question	Data	Findings / Propositions
Chen & Li (1999)	This study empirically assesses the impact of strategic alliances on new product development (p. 36).	Longitudinal secondary data were collected on U.S. semiconductor start-up firms from 1978 to 1989 (p. 45).	Learning through strategic alliances has two sources. One is learning the capabilities in certain functional areas, including technological, manufacturing, and marketing; this is content learning. The other is learning the managerial process, including how process knowledge relates to managing interfirm cooperation and process knowledge that can be applied to a firm's internal activities; this is process learning (p. 56). The number of strategic alliances that provide access to technology, and the number of functional areas that are involved in the alliances positively affect product development for semiconductor start-up firms. But the number of strategic alliances that provide access to manufacturing and marketing areas has no impact on product development (pp. 55–56).
Deeds & Hill (1996)	This study examines the relationship between the number of alliances an entrepreneurial firm engages in and its rate of new product development (p. 42).	Secondary data were collected on 132 biotechnology firms, *in vivo* therapeutics, and diagnostics (p. 47).	There is "an inverted, U-shaped relationship between the number of alliances a firm is engaged in and the rate of new product development" (pp. 52–53). "On average, malperformance problems start becoming serious when firms increase their number of alliances beyond about 25, although diminishing returns set in much earlier" (p. 53).
Deeds & Hill (1999)	This study compares the effectiveness of proposed deterrents to opportunism by two views: transaction cost economics and relational contracting (p. 144).	Cross-sectional data were collected through structured (p. 149) personal and phone interviews for 109 alliances by 57 dedicated biotechnology firms in four geographical areas (p. 150).	Strong relationships between the partners, such as congruent background and frequent communication, serve as a much more effective deterrent to opportunistic action than structural deterrents, such as hostage investments or contingent claims contract (p. 157). The inverted U-shaped relationship between age and opportunism demonstrates an existence of a honeymoon period in the research alliances, which lasts about 4.6 years, and a liability of adolescence among such alliances (pp. 157–158).

Doz (1988)	This chapter deals with issues that are critical to success of technology partnerships between larger and smaller firms, and proposes approaches that can circumvent the pitfalls (p. 319).		"Yet, even a cursory observation of such partnerships suggests that many are a disappointment to partners. They do not actually yield the results expected by either or both partners, and even when a measure of success is achieved the tensions in making partnerships work sometimes dwarf their success in the eyes of the participants" (p. 318). Three sets of issues are critical to success of partnerships between larger and smaller firms: convergence of purpose, consistency of position within the large firm, and interface (pp. 318–319). The issue of convergence of purpose stems from cultural distance, uncertainty and misunderstandings, and hidden agendas (pp. 319–324), but these problems can be minimized by carefully working out concepts of partnerships at the following levels: technological complementarity, joint business system complementarity and viability, value of outcome versus cost to partners, focus and boundaries, strategic continuity, and precision of agreement (pp. 324–326). The issue of consistency of position within the large firm stems from vested interests and politics of resource commitments (pp. 326–331); and solutions include creating horizontal groups and task forces in the large firms rather than relying on the hierarchy, and communicating regularly and frequently at the top (p. 331). For the issue of interface and boundary spanning, the solutions include organizing joint sessions between members of both firms (p. 332), expanding interface function beyond R&D (p. 334), and setting up a coordination committee comprising all the interfaces (p. 336).
Eisenhardt & Schoonhoven (1996)	This study examines strategic and social factors that lead entrepreneurial firms into forming alliances (137).	Data were collected through interviews with executives of product development alliances of 98 new semiconductor firms that were founded between 1978 and 1985 (pp. 141–142).	Entrepreneurial firms that were in vulnerable strategic positions, i.e., in emergent markets with high competition and using innovative technologies, formed more alliances (p. 146). Entrepreneurial "firms with top management teams that were large, experienced, and well-connected through former employers and high-level previous jobs formed product development alliances at higher rates" (p. 146). A surprising finding is that "growth-stage markets have the lowest rates of alliance formation" (p. 146).

(continued)

TABLE 14.1 (continued) Alliance Studies Involving Entrepreneurial Firms

Study	Research Question	Data	Findings / Propositions
Forrest & Martin (1992)	This study investigates the alliance experiences and the factors that make technology-related alliances between small biotechnology firms and large pharmaceutical and chemical firms successful (p. 42).	Survey data were collected on 42 dedicated biotechnology companies (DBCs) and 21 large companies (p. 43).	"The primary reasons for alliance formation for dedicated biotechnology companies (DBCs) could be grouped together and defined as 'seeking input of certain resources,'" including financial resources, product development resources, regulatory expertise, marketing channels, or competitive intelligence (pp. 44–45). In contrast, DBCs do not need alliance to gain access to general management skills, to ward off acquisition, or to preempt competition (p. 45). The top reason for alliance formation by large firms is technology acquisition (p. 48). DBCs reported higher rates of success (83%) than large firms (47.5%); "the lower perception of success for the large firms appears to be derived from their more rigorous standards of accountability" (p. 49). DBCs and large firms agree on similar reasons for successful alliances: "continuing, compatibility, and commitment" (p. 49). It seems that, according to the author, the entrepreneurial firms look at the financial resources of the large firm, because "many DBCs see the large firms as a 'venture capital source'" (p. 50). Large firms choose small alliance partners on technical and managerial capabilities, trust, compatibility, shared philosophies and attitudes, whether or not the DBC "was tied to other large firms who were current or potential competitors" because of possible leakage of sensitive information to competitors (p. 50). Large firms learned to focus on the business, the product, need and commitment, rather than the technological fit (p. 50).
Harrigan (1988)	This study investigates how differences, i.e., size, national origin, and venturing	Survey data were collected on 895 strategic alliances competing in 23 industries during	"The asset-size variable adds weak predictive power in regression models of venture survival, duration, or success" (p. 225); that is, ventures between partners of similar size in asset are not more successful than those between dissimilar partners. "This result suggests that simply 'sticking to one's knitting' alone—venturing in

	experience levels (p. 206) among sponsoring firms with respect to each other, influence the efficacy of their strategic alliances (p. 205).	the years 1974–1985 (p. 209).	activities that are close to sponsoring firm's strategic cores—is not enough to insure venture success" (p. 213). On the other hand, "ventures unrelated to both sponsoring firms are less likely than other to be successful" (p. 217). "Ventures that are horizontally related to both sponsoring firms are more likely than others to be judged a success by both sponsoring firms" (p. 215), while "ventures that are vertically related to both sponsoring firms are less likely to be operating after 1985" (p. 216). Although cultural distance was not used in the analysis, "comments from interviewed managers lead me to suspect that cultural homogeneity among sponsors is more important to venture success than symmetry in their national origins" (p. 222). The impact of dissimilarity in venturing experience levels on venture success is negative, but not statistically significant (p. 223).
Hoffmann & Schlosser (2001)	This study "aims to identify critical success factors of SME alliances as well as the perception of success factors by SME owners and managers" (p. 358).	Survey data were collected on 164 SMEs in Austria (p. 365).	"Our empirical results show that both content-oriented variables, such as 'Precise definition of rights and duties' and 'Contributing specific strengths,' and process-oriented variables, such as 'Deriving alliance objectives from business strategy' and 'Speedy implementation and fast results,' prove decisive for alliances success" (p. 375). Many of the statistically critical success factors are not perceived by SME managers as important, such as "Establishing required resources" and "Deriving alliance objectives from business strategy" (p. 375). "The critical success factors were underestimated mostly by the unsuccessful SMEs" (p. 375). Proposed important partner selection criteria are established trust, "strengths in the field of co-operation," complementary resources and strategies, and cultural fit (p. 361). But none of them is empirically critical success factors (p. 368). However, "complementary contributions," "established trust," and "agreement of fundamental values" are perceived by SME managers as success factors, although not the most important ones (p. 371). On the other hand, SME managers in failed alliances perceived "excellence in field of cooperation" as very important, probably influenced by their experience of failure (p. 373).

(continued)

TABLE 14.1 (continued) Alliance Studies Involving Entrepreneurial Firms

Study	Research Question	Data	Findings / Propositions
Hu & Korneliussen (1997)	This study examines the impact of social norms and interpersonal relationships on the performance of small firms in strategic alliances (p. 160).	Survey data were collected on 90 small and medium-sized firms from Norwegian fisheries, woodworking, furniture, plastics, information technology, and steel industries (pp. 164–165).	"Personal ties are positively related to reciprocity," and both personal ties and reciprocity have a positive effect on performance (p. 168).
Hull, Slowinski, Wharton, & Azumi (1988)	This study compares "the approaches to small-firm-large-firm cooperation in Japan U.S. by evaluating the extent to which cooperative ventures are advantageous between small and large firms in technology-based industries and which factors affect the conditions of mutual advantage" (p. 446).	Preliminary survey data were obtained from 15 large corporations in the U.S. and 6 in Japan (p. 452).	"Organizations in Japan mix mechanistic and organic design characteristics. In some ways, they are easier for organic entrepreneurial firms in the United States to deal with to the extent that Japanese management takes a more evolutionary and less bureaucratic approach than American managers (Kagono, Nonaka, Sakakibara and Okumura, 1985)" (p. 451). "Patience is required for successful partnering in high technology because developments may take considerable time to come to fruition" (p. 453). "Giving entrepreneurs considerable autonomy seems to be a key factor in the success of partnerships with large corporations" (p. 453). "The patience Japanese corporations seem to show with their entrepreneurial partners may be in part due to the probability that in the long run, much of the manufacturing process required to succeed will become a kind of in-house trade secret, especially in electronics and to a lesser extent in bioprocess" (p. 454). "Process technology and manufacturing capability need to receive increased appreciation" (p. 454). "If partners focus impatiently on the immediate drama of new-product development, their competitive position downstream may be risked" (p. 454).

Kelley, Rice, & Peters (2001)	This study's "objective is to determine whether there is an association between a firm's technology-based and product-based knowledge and its formation of alliances (p. 145).	Longitudinal secondary data between 1985 and 1996 were collected on 67 firms from computer and telecommunications industries (p. 148).	New firms with extensive technology-based knowledge are more likely to form alliances (p. 151). Product-based knowledge is also correlated with alliance formation, but the data, collected at the same time, cannot determine the direction of the relationship (p. 152).
Larson (1992)	This is an exploratory ethnographic study to understand the processes that cooperative alliances exercise control, especially social control (pp. 78–79).	Interviews were conducted on 7 dyadic relationships of 4 entrepreneurial firms that had experienced rapid growth between 1980 and 1986 (pp. 79, 98).	This study proposes a 3-phase process model of the formation of entrepreneurial dyads: preconditions, conditions to build the exchange structures, and the final phase of integration and control (pp. 97–98). The relatively stable and sustained relationships "were governed in important ways by social controls arising from norms of trust and reciprocity," and "governance was explained in large part by understanding the subtle control of interdependent and self-regulated players engaged in and committed to mutual gains" (p. 98).
Lee, Lim, & Tan (2000)	This paper explores whether strategic alliances can help SMEs enter markets that are already well-established and dominated by major corporations (p. 44).	Two case studies are used to illustrate the conclusions (p. 49).	Strategic alliances can help SMEs overcome resource disadvantage or achieve cost advantage, therefore gain competitive advantages over its bigger rivals (p. 46). "Hence, as a deterrence strategy, credible commitment to stay in the market by the SME through strategic alliance is achieved by the alliance's increased ability to sustain a prolonged intense competition with the bigger firm" (p. 49). SMEs should strategically select partners who possess complementary strengths and expertise, so that the alliance could achieve greater synergistic gains (p. 49).

(continued)

TABLE 14.1 (continued) Alliance Studies Involving Entrepreneurial Firms

Study	Research Question	Data	Findings / Propositions
Lu & Beamish (2001)	This study explores the impact of various internationalization strategies, including local strategic alliances, used by SMEs on their performance (p. 566).	Secondary data were collected on 164 Japanese entrepreneurial firms between 1986 and 1997 (pp. 566, 572).	"These results demonstrate the importance of alliance partner selection and suggest that local partners provide more value to SMEs than partners from the home country" (p. 578).
Miles, Preece, & Baetz (1999)	This study explores the use of strategic alliances by early-stage technology-based firms (ESTBFs) and factors that might indicate how and when alliances might benefit such firms (p. 21).	Survey data were collected on 112 ESTBFs that participated in a provincial funding program in Canada (p. 23).	"There was no difference in performance between those firms who were involved in alliances and those firms who were not" (p. 27). "Only when firms used alliances out of choice rather than to manage resource dependencies were alliances associated with firm success" (p. 27). "Those firms who felt that they were dependent on strategic alliances would be left in an inferior bargaining position when it came to negotiating the details of the alliance. As such, these firms would be likely to gain less even if the alliance turned out to be successful" (p. 27). Also, "having a limited choice of partners was associated with poorer performance" (p. 27).
Oliver (2001)	This study explores a pattern in the formation of strategic alliances for dedicated biotechnology firms (DBFs) over time (p. 473).	Secondary data of public citations of biotechnology agreements between 1976 and 1990 (p. 474).	New biotechnology firms increase alliance formation during the early years, which is the exploration stage of the organizational learning cycle, and then reduce alliance formation during the exploitation stage (p. 483). The data showed that DBFs steadily formed more new alliances in the first 4 years, and then the number of new alliances declined until age 11, after that, an inconclusive increase appeared at age 14 (p. 483).

Powell & Brantley (1992)	This study is to explore "the type and number of interorganizational relationships pursued by new biotechnology firms" (p. 372) and to decide whether new biotechnology firms "must be expert at both in-house research and cooperative research with external parties" (p. 371).	Data were collected from the industrial directory *Bioscan* (1990) on small, start-up new biotechnology firms (NBFs, p. 369) that were independently owned, with more than 10 employees, with a product orientation primarily in therapeutics or diagnostics, and were founded in 1987 or earlier (p. 373). Altogether there were 129 NBFs engaging in 765 bilateral agreements (p. 374).	In the biotechnology industry, "the relevant know-how is broadly dispersed and innovation depends on cooperative interaction among different types of organizations" (pp. 388–389), such as federally funded agencies, pharmaceutical companies, and universities (p. 376). Different types of alliance agreements are strongly complementary rather than substitutable (p. 379), which suggests that "firms are continuing to stay involved in external relationships even as they build up internal capabilities" (p. 389). As for the determinants for the number of ties, larger (more employees), older, more diversified (both diagnostics and therapeutics), and publicly owned firms have more agreements (p. 380).
Preece, Miles, & Baetz (1999)	This study examines what effects strategic alliances have for early-stage technology-based firms' (ESTBFs, p. 260) international sales and the diversity of global markets (p. 261).	Survey data were collected on 75 ESTBFs that participated in a provincial funding program in Canada (p. 267).	"An expected finding was the fact that strategic alliances were not a factor in explaining either international intensity or global diversity" (p. 273). The risks of international alliances "may keep firms from using alliances as a means of internationalizing" (p. 273).

(continued)

TABLE 14.1 (continued) Alliance Studies Involving Entrepreneurial Firms

Study	Research Question	Data	Findings / Propositions
Shan (1990)	This study empirically investigates a statistics model of the determinants of entrepreneurial high-technology firms to form cooperative relationships (pp. 129, 130).	Secondary data were collected on cooperative relationships and product development activities of new biotechnology firms (NBFs) (p. 134).	New biotechnology firms enter cooperative agreements more often if they are market followers not leaders (p. 136), if they have fewer employees (p. 136), or if they are commercializing new biotechnology products in foreign markets (p. 137). Product diversity (number of biotechnology products; p. 136) is not significantly related to alliance formation (p. 137).
Shan, Walker, & Kogut (1994)	This study examines the relationship between innovation and cooperation between small start-up and large established firms in biotechnology industry (p. 387).	Secondary and survey data were collected on 114 start-up biotechnology firms that had cooperative agreements before 1989 (p. 390).	"Startup innovation output," which is measured by the number of patents granted, "does not attract large firm relationships but rather depends on them" (p. 393). "Large startups do not attract more established firm partners than small startups" (p. 393). "The finding for PUBLIC FUNDING suggests that an established firm looks for confirmation of a startup's potential in the capital market before entering into an agreement with it. Startup participation in equity markets does not substitute for cooperation but encourages it" (p. 393). No partner-selection criteria. But the findings may imply that the existing number of patents as innovation output of start-up firms is not viewed as a partner-selection criterion for large established firms. Neither is size. And public funding is used as a criterion and encourages established firms to form cooperative agreements with start-up firms.

Steensma, Marino, & Dickson (2000)	This study investigates how cultural values influence the likelihood that entrepreneurial manufacturing firms will pursue technology alliances and the use of equity ties when technology alliances are pursued (p. 952).	Survey data were collected on 494 small-to-medium-sized manufacturing firms in Australia, Indonesia, Mexico, Norway, and Sweden (pp. 958–959).	"SMEs in uncertainty-avoiding nations (for instance, Mexico) had a lower threshold for technological uncertainty and were more likely to pursue technology alliances when such uncertainty increased than were SMEs in countries more tolerant of uncertainty (Sweden, for example)" (p. 966). "Overall, SMEs in countries with high levels of masculinity (such as Australia) were less likely to pursue technology alliances than SMEs in societies that are more feminine and cooperative (like Sweden and Norway)" (p. 966). "SMEs in countries with collectivist values (such as Indonesia and Mexico) were more likely to form technology alliances involving equity ties than SMEs in individualistic countries (such as Australia) " (pp. 966–967). "However, we found that SMEs in individualistic societies were more likely to use equity ties as technological uncertainty increased than were SMEs in collective societies" (p. 967).
Stuart, Hoang, & Hybels (1999)	This study examines how perceptions of the value of entrepreneurial firms are affected by interorganizational relationship with prominent partners (p. 317).	Secondary data on 301 private dedicated biotechnology firms that were in the development of human diagnostics and therapeutics from 1978 to 1991 and that were funded by venture capitals (pp. 323–324).	In uncertain contexts, i.e., when the entrepreneurial firms were young and had raised smaller amounts of private funding (p. 342), the prominence of their exchange partners—alliance partners, equity investors, and investment banks—enhanced their ability to attract resources (p. 344), and they went to initial public offering (IPO) faster and earned greater valuations at IPO (p. 315).

gence of purpose, consistency of position within the large firm, and interface. However, small and large firms in a partnership may also differ in other ways. For example, entrepreneurial and established firms are different in terms of resources, economic power, legitimacy, and innovative abilities. The resulting interdependency makes strategic alliances between small and large firms not only desirable but also risky. Moreover, small and large firms are potentially competitors because small, technologically innovative firms challenge the existing products and businesses of established firms. Partnerships between them are especially unstable as they race to learn from each other. Finally, the lack of a track record makes alliances with large established firms especially desirable for entrepreneurial firms in order to gain ready legitimacy in the marketplace.

We identified 15 key difference factors and grouped them into two categories: intrinsic factors and alliance making factors (see Table 14.2). Intrinsic factors capture the differences between an entrepreneurial firm and an established firm when they are examined as single organizations. Interfirm alliancing factors cover the differences between them when they are engaged in strategic alliances with each other. In other words, interfirm factors are relevant only when a partnership between an entrepreneurial firm and an established firm exists or is under consideration.

DIFFERENCES IN INTRINSIC FACTORS

Intrinsic difference factors, just defined, include resources, innovativeness, status in competition, legitimacy, history/track record, power, organizational characteristics, business focus, and planning horizon (see Table 14.2).

Resources

Entrepreneurial firms typically have limited financial, manufacturing, and marketing resources. Investors are unsure about the prospect of commercialization of the new products, and therefore hesitate to invest large amounts of capital in new companies. Compared to established and large companies, which have multiple sources of cash flow from different lines of businesses to compensate temporarily unprofitable ones, new companies do not have rich internal sources of capital to finance their sole business.

Alliances provide entrepreneurial firms access to the resources they need, especially access to the large firms' financial resources, manufacturing capabilities, and marketing expertise. Shan et al. (1994) report that biotechnology start-ups, which typically lack financial, marketing, and distribution resources, have cooperative relationships primarily with estab-

TABLE 14.2 Intrinsic and Alliancing Difference Factors in Entrepreneurial and Established Firms

	Entrepreneurial Firms	Established Firms
Intrinsic Factors		
1. Resources	Short of financial, manufacturing, and marketing resources	Affluent in financial, manufacturing, and marketing resources
2. Innovativeness	More innovative	Less innovative
3. Status in competition	Challengers in competition	Defenders, vulnerable to competition from newcomers
4. Legitimacy	Less	More
5. History/track record	Scarce	Sufficient
6. Economic/political power	Little influence over the environment	More economic and political power
7. Organizational characteristics	*Structure*: Clan, informal *Communication*: Fewer levels, frequent, informal, more horizontal *Decision making*: Speedy, flexible, informal, centralized from the top, keeping options open, opportunist	*Structure*: Bureaucratic, formal, fragmented *Communication*: More levels, slower, infrequent, open to distortion, barely horizontal *Decision making*: Slow, consensual, decentralized at the intermediate levels, long-term strategies
8. Business focus	Products and services	Expansion in scale and scope
9. Planning horizon	Speedy development	Not in a hurry
Alliancing Factors		
1. Control over technology	Retain control over its technology	Capture the technology
2. Confidence in technology	Confident, overly committed	Skeptical
3. Interorganizational interfacing	Decisions makers are the executors	Decision makers are not the executors
4. Criticality of alliancing	The alliance is a matter of survival	The alliance is not a matter of survival
5. Strategic purpose	Survival, growth	Sometimes only as a blocking strategy
6. Consistency of commitment	Subject to change	Consistent

lished firms (p. 390). They also report that alliancing with established firms leads to more innovative outputs, in the form of patents, for start-up firms. Larson's (1992) field study of dyadic alliances finds that "limited but dense networks of formal and informal exchange relationships" are the source of growth for "resource-poor entrepreneurial organizations" (p. 100).

Innovativeness

The literature shows consistently that entrepreneurial and small firms have higher rates of innovation. Powell and Brantley (1992) report that in science-based industries, such as computer, semiconductors, and biotechnology, established firms have lagged behind entrepreneurial firms in innovativeness during each industry's early stages. Very often, an innovation or a novel modification of an old product or service is the driver for the establishment of a new company. Indeed, small high-technology ventures rely on the commercialization and marketing of innovative products to survive and grow (Poutziouris, 2003, p. 202). Established firms, in turn, are known to take advantage of the innovativeness of entrepreneurial firms by collaborating with them. For example, Pfizer has alliances with more than 400 companies, over 250 of which are devoted to R&D, and its alliance partners are often smaller pharmaceutical companies and biotech labs working on promising "late-stage compounds" (Muson, 2002, p. 21).

Status in Competition

Entrepreneurial firms challenge established firms with innovations, making the existing products or services obsolete, attracting new customers, or taking away patrons from the established firms. As firms get older, they become increasingly vulnerable to competition from newcomers in the market. Facing entrepreneurial firms' challenge, established firms could of course take a variety of actions. Some established firms stay put until they are convinced of a real threat from a challenger. Others take proactive actions when potentially threatening ideas or findings are still in their preliminary stages. Strategic alliances are an example of a proactive option that established firms could take to thwart the challenges posed by entrepreneurial firms. For example, in the competitive pharmaceutical industry, where innovation is the major driving force of performance, established firms such as Eli Lilly routinely enter into strategic alliances with smaller biotechnology firms to strengthen their drug development efforts (Futrell, Slugay, & Stephens, 2001).

Legitimacy

Legitimacy is "a social judgment of acceptance, appropriateness, and desirability" (Zimmerman & Zeitz, 2002, p. 414). Organizations can derive legitimacy from regulative, normative, cognitive, and industrial norms, rules, values, and models (Scott, 1995). To gain legitimacy, entrepreneurial firms can conform, select, manipulate, and create norms and practices, such as registering with the SEC, hiring experienced top managers, locating in Silicon Valley, emphasizing potential technological breakthrough rather than existing profitability, and cultivating a new consumption mode of Internet shopping (Zimmerman & Zeitz, 2002, p. 423). Singh, Tucker, and House (1986) found that the propensity of young voluntary social service organizations to dissolve was significantly reduced by activities leading to external legitimacy, such as being listed in the community directory, having a charitable organization registration number, and creating a large board of directors.

History/Track Record

Being new also means a lack of history and track record for entrepreneurial firms. The short duration of existence of an entrepreneurial firm creates uncertainty about its quality for investors, customers, distributors, and suppliers. In contrast, established firms have a history, and also perhaps a good track record, that enhances their legitimacy and attractiveness. The lack of both legitimacy and track record in small firms can be compensated by forming strategic alliances with established firms that have both these attributes. A study by Goldberg, Cohen, and Fiegenbaum (2003) in the Israeli software industry confirms that strategic alliances with important partners, among other efforts such as strengthening internal core competencies, contribute toward a high corporate reputation of small firms (pp. 183–184).

Economic/Political Power

Large established companies may dominate the markets and are able to influence the evolution of their environment, both economically and politically. In contrast, small entrepreneurial firms can exercise little influence over their environment. Such a lack of power compels entrepreneurial firms to be highly flexible and responsive to environmental changes.

Organizational Characteristics

Entrepreneurial firms and established firms have different organizational characteristics in terms of structure, communication, and decision making. In the early stages of the organizational life cycle, entrepreneurial firms are generally informal, whereas large established firms are bureaucratic and most often fragmented internally. Entrepreneurial firms are agile and nimble in decision making, and alliance-related decisions are made from the top, while established firms have a certain influence over their environment and have, therefore, the luxury of being able to stick to their long-term strategies.

Business Focus

Entrepreneurial companies are founded to exploit new business opportunities, usually in relation to manifested or potential needs of customers for certain products or services. In order to survive, a new company needs to create markets, and the consumption of its products and services becomes the focus of their business. In comparison, established firms, especially those that already have a stable hold on their market shares, are eager in their pursuit of growth. In order to keep up with a high rate of expansion, established firms are unsatisfied with just extending the existing product lines. They are more likely to engage in acquiring other businesses, whether related or unrelated, and grow through diversification. Compared to the risk-taking entrepreneurial firms, established firms are cautious about entering into emerging technical subfields, worried about product cannibalization and uncertain investment payoffs.

Planning Horizon

Entrepreneurial and established firms may possess different planning horizons. Large established firms usually enjoy the benefits of relative stability and can implement strategies and activities with a long-term planning horizon (Das, 1991, 2004a). Entrepreneurial firms, on the contrary, are pressed for financial resources and face threats of dissolution all the time. Moreover, large established firms can afford long periods of stagnant or even poor performance by reducing their scale of operations if necessary. Constant dire threats do not allow entrepreneurial firms to easily manage the risks inherent in long-term planning (Das, 2004b, 2005; Das & Teng, 1997a). Such differences in the planning horizon between an entrepreneurial firm and an established firm have significant impact on their strategy and behavior when they enter into a partnership. For example, speedy development of a product is usually pursued urgently and vigorously by an entrepreneurial firm, while its established partner only wants to get access and keep updated with the new technology and is not usually in a hurry to replace its own mature products. On some occasions, the established firm may intend to use the partnership to control the new technology and new products so that its own existing profitable products will not be replaced too soon.

DIFFERENCES IN ALLIANCE-MAKING FACTORS

Alliance-making (alliancing) difference factors, when considering a partnership between an entrepreneurial firm and an established firm, include control over technology, confidence in the technology, interorganizational interfacing, criticality of alliancing, strategic purpose, and consistency of commitment (see Table 14.2).

Control Over Technology

When a new technology is involved in a partnership between an entrepreneurial firm and an established firm, which is most often the case, a struggle over the control of technology is more or less present between the partners. The established firm, which is usually the one that is seeking the innovative technology from the entrepreneurial partner, often attempts to capture the technology, transfer it to its own operations, and ultimately, appropriate it. At the other end of the competition is the entrepreneurial firm, which always tries to retain control over its technology. Such competition for the control over the technology usually results in tensions between the partners, and is a constant challenge for both the established firm and entrepreneurial firm in strategic alliances. This is especially important in the case of technology firms because, as Narula (2004) observes, a small firm's control over its technology and consequently its technology competence can be easily lost if the alliance with a large firm fails.

Confidence in Technology

The established firm and the entrepreneurial partner may differ at the level of confidence about the technology that is involved in the alliance. Whether a new technology is feasible or a new product is promising is always difficult to precisely predict. Entrepreneurial firms obviously are confident with their technologies, and sometimes overly committed, so that its established partner may well be skeptical. Moreover, it is unwise for the entrepreneurial firm to fully disclose the technology for the sake of convincing the potential partner, because of the risk of leakage of proprietary knowledge. Therefore, an entrepreneurial firm seeking a strategic alliance partner should pay attention to the skepticism of the established firm. A skeptical partner will hesitate to fully commit and, even when committed, will be likely to withdraw the support when satisfactory results are not achieved quickly.

Interorganizational Interfacing

The strategic alliance interface refers to the personnel from each side of the partnership who continuously interact with the other side throughout the alliances. Because of the multiple hierarchical levels in large established firms, the decision to establish a partnership is usually made by the top management but implemented by middle managers and technical specialists. In entrepreneurial firms, in contrast, the decision makers regarding formation of strategic alliances are usually the same as those who manage the alliances. The discontinuities in personnel interfaces, while moving from the formation stage to the operational stage in large established firms, is complicated by the ambiguity of the simultaneously collaborative and competitive nature of relations in strategic alliances (Das & Teng, 1997b, 2000b), and leads to difficulties for the middle managers in implementation activities. Sometimes even sabotage at the operational level will ruin the partnership that was hastily formed by the top management. The interfacing difficulties are sometimes rooted in conflicting personalities from the partnering companies, especially if the companies are at different stages of the corporate life cycle. It is reported, for example, that Lotus does not partner with start-ups, as a general rule, to avoid the clash of egos (Segil, 1998).

Criticality of Alliancing

Strategic criticality refers to the importance of a partnership to the continued viability of a firm. An entrepreneurial firm, which is restrained by financial, marketing, and manufacturing resources; legitimacy; and track record, would be in some need for a partnership with an established firm. In the case of the biotech industry, small firms are especially dependent on strategic research partnerships with large firms for overcoming their disadvantage of limited resources (Audretsch & Feldman, 2003, p. 285). While a particular alliance may be a matter of survival for a start-up, established firms have the resources to engage in multiple alliances, so that one failed alliance will not lead to the collapse of the whole company. With a larger scale and multiple areas of operation, established firms are more likely to survive a single failed alliance. Such a substantive difference in strategic criticality between an established firm and an entrepreneurial firm in a partnership can easily become a relational source of opportunism if the established firm is not committed to the alliance. Entrepreneurial firms should be vigilant in selecting a reliable and committed partner. Indeed, Narula's (2004) research with small and medium technology firms in electronic hardware industries confirms that these firms have to be extremely careful about picking alliance partners, given the reality of high rates of

R&D alliance failures (p. 160). In contrast, large firms often have redundant, back-up agreements with several firms so that they can easily find alternative avenues for needed resources (p. 160).

Strategic Purpose

With almost no exceptions, entrepreneurial firms enter strategic alliances in order to survive and grow. Even if they aim to become an acquisition candidate for the established partner later on, it is still better if they first reach certain maturation and gain sufficient bargaining power. In fact, selling a company after it already has become part of an alliance may be particularly disadvantageous. A strategic alliance with an entrepreneurial firm (with a promising technology) may sometimes be used by an established firm to prevent it from entering into an alliance with another established firm, especially a rival. Entrepreneurial firms need to be aware of such possibilities and carefully select an established firm that believes in developing its junior partner.

Consistency of Commitment

The commitment of member firms in an alliance has been emphasized by both academics and practitioners as critical to the success of partnerships. Large established firms are multiple-unit and complex organizations, and an alliance, while it benefits some people or units, almost inevitably poses threats to other units of the organizations. For example, an alliance with an entrepreneurial firm with superior technologies and product development potentials will be welcomed by the top management and the marketing department, but will pose a threat to the internal research personnel. Therefore, it is important that an entrepreneurial firm be aware of such possibility of inconsistent commitment on the part of an established firm and select the most reliable partner in terms of its ability to effectively deal with internal changes.

RESEARCH ON PARTNER SELECTION BY ENTREPRENEURIAL FIRMS

Our examination of the extant literature on partner-selection criteria revealed several characteristics, which include a focus on established firms, a focus on international alliances, a dominant framework, certain contextual factors, and some common criteria.

A Focus on Established Firms

Not surprisingly, the literature on alliance partner-selection criteria is focused on large and established firms, with very few exceptions (Adler & Hlavacek, 1976; Forrest & Martin, 1992).

A Focus on International Alliances

The literature is also focused on international alliances, a majority of which are international joint ventures. Since small entrepreneurial firms rarely have the resources, capabilities, or even interest in expanding into international markets, they are understandably left unnoticed by most researchers on partner-selection criteria. Moreover, major alliances, involving well-known large firms, are much more likely to be reported in the press (see, e.g., Glaister & Buckley, 1997). Therefore, large firms are likely to be overrepresented in those studies that compiled their datasets primarily from press resources. Moreover, small entrepreneurial firms are especially cautious about potential hazards of entering international strategic alliances. A study by Preece et al. (1999) found that the risks of international alliances might have kept early-stage technology-based firms "from using alliances as a means of internationalizing" (p. 273). Therefore, it is not surprising that small entrepreneurial firms are seldom included in international strategic alliances studies, and thus in partner-selection criteria research. An exception is Supphellen, Haugland, and Korneliussen's (2002) survey of Scandinavian small- and medium-sized businesses engaged in international strategic alliances (p. 789), although they used only personal information sources in evaluating potential partners.

A Dominant Framework

The categorization of task-related and partner-related criteria (Geringer, 1988, 1991) is widely accepted in empirical studies. However, the items under each category vary from study to study, and some task-related items in one study became partner related in another. For example, reputation, financial resources, and marketing system are task-related criteria in Geringer (1991), but partner related in Glaister (1996). Adding to the confusion, "distribution channels" is a task-related criterion (Glaister, 1996, p. 17) while "established marketing and distribution system" is partner related (p. 21) in the same study.

Contextual Factors

Some researchers have considered contextual factors in determining the importance of individual selection criteria in different situations. In one of the early studies, Tomlinson (1970) found that parent firms of different size (larger and smaller), in different industries (e.g., oil, electricals, vehicles, tobacco/food), and with different reasons for entering into a joint venture, use different partner selection criteria. Other contextual factors studied include "perceived task environment uncertainty" and "diversity of line functions" (Geringer, 1988), form of agreement, objectives of the project, type of collaborator, and the characteristics of the selecting company (Bailey, Masson, & Raeside, 1998), and size and experience of the company and the education and experience of the CEO (Al-Khalifa & Peterson, 1999). Both Glaister (1996) and Luo (1998) found significant influence of alliance motives on the selection criteria. However, Glaister and Buckley's (1997) study, based on a sample slightly different from Glaister (1996), found that the purpose of the venture, as well as partner nationality, industry of the joint venture, and the relative partner size, do not influence the relative importance of different selection criteria.

Common Criteria

The following is a list of the common criteria that have been deemed as important in the alliance partner selection criteria literature:

> (A) Task-related criteria: complementary products or skills; financial resources; technology capabilities or uniqueness; location; marketing or distribution systems, or established customer base; reputation and image; managerial capabilities; government relationship, including regulatory requirements and government sales; help in faster entry into the target market; and industry attractiveness.
>
> (B) Partner-related criteria: strategic fit or interdependence, or compatible goals; compatible or cooperative culture and ethics; prior ties and successful prior association; trust between top managers; strong commitment; similar status, including size and structure; reciprocal relationship; commensurate risk; and ease of communication.

ANALYSIS OF PARTNER SELECTION CRITERIA

The topic of partner-selection criteria covers almost every aspect of a firm, from financing, marketing, manufacturing, technology, and product, to goals, commitment, size, culture, management, and past ties with partners. To make better sense of these criteria, we grouped the criteria studied into 21 categories: (in alphabetical order) Commitment, Cost, Culture, Finance, Goals, Government, Industry, Internationalization, Learning, Location, Management, Manufacturing, Market, Past ties, Product, Reciprocity, Reputation, Risk, Size, Technology, and "Other"(a multi-area criterion that refers to complementary capabilities, resources, and strengths in cooperative activities). We then placed the studies on partner-selection criteria in different sets according to the nature of the alliance samples S namely, large-large alliances, large-small alliances, small-small alliances, and small-large alliances. Most of the studies fall in the group labeled "mixed and unspecified size," which include studies that do not specify the size of the partners in the alliances studied, or only specify the size of one party in an alliance while ignoring the relative size of its partners. For example, Geringer (1988, 1991), Glaister (1996), Glaister and Buckley (1997), Al-Khalifa and Peterson (1990), and Kumar (1995) do not specify the size of any of the partners in the alliances. Beamish (1987), Dacin, Hitt, and Levitas (1997), Hakanson and Lorange (1991), Hitt, Dacin, Levitas, Arregle, and Borza (2000), Tatoglu (2000), Tomlinson (1970), and Tyler and Steensma (1995) specify that the selecting party (focal firm) is a large firm, and the selected partners are either unspecified in size or specified as mixtures of large and small firms. Arino, Abramov, Skorobogatykh, Rykounina, and Vila (1997) and Wang, Wee, and Koh (1999) include both small and large firms as the selectors but do not specify the relative size of their partners. Bailey et al. (1998) and Brouthers, Brouthers, and Wilkinson (1995) specify that they have small and large firms both as selectors and selected firms. Luo (1997, 1998) specifies that the selected partners are all large firms but does not specify the size of the selectors. Supphellen et al. (2002) specify that the selectors are small- and medium-sized companies but are silent on the status of their partners.

Our analysis showed that very few studies (only 6 of them) have small-large alliances as their research subjects. Only one of them (Forrest & Martin, 1992) investigates the selection criteria small firms used to select their larger partner. The conclusions of three other studies may suggest some of the attributes of large firms that the small firms might be looking for (see Doz, 1988; Hull et al., 1988; Stuart et al., 1999).

Our examination of the studies on strategic alliances of entrepreneurial or small firms reveals that most of the studies do not look at partner-selection criteria used by the entrepreneurial firms or their partners (see Table 14.1). However, the results of many of the studies provide important information on what partner selection criteria could be.

Forrest and Martin (1992) investigated the alliance experiences and factors that make technology-related alliances between small biotechnology firms and large pharmaceutical and chemical firms successful. Their study found that large pharmaceutical and chemical firms chose entrepreneurial firms based on technical and managerial capabilities, trust, compatibility, shared philosophies and attitudes, ties of the entrepreneurial firm with potential competitors, and commitment. Although not much information is given concerning the partner-selection criteria used by the small firms, the authors implied that the small firms look at the financial resources of the large firm. An intangible factor, having to do with the gut feelings of the partners ("essential chemistry"), was found by Forrest and Martin (1992) to be important for both small and large partners.

Although Forrest and Martin (1992) reported a higher success rate for dedicated biotechnology alliance firms in alliances than their larger partners (83% versus 47.5%), it has also been found that start-up biotechnology firms that initially allied with established potential rivals performed worse on average (Baum et al., 2000). In contrast, Harrigan (1988) found that size did not predict the success of strategic alliances; that is, alliances between partners of similar size are not more successful, in terms of venture survival, duration, or subjective assessments of success by the partners, than those between dissimilar partners. In addition, similarity in status, such as size, has been emphasized in many studies (e.g., Chung, Singh, & Lee, 2000; Daniels, 1971; Geringer, 1991; Li & Rowley, 2002; Podolny, 1994) on partner-selection criteria for established firms as an important and effective criterion. Thus, there is no consistency in the results concerning the dissimilarity of size that always exists in alliances between entrepreneurial firms and established firms.

Larson's (1992) case studies of four entrepreneurial firms engaged in seven cooperative alliances proposed several criteria that should be considered for entrepreneurial firms in the selection of partners: personal reputations and prior relations, including histories, individual friendships, capabilities, commitment, and mutual benefits; firm's reputation, including long-term learning opportunities of expertise and innovative capabilities of key suppliers and customers, ease of communication and working relationships, enhancement of reputation, and potential impact on growth; mutual economic advantage; and trust developed in the trial period (pp. 84–88). Some of these criteria have received empirical support in other studies. For example, Hu and Korneliussen (1997) found that personal ties have a positive effect on the performance of small firms in strategic alliances (p. 168). BarNir and Smith (2002) also found that personal ties of managers in small businesses lead to more interfirm alliances (p. 228). The importance of ease of communication has been confirmed by Deeds and Hill (1999) in an investigation on the effectiveness of opportunism deterrence in dedicated biotechnology firms. They found that strong relationships between the partners, such as congruent backgrounds and frequent communication, serve as a much more effective deterrent to opportunistic actions than alliance-specific investments or contingent claims contracts, suggesting that these should be used as selection criteria by entrepreneurial firms.

The exploration of the determinants of involvement in strategic alliances for entrepreneurial firms represents another research avenue. Kelley, Rice, and Peters (2001) found that technology-based and product-based knowledge are both positively related to the number of alliances formed. Powell and Brantley (1992) found that relatively larger, older, more diversified, and publicly owned entrepreneurial firms have more agreements, suggesting that the partners of entrepreneurial firms used size, age, product diversification, and public funding as the selection criteria. However, Shan et al. (1994) found that larger start-up biotechnology firms, with more existing innovation output, did not attract more large firms into cooperative relationships. Only public funding was related to alliance formation, suggesting that perhaps neither innovative output nor size were used by established firms in choosing start-up firms as partners. In fact, Shan's (1990) study of a similar sample found that those new biotechnology firms that were smaller and used imitative rather than innovative technology entered into more cooperative agreements.

Chen and Li (1999) found that the number of strategic alliances that provide access to technology, not to manufacturing and marketing areas, has a positive impact on product development for U.S. semiconductor start-up firms. This result suggests that entrepreneurial firms should choose partners that can provide access to technology, not necessarily manufacturing or marketing, if they are focused on new product development. However, an exclusive focus on new product development may not be enough for the long-term survival and growth of entrepreneurial firms. An emphasis on access to process and manufacturing learning is often needed for an entrepreneurial firm to grow out of the technology-only stage, so that alliance partners with potential contributions to manufacturing and marketing should be preferable.

It is apparent that some of the contextual factors that have been identified in the partner selection criteria literature, such as motivation of the partnership and partner's size and other characteristics, distinguish strategic alliances between entrepreneurial and established firms from those between established firms only. For both entrepreneurial firms and established firms, the differences of size, status, and other characteristics should provide sufficient justification for extra caution when considering the formation of strategic alliances, starting from the selection of the partner.

GUIDELINES FOR PARTNER SELECTION BY ENTREPRENEURIAL FIRMS

Studies have generally proposed or found empirically that partner-selection criteria are influenced by the motivations for entering into alliances as well as the characteristics of the firms, such as size, organizational type, industry, and organizational culture. When an entrepreneurial firm teams up with an established firm or even another entrepreneurial firm, it is likely that the partners in both scenarios differ in size, motivation, and organizational culture. Entrepreneurial firms and established firms are quite different from each other (see Table 14.2). Such differences usually result in conflicts between them. As our earlier discussion shows, entrepreneurial firms should not follow the conventional partner-selection criteria without a great degree of caution.

When alliancing with an established firm, the entrepreneurial firm should keep in mind that the partner is different from itself in structure, communication, decision making, and so on, and be aware of possible conflicts or risks that may arise from these differences. We propose the following list of partner-selection criteria that an entrepreneurial firm should adopt when it considers forming strategic alliances with established firms.

Compatible Motivations

Sometimes established firms form strategic alliances with entrepreneurial firms that possess promising technology just to preempt possible partnerships between the entrepreneurial firms with their competitors, or to forestall the potential threats to their own mature products posed by the new technology. Such self-interested motivations would not of course be overtly a part of the negotiations. The entrepreneurial firms have to pay attention to other cues for whether or not the established firms' real motivations to form strategic alliances with them are to develop new products, so that there would be compatible objectives for survival and growth. The existence of a few major competitors (of the established firm) that are also actively seeking to develop new products using the same new technology through interfirm alliances is usually a sign that a blocking strategy is being attempted. Such signs are even stronger when the entrepreneurial firm is leading the technological development. A lack of a detailed action schedule for the alliance is another cue that the established firm is not really interested in developing the technology but in diverting the immediate threats.

An example is the alliance between Telefonica S.A. and Bidland Systems. Because the valuable resources of technology start-ups are often intangible knowledge or information, learning races can actually finish even before the alliances enter into the operation stage. Established firms' possible motivations are especially important for entrepreneurial firms. The hidden motivation of Telefonica made it almost impossible for Bidland Systems, a San Diego-based start-up, to survive at all (Peterson, 2001). Bidland Systems was a leading provider of easy and affordable online auction solutions (Business Wire, 2000). It was enticed into strategic alliance talks with Telefonica S.A., the Spanish telecommunication giant, and its American subsidiary, Telefonica B2B, which reached a joint venture and investment agreement with Bidland in August 2000 (Business Wire, 2000). However, several months later, Telefonica refused to abide by the agreement. Bidland then filed a lawsuit contending that Telefonica launched its own venture after having "obtained complete access to Bidland's proprietary business-to-business auction and dynamic e-commerce business information and technology" (Business Wire, 2000). Telefonica apparently had an opportunistic motivation toward Bidland's attractive technology, which was at the same time relatively easy to appropriate.

Access to Manufacturing and Marketing Functions

Long-term survival and growth objectives necessitate entrepreneurial firms to obtain manufacturing and marketing facilities to exploit their innovative capabilities in technology. That would improve their chances for transforming themselves from a fragile organization into a stable one. However, one of the weaknesses of technology-based entrepreneurial firms is the lack of attention paid to marketing strategies (Jones-Evans & Westhead, 1996), and the literature on marketing and technology-based entrepreneurship has not done a good job in explaining how technology-based entrepreneurs take on marketing their innovations successfully (Boussouara & Deakins, 1999, p. 207). We propose that forming strategic alliances with established firms can be one avenue for entrepreneurial firms to learn about markets and build up marketing resources and experience. Hence, entrepreneurial firms should choose established firms that are willing to offer access to manufacturing and marketing resources.

As an illustration, consider the successful partnership between Glaxo Holdings PLC and ICOS Corp. This alliance marked a major transition in alliance-making between entrepreneurial biotechnology firms and established pharmaceutical firms during the early 1990s, a transition from "mere money-for-ideas or money-for-products swaps" (Axinn, 1992, p. SR10) to marketing agreements in which the entrepreneurial firms are more involved. Based on the complementary strengths of ICOS's molecular biology expertise and Glaxo's drug discovery expertise, a shared R&D and co-promotion agreement was signed in 1991 (Biotech Patent News, 1991) for developing therapeutic agents for cardiovascular disease and asthma (PR Newswire, 1994). Just 2 years after the compounds they jointly developed entered Phase 1 testing (PR Newswire, 1995), ICOS gained all commercial rights to the compounds and was well-positioned for further research and commercialization independently (Worldwide Biotech, 1997). In alliances that go beyond mere technology or product transfer, start-ups like ICOS can learn from their partners' technology expertise and get involved in interacting with consumers, thereby strengthening their capability to survive and grow by themselves.

Involvement and Commitment of Middle Managers

Although alliance deals are made between the top managers of both partnering firms, the middle managers in established firms are the ones who usually carry out the operations. In order to avoid alienation or even sabotage by the middle managers, who sometimes do not understand the opportunities of alliances but rather feel threatened by outsiders, the entrepreneurial firms need to emphasize the importance of involving middle managers from the very beginning. Whether the middle managers from the established firms are involved and committed to the alliance should be one of the important criteria that entrepreneurial firms should use in selecting partners.

Consider the case of the partnership between Alza and Ciba-Geigy, terminated later. This research alliance between Alza Corp., a California-based entrepreneurial company, which has been a subsidiary of Johnson & Johnson since 2001, and Ciba-Geigy of Switzerland, which is now part of Novartis AG after it merged with Sandoz Inc. in 1996, showcases the clash of organizational cultures between an entrepreneurial company and an established pharmaceutical giant and the resulting resentment of the middle managers (Doz, 1996, pp. 65–66). The real reason for the dissolution, however, as revealed in Doz's interview with executives from both companies, is the fact that Alza personnel were deeply frustrated by the bureaucratic structures and lengthy and formal procedures in Ciba-Geigy. When interfirm cooperation was needed between top managers or lab scientists, it was seldom possible without middle managers being involved. The lack of involvement by middle managers in Ciba-Geigy apparently thwarted the interaction attempts of Alza's personnel, despite the enthusiasm of the top management. The separation of middle managers from the top management in large established firms makes it crucial to involve middle managers in the negotiation stage and, thereafter, the operation of alliances. Whether the established firm can take measures to make its middle managers accessible for its entrepreneurial partner should be a vital criterion that a start-up firm should emphasize in selecting its alliance partner.

Dedicated Task Forces

In addition to committed middle managers, the prospect that a task force dedicated to the coordination of the alliance partners will be set up should also receive emphasis. The reason is that even if the middle managers are committed, the slow, multilevel communication within the established firms is very often the source of frustrations and conflicts. The importance of a dedicated alliance task force has already been demonstrated by the fact that many companies have set up separate departments that deal with strategic alliances. When such a department is not set up, at least a dedicated task force should be envisioned by the established firm. The entrepreneurial firm, therefore, should keep this in mind as a selection criterion.

A good example here is the success of the partnership between, again, Alza Corp (later a subsidiary of Johnson & Johnson) and Theratechnologies Inc. (a Canadian biopharmaceutical company) since 2001. This success can be attributed to Alza's dedicated task force composed of personnel across the various stages of the cooperation, and the additional support of the alliance management department, according to Theratechnologies' Chief Scientific Officer, Dr. Abribat (Delivery Times: An Alza Publication, 2003). These dedicated task forces have enabled Alza to tailor their approach to each partner and respond quickly to their needs. Only 3 months after their first meeting in a conference, the two companies reached a cooperative agreement with a clearly defined strategy, detailed R&D activities, and time frames. Now three development projects between the two companies are progressing "extremely well." Although a separate department for alliance management is not always necessary, at least a project-level task force should be put together. The ability of an established firm to devote a task force for a partner should be one of the top criteria that an entrepreneurial firm should consider when selecting alliance partners.

Intention to Act with Speed

The difference in the criticality of an alliance between two partners may result in conflicts when the entrepreneurial firm is eager to make the alliance work while the established firm wants to take some time. Therefore, the entrepreneurial firms should make sure that the potential partner is just as keen to act with speed as they are to make the alliance work. Such intentions can be best manifested in detailed action plans and specific schedules. A lack of intention to act with speed can be traced to mere enthusiasm without genuine action plans.

Consider the case of the successful partnership between Roche Holdings Ltd., a giant Swiss pharmaceutical company, and Trimeris Inc., a North Carolina-based biotech rising star, in developing anti-HIV drugs (Seachrist, 1999). Trimeris' vice president, Michael Rechny, was convinced by Roche's corporate profile as a leader in drug development, and believed that Roche was as anxious as Trimeris about "a timely introduction of a whole new class of anti-retroviral agents," and would help them speed up the timely development of the two promising anti-HIV fusion inhibitors, T-20 and T-1249 (Seachrist, 1999). Within 2 years of the formation of the partnership in 1999, the two products were successfully developed and were granted fast-track status by the FDA, and the two companies extended their partnership for at least 3 more years (Coghill, 2001). The intention to act with speed, which was a major attraction for Trimeris, is a big concern for entrepreneurial firms, because their investors usually demand immediate success in technology advancement and product development. Failure to have quick results often is a matter of survival for start-up firms. This case shows how significant the intention to act with speed on the established firm's part is in an alliance with entrepreneurial start-ups.

CONCLUDING REMARKS

Entrepreneurial firms have increasingly entered into strategic alliances, especially in technology-based industries. They seek developmental resources from established partners. However, the asymmetries in power, motives, and learning ability between entrepreneurial firms and their established partners make it imperative that careful attention is given to the selection of alliance partners.

We have noted how entrepreneurial firms are different from established firms in terms of intrinsic and alliance-making factors, including resources, innovativeness, status in competition, legitimacy, history/track record, economic/political power, organizational characteristics, business focus, planning horizon, control over technology, confidence in the technology, interorganizational interfacing, criticality of alliancing, strategic purpose, and consistency in commitment. Such differences should result in different approaches for entrepreneurial firms in strategic alliance management than those between established firms, which are the major subject of strategic alliance research. Our focus in this chapter was on partner-selection criteria, the first concern in strategic alliance management. We found that very few partner-selection criteria studies have been done with particular reference to entrepreneurial firms.

For empirical testing of whether the guidelines proposed here lead to more effective performance of entrepreneurial firms engaging in strategic alliances with established firms, care should be taken in measuring success in appropriate terms. For instance, alliance terminations should not be automatically considered as failures—as some researchers have done—because many alliances are agreements that are essentially temporary in nature (Das & Teng, 2000b). Similarly, an acquisition of an entrepreneurial firm by its established partner, or a third party, may or may not be an indicator of alliance failure, depending on the entrepreneur's expectations. Contextual factors, such as industry, stage of technology development, size of the alliance partner, location of the firms, and motives of the alliances, may also need to be considered. Future researchers need to examine if there are moderating factors that influence the relative importance of the guidelines we have proposed here. Another significant research question is how entrepreneurial firms can better exploit the resources in established firms once the alliances are set up.

Based on our analysis of how entrepreneurial firms differ from established firms along a number of dimensions, we framed several recommendations urging entrepreneurial firms to take note of certain characteristics of established firms in selecting them as alliance partners. Entrepreneurial firms should choose those established firms that are motivated to develop technology or product rather than simply to meet the threat of a new technology, that are willing to provide access to manufacturing and marketing functions, that involve committed middle managers in addition to enthusiastic top managers, that will set up dedicated task forces dealing with the alliances, and that are committed to acting immediately and with speed. We believe that by being especially attentive to these factors in selecting established firms as partners, entrepreneurial firms would have better prospects for survival and growth.

ACKNOWLEDGMENT

This chapter, save some minor changes and abridgment, was earlier published as Das and He (2006).

REFERENCES

Adler, L., & Hlavacek, J. D. (1976). *Joint ventures for product innovation.* New York: American Management Association.

Al-Khalifa, A. K., & Peterson, S. E. (1999). The partner selection process in international joint ventures. *European Journal of Marketing, 33,* 1064–1081.

Almeida, P., Dokko, G., & Rosenkopf, L. (2003). Startup size and the mechanisms of external learning: Increasing opportunity and decreasing ability? *Research Policy, 32,* 301–315.

Alvarez, S. A., & Barney, J. B. (2001). How entrepreneurial firms can benefit from alliances with large partners. *Academy of Management Executive, 15*(1), 139–148.

Arino, A., Abramov, M., Skorobogatykh, I., Rykounina, I., & Vila, J. (1997). Partner selection and trust building in west European-Russian joint ventures: A Western perspective. *International Studies of Management and Organization, 27*(1), 19–37.

Audretsch, D. B., & Feldman, M. P. (2003). Small-firm strategic research partnerships: The case of biotechnology. *Technology Analysis & Strategic Management, 15,* 273–288.

Axinn, D. (1992). Pharmaceuticals '92: Pick your partners. *Chemical Market Reporter, 241*(10), SR10–SR14.

Bailey, W. J., Masson, R., & Raeside, R. (1998). Choosing successful technology development partners: A best-practice model. *International Journal of Technology Management, 15,* 124–138.

Barley, S. R., Freeman, J., & Hybels, R. C. (1992). Strategic alliances in commercial biotechnology. In N. Nohria & R. Eccles (Eds.), *Networks and organizations: Structure, form and action* (pp. 311–347). Boston: Harvard Business School Press.

BarNir, A., & Smith, K. A. (2002). Interfirm alliances in the small business: The role of social networks. *Journal of Small Business Management, 40,* 219–232.

Baum, J. A. C., Calabrese, T., & Silverman, B. S. (2000). Don't go it alone: Alliance network composition and startups' performance in Canadian biotechnology. *Strategic Management Journal, 21,* 267–294.

Beamish, P. W. (1987). Joint ventures in less developed countries: Partner selection and performance. *Management International Review, 27*(1), 23–37.

Biotech Patent News. (1991, December 1). Glaxo collaboration seeks to modify phosphodiesterase activity. *Biotech Patent News.*

Boussouara, M., & Deakins, D. (1999). Market-based learning, entrepreneurship and the high technology small firm. *International Journal of Entrepreneurial Behaviour & Research, 5,* 204–223.

Brouthers, K. D., Brouthers, L. E., & Wilkinson, T. J. (1995). Strategic alliances: Choose your partners. *Long Range Planning, 28*(3), 18–25.

Busenitz, L. W., West, G. P., III, Shepherd, D., Nelson, T., Chandler, G. N., & Zacharakis, A. (2003). Entrepreneurship research in emergence: Past trends and future directions. *Journal of Management, 29,* 285–308.

Business Wire. (2000, December 12). Bidland Systems sues Telefonica for breach of contract; Multimillion dollar lawsuit filed against telecommunication giant. *Business Wire.*

Chen, R., & Li, M. (1999). Strategic alliances and new product development: An empirical study of the U.S. semiconductor start-up firms. *Advances in Competitiveness Research, 7*(1), 35–61.

Chung, S. A., Singh, H., & Lee, K. (2000). Complementarity, status similarity and social capital as drivers of alliance formation. *Strategic Management Journal, 21,* 1–22.

Coghill, K. (2001, June 20). Trimeris, Roche extend alliance to develop HIV fusion inhibitors. *BioWorld Today, 12*(119).

Dacin, M. T., Hitt, M. A., & Levitas, E. (1997). Selecting partners for successful international alliances: Examination of U.S. and Korean firms. *Journal of World Business, 32*(1), 3–16.

Daniels, J. D. (1971). *Recent foreign direct manufacturing investment in the United States: An interview study of the decision process.* New York: Praeger.

Das, T. K. (1991). Time: The hidden dimension in strategic planning. *Long Range Planning, 24*(3), 49–57.

Das, T. K. (2004a). Strategy and time: Really recognizing the future. In H. Tsoukas & J. Shepherd (Eds.), *Managing the future: Foresight in the knowledge economy* (pp. 58–74). Oxford, UK: Blackwell.

Das, T. K. (2004b). Time-span and risk of partner opportunism in strategic alliances. *Journal of Managerial Psychology, 19,* 744–759.

Das, T. K. (2005). Deceitful behaviors of alliance partners: Potential and prevention. *Management Decision, 43,* 706–719.

Das, T. K., & He, I. Y. (2006). Entrepreneurial firms in search of established partners: Review and recommendations. *International Journal of Entrepreneurial Behavior & Research, 12,* 114–143.

Das, T. K., & Teng, B. (1997a). Time and entrepreneurial risk behavior. *Entrepreneurship Theory and Practice, 22*(2), 69–88.

Das, T. K., & Teng, B. (1997b). Sustaining strategic alliances: Options and guidelines. *Journal of General Management, 22*(4), 49–64.

Das, T. K., & Teng, B. (2000a). A resource-based theory of strategic alliances. *Journal of Management, 26,* 31–61.

Das, T. K., & Teng, B. (2000b). Instabilities of strategic alliances: An internal tensions perspective. *Organization Science, 11,* 77–101.

Das, T. K., & Teng, B. (2003). Partner analysis and alliance performance. *Scandinavian Journal of Management, 19,* 279–308.

Deeds, D. L., & Hill, C. W. L. (1996). Strategic alliances and the rate of new product development: An empirical study of entrepreneurial biotechnology firms. *Journal of Business Venturing, 11,* 41–55.

Deeds, D. L., & Hill, C. W. L. (1999). An examination of opportunistic action within research alliances: Evidence from the biotechnology industry. *Journal of Business Venturing, 14,* 141–163.

Delivery Times: An Alza Publication. (2003). Anatomy of a partnership: A conversation with Dr. Thierry Abribat, Chief Scientific Officer. *Theratechnologies, 2*(4), 4–5, 8.

Dougherty, D., & Hardy, C. (1996). Sustained product innovation in large mature organizations: Overcoming innovation-to-organization problem. *Academy of Management Journal, 39,* 1120–1153.

Doz, Y. L. (1988). Technology partnerships between larger and smaller firms: Some critical issues. In F. J. Contractor & P. Lorange (Eds.), *Cooperative strategies in international business* (pp. 317–338). Lexington, MA: Lexington Books.

Doz, Y. L. (1996, Summer). The evolution of cooperation in strategic alliances: Initial conditions or learning processes? *Strategic Management Journal, 17*(Special Issue), 55–83.

Eisenhardt, K. M., & Schoonhoven, C. B. (1996). Resource-based view of strategic alliance formation: Strategic and social effects in entrepreneurial firms. *Organization Science, 7,* 136–150.

Forrest, J. E., & Martin, M. J. C. (1992). Strategic alliances between large and small research intensive organizations. *R&D Management, 22*(1), 41–53.

Freeman, C., & Soete, L. (1997). *The economics of industrial innovation* (3rd ed.). Cambridge, MA: MIT Press.

Futrell, D., Slugay, M., & Stephens, C. H. (2001). Becoming a premier partner: Measuring, managing and changing partnering capabilities at Eli Lilly and Company. *Journal of Commercial Biotechnology, 8*(1), 5–13.

Geringer, J. M. (1988). *Joint venture partner selection: Strategies for developed countries.* New York: Quorum Books.

Geringer, J. M. (1991). Strategic determinants of partner selection criteria in international joint ventures. *Journal of International Business Studies, 22,* 41–62.

Glaister, K. W. (1996). UK-Western Europe strategic alliances: Motives and selection criteria. *Journal of Euromarketing, 5*(4), 5–35.

Glaister, K. W., & Buckley, P. J. (1997). Task-related and partner-related selection criteria in UK international joint ventures. *British Journal of Management, 8,* 199–222.

Goldberg, A. I., Cohen, G., & Fiegenbaum, A. (2003). Reputation building: Small business strategies for successful venture development. *Journal of Small Business Management, 41,* 168–186.

Hakanson, L., & Lorange, P. (1991). R&D based co-operative ventures. In L. G. Mattsson & B. Stymne (Eds.), *Corporate and industry strategies for Europe* (pp. 235–262). Amsterdam: North-Holland.

Harrigan, K. R. (1988). Strategic alliances and partner asymmetries. In F. J. Contractor & P. Lorange (Eds.), *Cooperative strategies in international business* (pp. 205–226). Lexington, MA: Lexington Books.

Hindle, K., & Yencken, J. (2004). Public research commercialization, entrepreneurship and new technology based firms: An integrated model. *Technovation, 24,* 793–803.

Hitt, M. A., Dacin, M. T., Levitas, E., Arregle, J.-L., & Borza, A. (2000). Partner selection in emerging and developed market contexts: Resource-based and organizational learning perspectives. *Academy of Management Journal, 43,* 449–467.

Hoffmann, W. H., & Schlosser, R. (2001). Success factors of strategic alliances in small and medium-sized enterprises—An empirical survey. *Long Range Planning, 34,* 357–381.

Hu, Y., & Korneliussen, T. (1997). The effects of personal ties and reciprocity on the performance of small firms in horizontal strategic alliances. *Scandinavian Journal of Management, 13,* 159–173.

Hull, F., Slowinski, G., Wharton, R., & Azumi, K. (1988). Strategic partnerships between technological entrepreneurs in the United States and large corporations in Japan and the United States. In F. J. Contractor & P. Lorange (Eds.), *Cooperative strategies in international business* (pp. 445–456). Lexington, MA: Lexington Books.

Jones-Evans, D., & Westhead, P. (1996). The high technology small firm sector in the UK. *International Journal of Entrepreneurial Behaviour & Research, 2,* 15–35.

Kagono, T., Nonaka, I., Sakakibara, K., & Okumura, A. (1985). *Strategic vs. evolutionary management: A U.S-Japan comparison of strategy and organizations.* Amsterdam: North-Holland.

Kelley, D. J., Rice, M. P., & Peters, L. S. (2001). The relationship between technology-based and product-based knowledge and alliance formation in new firms. *International Journal of Entrepreneurship and Innovation Management, 1,* 143–156.

Kumar, B. N. (1995). Partner-selection-criteria and success of technology transfer: A model based on learning theory applied to the case of Indo-German technical collaborations. *Management International Review, 35*(Special Issue), 65–78.

Larson, A. (1992). Network dyads in entrepreneurial settings: A study of the governance of exchange relationships. *Administrative Science Quarterly, 37,* 76–104.

Lee, K. S., Lim, G. H., & Tan, S. J. (2000). Feasibility of strategic alliance as an entry strategy into markets dominated by major competitors. *Journal of Small Business and Enterprise Development,* 7(1), 43–57.

Li, S. X., & Rowley, T. J. (2002). Inertia and evaluation mechanisms in interorganizational partner selection: Syndicate formation among U.S. investment banks. *Academy of Management Journal, 45,* 1104–1119.

Lu, J. W., & Beamish, P. W. (2001). The internationalization and performance of SMEs. *Strategic Management Journal, 22,* 565–586.

Luo, Y. (1997). Partner selection and venturing success: The case of joint ventures with firms in the People's Republic of China. *Organization Science, 8,* 648–662.

Luo, Y. (1998). Joint venture success in China: How should we select a good partner? *Journal of World Business, 33,* 145–166.

Miles, G., Preece, S. B., & Baetz, M. C. (1999). Dangers of dependence: The impact of strategic alliance use by small technology-based firms. *Journal of Small Business Management, 37*(2), 20–29.

Muson, H. (2002). Friend? Foe? Both? The confusing world of corporate alliances. *Across the Board, 39*(2), 18–25.

Narula, R. (2004). R&D collaboration by SMEs: New opportunities and limitations in the face of globalisation. *Technovation, 24,* 153–161.

Oliver, A. L. (2001). Strategic alliances and the learning life-cycle of biotechnology firms. *Organization Studies, 22,* 467–489.

Peterson, K. (2001, March 24). Bidland Systems puts itself into inactive mode. *San Diego Union-Tribune,* p. C2.

Podolny, J. M. (1994). Market uncertainty and social character of economic exchange. *Administrative Science Quarterly, 39,* 458–483.

Poutziouris, P. (2003). The strategic orientation of owner-managers of small ventures: Evidence from the UK small business economy. *International Journal of Entrepreneurial Behaviour & Research, 9,* 185–214.

Powell, W. W., & Brantley, P. (1992). Competitive cooperation in biotechnology: Learning through networks. In N. Nohria & R. Eccles (Eds.), *Networks and organizations: Structure, form and action* (pp. 366–394). Boston: Harvard Business School Press.

Preece, S. B., Miles, G., & Baetz, M. C. (1999). Explaining the international intensity and global diversity of early-stage technology-based firms. *Journal of Business Venturing, 14,* 259–281.

PR Newswire. (1994, April 14). ICOS reports 1994 first quarter results. *PR Newswire.*

PR Newswire. (1995, November 8). ICOS announces Phase 1 study. *PR Newswire.*

Scott, W. R. (1995). *Institutions and organizations.* Thousand Oaks, CA: Sage.

Seachrist, L. (1999, July 13). Trimeris teams with Roche in $88M deal for HIV drugs alliances. *BioWorld Today, 10*(133).

Segil, L. (1998). Strategic alliances for the 21st century. *Strategy & Leadership, 26*(4), 12–16.

Shan, W. (1990). An empirical analysis of organizational strategies by entrepreneurial high-technology firms. *Strategic Management Journal, 11,* 129–139.

Shan, W., Walker, G., & Kogut, B. (1994). Interfirm cooperation and startup innovation in the biotechnology industry. *Strategic Management Journal, 15,* 387–394.

Shefer, D., & Frenkel, A. (2005). R&D, firm size and innovation: An empirical analysis. *Technovation, 25*(1), 25–32.

Singh, J. V., Tucker, D. J., & House, R. J. (1986). Organizational legitimacy and the liability of newness. *Administrative Science Quarterly, 31,* 171–193.

Steensma, H. K., Marino, L., & Dickson, P. H. (2000). The influence of national culture on the formation of technology alliances by entrepreneurial firms. *Academy of Management Journal, 43,* 951–973.

Stinchcombe, A. L. (1965). Social structure and organizations. In J. G. March (Ed.), *Handbook of organizations* (pp. 142–193). Chicago: Rand-McNally.

Stuart, T. E., Hoang, H., & Hybels, R. C. (1999). Interorganizational endorsements and the performance of entrepreneurial ventures. *Administrative Science Quarterly, 44,* 315–349.

Supphellen, M., Haugland, S. A., & Korneliussen, T. (2002). SMBs in search of international strategic alliances: Perceived importance of personal information sources. *Journal of Business Research, 55,* 785–795.

Tatoglu, E. (2000). Western joint ventures in Turkey: Strategic motives and partner selection criteria. *European Business Review, 12*(3), 137–147.

Tomlinson, J. W. C. (1970). *The joint venture process in international business: India and Pakistan.* Cambridge, MA: MIT Press.

Tyler, B. B., & Steensma, H. K. (1995, Summer). Evaluating technological collaborative opportunities: A cognitive modeling perspective. *Strategic Management Journal, 16*(Special Issue), 43–70.

Wang, P., Wee, C. H., & Koh, P. H. (1999). Establishing a successful Sino-foreign equity joint venture: The Singapore experience. *Journal of World Business, 34,* 287–305.

Worldwide Biotech. (1997, March 1). ICOS and Glaxo Wellcome change terms on PDE program. *Worldwide Biotech.*

Zimmerman, M. A., & Zeitz, G. J. (2002). Beyond survival: Achieving new venture growth by building legitimacy. *Academy of Management Review, 27,* 414–431.

ABOUT THE CONTRIBUTORS

Merve Bener is a Joint Ventures Manager in Qatari Diar Real Estate Investment Company, fully owned by the Qatar Investment Authority. She obtained her PhD from the Management School, the University of Sheffield. Her doctoral research examines the management and performance of international joint ventures. Her research interests include the management of strategic alliances, joint ventures, mergers and acquisitions. E-mail: mervebener@hotmail.com

Harry Bremmers is senior researcher and lecturer in the position of associate professor in law and economics at Wageningen University. He graduated in Business Economics (Tilburg University, 1977) and Law (Erasmus University, 1993). He obtained a PhD in 1995 at Erasmus University with a study on the effects of environmental standards and legislation on financial accounting theory and practice. He joined Wageningen University in 1993, with subsequent appointments at the Business Administration and Law & Governance group. He specializes in green law (food law and environmental law) and its managerial and economic impact on the food industry. He has published more than 100 papers, books, and articles, mainly on the managerial and economic impact of sustainability requirements in the food industry. He participated in several projects for the European Union addressing the competitiveness and sustainability of the European food and drink industry, which at present are used to set out new policies. E-mail: harry.bremmers@wur.nl

Strategic Alliances for Value Creation, pages 361–371

Ariela Caglio is associate professor of management accounting and control at Università Bocconi and Professor of SDA Bocconi School of Management. She has published several contributions in books and academic journals. Her research interests relate to the evolution of the accounting profession, CFOs compensation, and interorganizational management accounting. She is the Book Review Editor for the *European Accounting Review*. E-mail: ariela.caglio@sdabocconi.it

César Camison is professor of strategic management in the Department of Business Management, Faculty of Economics, University of Valencia. He has a Bachelor of Economic and Business Sciences (1980) with Extraordinary Prize, and PhD in Economics and Business Sciences on (1984) with Cum Laude and Extraordinary Prize. He is a Principal Researcher for *Research Group on Strategy, Competitiveness and Knowledge and Innovation Management (GRECO)* (www.greco.uji.es). He has experience of 30 years in teaching, researching, and university management, which he has developed in some Spanish universities, and has been a visiting professor in different European and American Universities (London School of Economics and Political Science, Surrey; Universitá Commerciale Luigi Bocconi de Milán; Vienna University; Université de Montpellier I; Texas A&M University). His fields of expertise are strategic management, especially the sources of international competitive advantages based on intangible assets and dynamic/innovation capabilities, firms as knowledge and learning organization, and strategic alliances and competitive dynamics inside interorganizational networks and industrial districts. He has worked on these topics in tourism, and small and medium-sized firms. He has published more than 60 books as author, co-author, or coordinator for publishers such as Prentice-Hall, Elsevier Science, John Wiley & Sons, Information Science Reference, Idea Group Publishing, Sage, Routledge, and Office for Official Publications of the European Communities. Likewise, he has published over 100 articles in academic journals such as *Scandinavian Journal of Management, British Journal of Management, European Journal of Management, Organization Studies, International Journal of Operations and Production Management, Journal of Small Business Management, Journal of Business Research, Environment and Planning A, Environment and Planning C, International Business Review, and Tourism Management.* E-mail: camison@emp.uji.es

Refik Culpan is professor of management and international business at the School of Business Administration, The Pennsylvania State University-Harrisburg. He holds a PhD from New York University. He teaches strategic management and international business at both graduate and undergraduate levels. He has extensive international experience in teaching at various universities and conducting seminars and workshops in many countries. He has published three books and numerous articles in business and management journals. His recent book, *Global Business Alliances: Theory and Practice*, has been translated into Chinese. He is the editor-in-chief of *International Journal of Strategic Business Alliances*. E-mail: rculpan@psu.edu

T. K. Das is professor of strategic management and area coordinator (Strategic Management and Business & Society) at the Zicklin School of Business, Baruch College, City University of New York. He is concurrently a member of the university's doctoral faculty. Professor Das received his PhD in Organization and Strategic Studies from the Anderson Graduate School of Management, University of California at Los Angeles (UCLA). He also has degrees in physics, mathematics, and management, and a professional certification in banking. Prior to entering the academic life, Professor Das had extensive experience as a senior business executive. He has research interests in strategic alliances, strategy making, organizational studies, temporal studies, and executive development. Professor Das has published a number of books and monographs, and his research has appeared in over 45 journals, of which some of the later ones include *Academy of Management Executive, Academy of Management Review, British Journal of Management, Journal of International Management, Journal of Management, Journal of Management Studies, Organization Science, Organization Studies*, and *Strategic Management Journal*. Professor Das currently serves as a senior editor for *Organization Studies*, and is or has been associate editor or editorial board member of a number of other journals. He is the founding series editor of *Research in Strategic Alliances* (Information Age Publishing). E-mail: TK.Das@baruch.cuny.edu

Helene Delerue is professor at the Management and Technology Department, ESG-UQAM (Business School, University of Quebec at Montreal). She received her doctorate in strategic management from Paris-Dauphine University. She also has an MA in statistics and an MA in sociology. Prior to earning her doctorate, Professor Delerue worked as a statistician in public and private organizations. She is a member of the International Expert Group on Biotechnology, Innovation and Intellectual Property, an international, multidisciplinary research group organized by the Centre for Intellectual Property Policy, McGill University. Her current research interests include alliance relationships and networks, business practices and intellectual property protection, and secrecy and trade secrets in international business. She is also a member of Project Management Research Chair at UQAM. She is also involved in a number of collaborative research efforts addressing innovation projects. E-mail: vidot-delerue.helene@uqam.ca

Angelo Ditillo is associate professor of management accounting and control at Università Bocconi and Professor of SDA Bocconi School of Management. He has published several contributions in academic journals. His current research interests relate to interorganizational management accounting, and management control in knowledge-intensive firms and creative settings. E-mail: angelo.ditillo@unibocconi.it

Geert Duysters is professor of entrepreneurship at Eindhoven University of Technology and Tilburg University. He currently acts as the scientific director of the Brabant Center of Entrepreneurship, a joint center of Tilburg University and the Eindhoven University of Technology. In 2010 he was awarded a distinguished Chutian Professorship at Wuhan University of Technology (China). He holds a PhD in economics and has worked at the University of Maastricht and the TU Eindhoven as subsequently, researcher, assistant professor, associate professor, and full professor. He is a former professorial fellow of UNU-MERIT (a research and training center of the United Nations and Maastricht University). He worked as an alliance expert for the European Commission and the OECD. During 2000–2003 he was the director of the Eindhoven Centre for Innovation studies (ECIS). He also acted as associate dean of the faculty of technology management from 2004 to 2006. His academic research mainly concerns corporate entrepreneurship, international business strategies, innovation strategies, mergers and acquisitions, network analytical methods, and strategic alliances. He has published over 80 international refereed articles and book chapters. His interest in business strategies and innovation strategies is not only academic, as he worked as a consultant (senior manager) for KPMG Alliances at the international headquarters in Amstelveen (The Netherlands). He also acts as a founding global board member of the Association of Strategic Alliance Professionals (ASAP). As an entrepreneur, he founded three Internet companies over the past decade. E-mail: G.M.Duysters@tue.nl

Lorraine Eden is professor of management and Mays Faculty Fellow at Texas A&M University in College Station, Texas. She received her PhD in economics with Distinction from Dalhousie University in Halifax, Nova Scotia, Canada. Her research interests include strategies of multinational enterprises (MNEs), transfer pricing (the pricing of products with MNEs), and MNE-state relations. More than 100 of her publications appear in journals such as *Academy of Management Journal, Academy of Management Review, Accounting, Organizations and Society, Asian Survey, Canadian Journal of Economics, International Trade Journal, Journal of International Business Studies, Journal of International Management, Management International Review, Millennium, Organization Science,* and *Public Finance/Finances Publiques.* She has received several research awards, including a Canada–U.S. Fulbright Research Fellowship at Harvard University (1992–1993), a Pew Faculty Fellowship in International Affairs Case Teaching and Research at Harvard University (1991–1992), and a Texas A&M University Faculty Fellowship (2002–2007). Professor Eden was vice president and 2002 program chair for the Academy of International Business, and in 2004 was elected a Fellow of the Academy of International Business. Previously a departmental and deputy editor for the *Journal of International Studies* and guest editor at several scholarly journals, Professor Eden completed her 3-year term as editor-in-chief of the *Journal of International Business Studies* in December 2010. E-mail: leden@mays.tamu.edu

Keith W. Glaister is dean of the Management School, University of Sheffield, and Professor of International Strategic Management. His main research focuses on the analysis of formation, partner selection, management, and performance of international joint ventures and strategic alliances. E-mail: k.glaister@sheffield.ac.uk

Don Goeltz is a visiting professor at Fairleigh Dickinson University, an adjunct professor at Pace University, and a consultant to venture companies. His research interests include organizational learning, learning portfolios, strategy, and entrepreneurship. Venture clients have included a Lucent spinout, a video compression company, and a networking company for trade show attendees. Prior venture experience includes management positions with a notification services company, a national two-way voice/data service company, and BellSouth/RAM Mobile Data, the first wireless email and mobile data services in the United States. Prior experience also includes a founding partner of NorthEast Ventures, a senior consultant with Booz, Allen & Hamilton, and management positions with United Technologies and AT&T. Dr. Goeltz has doctoral degree from Pace University, an MBA from New York University, and an MS in Computer Science from Stevens Institute of Technology.

Irene Y. He is a former doctoral student at the City University of New York.

Michael Hitt is distinguished professor of management at Texas A&M University and holds the Joe B. Foster Chair in Business Leadership. He received his PhD from the University of Colorado. Dr. Hitt has co-authored or co-edited 26 books and authored or co-authored many journal articles. A recent article in the *Journal of Management* listed him as one of the ten most cited authors in management over a 25-year period. Additionally, the *Times Higher Education* in 2010 listed him among the top scholars in economics, finance, and management based on the number articles with a high citation rate on the Web of Science. He has served on the editorial review boards of multiple journals and is a former editor of the *Academy of Management Journal* and the *Strategic Entrepreneurship Journal.* He is a fellow in the Academy of Management and in the Strategic Management Society, a research fellow in the National Entrepreneurship Consortium, and received an honorary doctorate from the Universidad Carlos III de Madrid. He is a former president of the Academy of Management, a former president of the Strategic

Management Society, and a member of the Academy of Management Journals' Hall of Fame. He received awards for the best article published in the *Academy of Management Executive* (1999), *Academy of Management Journal* (2000), and the *Journal of Management* (2006). He received the Irwin Outstanding Educator Award and the Distinguished Service Award from the Academy of Management and the Falcone Distinguished Entrepreneurship Scholar Award from Syracuse University. E-mail: mhitt@indiana.edu

R. Duane Ireland is a university distinguished professor and holds the Conn Chair in New Ventures Leadership in the Mays Business School at Texas A&M University. Previously an associate editor for the *Academy of Management Journal,* the *Academy of Management Executive* and *Entrepreneurship Theory and Practice,* he completed his term as the editor for the *Academy of Management Journal* on December 31, 2010. He has been a co-editor for special issues of *Strategic Management Journal, Strategic Entrepreneurship Journal* (forthcoming), *Academy of Management Review, Academy of Management Executive* (twice), and *Organizational Research Methods.* He served as the program chair of the Corporate Strategy and Governance Interest Group in the Strategic Management Society. He is the author or co-author of many articles appearing in journals such as the *Strategic Management Journal, Academy of Management Journal, Academy of Management Review, Academy of Management Executive, Administrative Science Quarterly, Strategic Entrepreneurship Journal, Organization Science* and *Journal of Management,* among others. He received awards for the best article published in *Academy of Management Journal* (2000) and *Academy of Management Executive* (1999). A paper published in *Academy of Management Executive* in 2001 received an award from the U.S. Association for Small Business & Entrepreneurship (USASBE) as the best article published in corporate entrepreneurship during 2001–2002. He is a fellow of the Academy of Management, a fellow of the Strategic Management Society, and a research fellow in the Global Consortium of Entrepreneurship Centers. He is the incoming vice-president elect and program chair for the Academy of Management. E-mail: direland@mays.tamu.edu

Yuval Kalish is from the Leon Recanati Graduate School of Business Administration at Tel Aviv University. His interests include the modeling of social networks, organizational psychology, organizational learning, leadership, and conflict management. He published his work in journals such as *Social Networks,* and he was invited to write chapters on organizational network analysis for the American Psychological Association and for Cambridge University Press. He is currently academic manager of the leadership program at the executive training program at Tel Aviv University. E-mail: yuvalk@post.tau.ac.il

Dovev Lavie is associate professor at the Technion, a Sloan Industry Studies Fellow, and a recipient of the INFORMS TMS Best Dissertation Award and the Academy of Management Newman Award for Best Paper based on a Dissertation. He earned his PhD at the Wharton School and served as an assistant professor at the University of Texas at Austin. Focusing on strategic management, his research interests include value creation and appropriation in alliance networks, relational capabilities and performance implications of alliance portfolios, as well as applications of the resource-based view in interconnected technology-intensive industries. His work has been published in the *Academy of Management Journal, Academy of Management Review, Strategic Management Journal, Organization Science,* among other leading journals. He has served on the editorial boards of the *Strategic Management Journal, Academy of Management Journal, Academy of Management Review, Administrative Science Quarterly, Organization Science,* and *Strategic Organization.* E-mail: dlavie@ie.technion.ac.il

Christoph Lechner holds the Chair of Strategic Management at the University of St. Gallen. He is the managing director of its Institute of Management and academic director of its PhD program in Strategy & Management. During his career, he has received the Cap Gemini Ernst & Young Award for the Best German Business Book, the Best Conference Paper Award of the Strategic Management Society, the Distinguished Paper Award of the BPS Division of the Academy of Management, and the Sumantra Ghoshal Research and Practice Award. His research interests are in the area of strategic initiatives, alliance and network strategy, and business models. He has written five books as well as numerous articles in journals such as *Academy of Management Journal, Strategic Management Journal,* and *Journal of Management,* among others. He is a member of the editorial boards of *Strategic Management Journal, Journal of Management Studies, Long Range Planning,* and *Journal of Strategy and Management.* Besides the university, he serves as a member of the boards of Helvetia (insurance) and Hügli (food), both listed at the Swiss Stock Exchange. E-mail: christoph.lechner@unisg.ch

Dan Li is assistant professor of international business in the Kelley Business School at Indiana University. She received her PhD in management from Texas A&M University. Her research focuses on the management of multinational enterprises, particularly in the areas of international strategic alliances. Professor Li's research appears in journals such as the *Academy of Management Journal, Journal of International Business Studies, Entrepreneurship Theory & Practice, Journal of Management, Management International Review, Multinational Business Review, Scandinavian Journal of Management, Group and Organization Management, Journal of Asian Business Studies,* and *Journal of Mathematical Sociology.* She has served on the editorial review boards of the *Academy of Management Journal* and *Journal of Business Venturing.* Professor

Li is a founding member of the International Association of Chinese Management Research and senior associate of the Research Center for Chinese Politics & Business at Indiana University. E-mail: lid@indiana.edu

Xiaohua Lin is professor of international business and entrepreneurship, and director of the International Research Institute at the Ryerson University's Ted Rogers School of Management. He previously taught at Penn State's School of Professional Graduate Studies and University of Windsor. He has a PhD from Oklahoma State University. He is Canada Chapter Chair of the Academy of International Business, Vice President (Research) of the Canadian Council for Small Business & Entrepreneurship, and serves on the editorial boards of three journals. He has published his research in scholarly journals such as *Strategic Management Journal, Journal of International Business Studies, Management International Review, Journal of World Business, Journal of International Marketing,* and *Journal of Business Ethics.* He is ranked 70th among the most prolific authors in the six leading international business journals during the years 1996–2006 according to a survey published in *APJM* (2008/25, pp.189–207). His current research is focused on emerging market-based multinational enterprises, cross-border mergers and acquisitions, and transnational entrepreneurship. He is the founder of the Canadian Entrepreneurship & Innovation Platform, a nonprofit organization that promotes and facilitates Canada-based transnational entrepreneurship. E-mail: hlin@ryerson.ca

Ángeles Montoro-Sánchez is associate professor of management at the Complutense University of Madrid (Spain), where she obtained her PhD in business administration. Her research interests include strategic alliances, mergers and acquisitions, innovation, and entrepreneurship. Her research has been presented at the Academy of Management, Strategic Management Society and European International Business Academy meetings, and published in *Research Policy, Transport Policy, Journal of Organizational Change Management, International Journal of Manpower, Canadian Journal of Administrative Science, Group Decision and Negotiation, International Journal of Technology Management,* and the *Service Industries Journal,* among others. E-mail: mangeles@ccee.ucm.es

Eva-María Mora-Valentín is associate professor of management at Rey Juan Carlos University, where she obtained her PhD in business administration. Her research interests include strategic alliances, cooperative agreements, and firm-research organizations relationships. Her research has been presented at the Strategic Management Society and European International Business Academy annual meetings and published in *Industry and Higher Education, Science and Public Policy, International Journal of Technology Management* and *Research Policy,* among others. E-mail: evamaria.mora@urjc.es

Amalya L. Oliver is George S. Wise Chair in Sociology at the Hebrew University. Her areas of interest include organizational sociology, networks and knowledge exchanges, university-industry technology transfer, trust, the emergence of professions, leadership and responsibility, and scientific misconduct. She has published in journals such as *Organization Science, Organization Studies, Research Policy,* and *Social Networks.* Her recent book, *Networks for Learning and Knowledge Creation in Biotechnology,* was published by Cambridge University Press in 2009. She is currently the chair of the Library Authority and the Hoffman Program for Leadership and Responsibility at the Hebrew University and is writing a book on academic leadership and responsibility. E-mail: amalyao@cc.huji.ac.il

Onno Omta is chaired professor in business administration at Wageningen University and Research Centre (WUR), The Netherlands. He received a PhD in innovation management and an MSc in biochemistry, both from the University of Groningen, where he also held the position of associate professor for 5 years. He has published numerous articles in leading scientific and professional journals. He was the co-author of a number of Best Paper Award-winning articles presented at different conferences and published in different scientific journals. He received the Citation of Excellence, Highest Quality Rating for research implications by ANBAR Management Intelligence Accreditation Board for his article in *Technovation* (1997). His book, *Critical Success Factors in Biomedical Research and Pharmaceutical Innovation,* has been sold all over the world. He serves on the organizing and editorial committees of a number of international conferences, and he is the founder and editor-in-chief of *The Journal on Chain and Network Science,* which was indexed in Scopus in 2008. E-mail: onno.omta@wur.nl

Marta Ortiz-de-Urbina-Criado is assistant professor of management at Rey Juan Carlos University (Spain), where she obtained her PhD in management. Her research focuses on alliances, mergers and acquisitions, innovation, and entrepreneurship. Her research has been published in *Group Decision and Negotiation, Service Industrial Journal, Canadian Journal of Administrative Science, International Journal of Technology Management, International Journal of Manpower,* and *Universia Business Review,* among others. E-mail: marta.ortizdeurbina@urjc.es

John E. Prescott is the Thomas O'Brien Chair of Strategy in the Katz Graduate School of Business at the University of Pittsburgh. John is the author and/or editor of five books, the most recent being *Establishing a World-Class Competitive Intelligence Function—Workbook* and over 90 articles. Dr. Prescott's research focuses on dynamic competitive rivalry, competitive intelligence, alliance networks, governance structure, and technology strategy. He is the competitive intelligence content expert at the American Productivity and Quality Center (APQC.org). He was the dean of the Business Analyst Program at Texas Instruments. Dr. Prescott consults internationally. E-mail: prescott@katz.pitt.edu

Anna Sabidussi is associate professor of Innovation and Entrepreneurship at TIASNimbas Business School, Tilburg University. Previously, she was assistant professor at Eindhoven University of Technology and at Wageningen University and Research Centrum. She received her PhD from Wageningen University on a joint cooperation project with the School of Economics, Utrecht University. Before entering academia, she worked several years as a professional investor for financial institutions. Her research focus is at the crossroads of innovation management and entrepreneurship, and mainly concerns corporate entrepreneurship, open innovation and external technology sourcing strategies. E-mail: A.Sabidussi@tiasnimbas.edu

Weilei (Stone) Shi is assistant professor of strategy at Zicklin School of Business, Baruch College, City University of New York. He obtained his PhD in strategic management from the University of Pittsburgh in 2008. His research centers on the interaction between strategy and international management. Specifically, he is interested in examining M&As and alliances from both temporal and network perspectives. His papers have been published in the *Journal of Management*, *Journal of Management Studies*, *Multinational Business Review*, and the *Academy of Management Best Paper Proceedings*. His book chapters appear in *Advances in Mergers and Acquisitions* (2008) and *Researching Strategic Alliances: Emerging Perspectives* (2010). He has been awarded the Outstanding Reviewer Award three times by the International Management Division of the Academy of Management at their annual conferences from 2005 to 2007. E-mail: weilei.shi@baruch.cuny.edu

Harbir Singh is the William and Phyllis Mack Professor of Management, codirector of the Mack Center for Technological Innovation, and vice dean for global initiatives at the Wharton School of the University of Pennsylvania. His main areas of research focus on strategic alliances and network formation, alliance management, corporate acquisitions, management buy-outs, and corporate restructuring. His work has been published in journals such as the *Academy of Management Journal*, *Strategic Management Journal*, and *Administrative Science Quarterly*. He has served on the editorial boards of *Strategic Management Journal* and the *Academy of Management Journal*. His research on the role of cultural distance won the JIBS Decade Award, he served as a chair of the Business Policy and Strategy Division of the Academy of Management, and currently serves on the academic board of the Indian School of Business. He has worked with several Fortune 500 companies, including Hewlett Packard, Verizon, and IBM. E-mail: singhh@wharton.upenn.edu

Charles C. Snow is the Mellon Foundation Professor of Business Administration in the Smeal College of Business, Pennsylvania State University. He is also a professorial fellow in the Department of Management and Marketing at the University of Melbourne, and a Visiting research scholar at the Aarhus School of Business, Aarhus University, Denmark. He is the co-editor of the *Journal of Organization Design* (an open-access journal). His areas of research are innovation management, organization design, and new organizational forms. He has taught MBA students and executives in more than 25 countries. E-mail: csnow@psu.edu

INDEX

Strategic Alliances for Value Creation, pages 373–391

B

C

D

E

F

G

I

M

T

Y

Z

Printed and bound by CPI Group (UK) Ltd, Croydon, CR0 4YY

24/09/2026

14968994-0001